Victims and Criminal Justice

CLARENDON STUDIES IN CRIMINOLOGY

Published under the auspices of the Institute of Criminology, University of Cambridge; the Mannheim Centre, London School of Economics; and the Centre for Criminology, University of Oxford.

RECENT TITLES IN THIS SERIES:

A Precarious Life: Community and Conflict in a Deindustrialized Town
Willis

Exporting the UK Policing Brand 1989–2021
Sinclair

Penality in the Underground: The IRA's Pursuit of Informers
Dudai

Assessing the Harms of Crime: A New Framework for Criminal Policy
Greenfield and Paoli

Armed Robbers: Identity and Cultural Mythscapes in the Lucky Country
Taylor

Crime, Justice, and Social Order: Essays in Honour of A. E. Bottoms
Liebling, Shapland, Sparks, and Tankebe

Policing Human Rights
Martin

Normalizing Extreme Imprisonment: The Case of Life Without Parole in California
Vannier

Respect and Criminal Justice
Watson

Neighbourhood Policing: The Rise and Fall of a Policing Model
Innes, Roberts, Lowe, Innes

Respectable Citizens—Shady Practices: The Economic Morality of the Middle Classes
Farrall and Karstedt

Victims and Criminal Justice

A History

Pamela Cox

Professor of Sociology and Social History, University of Essex

Robert Shoemaker

Emeritus Professor of History, University of Sheffield

Heather Shore

Professor of History, Manchester Metropolitan University

OXFORD
UNIVERSITY PRESS

OXFORD
UNIVERSITY PRESS

Great Clarendon Street, Oxford, OX2 6DP,
United Kingdom

Oxford University Press is a department of the University of Oxford.
It furthers the University's objective of excellence in research, scholarship,
and education by publishing worldwide. Oxford is a registered trade mark of
Oxford University Press in the UK and in certain other countries

First Edition published in 2023

Published in the United States of America by Oxford University Press
198 Madison Avenue, New York, NY 10016, United States of America

British Library Cataloguing in Publication Data

Data available

Library of Congress Control Number: 2023943445

ISBN 978–0–19–284648–8

DOI: 10.1093/oso/9780192846488.001.0001

Printed and bound by
CPI Group (UK) Ltd, Croydon, CR0 4YY

In memory of Clive Emsley, inspirational scholar and friend

General Editors Introduction

The *Clarendon Studies in Criminology series* aims to provide a forum for outstanding theoretical and empirical work in all aspects of criminology and criminal justice, broadly understood. The Editors welcome submissions from established scholars, as well as manuscripts based on excellent PhD dissertations. The Series was inaugurated in 1994, with Roger Hood as its first General Editor, following discussions between Oxford University Press and Oxford's then Centre for Criminological Research. It is edited under the auspices of three centres: The Centre for Criminology at the University of Oxford, the Institute of Criminology at the University of Cambridge, and the Mannheim Centre for Criminology at the London School of Economics. Each supplies members of the Editorial Board and, in turn, the Series General Editor or Editors.

Victims and Criminal Justice: A History is a welcome addition to the Series. Its authors—Pamela Cox, Robert Shoemaker, and Heather Shore—explore crime victims' experiences of, and engagement with, the criminal justice system in England and Wales between the late seventeenth and late twentieth centuries. It tells a compelling and sometimes surprising story of a shift in the influence of victims from key players to mere witnesses for the state. In an elegantly written and authoritative account of the victim, the authors explore their place in a changing social, cultural, and economic landscape as well as under an evolving legal system, drawing on legal history, victimology, and the history of crime to provide a compelling account of the social history of victims.

While victimological research has grown considerably in the past three decades or so, there have been few attempts to bring together rich empirical evidence and theoretical accounts of the standing and role of victims in response to crime. This critical account of the governance of victims and developing victim policy more widely fills this lacuna and in so doing, tells us almost as much about the history of prosecution as it does about victims' access to justice over time.

Taking a rigorous mixed-methods approach, the authors draw on news media and other sources of qualitative data as well as statistical and digital resources to show who victims were, what resources were available to them, and what outcomes followed their complaints. Accounts of victims from Old Bailey data make clear complex issues around class, ethnicity, and gender, and while the book focuses on more serious crime, particularly violence against women and minorities, it does not make for difficult reading. For those interested in victim policy and its place in the wider justice system, this is essential reading. We are pleased to include it in the Clarendon Studies in Criminology.

Mary Bosworth and Carolyn Hoyle
General Editors
Centre for Criminology, University of Oxford
March 2022

Acknowledgements

We would like to thank the Economic and Social Research Council for funding the 'Victims' access to justice through English criminal courts, 1675 to the present' project (ES/R006962/1). Research conducted as part of this interdisciplinary initiative underpins this book, together with linked publications, presentations, datasets, and reports. We would also like to thank all members of the interdisciplinary team involved in the wider project: Professor Barry Godfrey, Professor Sandra Walklate, and Dr Lucy Williams (all of the University of Liverpool), Dr Ruth Lamont (University of Manchester) and Dr Elisa Impara (University of Essex), as well as Jamie McLaughlin, of the Digital Humanities Institute at the University of Sheffield.

We are also very grateful to all those beyond this team who helped to shape our thinking, especially members of our project advisory board and those responding to our papers presented at events organized or hosted by the European Social Science History Conference, the Social History Society, British Crime Historians Group, the British Society for Criminology, Yale University Legal History Forum, the British History seminar at the Université de Picardie Jules Verne, the *Modern Law Review* workshop on 'Reconceptualising Children's Rights', the University of Essex's Law and Criminal Justice Group, and the Office of the Victims Commissioner for England and Wales. We extend particular thanks to those who read and offered generous comments on our draft manuscript: David Churchill, Ruth Lamont, and Paul Rock. Finally, we are indebted to the creators of the pre-existing datasets we have used in this research: The Old Bailey Proceedings Online (Tim Hitchcock, Robert Shoemaker, Clive Emsley, Sharon Howard, and Jamie McLaughlin), and the Old Bailey Corpus (Magnus Huber, Magnus Nissel, and Karin Puga).

Contents

List of Tables and Figures

Tables

Figures

List of Abbreviations

BVSS	Bristol Victim Support Scheme
CICB	Criminal Injuries Compensation Board
CDF	Cyclists' Defence Fund
CPS	Crown Prosecution Service
CRS	Commission for Racial Equality
DORA	Defence of the Realm Act
DPP	Director of Public Prosecution
Edw.	Edward
Eliz.	Elizabeth
Geo.	George
GLF	Gay Liberation Front
HC Deb	House of Commons Debates
HISCO	Historical International Classification of Occupations
HMRC	HM Revenue & Customs
ICS	Islington Crime Survey
JP	Justice of the Peace
MP	Member of Parliament
NACRO	National Association for the Care and Resettlement of Offendors
NAVSS	National Association of Victim Support Schemes
NSPCC	National Society for the Prevention of Cruelty to Children
OBC	Old Bailey Corpus (https://fedora.clarin-d.uni-saarland.de/oldbailey)
OBO	Old Bailey Proceedings Online (www.oldbaileyonline.org); subsequent text (such as t17160906-29) indicates the trial reference number
OBP	Old Bailey Proceedings
Phil. & Mar.	Philip & Mary
PP	Parliamentary Papers
PP, HC Deb	House of Commons Debates
QC	Queen's Counsel
RSPCA	Royal Society for the Prevention of Cruelty to Animals
Vict.	Victoria
UNODC	United Nations Office for Drugs and Crime
Will.	William

1
Introduction

In September 1716, Abraham Major appeared as a complainant at London's Old Bailey court to accuse six women of luring him to a house, binding him, and taking two gold rings, one pair of silver buckles, a silver tobacco box, and twenty-six guineas and other coins. He told the court that, having freed himself from his constraints, he had attracted the attention of a parish constable who had helped him to search for his assailants. Not finding them that night, Major investigated further and made arrangements with another member of the gang to return the stolen rings in return for two guineas reward. Following the agreed exchange in a nearby pub, Abraham accepted an invitation to have a glass of rum back at the house where he had been robbed, whereupon the same women set upon him once again. This time, his wife extracted him from the situation. In the ensuing trial at the Old Bailey, Major led the prosecution himself and, after hearing all the evidence, the jury convicted five women of robbery and the judge sentenced them to death by hanging. Four escaped the gallows because they were pregnant. One woman, Elizabeth Slate [or Slatt] was hanged in public at Tyburn less than two weeks after the trial (OBO, t17160906-29, OA17160919).

The report of the trial in the *Proceedings* of the Old Bailey described Abraham Major as 'a very stupid fellow' who had risked his safety in a 'most notorious place'. The *Proceedings* report also describes him as 'the Prosecutor' of the case. Nowadays we would refer to him as the 'victim' of the crime, but that term is barely used in the *Proceedings* and never to describe someone bringing a case. From the perspective of the law at the time, Major was fulfilling an obligation. A subject of the monarch who suffered a serious wrong (a felony) had a duty to initiate a prosecution on behalf of the king. They had both a right and a duty to lead in criminal justice proceedings, but this gave them opportunities to attempt to illegally settle cases out of court, as Major attempted to do in this case.

By the mid-nineteenth century, however, the situation had changed considerably. Parish watchmen had been replaced by local police forces paid

Victims and Criminal Justice. Pamela Cox, Robert Shoemaker, and Heather Shore,
Oxford University Press.
DOI: 10.1093/oso/9780192846488.003.0001

for by public funds in the form of local rates and operating under new statutory regulations. These police forces played an increasingly important part, alongside the prosecutor, in bringing prosecutions, and the discretion exercised by victims was reduced.

On 21 April 1860, Jane Bellamy, the thirty-year-old wife of a shoemaker, experienced a robbery (OBO, t18600507-494). Mrs Bellamy had left a Southwark pub with a female friend one evening in May, but was followed by a man and a woman who accosted her, knocked her to the ground and stole fifteen shillings and her shawl. Her friend deposed in the Old Bailey that the robbery had taken place in a 'very bad neighbourhood'. There were police patrols nearby, as an officer of the Metropolitan Police told the court that he heard the commotion and attended the scene, where he took into custody the two suspects who had been apprehended by witnesses. Although the report of the trial in the *Proceedings* describes Mrs Bellamy as the 'prosecutrix', the actual prosecution in court was conducted by a barrister, 'Mr Caarten'. The suspects were defended by another barrister, 'Mr Lilley', who cross-examined Bellamy and her friend. The jury found both defendants guilty and they were imprisoned for eight days.

Although Jane Bellamy played an active part in these proceedings as the complainant, she did so at the direction of her legal counsel, John Marinus Bicker Caarten. Mr Caarten appears in the *Proceedings* as counsel in seventy-eight Old Bailey trials between 1853 and 1860. As Bellamy's case, and those of many others analysed for this book exemplify, by 1860 the relationship between the state and the victim of crime was changing: the role of prosecutor was gradually being assumed by professional counsel and the police. The 'prosecutor' and 'prosecutrix' of old were being reduced to mere witnesses.

The relationship would shift again over the course of the twentieth century. In 1975, a widower in his sixties, Leslie Denham, was driving near his home in Wimbledon, South London when he was flagged down by two men brandishing what they claimed was a police badge. Informed by the men that he was under arrest for driving under the influence of alcohol, he agreed to accompany them to a police station. Instead, they stopped at Wimbledon Common and made him empty his pockets of money and a watch. After subjecting Mr Denham to what *The Times* described in their coverage of the ensuing Old Bailey case as 'sexual indignities', the men pushed him into a ditch. Mr Denham reported the case to the Metropolitan Police who investigated and arrested the two men. They claimed the incident had started as a joke which then got out of hand. A case was prepared by the Metropolitan Police Solicitor's Department, who undertook the prosecution and instructed counsel (a barrister, Mr C. J. Crespi) to prosecute. In court, the two accused pleaded guilty, expressed their remorse and through their defence counsel they apologized to Denham, offering him compensation. This was an informal offer, but the court could—by the 1970s—have ordered criminal injury compensation to be paid as part of the sentence. The Recorder—or circuit judge—sentenced both men to five years' imprisonment (*Times*, 15 Feb. 1975; PP, 1979, 19). The victim in this case played virtually no role in the prosecution. Once he reported the case, its investigation and prosecution was left entirely in the hands of police and counsel, and, since the accused pleaded guilty, he did not even need to appear in court.

As these three cases demonstrate, crime victims' experiences of, and engagement with, the process of criminal justice changed dramatically between the late seventeenth and late twentieth centuries. At the start of our period, 'victims' drove the English criminal justice system but would never have described themselves as such. They could bring prosecutions as complainants and prosecutors, give evidence as witnesses, put up personal rewards for the recovery of lost goods or claim rewards for securing convictions. As Gwenda Morgan and Peter Rushton (1998, 30) noted: 'It would be no exaggeration to say that individuals created the crime, with the assistance of the constables and justices, by turning personal wrongs into official accusations'. By the end of our period, 'complainants' had been reframed as 'victims' and had been firmly displaced as the state, through the Crown Prosecution Service (CPS), took virtually full responsibility for the process of prosecution. This was the result, primarily, of the state's efforts to encourage efficient prosecution in order to reduce criminal offending. This story is quite different from those in Scotland or continental Europe where state prosecutors had existed since at least the fifteenth century.

This book examines the origins and impacts of key legal, procedural, and institutional changes introduced in England and Wales in order to encourage and govern prosecution. These included: the use of rewards from the 1690s; the increasing use of prosecution counsel from the 1730s; financial support to cover victims' costs and 'time and trouble' from the 1750s; the rise of voluntary prosecution associations in the 1770s; the emergence of 'police prosecutions' from the 1780s; the creation of the 'new police' in the 1830s; the establishment of a Director of Public Prosecutions (DPP) in the 1870s; the introduction of criminal injuries compensation in the 1960s;

the birth of victim support organizations and victim-related activism in the 1970s; and, the creation of the CPS in the mid-1980s.

The establishment of the CPS was a landmark development for England and Wales. For the first time, a public prosecution agency, independent from victims and the police, would determine which allegations should be prosecuted. This finally sealed the dominance of the state over the private complainant in court and led to a further narrowing of victims' participation in criminal justice proceedings. Victims became 'aggrieved persons' who appeared in court as witnesses rather than complainants. Only in exceptional circumstances could they appear as prosecutors. Reflecting on this shift, criminologists Joanna Shapland and David Cohen (1987, 28) suggested that:

> victims [are now] largely unnecessary in the operation of the criminal justice system. Though most offences are reported by victims . . . victims are no longer needed in the vast majority of cases. Most offenders are not caught, most defendants plead guilty, and, even if there is a trial, the victim is only one prosecution witness among many, with no special status in law.

Unlike most studies in criminal justice history, this book is not centred on the defendant, but on the complainant or, more colloquially, the victim. It explores—at different points in time—how victims were defined in law, what the law allowed and encouraged them to do, who they were in social and economic terms, how they participated in the criminal justice system, why many were unwilling or unable to engage in that system, and why some campaigned for specific rights. In short, the book offers a critical history of victims and criminal justice in England over three centuries.

1.1 Researching the History of Victims

Given their centrality in criminal justice, we know remarkably little about the history of victims. Crime historians have, in the main, focused on those accused of offences rather than those who experienced or prosecuted them. Criminologists have, through the sub-discipline of victimology, studied modern victims in detail but lack a long historical perspective. Legal historians and scholars have charted the development of statutes and practices relating to crime victims but have not extensively examined their broader context or impact. This book aims to bridge these gaps by bringing together scholarship in these fields, sharing new historical data on victims, and proposing new ways of understanding their shifting relationship with the state.

The dual nature of victimhood made this relationship an uneasy one. Historically, a crime victim in England and Wales was both an individual who personally experienced an offence but also a royal subject with an obligation to act as the monarch's 'prosecutor' if that offence was deemed a serious one. The criminal justice system encouraged the prosecution of offences in the public interests of the state, not the private interests of the victim. Recognizing this, the first generation of British crime historians explored the operation of the criminal law as part of a wider dynamic of state power that protected elite interests. Written within a broadly critical Marxist paradigm and focusing on the social conflicts of the eighteenth and early nineteenth centuries, these studies typically assumed that those accused of crimes were oppressed and powerless and that the prosecuting victims held all the legal cards, together with the power to play them in their own class interest (Hay et al., 1975).

This paradigm was questioned by further historical research which suggested that the criminal law was more open to, and used by, a broader range of people (Brewer and Styles, 1980). John Langbein (1983, 105) argued that '[w]ithin the confines of a system that lacked professional prosecution, steps were taken to make the system serve the interests of the non-élite prosecutors who predominated'. Peter King (1984, 2000) found that the majority of eighteenth- and early nineteenth-century complainants were drawn from 'the middling sort'. Similarly, George Rudé (1985) argued that the emergent urban middle class drove the nineteenth-century prosecution process and forced key reforms to it. Together with other social histories of criminal justice (Phillips, 1977; Beattie, 1986, 2001; Conley, 1991; Linebaugh, 1991; Shoemaker, 1991; Gray, 2009), these studies shed new light on the history of prosecution. They also inspired further work, on the role of policing in prosecution (Hay and Snyder, 1989; Beattie, 2012; Smith, 2006, 2007; Churchill, 2017; Bland, 2022), the exercise of prosecutorial discretion (King, 2000), the experiences of women and children as victims (Tomes, 1978; Conley, 1986, 2014; Clark, 1987; D'Cruze, 1998, 1999; Jackson, 2000; D'Cruze and Jackson, 2009), complainant profiles (Godfrey, Cox, and Farrall, 2007, ch. 6), the slow growth of public prosecution (Hay, 1983; Smith, 2006, 2007), and the limits of the state's monopoly over prosecutorial practice (Hay, 1983; Godfrey, 2008; Churchill, 2014). Building on this substantial scholarship, our book explores many of these themes over a longer time span. In so doing, it focuses on the specific issue of public access to justice over time.

The concept of 'access to justice' has been explored by legal scholars but has not, to date, featured strongly in crime history, historical criminology, or legal history. A society with fair access to justice has been defined as one with criminal justice and legal systems that are fair, accessible to all and deliver outcomes that are individually and socially just (adapted from Cappelletti and Garth, 1978). This idea is clearly connected to broader concepts of the public good or the public interest. A given society, may for example, offer wide access to unfair or corrupt systems, or narrow access to fair systems, neither of which serve the public interest. Recent research on access to justice has addressed a range of different issues including the reform of justice services (Law Society, 1992; Ministry of Justice, 2011), rights-based access to the law (Sandefur, 2009), and the lack of access experienced by marginal communities (Ghai and Cottrell, 2009; Mayo, Koessl, and Scott, 2014), but it has not addressed these matters from an historical perspective.

Our book approaches this in three ways: firstly, by narrating shifts in public obligations and entitlements to report, prosecute, and influence the outcome of a criminal complaint; secondly, by tracking shifts in the public uptake or exercise of these entitlements; and thirdly, by analysing the impact of both of these shifts on the ways different groups of victims participated in the justice system. At all stages, we aim to place these matters in their wider historical context, and to weigh the impact of particular criminal justice reforms against that of broader socio-cultural changes. We also seek to highlight, with the benefit of historical hindsight, the unintended consequences of particular reforms. A striking early example of the latter, discussed in more detail in the following chapters, are the repercussions of the state's introduction in the 1690s of financial rewards for those victims who brought successful prosecutions. This innovation produced both desired and undesired effects: prosecutions increased but so did forms of corruption connected to them. This led to further state actions to rein in that corruption, including the reform of earlier forms of policing from the mid-eighteenth century and then the introduction of the 'new police' in the early nineteenth. The new police came to exert a dual power to both investigate and prosecute, which later became highly problematic.

This example points to a common thread running through this book: that the state sought to govern prosecution from a distance until the 1980s, and that the main aim of this governance was to assert its own legitimacy by reducing crime and preserving public order through facilitating certain types of public access to justice. The personal, private, or emotional needs of individual victims were rarely a matter of state concern throughout the long time period addressed in this book. They only became so in the late twentieth century, with the contentious and highly politicized re-imagining of 'the victim'. The post-war drivers of that politicization have been much debated by criminologists (Mawby and Walklate, 1994; Rock, 1990, 2004b; Walklate, 2007, 2009, 2017; Zedner, 2002), but they have rarely been related to longer term historical shifts in the governance of victims. Historically oriented criminological research has addressed elements of this story, and this book acknowledges and builds on this scholarship. Studies of the rise of public prosecution (Rock, 2004a, 2004b; Spencer, 2011), the framing of victims as objects of public policy (Kearon and Godfrey, 2007; Godfrey, Cox, Shore, and Alker, 2017; Rock, 2019), and genealogical approaches to victims' legal rights (Kirchengast, 2006, 2010, 2016; Holder, 2018a) are key foundations for our study. Local government power, often overlooked in theorizations and empirical investigations of governmentality, played a vital part here. Tyrone Kirchengast rightly views the criminal trial as a form of 'local governance' and as an 'institution of social power' (2016, 40–64), while Robert Morris (2001, 114) notes 'the persistence of localised forms of criminal justice administration' into the twentieth century.

In this book, we offer an empirically-grounded account of shifts in the governance of victims in terms of the tactics and techniques (O'Malley, Weir, and Shearing, 1997; Rose, 1999) used by the local and central state and others to encourage, finance, and manage the flow of their participation in the justice system over time. We suggest that although victim policy per se did not emerge until the mid-twentieth century, victims were made visible, and mobilized, as subjects of governance long before this. We argue that victim policy in England in the post-war period has been forged through efforts to resolve deep-seated tensions arising from the state's adopted role as the primary prosecutor of crime, a role which emerged only gradually over the course of three centuries.

Criminological research on victims has grown rapidly since the 1980s. There are many strands to this now global field but two overarching approaches stand out: one that is deeply sceptical about the politicization of 'the victim' and views this as contributing to populist and illiberal cultures of control (see e.g. Garland, 2001) and one that views this politicization as a key means of ensuring that victims, especially those from socially marginal or minoritized groups, receive the progressive policy attention and resources that they need (see e.g. Goodey, 2004). There is relatively little cross-over or dialogue between those working within these two broad approaches. Critical victimology has, however, sought to facilitate this (see, for example, Spencer and Walklate, 2016; Duggan, 2018) by recognizing the value of victims' concerns while, at the same time, contextualizing the complex emergence of those concerns and critiquing the contentious co-opting of those concerns by politicians. This book takes a similar approach but also contributes a distinctive historical perspective.

In the past, public access to justice was highly uneven. As we will go on to explore, those with greater levels of economic, social, and cultural capital were more likely to engage with the justice system. White men of some means have long been the primary victim-participants in the English criminal justice system, initiating the majority of criminal complaints yet identifying the least with modern public narratives of victimhood. The experiences of women, children, and socially marginal and minority ethnic groups in this context require attention. Even today, public access to justice in England and Wales remains unequal. Recent victim surveys demonstrate low rates of crime reporting among these and other groups leading to low rates of arrest, prosecution, and conviction; high rates of attrition; difficulties in accessing relevant information; long delays in proceedings; and prohibitive financial and personal costs of engaging in those proceedings (Spencer and Walklate, 2016; Hunter, Jacobson, and Kirby, 2013; Jacobson and Cooper, 2020; Cox, Impara, Lamont, and Walklate, 2021). Why has our criminal justice system evolved in ways that have left so many victims facing what they perceive as a 'justice gap'? How can future efforts to close that gap be informed by efforts that were made in the past?

Our book addresses these issues via an empirically grounded mixed-methods analysis of a range of historical sources. We combine qualitative analysis of textual primary sources with quantitative analysis of datasets of criminal prosecutions. Our datasets are explained below, and in more detail in the Appendix. The proscriptive law has been documented through statutes, legal commentaries, and advice manuals for magistrates and other legal officials. Evidence of actual policing and prosecution practice has been sourced from parliamentary investigations, published commentary, magistrates' notebooks and, as explained in the next section, quantitative analysis of the records of criminal prosecutions. While our principal primary source evidence concerns London, we have consulted the extensive secondary literature for evidence of prosecution practices in other parts of England and Wales (Scotland, of course, had a different judicial system, and merits a separate study). Our in-depth examination of prosecutions in London is thus supplemented by a wide range of evidence pertaining to criminal justice in the rest of the country.

Before outlining our principal datasets, it is necessary to consider the ambiguities of the words 'prosecution', 'prosecutor/prosecutrix', and 'to prosecute'. In English law the role of 'prosecutor' has never been assigned to a single individual or institution; even after the creation of the CPS in 1986, crown prosecutors did not undertake the investigation of the crime and did not have full responsibility for charging suspects and dealing with witnesses (see Chapter 4); nor did they exercise a complete monopoly over prosecution. Throughout our period, the various tasks involved in bringing a criminal case to court and presenting it before a judge and jury, which include discovering the crime and identifying it as such, naming and finding the suspect, assembling the evidence, securing witnesses, presenting to the jury, testifying, and cross-examining witnesses, have been divided up between victims, magistrates, policing agents, lawyers, and court officials. As we will go on to show, over the course of the three centuries examined, the balance of responsibilities between these actors shifted considerably away from the victims. However, because these tasks have always been shared to varying degrees between these parties, in most cases it is virtually impossible to identify a single 'prosecutor' who was responsible for 'the prosecution'. In most criminal trials we cannot identify who was primarily responsible for the prosecution, including the payment of costs, securing of witnesses, and hiring of counsel. Consequently, where we use the term 'prosecutor' we are often referring to more than one individual, and when we discuss the shifting responsibility for conducting 'prosecutions' towards police, counsel, or public prosecutors, we do so with a recognition that other parties may have continued to play a role.

A key theme of the book concerns the emergence of 'public prosecution' from what we would today call 'private prosecution', a development which fundamentally changed the nature of the English criminal trial. This, too, is a multi-faceted concept, and in Chapter 4 we distinguish between 'state prosecution', 'police prosecution', and 'public prosecution', which developed over time in that order. The origins of prosecution in England lie in the right and obligation of the aggrieved individual to take action against their malefactor—'private prosecution' was the norm. What we term 'state prosecutions' were undertaken at the behest of crown officials, including the Attorney General and Treasury Solicitor, and quasi-state agencies such as the Mint and the Bank of England. These prosecutions, which concerned offences which directly challenged state authority such as treason, sedition, and counterfeiting the currency of the realm, had occurred since at least the medieval period, but rarely accounted for more than a small fraction of trials. Police prosecution, on the other hand, developed at scale at the local level in the nineteenth century, as the police began to work closely with counsel to take responsibility for cases where the victim alone was not able, willing, or trusted to bring the case on his or her own. As we will see in Chapter 4, prosecutions by quasi-state agencies or the police were not necessarily mutually exclusive. There were also some 'non-state' crimes which involved the Attorney General or Treasury Solicitor, but these concerned offences involving serious threats to public order or finance such as murder, forgery, and fraud. Finally, public prosecution emerged from the late nineteenth century, following the creation of the Director of Public Prosecutions (DPP), and therefore the adoption, initially in limited circumstances, of the role of a public prosecutor. Today, public prosecution through the CPS is the norm, private prosecution is rarely used, and police prosecution has been abolished.

In his influential article exploring 'conflicts as property', criminologist Nils Christie (1977) famously argued that criminal justice officials are 'professional thieves' who 'steal' people's conflicts and transform them into legal disputes between state bureaucracies and defendants, thereby undermining citizens' participation in the resolution of their own conflicts. This argument has become 'foundational' to the community and restorative justice movements, 'both as a normative critique of expert power and as a sketch of alternatives to traditional criminal justice practices' (Halvorsen, 2014, 335). Our book challenges Christie's characterization of criminal justice agents as 'conflict thieves' by showing how, in the course of the journey to public prosecution in England and Wales, the labour of prosecution was divided and increasingly assumed by local and national state officials in order to ensure the more systematic prosecution of crime, and enable more people to access justice. We fully acknowledge that this process primarily served state interests by confirming its legitimacy and upholding the rule of law. We suggest, however, that rather than 'stealing' conflict, the state socialized its resolution. Over time, and as our opening vignettes illustrate, the labour of parish constables, magistrates, juries, local police forces, local government officers, prosecution and defence counsel and judges, was directed towards the receipt, investigation, and prosecution of people's complaints. The work of all these parties was flawed in many respects and subject to rightful and rigorous critique at numerous points in time. But taken together, their labour and the modes of governance that supported and funded it made it possible for citizens to exercise their choice to access justice albeit at the same time constraining those choices.

As we go on to show, though their participation was still necessary, individual victims were gradually 'relieved' of much of the labour of prosecution as this was taken on by other agencies. Terminology is a challenge here, especially in the emotive atmosphere in which political discussions of victims' position in the justice system are now conducted. We frame the sharing or socialization of the labour of prosecution in terms of how this gradually 'displaced', 'supplanted', 'minimized', 'side-lined' and 'marginalized' victims. We use these terms because we feel that they allow us to capture and explain an undeniable, significant, and much-misunderstood historical transformation. We nevertheless seek to explore the extent to which that transformation—the sharing of prosecution labour—served the wider public interest. While it gave some victims more effective access to justice, it left others to contend with what we have termed the 'pains of prosecution'.

1.2 Criminal Prosecutions and Victims at the Old Bailey

A key reason why criminal justice sources have been principally mined for stories and statistics relating to offenders rather than victims is that state-generated records of the criminal justice process are largely organized around the accused. Reading against the grain, however, historians newly interested in the experiences of victims were able to shift the focus, but their foundational scholarship on victims (discussed above) was based on close analysis of relatively small samples of criminal justice data gathered manually from physical archives. George Rudé was the first historian to pose the direct question, 'who were victims of crime?' but, at the time, he could only answer it through the manual comparison of samples of early nineteenth century court records from three English counties, including Middlesex (Rudé, 1985, 2–3). Digitization of key criminal justice records and advances in computational quantification have, however, enabled this research to be conducted at scale, allowing historians to identify broad patterns in experiences of victimization, the identities of victims, and practices of prosecution over time. Godfrey, Cox, and Farrall's (2007) study of historical court records from the northwest of England was one of the first to analyse victims using digitized archival material.

Our book takes up and expands the use of digital resources. It makes extensive use of the records of cases heard at the Old Bailey in London and reported in the quasi-official published *Proceedings* of the court for the period from 1674 to 1913, or in *The Times* newspaper for two sample periods, 1910–25 and 1960–75.[1] Since the middle ages, the Old Bailey has been the principal court for the prosecution of serious crime—felonies—in London. Until 1967, English law maintained a mediaeval distinction between crimes classified as felonies (serious offences, punishable by the forfeiture of land or goods up to 1870, and by death in certain circumstances up to 1965) and those regarded as misdemeanours (lesser offences punishable by other means). There were different legal procedures for each. Nonetheless, the victim was expected to bear the principal responsibility for prosecuting both types of crime until well into the nineteenth century. The most common felonies prosecuted in the Old Bailey were simple thefts (known as larcenies), various forms of deception (forgery, fraud, coining, and counterfeiting), property offences involving force or violence (robbery, burglary), and the most serious forms of violence (murder and rape).

Some offences straddled the boundary between felonies and misdemeanours, generally where the misdemeanour was a less serious version of the felony, such as assault with intent to rape (where no rape was committed) or receiving stolen goods (rather than stealing them). The biggest area of overlap was in the case of theft, where the one shilling borderline between grand and petty larceny led to the latter's ambiguous status as a 'non-capital felony' which was prosecuted as if it were a misdemeanour. This borderline was clearly discretionary and, as the value of a shilling declined over time, more and more larcenies became grand larcenies. This trend came to its logical end in 1827 when the distinction between grand and petty larceny was abolished (7 & 8 George IV, *c.* 29).

While the cases at the Old Bailey primarily came from London, the court's significance was national. For much of the early part of our period, the Old Bailey accounted for a major proportion of all the serious crime trials held in England and Wales. Although this declined in the first half of the nineteenth century owing to the rapid growth of other towns and cities, the Old Bailey consistently accounted for a significant proportion, a

[1] Throughout this book, we use the term 'Old Bailey' to refer to this court throughout its history, including after 1834 when it was formally titled the 'Central Criminal Court'.

quarter, of national commitments to the assizes courts between 1855 and the eve of the Second World War (Parliamentary Papers dataset). Given its London location, the court's influence extended nationally, since the high court judges, who sat both in court and in the legislative House of Lords, influenced judicial decision-making and government policies on crime, policing, and punishment. As explained below, during the nineteenth century the Old Bailey's jurisdiction expanded beyond London into south-east England and, in some cases, nationally. Moreover, crime reporting in the popular press was heavily dominated by crimes and trials which took place in London (King, 2007; Devereaux, 2013; Shore, 2015). As such, the court's business had the potential to shape both perceptions of justice and victims' experiences in courts and in the public sphere more generally throughout this period.

Our principal source for historical Old Bailey trials is the *Proceedings* of the court, which were regularly published following each meeting ('sessions') of the court between April 1674 and April 1913. While the nature of the reporting and level of detail provided changed, the *Proceedings* provide an extraordinarily consistent record of criminal justice practice over three centuries, as, with only minor exceptions, they provide basic facts of each case (names of victims and defendants, nature of the criminal charge, plea, verdict, and punishment sentence). When the *Proceedings* were digitized by the Old Bailey Online project between 2000 and 2008, this information, pertaining to 197,245 trials, was tagged, allowing a dataset to be created which facilitates statistical analysis.[2] The wider research project upon which this book is based enhanced the Old Bailey Online data by improving the information pertaining to victims, principally by adding coding for missing victim occupations. It is important to note that the *Proceedings* do not provide full transcripts of trials (although they often read like them), as much of what was said in court was not reported. Statements from counsel and defendants were routinely abbreviated or omitted, and questions and answers were often combined in reports of witness testimonies. Nonetheless, victims' testimony was most likely to be reported and most trials were reported at sufficient length to enable the identification of the key participants and the circumstances surrounding the crime and arrest of the defendants (Shoemaker, 2008b; Emsley, Hitchcock, and Shoemaker, 2018c). Our analysis includes acquittals as well as those convicted of a charge, thus

[2] The Proceedings of the Old Bailey, 1674 to 1913, https://www.oldbaileyonline.org.

including victims whose criminal complaints were deemed worthy of a formal prosecution, even if the trial jury or judge did not agree.

Two additional datasets, both detailed in the Appendix, provided us with more detailed information about the ways criminal trials, as recorded in the *Proceedings*, were conducted at the Old Bailey. The Trial Participants dataset, compiled from a manual reading of a sample of nineteenth-century trial accounts, allowed us to examine more closely who was present at trials and, if they spoke, whether they were the first, second, third, or fourth speaker. Similar information was derived from the Old Bailey Corpus, a dataset of spoken speech extracted from the trial accounts.

The *Proceedings* ceased publication in April 1913, so for data on Old Bailey trials for the rest of the twentieth century we turned to reports in *The Times* newspaper. We chose *The Times* owing to its status as an authoritative publication which 'was and is a marker of the way in which the law (including the criminal justice process) has been presented for mass consumption' and 'provided a model copied by others' (Rowbotham, Stevenson, and Pegg, 2013, 11). We included every reported Old Bailey case in two sample periods, 1910–25 and 1960–75, resulting in a total of 5,816 prosecutions. The first three years and four months duplicate the period covered by the final issues of the *Proceedings*, which allowed us to compare *The Times* reporting with the *Proceedings* and understand the selectivity of *Times* reporting. For the remaining years, we sought to include both a period which captured the early twentieth century, before and after the First World War, in the early years of the office of the Director of Public Prosecutions, and a period after the Second World War when new attitudes towards victims emerged. We note from the outset that there are questions over the consistency of the data across these two sources and the long time period of our survey. We outline and address these in more detail in the Appendix. For all its challenges, our *Times* dataset offers a rare insight into the twentieth-century history of crime victims in court. It helps to bridge a data gap in that it offers an overview of a subset of victims engaging with the criminal justice system from the 1910s to the 1970s, in the era before large victim surveys began in the 1980s (Hough and Mayhew 1983; Jones, MacLean, and Young, 1986).

Our focus on cases tried at the Old Bailey means that this book is similarly focused on prosecutions in the London area, and on serious crimes. Until 1834, the court's jurisdiction covered the City of London and the county of Middlesex, which meant it heard the vast majority of prosecutions for serious crime in the metropolis at the time. After its re-constitution as the Central Criminal Court in November 1834, its jurisdiction extended to incorporate the growing metropolitan parts of the neighbouring counties of Essex, Kent, and Surrey. In 1856 its jurisdiction was further extended to include a small number of cases from the rest of England and Wales for which it was determined that a fair trial could not be obtained locally; or, as established in 1925, if such a trial was 'more convenient'. In 1972 it became a crown court, whose jurisdiction was no longer geographically prescribed (Crew, 1933. 276–7; Shoemaker, 2008a). Nonetheless, metropolitan cases predominated. To widen our coverage, we created a further Parliamentary Papers dataset derived from published statistics of the annual number of national prosecutions for indictable offences from 1805 to 1979, broken down where possible by cases heard by summary jurisdiction and commitments for trial at the quarter sessions and assizes courts. As explained in the Appendix, this dataset also includes statistics on the number of government-funded prosecutions, and those conducted by the Director of Public Prosecutions and other government agencies.

As an assize court and later crown court, the Old Bailey primarily heard felonies. As we explain in Chapter 2, the legal obligations of victims, witnesses, and, to a lesser extent, the broader public, were restricted to felonies, whereas with misdemeanours, judicial officials and the public had greater flexibility in how they responded to offences. While the court's remit dictated our focus on felonies, the ambiguous and changing legal status of many offences meant that we have also necessarily paid some attention to offences which were also often tried in lower courts. Depending on the specific circumstances of the offence, many cases of simple theft (petty larceny and other thefts without aggravating circumstances) and serious assault could be tried both at the assizes and the quarter sessions courts and, primarily from the second half of the nineteenth century, by summary jurisdiction in magistrates' courts. It is impossible to fully assess victims' experience of justice at the Old Bailey without recognizing these ambiguities and changes in how some offences were tried. We therefore draw on existing studies of lower courts and summary jurisdiction (see e.g. Auerbach, 2021; Gray, 2009; Davis, 1984, 1989; Godfrey, Cox, and Farrall, 2007; Shoemaker, 1991).

What we do not examine in any detail is the large number of regulatory misdemeanours (such as keeping disorderly houses, drunkenness, and motoring offences) since there was typically no identifiable individual who was harmed and could be expected to report and prosecute the offence. Since the prosecution of such offences raises very different issues from those we address in this volume, they are largely excluded from this study, though we acknowledge that prosecutions of these offences constitute some of the earliest examples of state prosecution. Overall, therefore, our core focus is on the most serious victim-centred crimes tried in the English and Welsh courts.

1.3 Patterns of Prosecutions

We open our discussion of the history of crime victims by offering an overview of the broad patterns within our data and a preliminary explanation of the underlying factors which shaped these trends. These patterns profoundly affected victims' experiences of justice.

The *Proceedings* contain details of 230,646 'victim prosecutions': every criminal charge that is linked to a victim is counted separately (where a victim brought more than one charge, each is counted as a separate prosecution). As Figure 1.1 demonstrates, the number of victim prosecutions recorded in the Old Bailey varied dramatically over time. Incomplete reporting (and the loss of some early editions of the *Proceedings*) in the years up to 1715 account for some of the fluctuations in this period but

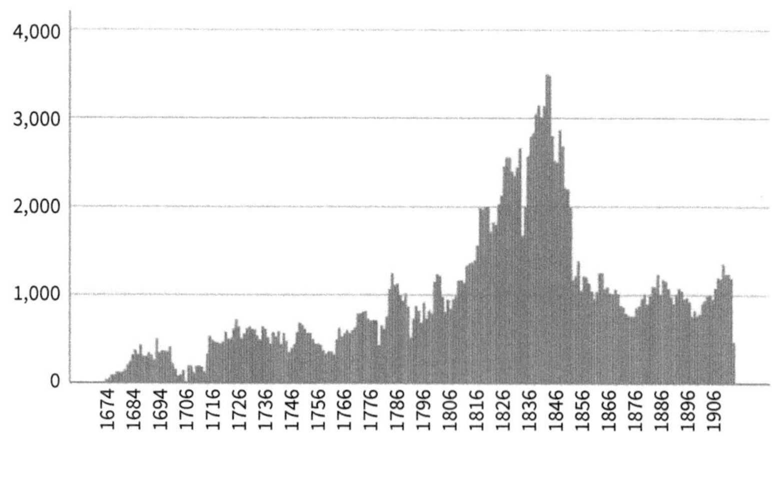

Figure 1.1: Old Bailey Victim Prosecutions by Year, 1674–1913
Source: Proceedings Dataset

the dramatic rise in victim prosecutions between 1790 and 1842, and the equally dramatic fall between 1843 and 1876, have more substantive explanations. A huge wave of prosecutions followed the end of the Napoleonic wars in 1815, as large numbers of young men were demobilized and returned to civilian life. This was inflated in the ensuing decades by rising levels of poverty and social unrest (Emsley, 2013a; Hay and Snyder, 1989; King, 2006).

The fall in prosecutions at the Old Bailey after 1842 is echoed in national statistics reported in the Parliamentary Papers, although the fall in Old Bailey cases was more dramatic (Parliamentary Papers dataset). 1842 saw the peak of mid-century unemployment, food price rises, and Chartist agitation. Over the following years, there was a significant decline in prosecutions for theft, the most common offence tried at the Old Bailey (Gatrell, 1980, 312–13). While it is likely that fewer crimes took place and it is possible that more victims responded to crimes without recourse to the courts, the primary cause of the decline in Old Bailey cases was a series of statutes dating from 1840, as explained in Chapter 3, which allowed more crimes to be dealt with summarily in the lower courts, by magistrates. Most importantly, the 1855 Criminal Justice Act enabled the summary prosecution of all thefts of goods valued less than five shillings, if the accused consented, and of all simple larcenies if the accused pleaded guilty (18 & 19 Vict., *c.* 126). As noted in the 1856 *Judicial Statistics*, this Act was primarily responsible for the decline in commitments for trial in that year (vii–viii). In 1879 the Summary Jurisdiction Act further expanded the range of larcenies triable by summary jurisdiction and also assigned most offences by juveniles under 16 to those courts (42 & 43 Vict. *c.* 49, s. 10-13; Gatrell and Hadden, 1972, 356; Tobias, 1967, 228). As the Old Bailey's geographical jurisdiction expanded, as explained above, the legal jurisdiction of the assizes courts narrowed.

With more and more offences being dealt with by summary jurisdiction, the number of Old Bailey victim prosecutions stabilized at around 1,000 per year from 1860 to 1913, at a time when the population of the metropolis doubled (Auerbach, 2021, 285). The proportion of London's population who appeared as victim prosecutors at London's highest criminal court thus declined significantly, as victims of crime increasingly saw their prosecutions tried in the lower courts.

These mid-nineteenth-century legal changes resulted in a dramatic shift in the composition of crimes prosecuted at the Old Bailey, as demonstrated in Figure 1.2 (the offence categories are explained in the Appendix;

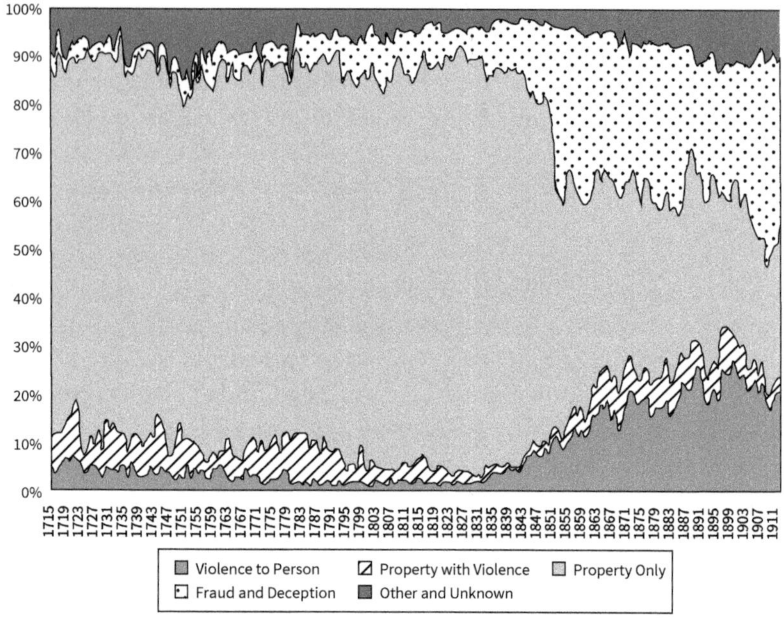

Figure 1.2: Offence Categories in the *Proceedings*, 1715–1913
Source: Proceedings dataset

here Killing, Personal Harm, and Sexual Injury have been combined into 'Violence to the Person'). Prior to the 1840s, acts against property only, including larceny, burglary, housebreaking, pickpocketing, and shoplifting (but excluding violent theft) accounted for between 69 and 87 per cent of all prosecutions. Between 1843 and 1883, however, the proportion of prosecutions at the Old Bailey accounted for by these offences fell by more than half as other offences, sometimes involving different methods of prosecution, became more prominent. Fraud and deception were proportionally much more common, including coining offences and cases with institutional victims (including quasi-state agencies, companies, and voluntary organizations); the former were frequently prosecuted by the police and officers from the Mint. Other offences acquiring greater prominence at the Old Bailey included violence to the person and property offences with violence. Within the 'other' category, there was also a growing number of offences categorized as violations of public order, including bigamy, perjury, and perverting the course of justice. Many of the former disproportionately affected female victims, while some of the latter can be characterized as 'victimless offences', in the sense that it was the broader state and society, rather than individuals, that were considered to be harmed and it was agents of the state who prosecuted.

Overall, as explored in Chapter 5, the composition of victims at the Old Bailey changed between 1674 and 1913 in two important respects. Firstly, those whose complaints involved non-violent property offences, other minor offences, and juvenile offenders increasingly had their offences tried by summary jurisdiction and did not experience a jury trial. Secondly, the victims whose complaints *were* tried at the Old Bailey increasingly became those who had suffered the most serious crimes (which disproportionately involved female victims). Also, more cases were tried involving institutional victims and where the state itself could be considered the victim. In such cases, the state had a significant interest in pursuing a conviction, thus potentially changing the role of the victim in the courtroom.

As outlined above, in order to explore patterns of Old Bailey prosecutions in the twentieth century we manually constructed a dataset of 5,816 crime reports appearing in *The Times* between 1910–25 and 1960–75. A comparison between reports in the more comprehensive Old Bailey *Proceedings* and *The Times* between 1910 and 1912, when both were published, shows that only 14.4 per cent of the cases reported in the *Proceedings* were also reported in *The Times* and that the percentage varied over time, presumably owing to changing editorial priorities. This helps to explain the fact that the number of cases reported varied substantially from year to year, as shown in Figure 1.3. The nature of the selectivity operated by the paper varied considerably over the twentieth century, as editorial practices changed and the newsworthiness of particular types of crimes waxed and waned. This makes it difficult to identify chronological trends of prosecutions in this data. For these reasons, we make greater use of the more comprehensive Old Bailey *Proceedings* data, although we use *Times* data to provide a twentieth-century perspective where sufficient evidence exists.

The distribution of offences recorded in *Times* reports was shaped by both the editorial policies of the paper and the changing mixture of offences tried at the Old Bailey. In 1910–12, when compared to the *Proceedings*, *The Times* disproportionately reported cases of fraud and violent offences, particularly those which led to the death of the victim. As a result, higher proportions of cases involving institutional and female victims were reported. On the other hand, *The Times* was less likely to report more mundane property and public order offences and, in the 1910–25 period, sexual offences.

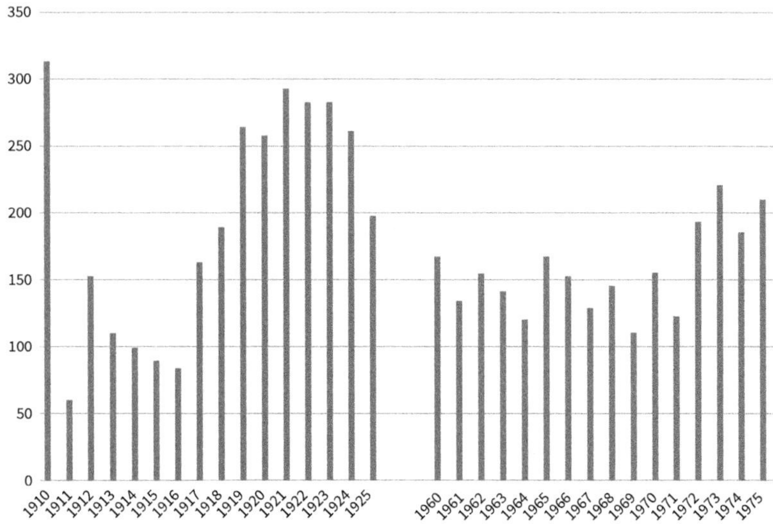

Figure 1.3: Victims in Old Bailey Cases Reported in *The Times*, 1910–25 and 1960–75

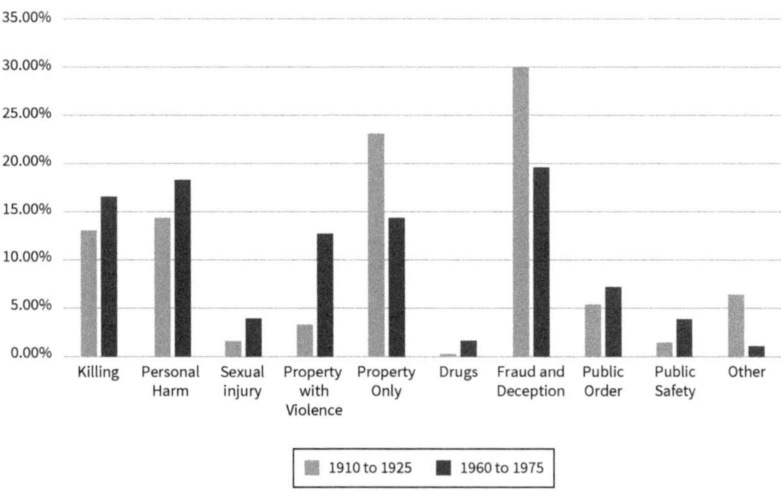

Figure 1.4: Offence Categories in *The Times*, 1910–25 and 1960–75

Nevertheless, the overall distribution of offences tried at the Old Bailey in our two sample periods, as reported in *The Times*, is broadly similar to that found in the *Proceedings* in the early twentieth century, with deception and property offences being the largest categories (Figure 1.4). There were also significant numbers of prosecutions for crimes involving violence. Significantly, when compared to the earlier period, the 1960–75 period has higher levels of prosecutions for public order, safety and security, and drugs offences, perhaps reflecting growing state involvement in prosecutions affecting the perceived wider public interest.

In sum, the changing distribution of crimes prosecuted at the Old Bailey between the late-seventeenth and the late-twentieth centuries is suggestive of changes in the types of victims and prosecutors which brought these prosecutions. The nature and causes of these changes are explored in further detail in subsequent chapters.

1.4 Aims and Structure of This Book

This book is the first of its kind to present a critical history of victims' changing involvement in English criminal trials and the wider criminal justice system from the early modern to the modern period. In exploring the long history of participation in criminal justice, it interrogates assumptions made in previous studies and returns us to the question asked by Rudé: who were the victims? It also moves beyond this to offer a unique analysis of the profiles of, resources available to, and outcomes for, around a quarter of a million individual complainants at the Old Bailey from the late-seventeenth to the late-twentieth centuries. In so doing, it explores the processes that led to the marginalization of victims within the justice system and subsequent efforts to re-centre them.

Rudé published his classic book, *Criminal and Victim*, in 1985—the year the Prosecution of Offences Act was passed, mandating the establishment of the CPS the following year. As indicated above, this was a landmark moment with far-reaching implications for the criminal justice process and the place of victims within it. As we will go on to show, it was the culmination of a historical narrowing of the victims' role, a complex process which began in the eighteenth century, as policing agents and lawyers assumed a right to lead the prosecution of offences, but which was not completed until 'police prosecution' was abolished and replaced by 'public prosecution' in the mid-1980s—the point at which our core historical analysis ends.

This opening chapter has introduced the broad terrain explored by this book, reviewed key themes in historical and criminological literature and explained our key datasets. Chapter 2 (Hidden Victims) explores the challenges of researching the history of the many victims whose complaints did not reach court or who were unwilling or unable to fully engage with the criminal justice system of the day. It offers an overview of the prosecution process, outlines the numerous disincentives to participating in it, profiles the types of victims who were least likely to engage with the judicial process and describes some of the alternative tactics available to them. While these victims cannot be included in our study, their absence is vital context, one that explains the state's substantial efforts over time to reduce those disincentives and ensure that more crimes were prosecuted, efforts which led to significant redefinitions of the role and entitlements of the victim.

Chapter 3 (From Prosecutors to Victims) documents these initiatives and investigates how they affected victims' access to justice over time. From the late-seventeenth century, the state sought to incentivize victims to initiate more prosecutions. These incentives took various forms. Initially the state offered rewards for convictions, and then reimbursed the costs of prosecution and introduced allowances for time and trouble. The chapter shows how early-modern English conceptualizations of victims as actors with legal obligations to prosecute endured even as nineteenth-century interventions by the state and voluntary organizations became more substantial. From the eighteenth century, and accelerating in the nineteenth century, professionals assumed a greater role in the criminal justice system, ostensibly supporting the victims' interests but simultaneously sidelining them as direct participants. The chapter ends by outlining the twentieth-century changes which completed the process of transforming victims into marginal figures in the courtroom and triggered campaigns for victims' 'rights'.

Chapter 4 (Public Prosecution) examines the complex and uneven rise of public prosecution in more detail, exploring how it developed on the ground through police and court practice, how it was framed in public political debate, and how compromises were made enabling the creation of the DPP in the 1880s and the CPS a century later. It argues for a conceptual differentiation between prosecutions conducted by the state or its quasi-agencies, and prosecutions conducted in the interests of private victims or institutions (including voluntary organizations and companies), which were increasingly delegated to the state-funded police and which led, ultimately, to forms of public prosecution. From the mid-nineteenth century to the late-twentieth century, a significant proportion of higher court prosecutions, and the investigations that preceded them, were managed by the police and their solicitors and barristers. The English police's dual role as investigators and prosecutors was unusual in global terms and the history of how it arose and why it came to an end is little known.

Chapter 5 (Victims at the Old Bailey) assesses the impact of the changing prosecution, policing, and support arrangements discussed in Chapters 3 and 4 on the participation of victims in arguably the most important criminal court in England. The chapter explores the extent to which marginalized groups, particularly female and working-class victims, young and elderly victims, and minority ethnic victims, prosecuted cases, and assesses the impact of statutes and practices which may have facilitated their appearances in court.

Chapter 6 (Trials and Outcomes) moves on to consider the events of the trials, in terms of who participated, when, and how much they spoke in court. It then offers an analysis of trial outcomes, in terms of verdicts and punishment sentences, as measures of whether prosecutions might be deemed 'successful' by victims. Together, Chapters 5 and 6 consider what was driving the changing profile of Old Bailey victims and their experiences of the criminal justice system, weighing the impact of state and legal reforms against that of wider cultural, social, and economic shifts.

Chapter 7 (Post-war Victims and the Pains of Prosecution) provides a new historical reading of the emergence of calls for victims' rights after the Second World War. It sets these in the context of the displacing of the victim in prosecution practice documented in the preceding chapters. It focuses on post-war Old Bailey trials relating to domestic violence, sexual offences, and what would become recognized as homophobic hate and racially-aggravated offences, exploring representations of the victims involved, the development of campaigns aiming to support them, and the state's response to these. It suggests that the victims of these offences experienced what we have termed particular 'pains of prosecution'. The chapter offers a new historical reading of the emergence of 'victim support' as a concept and as a set of cultural practices. Chapter 8 (Epilogue) draws our investigation to an end by bringing this story into the present and summarizing the value of historicizing both victims' participation and their increasing politicization.

Overall, this book seeks to deepen contemporary and historical understandings of changing conceptions of victimhood, using quantitative analysis of trial reports and a wide range of qualitative evidence to add a new dimension to current social, cultural, and economic histories of criminal justice. It also offers a critical and historically informed perspective on current efforts in England and Wales and beyond to encourage victims' engagement with, and participation within, the criminal justice system. In so doing, it seeks to establish a new interdisciplinary account of victims' access to justice over time.

2
Hidden Victims

Criminologists and crime historians have long been aware of the challenges posed by the 'dark figure' of unreported and unrecorded crime. Only a small fraction of overall crime is ever reported to the authorities; reports are not always pursued; and those that are may never reach court or a final verdict. This is a problem for historians seeking to discern patterns in overall victimization over time. But an examination of those victims who, for manifold reasons, failed to engage with criminal justice can be revealing. It helps to demonstrate the limitations in judicial processes which the state and voluntary associations attempted to address over the three centuries reviewed in this book. As we will argue, these efforts, which are outlined in Chapters 3 and 4 and whose impact is assessed in Chapters 5 and 6, had important consequences for the place of victims in criminal justice, as efforts to support victims paradoxically often resulted in their being supplanted in proceedings. This book concentrates on those victims who chose (or were compelled), and were permitted, to engage in prosecutions leading to trials from the late-seventeenth century onwards, and the factors shaping and governing that engagement. In other words, it is primarily based on the examination of reported and prosecuted crime. Before turning to this, however, we need to examine how levels of *unreported* and *unprosecuted* crime affect our investigation.

This chapter summarizes existing historical research on unreported, unprosecuted, and unsuccessfully prosecuted crime, on the use of informal settlements and alternatives to prosecution, and on rejected prosecutions. In doing so, it explores the range of disincentives to prosecution which led victims to choose alternative methods, and which prompted the state to introduce measures to counter them.

Victims and Criminal Justice. Pamela Cox, Robert Shoemaker, and Heather Shore,
Oxford University Press.
DOI: 10.1093/oso/9780192846488.003.0002

2.1 Unreported Crime

Until the late-twentieth century, victims and witnesses of serious crimes (felonies) had a legal obligation to attempt to apprehend the culprit and take them before a constable or justice of the peace (JP) (Hale, 1736, I, 588; Blackstone, 1769, 289). Failure to do this, and thus to cover up a crime, was itself a crime (*misprision of felony*) in England and Wales. 'Misprision', or deliberate concealment, had been applied to the crime of treason since the middle ages, but was expanded in the sixteenth century to include felonies in order to promote the reporting and therefore the control of crime. Legal manuals indicate that 'misprision of felony' continued to be recognized as an offence throughout the eighteenth and nineteenth centuries, and was only formally abolished in 1967 (Glazebrook, 1964; Hale, 1736, I, 371–5; Blackstone, 1769, 121; Burn, 1755, I, 69; Maule, 1869, I, 404; Criminal Law Act, 1967, *c.* 58, s. 1).

The obligation to *prosecute* felonies began with this duty to arrest the culprit and bring him or her before a constable or JP. As the late seventeenth-century jurist Matthew Hale wrote, referring to a hypothetical victim as 'A.', 'the law in this case makes A. an officer' (Hale, 1736, II, 76). This obligation only pertained to known felons, however. Those *suspected* of felony *could* be arrested by a private person, but there was no requirement to make such arrests (Hale, 1736, II, 82). There was also a duty in common law for the general public to join a 'hue and cry' in pursuit of an offender following a sudden death or the inflicting of a serious wound (Hale, 1736, I, 588; Burn, 1755, II, 16), although this was limited to adult men who actually witnessed the crime or came across the body; this duty included arresting any suspect identified (Glazebrook, 1964, 202–4; Hale, 1736, 75). In 1827, the Criminal Statutes Repeal Act (7 & 8 Geo 4 *c.* 27) ended this obligation, but the right (rather than the obligation) to make a 'citizen's arrest' still remained in force. Once the suspect was arrested and brought before a magistrate, victims were expected to take the lead in prosecuting the case. If the crime was a felony, under the Marian bail statutes (1555), the magistrate was obliged to take depositions and forward the case to the grand jury; this included binding over the victim by recognizance to appear in court and testify (Langbein, 1974; 1 & 2 Phil. & Mar. *c.* 13; 2 & 3 Phil. & Mar. *c.* 10).

There was, however, very little chance of a victim or witness being sanctioned for failing to carry out their legal duties. When combined with the disincentives to prosecution discussed below, this meant that the vast majority of crimes were not reported or prosecuted. Commentators have attempted to attach a number to the 'dark figure' of unreported crime. *The Times* observed in 1785 that 'nine-tenths of the breaches against the laws escape detection, from the trouble and charges consequent on prosecution', while in 1796 magistrate Patrick Colquhoun asserted that 'under the present system there is not above one offence in one hundred that is discovered or prosecuted' (*The Times*, 5 Dec. 1785; Colquhoun, 1796, vii; King, 2000, 11–12, 30, 132–4).

Crime historians, using a variety of evidence to try to illuminate this 'dark figure' of unreported and unrecorded crime, have reached similar conclusions. Robert Shoemaker's study of 217 years of entries in some of the most detailed diaries and correspondence kept by twelve Londoners from the period 1660–1800 found that they recorded a total of seventy-three crimes (including petty crimes) committed against the diarist or correspondent, their families, households, neighbours, friends, or acquaintances. Only nine of these seventy-three crimes (12 per cent) were reported to the magistrates, and only four (5 per cent) of these led to formal action against someone accused of committing the crime. These, as one might expect, included the most serious crimes reported: murder and housebreaking. Nonetheless, most break-ins and robberies were not reported (Shoemaker, 2017, 81–2). Similarly, Peter King looked at eight diarists from Essex between 1754 and 1810 who recorded thirty-nine felonious property appropriations in 132 years. These resulted in just three formal prosecutions (King, 2000, 18–19).

It has been suggested that the 'dark figure' decreased in the nineteenth century (Gatrell, 1980, 249–50), but contemporary observers continued to note that a high proportion of crimes remained unprosecuted and we cannot presume there was an increasing trend for crimes to be reported and prosecuted. Mid-Victorian lawyer C. S. Graves believed that, 'Of the multitude of offences that are committed, no doubt, only a small portion comes to the knowledge of the police' (Graves, 1866–7, 108, cited by Churchill, 2017, 25). In 1898, a parliamentary report noted that, owing to more merciful attitudes towards offenders, 'there is a somewhat greater reluctance to prosecute now than formerly' (PP, 1900).

Those researching the later twentieth century are fortunate to have comprehensive survey data to compare with official figures on recorded crime. In 1977 a study of victims of crime in three London boroughs (Brixton, Hackney, and Kensington)—the first of its kind—found a large number of unreported crimes, with victims' propensity to report them to the police varying according to the severity of the crime and where they lived (Sparks,

Genn, and Dodd, 1977). In 1981, the Home Office agreed to scale up these community crime surveys to a national level. The first British Crime Survey was conducted in 1982 and it continues to be carried out periodically today as the Crime Survey for England and Wales. The initial survey indicated that respondents had experienced 'four times more offences of property loss and damage than [in] official statistics and around five times more offences of violence (wounding, robbery, and sexual offences)' (Hough and Mayhew, 1983, 32). It also offered new evidence on how victims responded to specific crimes, finding that 'the lowest reporting rates ... were shared by vandalism and theft in a dwelling' followed by sexual offences, theft from a vehicle, and theft from a person. The crime by far most likely to come to the attention of the police was theft of a vehicle. Respondents' reasons for not reporting included the commonly expressed belief 'that the police would not have been able to do anything' and 'that their incidents were inappropriate for the police' (ibid, 10–11). Ever since, crime surveys have continued to generate substantial data on the nature and extent of hidden victimization and victims' exercise, or lack, of agency. As this chapter shows, the broader history of these questions has been less fully explored owing to incomplete evidence, but it offers valuable insights into who such victims were, what they were victims of and what actions they took—or did not take—over time as a result.

Types of offences

The extent to which victims chose to report crimes (or not) varied according to the type of offence, the identity of the victim and the offender, and the wider context in which the offence occurred. The offence most likely to be prosecuted was homicide, an offence for which an official investigator, the coroner, had long existed. But even this offence was not consistently dealt with. Coroners had a legal responsibility to investigate all sudden, violent, or suspicious deaths, and it has been argued that the seriousness of the crime encouraged reports and prosecutions. It is difficult to dispose of a body and both policing agents and the public were keen on the prosecution of murder (Forbes, 1978, 1–52; Shoemaker, 2001, 191). However, in the absence of modern forensic and medical skills, assigning criminal responsibility for a death can be difficult. Archer's investigation into 'mysterious and suspicious deaths' reported in late nineteenth-century newspapers or investigated by coroners found that several types of violent deaths were not reported as murders, including those resulting from male-on-male fights, domestic violence, and all cases where a culprit could not be found or the police anticipated difficulties in obtaining a conviction (Archer, 2008). A good example of the latter is infanticide, where there were often no witnesses to a birth and it was difficult to determine whether the victim was stillborn or choked to death (Kilday, 2013).

At the heart of these failures to investigate, report, and prosecute homicide were both public views about the acceptability, or otherwise, of certain types of violence, and the difficulty of proving that injuries had led to death, particularly if the victim had been poisoned or had existing medical problems (Archer, 2008; Watson, 2004). These findings support Taylor's argument that between 1850 and 1998 'most murders and suspicious deaths went uninvestigated', although not necessarily his controversial explanation that the number of such deaths reported was deliberately kept artificially low by the limited amount of resources the state was willing to devote to supporting prosecutions (Taylor, 1998, 588; for a critique, see Godfrey, 2008, 178–80). While the state took responsibility for investigating this offence in place of the deceased victim, familiar issues of limited time, funding and prevailing social attitudes combined to discourage prosecutions (Morris, 2001). The fact that even an offence widely condemned by the public was not consistently prosecuted illustrates just how high the dark figure of unreported crime was.

Crimes that were particularly unlikely to be formally reported included non-fatal domestic violence, sexual assault (discussed in a separate section at the end of this chapter), petty thefts, and minor assaults. In the eighteenth and nineteenth centuries, 'moderate physical correction' of subordinates (wives, servants, apprentices, and children) was socially acceptable, which meant that even when such violence was extreme, it was likely to go unreported (Smith, 2007; Conley, 1991, 126–7). It was difficult to draw a clear line between acceptable and unacceptable violence and, in any case, the inferior position of the victims vis-a-vis the perpetrators made it difficult for them to prosecute. This was an area where, from the mid-nineteenth century onwards, voluntary bodies and the state attempted to assist. However, despite the passage of statutes intended to facilitate such prosecutions in 1853 and 1861, the number of prosecutions of 'aggravated assaults' on women and children actually declined in the summary courts (where they were now tried; Edwards, 2005, 252–3). There were many reasons for underreporting such crimes including, in the case of husbands' attacks on wives, the victims' tendency to blame themselves for provoking the violence, a lack of trust in the police, women's economic dependence on their male attackers, fear of retribution, and the fact the police and the courts did not appear to take such cases seriously (Edwards, 2005; Clark, 2000). Social reformer Harriet Taylor and her husband John Stuart Mill published an anonymous report about a trial for attempted spousal murder in the *Morning Chronicle* in 1851. They commented:

> we scarcely believe there is an offence in the whole criminal code of which a prisoner would have been acquitted, in the face of such evidence, except that of an attempt at wife-murder ... There is no crime in the whole catalogue of offences in which the single act which incurs the penalty of the law is an index to such an amount of undetected and unpunished wickedness' (*Morning Chronicle*, 28 August 1851, 4).

Churchill notes that the nineteenth-century police tended to ignore 'family quarrels' and that, as a result, cases of domestic violence were 'amongst the least likely to come to court' (2017, 62, 196).

Petty theft (broadly defined), probably the most prevalent crime throughout this period, was also seriously underreported, and even when reported, often not pursued to conviction. According to Churchill (2017, 25), in the nineteenth century:

> Contemporaries identified several varieties of crime (chiefly forms of petty theft) which were especially likely to go unreported: embezzlement from the workplace; thefts committed by servants; theft of fuel and materials; theft of letters from the postal system; shoplifting; theft of exposed goods outside shops or on the dockside; thefts from sailors and travellers; obtaining goods by false pretences; and frauds committed by 'respectable' persons.

In the 1860s, William Palin, Chief Constable of Manchester, complained that even where cases were reported to the magistrates with sufficient evidence to prosecute, 'the persons charging declined to attend' (cited by Churchill, 2017, 192). Despite the relative ease of prosecuting thefts by employees in the police courts, research by Davis found that 'employers apparently overlooked vast quantities of law-breaking' in late nineteenth-century London (Davis, 1989, 401–2). Some of this unwillingness to prosecute was probably due to the relatively low value of the stolen goods compared to the likely costs of prosecution. But while many of the thefts discussed here were of low-value items, others, particularly those involving aggravated circumstances such as theft from shops and the post, and thefts from the person, were felonies, and considered as serious crimes.

In general, less serious crimes—misdemeanours—were less likely to be prosecuted. Apart from the absence of legal compulsion, these were often very minor offences. One of the most common offences, assault, was so broadly defined in eighteenth-century legal advice as to include 'any injury done to the person of a man, in an angry insolent manner, be it ever so small ... for example, spitting in his face, jostling him, treading on his toes, or any way touching him in anger' (Trusler, 1786, 130). With increasingly demanding standards for 'civilized' behaviour over the ensuing centuries, it is likely that the remit of this common law offence only became broader (Wiener, 1998; Wood, 2004). But the criminalization of what might have been previously perceived as non-criminal behaviour may have only increased the amount of non-reported crime. In such cases the trouble involved in initiating a prosecution could seem disproportionate to the harm received and, as discussed below, there were simpler, less formal methods of resolving such accusations. Moreover, some misdemeanours, such as fraud and damage to property, were borderline civil offences, which could be dealt with outside the criminal court system.

Types of victim

Certain types of victims were particularly unwilling or unable to report and prosecute, the result of both the nature of the crimes they experienced and their social position. We can see this as the reverse image of the social and gender composition of those victims who did decide to prosecute. As we shall see in Chapter 5, the proportions of lower-class and female victims at the Old Bailey were far lower than in the overall population. While we cannot assume that levels of victimhood were evenly distributed throughout the population (see Hope and Trickett, 2008), there is evidence to suggest that both these groups were particularly dissuaded from reporting and prosecuting crime, along with other groups, including children and people with disabilities. It is also likely that homosexual victims and those from minority ethnic groups are underrepresented in the judicial records, but we lack firm evidence on this point (Shore and Williams, 2022).

The largest group of non-prosecuting victims was undoubtedly women, who accounted for only 14.4 per cent of the victims at the Old Bailey between 1674 and 1913, and 32.1 per cent of cases reported in *The Times* between 1910 and 1975 (*Proceedings* and *Times* datasets). While the proportion of women in the *Proceedings* increased in the late nineteenth century, *The Times* appears to have disproportionately selected cases involving women for reporting. Overall, the number of women prosecuting was remarkably low for a group which comprised more than half of the metropolitan population.

With the exceptions of those who were subjected to sexual offences and domestic violence, there is little historical research on female victims, but we can identify some clear obstacles and disincentives to prosecution for women. The most obvious is that, until 1882, most married women's property was deemed to be owned by their husbands. In principle, therefore, they could not be victims in property offences (the offence most frequently prosecuted at the Old Bailey) even when, for example, the stolen goods were clearly the wife's possessions, such as her jewellery or clothing. In practice, however, this law was not always followed in criminal cases, and married women did prosecute some cases at the Old Bailey. There were 803 married female victims recorded in the *Proceedings* between 1674 and 1834, including many who were prosecuting theft. While marital status was not routinely recorded, it is notable that these married women accounted for only 5.8 per cent of cases prosecuted by women in the period (OBO).

This changed after the Married Women's Property Act of 1882, which allowed married women to own property in their own right (45 & 46 Vict. *c*.75). Following its passage, the number of prosecutions on behalf of female victims increased by 31 per cent for theft, and by 56 per cent for fraud (based on a comparison of prosecutions ten years before and ten years after the passage of the Act: *Proceedings* dataset). In reports of *The Times*, where just 44.3 per cent women were given a marital status, 34.6 per cent of them were married, compared to 59.0 per cent single and 6.5 per cent widows (*Times* dataset). This suggests that, prior to 1882, their status as married women prevented many female victims from prosecuting crime.

Even when we remove property offences, women only account for 32.0 per cent of the victims identified by sex at the Old Bailey (*Proceedings* dataset). When female victims did appear in court, the trial reports analysed in Chapter 6 show that they were less likely than male victims to testify and that when they did speak they did so later in the trial. The Old Bailey courtrooms were male-dominated environments throughout this period. Until the early twentieth century, all the judges, jurors, court officials, and lawyers were men, and women were less likely to serve as witnesses. The passage of the 1919 Sex Disqualification (Removal) Act lifted the bar on women holding public office (including as judges and jurors) or entering a profession (including the law) but change was slow (9 & 10 Geo. 5 *c*. 71). The first female judge did not sit at the Old Bailey until 1972, and women entered the law and the police force only gradually. Even in 1966 they still accounted for fewer than 5 per cent of officers (Grant, 2019, 383, 391; D'Cruze and Jackson, 2009, 111–13).

Women may have found this male-dominated atmosphere intimidating, thought that they did not belong there, or thought that their accusations would not be believed. With the exception of the points made below about sexual crimes, we have little evidence on these possibilities, but contemporary prejudices about 'women's tendency to be governed too much by the passions and too little by reason' clearly had the potential, from the point of view of male officials and juries, to discredit female testimony, and to lead women to believe they would not be listened to (Edwards, 2005, 255–8; Shoemaker, 1998, 28–9). Taylor and Mill noted in 1846 that women 'in the lower ranks of life' were reluctant to initiate prosecutions because they 'do not expect justice from a bench or jury of the male sex' (quoted in Shoemaker, 1998, 292). Those suspicions were not without foundation; actual jury decision-making suggests such attitudes sometimes prevailed. At the Middlesex quarter sessions, a sample from around the turn of the eighteenth century found that indictments initiated by women were 37 per cent more likely to be rejected by the grand jury than those initiated by men (Shoemaker, 1991, 211).

Women's relative absence cannot simply be explained by noting that men were more likely to spend time in public spaces where they were more likely to become victims of crime. In practice, gendered notions of 'separate spheres' were often not followed in women's day-to-day lives (Shoemaker, 1998). In fact, women did frequently prosecute crime, but not at the Old Bailey. Throughout this period, women often chose alternatives to formal prosecution by indictment. They were proportionally more likely to participate in cases resulting in informal settlements, binding over, and summary jurisdiction. These alternatives, discussed below, were most frequently used by women to prosecute offences against the peace such as assault and defamation, particularly in cases of domestic violence (Shoemaker, 1991, 207–12; Conley, 1991, 68–95). Nonetheless, female complainants could still be underrepresented, particularly in rural areas (Shoemaker, 1991, 208–9; Darby, 2015, 372). A survey of employment disputes recorded in justices' notebooks and petty sessions records in eighteenth and early nineteenth-century England found that women accounted for only 20.4 per cent of cases brought by servants, despite the fact female servants outnumbered male servants at the time (Chartrand, 2017, 122).

While women were marginalized at the Old Bailey by their gender, the other large (and overlapping) marginalized groups in the population were the working class and the poor. As documented in Chapter 5, while a substantial, and increasing, number of prosecutions came from the labouring poor, these groups remained less likely than those from other social classes to prosecute at the Old Bailey throughout the period. Evidence from earlier studies including other parts of the country confirms this conclusion. Rudé's investigation of prosecutions in early nineteenth-century Middlesex, Gloucestershire, and Sussex found that 'victims [tended to be] of the "middling" and upper classes' (Rudé, 1985, 117). Similarly, King concluded that 'the middling strata dominated the prosecution process in every county' in the late eighteenth and early nineteenth centuries, accounting for two-thirds to three-quarters of all prosecutors, because they 'were more likely to have the resources available to mount a prosecution' (King, 2000, 38–40). For the nineteenth century, David Philips, while noting the 'surprising' number of working-class prosecutors in the Black Country, observed that this was lower than their proportion in the population as a whole (Philips, 1977, 126). Given the absence of reliable data, we cannot confirm whether any social group was more or less likely to be actual victims of crime in the past, but all except the very poor possessed some items worth stealing, and the poor were less able to protect their possessions from theft. Jennifer Davis noted that 'the labouring poor were, according to the police and the criminal records, more likely to be the victims of theft, both violent and non-violent, than other social classes' (Davis, 1989, 414). Instead, the relatively low presence of the labouring poor among victims is better explained by their being dissuaded from acting by the legal costs and the time off work necessitated by a court prosecution (discussed below). While, as Chapter 3 will show, financial support did become available over time, it was never comprehensive.

Like women, the labouring poor were disproportionately more likely to seek cheaper forms of prosecution. In eighteenth-century London, JPs were often willing to hear their complaints informally for low or no fees. So called 'trading justices', socially inferior men who turned their office into a trade by hearing large volumes of cases from poor victims at low cost, offered an important quasi-official form of prosecution (Landau, 1984, 184–203; Landau, 2002, 46–70). When these justices were replaced by stipendiary magistrates with the Middlesex Justices Act in 1792, the latter served a similar function (32 Geo. III *c.* 53).

Cases involving child victims were also less likely to be prosecuted, in part because they were seen as unreliable witnesses. According to William Blackstone in 1773, children of any age were allowed to testify in court, and they could do so sworn if they understood the nature of the oath. Their evidence, however, had to be corroborated. The fact that child witnesses could be questioned about their basic understanding of truth (to determine whether they could be sworn) was likely to induce scepticism in the minds of judges and jurors (Blackstone, 1769, 214; Jackson, 1999; Jackson, 2000, 93–6, 214). Paradoxically, statutes passed between 1885 and 1933 which were intended to protect child witnesses and facilitate their testimony contributed to the perception of children's evidence as inherently questionable, since they deemed it unsafe without corroboration. It was only in the late twentieth century, with the passage of statutes from 1988 to 1999, that the tide turned and provisions enabled children under fourteen to testify unsworn, and without corroboration (Lamont and Cox, 2021). It is significant, too, that child victimization was obscured by child prosecutions. A large proportion of those aged under sixteen who appeared in court in the nineteenth and twentieth centuries charged with theft, truanting, or variants of vagrancy had experienced neglect or harm of some kind which often went unprosecuted (Shore, 1999; Cox, 2013; Godfrey, Cox, Shore, and Alker, 2017; Daly and Rap, 2019). Faced with these barriers to prosecution, many offences committed against children were not reported.

Disability was likely a further barrier to prosecution. Disabled victims were not routinely identified as such in the *Proceedings*, but it appears that only a few, identified via historical descriptors of disability, appeared as victims in eighteenth-century Old Bailey trials. David Turner found only fifty-one individuals labelled with a physical impairment in 35,780 trials between 1675 and 1775: just 0.14 per cent of victims (Turner, 2012). Despite the likelihood that a disability could make a person more vulnerable to crimes such as robbery, the apparently rare appearances of physically disabled people in court suggests that they are likely to have faced particular disadvantages 'in a system that placed the onus on the victims of crime to initiate prosecutions', in that they would have experienced difficulties in apprehending suspects, recruiting witnesses, and attending court (Turner, 2012, 47–64, 52). Some types of disability received at least marginally increased support from the late eighteenth century, when interpreters were allowed for deaf and mute witnesses and victims. From 1805, deaf people were allowed to present their evidence in writing (Stone and Woll, 2008, 231–3). On the other hand, it is possible that the medicalization of and reduced tolerance towards the perceived mentally deficient in the nineteenth century made it more difficult for these victims to testify in court (Jarrett, 2020, ch. 4). In addition, particularly in the twentieth century, they may have been deemed by the court not to be competent to provide evidence. The access to justice of victims with disabilities of all types is a topic much in need of further research.

In summary, all that we know about the history of crime indicates that the vast majority of offences were not prosecuted. As a result, the victimhood of those harmed was hidden from view. Even the most serious of crimes, murder, did not always lead to reporting and prosecution. For petty theft, a simple assessment of the likely costs and benefits of involving the law was enough to dissuade most victims from becoming prosecutors. Lower reporting of crime was more pronounced among women, the poorer classes, young people, and, it is likely, those with disabilities. Given both the reputational and financial resources needed to conduct a prosecution, more marginal members of society were least likely to prosecute, and in this way the criminal justice system served to reinforce established social hierarchies.

2.2 Reasons Not to Prosecute

There were many reasons why victims who might otherwise have been expected to seek access to the law chose not to report and prosecute crime. Chief among them were the costs involved, and the potential damage a prosecution might make to a victim's standing in the community. Moreover, victims of crime had several attractive options for settling criminal accusations outside the law. In addition, some victims failed to gain the support of policing agents in bringing the cases to the attention of magistrates.

Costs

Eighteenth- and nineteenth-century writers and more recent historical investigations agree that the biggest disincentive to prosecution was the costs involved (King, 2000, 30; Phillips, 1977, 110–16; Churchill, 2017, 194). Those initiating prosecutions had to pay a fee for each stage of the judicial process, including securing a warrant to arrest the suspect, drawing up the indictment, and bringing it before the grand jury. Other costs included the time and expense of searching for the culprit and what could be substantial fees for a solicitor to provide legal advice and counsel to appear in court. In 1833, Thomas Wontner, son of a governor of Newgate Prison and founder of a firm of solicitors which acted for the Metropolitan Police, estimated that prosecution costs at the Old Bailey averaged £3 18s 4d (Wontner, 1833, 271). It would take a carpenter about sixteen days of work, or a skilled engineer nearly eleven days, to earn that much (Emsley, Hitchcock, and Shoemaker, 2018a). Lost labour was also a crucial cost. Attending a preliminary hearing and then attending court to testify could be very time-consuming. Trials took place over a number of days and there was no way of knowing when the case would be heard; Wontner claimed the average time prosecutors were 'detained from their business' was five days (Wontner, 1833, 320).

Despite statutory provisions to reimburse expenses introduced in the eighteenth and early nineteenth centuries, discussed in Chapter 3, costs remained a disincentive to prosecution. Samuel Wilkinson, Town Clerk of the Borough of Walsall, told the parliamentary Select Committee on Public Prosecution in 1854–5 'There is no doubt in the world that many prosecutions are not gone into on account of the poverty of the prosecutor; he will not undertake the labour, and trouble, and cost of the prosecution, because he has not the means' (PP, 1855, 156). A Select Committee on Prosecution Expenses in 1862 found that prosecutions were not going forward because the allowance to prosecutors and witnesses was too low for the actual expenses of pursuing the prosecution. As witness Henry Leigh Trafford, stipendiary magistrate at Salford, told the Committee, 'the effect [of the allowances] is extremely prejudicial; and I can state two or three cases in which parties have refused to prosecute, saying at the time that the expenses allowed were too small' (PP, 1862, 45). As a consequence, victims adopted strategies to avoid having to prosecute, for example by failing to swear to the identity of the prisoner at a committal hearing. Despite further measures concerning costs implemented in the late nineteenth century, a parliamentary committee in 1903 found that the allowances provided to prosecutors and witnesses were still inadequate (PP, 1903).

The fundamental problems were that the provisions for payment of expenses did not meet all the costs of prosecution and, crucially, payments were always made in arrears, discouraging not only poorer victims but anyone who was doubtful whether the payments would actually be made.

Expenses awarded did not cover any efforts made by the victim (or the police) to identify the culprit, and inadequate provision was made for legal costs (Phillips, 1977, 113–16; Churchill, 2017, 194). This was a particular issue in London, where, according to James Hemp, Assistant Clerk of Arraigns, 'the allowance at the Central Criminal Court, for instance, to an attorney for a prosecution is almost absurd. Beyond the allowance of 2l [two pounds] or 3l which he has for the brief, he very frequently has to pay to the attorney a bill of 50l or 60l' (PP, 1854–5, evidence of James Hemp). Neither was the loss of time adequately covered: Churchill (2017, 194) cites the case of Benjamin Kay, a draper from Pudsey, who in 1860 refused to report a case of shoplifting to the police as the allowance for his attendance in court would not be sufficient to compensate for his loss of time.

Reputation

In deciding whether to prosecute, victims also considered the effect a prosecution might have on their social standing within their community, while those in dependent positions (such as children) may have feared retribution from those in positions of power. In areas where the authorities were distrusted, such as in some working-class or immigrant neighbourhoods, invoking the law and the police could be viewed as unwelcome and disruptive to community harmony (King, 2000, 31–2). Across all neighbourhoods, there is evidence to suggest that when the offender was young, or a person of status or reputation within the community, victims were less likely to pursue a case. Young offenders known to their neighbours, who were viewed as potentially reformable if dealt with informally, were less likely to be prosecuted than strangers (King, 2000, 33). For a different reason, some victims chose not to prosecute suspects from 'good families', whose reputations implied they could not have committed such a crime, particularly if it was a sexual offence (or if they had committed the crime, like juvenile offenders they were deemed more reformable) (Conley, 1991, 173–7; Shore, 1999). Some victims also feared retributive violence, or malicious prosecutions from friends and families of the accused, if they proceeded with a prosecution (King, 2000, 31; Churchill, 2017, 194).

Worries about the social stigma associated with prosecution were greatest when the offence was capital and the accused might suffer the death penalty. Prior to the revisions of the Bloody Code in the 1820s and 1830s, those convicted of thefts of even relatively low value items might hang, and some victims did not wish to be held responsible by their community for the execution of the defendant, particularly if he or she was a juvenile or young adult (King and Noel, 1993, 32–3; King, 2000, 31–2; Shore, 1999, 27–8). In such situations, and bearing in mind the perceived reformability of young offenders, victims either prosecuted on a reduced (non-capital) charge, sought an informal resolution, or pleaded for mercy at the trial. It is possible that the abolition of the death penalty for most offences helps explain the increases in prosecutions from the 1820s through the 1840s (discussed in the Introduction and Chapter 3), as victims could prosecute with the assurance that convicts would not hang but instead face a reformatory punishment in a penitentiary or through transportation (Philips, 1977, 135).

A different source of social stigma could derive from the circumstances of the crime, when the victim's own behaviour, particularly their sexual conduct, was embarrassing or could be deemed complicit, as in cases where men's pockets were picked by prostitutes, the victim was drunk at the time of the crime, or in cases of sexual assault (Shore, 2009; Churchill, 2017, 195). As discussed below, one of the reasons adult victims of rape rarely prosecuted was because, as is often the case today, they feared having their own behaviour subjected to close scrutiny and preferred to protect their reputations by covering up the crime. Crimes involving prostitutes and other sexual crimes were often reported sensationally in early editions of the Old Bailey *Proceedings*, though in the second half of the eighteenth century, under pressure from the City of London, the tone of reporting became more respectable, and in the nineteenth century trials for sexual offences were heavily censored (Emsley, Hitchcock, and Shoemaker, 2018c). Newspapers, however, which reached a far greater audience in the nineteenth and twentieth centuries, were not subject to such constraints, and victims who sought to avoid having their actions scrutinized in public were likely to fail to report such crimes.

Alternatives to prosecution

As a result of the above, many victims simply ignored their legal obligations to prosecute and sought recompense outside the law. The wide range of alternative means of responding to crime allowed victims to achieve their aims, whether they were compensation, retribution, or the reform of their antagonists, with far less expense and inconvenience when compared to a formal trial. These informal and semi-formal processes were sometimes welcomed, and even encouraged, by the authorities, who were conscious of the cost of more formal proceedings and satisfied with results which penalized the culprit and offered the possibility of reform.

Informal settlements

Depending on the nature of the offence and the position and attitudes of both the offender and the victim, victims could choose to seek compensation or retribution, or a combination of both (King, 2000, ch. 2; Shoemaker, 1991, ch. 4). In cases of theft, the most obvious form of compensation was the return of the stolen property. As already noted, failure to prosecute a felony—misprision—was a crime. The practice of reaching an agreement to avoid prosecution—known as 'compounding a felony'—was also illegal until 1967. However, as discussed in Chapter 3, misprision and compounding were very rarely prosecuted and informal settlements between criminal and victim were common. The magistrate Patrick Colquhoun noted this in 1796: 'Notwithstanding the severity of the law, the composition [compounding] of felonies and misdemeanours is carried to a much greater height than it is almost possible to believe' (Colquhoun, 1796, 252). In addition to the return of their stolen goods, victims often demanded, and received, further payments or services, including apologies, in return for not prosecuting (King, 2000, 24). In cases of assault and violence, damages were sometimes paid to compensate for the medical costs and pain caused by injuries (Shoemaker, 1991, 82–4). As a form of 'conflict resolution', some victims in the eighteenth and nineteenth centuries received printed public apologies in newspaper advertisements from their wrongdoers, in most cases in lieu of formal prosecutions, for a wide range of offences including cases of violent assault. This early form of 'restorative justice' declined in London from the 1790s, perhaps as a result of the introduction of stipendiary magistrates who offered judicial means of resolving such disputes, but it continued in the provinces until police prosecution became prevalent in the second half of the nineteenth century (Andrew, 2002; Cox and Devi-Mcgleish, 2020).

In law, victims were entitled to the restitution of their goods if the culprit was convicted (Hale, 1736, I, 541), but there is no evidence that this occurred in practice (perhaps because it required a special writ). The 1870 Forfeiture Act permitted 'any person aggrieved' to apply for compensation from the convicted person for a sum of less than £100 for loss of property due to a felony. The amount awarded was deemed a judgement debt from the convicted person (33 & 34 Vict. *c.* 23), but there is no evidence that this was a common practice. In this context of limited opportunities for official compensation, victims whose primary interest was in recovering their stolen goods or receiving compensation for their injuries had to seek informal arrangements outside the judicial system, which normally involved a promise not to prosecute.

In 1785, a coachman who stole a lady's watch in London was identified with the assistance of the 'populace' (bystanders on the street), which searched the coach and found the watch. While the 'mob' pressed for prosecution, the victim, whose watch had been returned, 'not only suffered him to go unpunished', but also was about to 'give him a gratuity of his dishonesty', until the crowd stopped her (*The Times*, 13 Sept. 1785; King, 2000, 29). Victims behaved similarly in the next century. In the 1830s, the social reformer Edwin Chadwick claimed, based on his interviews with repeat offenders, that 'there was not one gentleman in twenty' who would prosecute a pickpocket if the article in question was returned (Chadwick, 1868, cited in Churchill, 2017, 193). In 1855, Henry Trafford, stipendiary magistrate for Salford, testified to a parliamentary committee that 'Frequently cases occur before me where I am compelled to summon the prosecutor to appear, because the property of which he has been robbed has been returned to him, and he wishes to forgo the trouble; this is the case most frequently in the cases of old and repeatedly convicted offenders' (PP, 1854–5, 91).

Alternatively, victims, particularly those who were in a position of power over offenders, could exact retribution by lecturing them, issuing a warning, or resorting to other methods of punishment. Employers had the option of simply dismissing pilfering employees (King, 2000, 24; Davis, 1989, 407). During times of war, victims could follow the practice of some magistrates and turn the culprit over to military recruitment officers as an alternative to prosecution (King, 2002). An option available to strongly-knit communities was to ostracize an offender, refusing them employment opportunities and even charity (King, 2000, 26–8, 91–2).

With the growth of summary jurisdiction and the police courts (discussed in Chapter 3), it has been suggested that informal settlements decreased during the nineteenth century (Gatrell, 1980, 249–50). But as Churchill has noted, throughout this period victims sought to hold onto considerable control over responses to crime, and as a result of both the disincentives to prosecute and the attractions of other methods, a significant proportion continued to resolve their complaints without resorting to a formal prosecution. Victims, he writes,

> regarded their criminal encounters in a proprietorial manner. They tended to regard criminal conflicts as a private matter, analogous to a civil dispute, rather than a public wrong; thus, they refused to recognise a clear distinction between felonious and non-felonious offences which would limit their right to settle privately (Churchill, 2017, 204).

Even after the police got involved, many victims attempted to retain control of the case and avoid prosecution. The difficulty of doing so, however, led victims to attempt to address their complaints at an earlier stage of the criminal process, before the police could become involved. As a result, 'communal and private sanctions remained integral to the framework of conflict resolution of the Victorian city … The balance of power [still remained] crucially, upon the initiative of individual victims' (Churchill, 2017, 211).

Violence

Retributive violence, both symbolic and actual, communal and individual, was another option. In certain places in the eighteenth and nineteenth centuries, communities employed the ritual of 'rough music', when wife beaters and others who committed offences against traditional moral values were humiliated by crowds banging pots and pans; some alleged perpetrators were paraded sitting backwards on a horse. In the eighteenth century, London mobs who apprehended thieves often chose to combine shame and physical retribution by dunking them in a convenient horse pond or river, echoing the traditional formal shaming punishment of 'ducking' or the 'cucking stool' (Shoemaker, 2004, 132; King, 2000, 27). The myriad forms of 'rough music' continued into the nineteenth century, but they were rarely used to punish those accused of serious criminal offences, and they declined overall in the second half of the century, though less so in rural areas (Conley, 1991, 23–8; Churchill, 2017, 198; Nash and Kilday, 2010; Banks, 2014). Nonetheless, individual victims or their friends could still respond to crimes by beating the culprit, particularly in cases of juvenile crime. Despite claims that formal prosecutions replaced violent responses to crime in the second half of the nineteenth century, Churchill (2017, 206) argues that the latter continued. Noting that 'the use of violence to deal with offenders fed from a broader culture of communal disputes resolution and norm enforcement', he argues that we should be wary of concluding that such activities disappeared from the Victorian city (see also Wood, 2004, 56–61). In a similar vein, Miers (2000) shows that twentieth-century victims who '[took] the law into their own hands' were among those denied criminal injuries compensation once this was introduced in the 1960s. Beyond the individual level, research on English organized crime highlights the use of hidden violence to punish wrongdoing within protection rackets and the informal economy (Shore, 2015; Roodhouse, 2013; Hobbs, 2013).

Refused by the police

Even if victims wished to engage with the legal process, in some cases they failed at the first hurdle. The first step in the criminal process was for offenders, identified by victims, witnesses, or policing agents, to be brought before a magistrate, but this normally required the assistance of a policing agent, usually a night watchman or a constable, or, after 1829, a policeman. At this point, officers could decide the case was without merit and dismiss the suspect without bringing them before a magistrate. (In such cases determined victims could still go to a magistrate without the suspect, or they could take the case directly to a grand jury: Hay, 1983, 169, 179).

The increasing role of the police in the identification of suspects in the nineteenth century increased the significance of this stage of the judicial process (Bland, 2018; see also Chapter 4). In the late nineteenth century, according to Wim Mellaerts, following an arrest 'the police tended to apply a great measure of discretion before backing a private individual to take the matter further', either pressuring the victim to drop the case or take it further depending 'on the suspect's identity (and especially on this person's criminal record) as well as the specific nature of the crime' (Mellaerts, 2000, 25). It is likely that the identity and perceived trustworthiness of the victim was also important in shaping the police response to the case. While evidence of initial police decision-making is limited, the few surviving police 'Occurrence Books' and 'Refused Charge Books' indicate that a significant number of suspects were released without further legal action. This could be a result of insufficient evidence, victims refusing to press charges, or the police deciding the offence was not serious enough to take forward (Emsley, 2005, 7, 27); such cases were unlikely to appear in the statistics collected of the 'number of crimes known to the police'. In a review of early twentieth-century refused charge cases recorded by various Metropolitan Police divisions, Emsley highlights incidents of assault, sexual assault, and domestic violence (Emsley, 2005, 7, 27–8, 64). These types of offences continued to feature in late twentieth-century accounts of refused charge procedures (McConville, Sanders, and Leng, 1991). While historical detail is scant on this matter, the possibility that police would dismiss the case was another reason not to attempt to prosecute.

2.3 Engaging with the Law

Once a case was brought before him, a magistrate had four options: to attempt to resolve the dispute informally; to summarily convict the defendant; to refer the case to a higher court; or to dismiss the case entirely. Thus began a process which could have many different outcomes, of which a criminal trial was one of the least likely. The criminologist Steven Box and the historian Peter King have both used the metaphor of a long corridor of interconnected rooms to describe the process of prosecution, where at each stage (room) of the process victims and defendants could leave (or be forced to leave) by doors which terminated the prosecution or diverted it into non-trial procedures, and only one door led to a continuation of the formal process in the next room, towards an eventual trial (Box, 1981, 158; King, 2000, 1). Through this process of what criminologists have called 'attrition', the majority of reports and prosecutions failed to result in a formal trial or verdict (Wahidin and Carr, 2013, 10–12). This remained true in spite of the development of more proactive policing and prosecution in the nineteenth century (addressed in Chapters 3 and 4). For example, of 87,563 indictable crimes 'known to the police' in England and Wales in 1898, only 60,732 persons were apprehended or summoned to answer charges.[1] Of these, 7,904 (13.0 per cent) were discharged without further action, 40,574 (66.8 per cent) were tried summarily, and only 11,513 (19.0 per cent) were committed for trial at the assizes or quarter sessions. Of those, a further few per cent were not tried because the grand jury rejected the indictment or no prosecution case was made, and a further sixth were acquitted by the petty jury. As a proportion of the number of crimes known to the police, the

[1] Indictable offences (a nineteenth-century term) were serious crimes which were originally triable before a jury at quarter sessions or the assizes, though statutes may have subsequently rendered them triable summarily (Gatrell, 1980, 240, n. 9).

9,133 persons convicted on a jury trial constituted only about one-tenth of the number of crimes reported (PP, 1900).[2]

This process of attrition, driven by victim or official discretion and other factors, was at times advantageous to victims who sought to avoid appearing at a formal trial, but disadvantageous to those who sought a formal conviction. Indeed, for the latter, the large number of unsuccessful prosecutions acted as a further disincentive to initiating them in the first place. In this section, we consider historical outcomes which did not lead to a formal prosecution and criminal trial.

Informal arbitration by magistrates

It is notable that even when cases were reported to a magistrate, the desire for an informal settlement remained, particularly for less serious offences. Magistrates exercised significant discretion in choosing whether to authorize a case for formal prosecution. As Thomas Gisborne wrote in 1794, magistrates tended to ignore legal handbooks and statutes, and instead based their judgments on 'their own unauthorized ideas of equity' (Gisborne, [1794], 281). In the interests of community harmony and of reducing costs and trouble for all concerned, most justices were positively inclined to seek informal resolutions of all but the most serious cases. Over the late eighteenth and early nineteenth centuries, King argues that they acted 'as very powerful filters' to determine which cases should be sent on for jury trial; these pre-trial processes were a 'deeply discretionary and negotiative process that resolved the vast majority of disputes about property appropriation, leaving only a small residue to be dealt with by the judge and jurors of the major courts' (King, 2000, 98, 125). In many ways, these informal arbitration practices prefigure late twentieth-century forms of 'restorative justice' and 'victim-offender mediation' which have sought to avoid escalation and encourage community deliberation (Johnstone, 2002; Zehr and Toews, 2004), but which have also attracted criticism for their failure to address unequal power relations between the parties (Daly, 2006).

[2] Precise proportions cannot be calculated because the statistics provide the number of *crimes* known to the police, but then provide the numbers of *persons* who were discharged, acquitted, etc. Moreover, since the judicial process often crossed into more than one calendar year, the numbers for any one year do not always count the same individuals.

Over the course of the eighteenth century, the informal judicial business which traditionally took place in their own homes became formalized in meetings of small numbers of justices known as 'petty sessions'. In the City of London, these took place in regular hearings conducted by the Lord Mayor and Aldermen, and in Middlesex in divisional petty sessions and hearings conducted at magistrates' offices (most notably at Bow Street, conducted by the half-brothers Henry and John Fielding), and other 'rotation offices'. While there appears to have been no legal requirement to keep records of this judicial business, JPs or their clerks often did so in order to have a record of judicial outcomes and the subsequent actions required. The most important surviving records for magistrates' courts in the eighteenth century are those of the Lord Mayor and Aldermen of the City, known as the Lord Mayor's and Guildhall Justice Room Charge Books, which detail numerous cases which were dismissed, informally resolved, or summarily convicted, as discussed below. As individuals, eighteenth-century JPs were encouraged to keep notebooks recording all the cases which were brought before them (regardless of outcome). Unfortunately for historians, this practice was only rarely followed, but, as noted below, some illuminating notebooks survive (Landau, 1984, 175).

These and other records provide occasional glimpses into the pre-trial processes which diverted so many cases away from a jury trial. A return to the Home Office in 1783 reveals that only half of the accused felons brought before the Whitechapel Rotation Office in East London were sent on for jury trial (King, 2000, 93, 98, 125). Cases in rural areas were even less likely to come before the courts: only 2.4 per cent of the 1,400 warrants for a variety of offences recorded in the notebook of Justice Edmund Tew in the county of Durham between 1750 and 1764 were referred for trial (Morgan and Rushton, 2003, 61). This exercise of magisterial discretion continued despite the formalization of the process of conducting hearings in the police courts in the 1830s: only 19.9 per cent of the cases heard by metropolitan magistrates in 1855 were sent on for trial (Davis, 1984, 113). Similar figures apply for 1898, when only 22.5 per cent of persons apprehended or summoned were committed for trial in London, and 19.0 per cent nationally (PP, 1900).

Justices, often advised by their clerks, could choose from a range of possible outcomes for cases they did not wish to refer for trial. In cases that were not simply dismissed for lack of evidence, they could settle the case informally, bind the defendant over by recognizance, or summarily convict the defendant of a petty offence and order a punishment. Shoemaker's analysis of two JP's notebooks, from eighteenth-century Middlesex (Henry Norris) and Wiltshire (William Hunt), found that, respectively, 38 and 58 per cent of the cases were 'agreed' without further legal action, 18 and 22 per cent were dealt with summarily, and only 34 and 8 per cent were referred for further legal action (with the accused either bound over by recognizance or imprisoned to await trial; Shoemaker, 1991, 44–7). In Durham, Edmund Tew settled 17 per cent of theft cases, 32 per cent of employment disputes and 39 per cent of assault cases by agreement (Morgan and Rushton, 2003, 64, 70, 74). Relatively few cases (16 per cent) from the City of London summary courts in the late eighteenth century were sent to the higher courts (Gray, 2009, 27–8).

In all these sources, while petty crimes were the most common, cases not sent for further legal action included indictable thefts. In spite of the Marian bail statutes, property offences, even if felonious, were often settled by the London magistrates with an apology, payment, and/or return of the stolen goods (Gray 2009, 86). In King's study of property crime, 'only half of the summary hearings about potential felonies recorded by the eight main diarists surveyed resulted in the accused being sent on to the major courts' (King, 2000, 86). Such practices, facilitated by the expansion of summary jurisdiction (discussed in Chapter 3) continued into the nineteenth century: in 1837 James Traill, a London magistrate, told a parliamentary subcommittee that 'it [was] well known that magistrates [were] in the practice of applying their summary jurisdiction even beyond the spirit, certainly beyond the words, of the law; assuming to themselves the power of adjudicating in cases of actual felony, by treating them as misdemeanors' (PP, 1837–8, 218, appendix, no. 14). The most serious offences, however, more consistently resulted in committals for trial. According to data collected in the parliamentary papers, 78.6 per cent of arrests for homicide and 72.4 per cent of arrests for felonious and malicious wounding in England between 1856 and 1914 led to trials (the figure for sexual crimes, discussed below, was lower; Gatrell, 1980, 287–8). Nonetheless, this left a significant minority of even these cases diverted by magistrates from prosecution.

The most common outcome of cases heard by magistrates thus appears to have been an informal settlement, often recommended by the magistrate (but sometimes 'ordered'). These settlements, involving the payment of some kind of compensation to the victim, or sometimes just an apology, were very similar to the informal settlements agreed between the parties without the presence of a magistrate discussed above, and they had similar advantages for victims. Indeed, eighteenth-century justices were encouraged to arrange such settlements in non-felonious cases by both manuals of legal advice and community pressures (Shoemaker, 1991, ch. 4). These practices continued in the nineteenth-century police courts and were particularly availed by female complainants (Auerbach, 2021, 190–7).

A more formal version of judicial mediation was the practice of binding the accused over by recognizance to appear in court, or to keep the peace or be of 'good behaviour'. This legal tool was primarily used for misdemeanours and was not widely used for felonies, since those accused of felony were supposed to be kept in prison until their trials. It was, however, used for theft, accounting for 8.5 per cent of a sample of 2,092 defendants bound over to attend the Middlesex Quarter Sessions between 1660 and 1725 (Shoemaker, 1991, 96). While a requirement to appear in court implied further action, very frequently the issuance of a recognizance was the final legal action taken against the accused. In 72 per cent of these cases, the recognizance was discharged following the defendant's appearance in court and the victim did not take any further legal action. The implication is that the result of these recognizances was that the disputes were settled. Victims (who could have chosen to charge the defendants with an indictable offence) clearly found the recognizance to be a useful alternative to formal prosecution. The very practice of having to find sureties and enter into a recognizance, and attend court to get the recognizance discharged, could be considered a form of punishment, giving the victim satisfaction that their antagonist had been punished, at minimal cost to the victim. This was particularly true for women's complaints against their husbands for assault, since the recognizance placed the accused under a temporary threat of a legal penalty should they misbehave further (Shoemaker, 1991, 32 and ch. 5; Hurl-Eamon, 2001, 435–54). Similarly, Davis has shown that rather than request a summons, battered wives who appeared in the late nineteenth-century police courts sometimes asked for their husband to be 'bound over to keep the peace' (Davis, 1984, 322; see also Auerbach, 2021, 199–202, 215).

The magistrate also had the option to simply decide that the case had no merit, and dismiss the parties. Shoemaker's analysis of eighteenth-century JP's notebooks indicates that this happened relatively rarely, in only 9–12 per cent of cases, though the large number of unknown dispositions suggests that figure may have been higher (Shoemaker, 1991, 44–7). Gray's analysis of the records of summary courts in the City of London in the late eighteenth century found somewhat greater proportions of cases dismissed, including 28.9 per cent of property cases (Gray, 2009, 88, 107, 127). Of all indictable offences heard in London in 1898, 22.4 per cent of those charged were discharged without further legal action, significantly more than the national figure of 13.0 per cent (PP, 1900). Nonetheless, throughout our period magistrates were more likely to resort to proactive measures for resolving criminal complaints (whether informal or formal) as opposed to simple dismissal.

The relatively high proportion of property cases dismissed, however, is significant because some of these cases would have been felonies and therefore should have been referred to trial, given the minimum threshold of the value of the stolen goods for grand larceny was only one shilling (Gray, 2009, 86, 89). With felonies, the Marian bail statutes obliged magistrates to take depositions and forward the case to the grand jury (Langbein, 1974). In practice, however, magistrates were willing to discharge suspects without trial in cases where they did not believe there was sufficient evidence to convict, and this practice increased over time, facilitated by the 1848 Indictable Offences Act, which gave magistrates greater powers to dismiss weak cases (11 & 12 Vict, *c.* 42). The 1869 version of Richard Burn's eighteenth-century manual of legal advice for justices (now authored by John Maule), clarified the rules: 'in modern practice', it stated, when 'exculpatory evidence is received at the instance of the prisoner and certified with other depositions', [and] if 'it appears in the clearest manner that the charge is malicious, as well as groundless', magistrates could discharge suspects (Maule, 1869, IV, 405; Mellaerts, 2000, 26).

Summary justice

A final alternative to formal prosecution, though it could itself be deemed a form of prosecution, was summary justice. As the means by which 'more than anywhere else ... the people met and experienced the law in the eighteenth century' (King, 2004, 126), its impact expanded even further in the nineteenth century with the expansion of the number and jurisdiction of the magistrates' courts (Auerbach, 2021). For many petty offences, a single justice or a group of justices could, regardless of the wishes of the victim, convict the offender summarily, without a jury trial, and order punishment by fine, whipping, or imprisonment (Shoemaker, 1991, ch. 7). In some cases, magistrates used their discretion to convict people they deemed guilty of stealing higher value items (felonies) by undervaluing the stolen goods and summarily convicting them for petty larceny (King, 2000, 90; Gray, 2009, 68–9; see also Smith, 2013, xix, xxii).

The expansion of summary justice over the eighteenth and nineteenth centuries, a major development which arguably enhanced access to justice for women and the poor, is discussed in Chapter 3. Here, it is sufficient to note that, as with all other forms of prosecution, summary cases were often dropped before final resolution, often at the request of the victim (King, 2004, 148; Auerbach, 2021, 203, 228). Davis argued that working-class victims frequently resorted to the law without actually following a charge through to its conclusion, 'perhaps feeling that the arrest of an offender and possibly a night in the police cells might be enough to achieve their original aim in invoking the law' (Davis, 1989, 415). In particular, such a short period of imprisonment was used to 'frighten' children, before releasing them without charge (King, 2000, 96). Such partial prosecutions were also common when wives prosecuted abusive husbands. In such cases, magistrates 'cooperated by allowing the charges to drop, often urging the parties to settle out of court' (Davis, 1984, 322; see also Darby, 2015, 373). In addition, a minority of summary trials led to an acquittal: 19.1 per cent of cases nationally, and 15.4 per cent of cases in London, in 1898 (PP, 1900).

Victims, often with the cooperation of magistrates, could thus avail themselves of a number of legal or quasi-legal practices for addressing their complaints without taking the case to court for trial. Given the lower costs and simpler procedures, these were attractive to those who did not have sufficient means, or confidence, to engage in more formal prosecutions. But, because such procedures typically led to reduced punishments, it is likely that they did not always succeed in meeting victims' goals of reforming the behaviour of their antagonists, or of exacting sufficient retribution against them. This provides some of the background to the state's efforts to support victims in making more formal prosecutions, discussed in Chapter 3. Nonetheless, throughout our period these alternative means of prosecution far outnumbered the number of cases which went to the crown courts, an important point to bear in mind when we examine the considerably better documented caseloads of the latter.

2.4 Rejected Prosecutions

Cases that were not dismissed, informally settled, or resolved by summary jurisdiction were forwarded on to a criminal trial, but there were still several points at which cases could be dropped or rejected. An examination of these aspects of the judicial process demonstrates why so many cases which reached the indictment stage were never actually tried in a courtroom, acting as a further disincentive to prosecution.

As we have seen, in all felony cases where there was significant evidence against the accused, JPs were obliged by the Marian bail statutes to proceed to further legal action. They were required to compile statements from the accused, the complainant, and material witnesses; to forward these documents to a trial court; and to take steps to ensure the parties involved would appear in court (Langbein, 1974; 1 & 2 Phil & Mar, *c.* 13; 2 & 3 Phil & Mar, *c.* 10). Felony suspects were typically committed to prison to await trial, but the law also attempted to ensure that victims fulfilled their duty to appear in court. They were usually bound over by recognizance, in which they (and typically two sureties) promised to forfeit a large sum (typically £40 in the eighteenth century) if they failed to carry out the condition of the recognizance, which was to appear at the next meeting of the relevant court to prosecute the case.

Before a felony case could be heard, the indictment had to be drawn up by the clerk based on the documents forwarded from the JP and evidence from the victim and the police (if involved). This was then presented to a grand jury, a group of propertied men (and women after 1919) who were given the responsibility to determine whether there was sufficient evidence against the defendant to merit trial by a petty jury, which determined the verdict (Hanly, 2021a). At the Old Bailey, there were separate grand juries for the City of London and the County of Middlesex. Victims were expected to testify before the relevant grand jury, and if the jury found the charge a 'true bill' (justified and made in good faith), they would have to attend the ensuing Old Bailey sessions, waiting in the vicinity of the courtroom potentially for days until the trial took place. Charges rejected by the grand jury were labelled 'ignoramus' (we do not know) or 'not found', and suspects were normally discharged.

Since their deliberations were secret, we know little about the criteria grand jurors used to make their decisions, but until the mid-nineteenth century they rejected a significant minority of indictments. We do not have statistics for the eighteenth-century assizes courts, but at the Middlesex Quarter Sessions between 1660 and 1725 and Essex between 1740 and 1805 the figure was 14 per cent (Shoemaker, 1991, 142, 146–9; King, 2000, 231). There is some evidence that victims in marginal positions were more likely to have their cases rejected. As noted above, cases involving female victims in Middlesex were more often found 'ignoramus'. Evidence of the impact of the victim's social status on the grand jury's decisions is mixed. In Middlesex there is no evidence of any differences by status, whereas in Essex, gentry, tradesmen and craftsmen, and professional victims were more likely to have their charges approved than farmers and labourers (Shoemaker, 1991, 148; King, 2000, 235).

The proportion of indictments rejected by the grand jury declined in the nineteenth century. Between 1814 and 1834, the indictments against 13.1 per cent of persons committed for trial at Quarter Sessions and at the Old Bailey in London and Middlesex were 'not found' by the grand jury or not prosecuted, and 11.9 per cent nationally (PP, 1835, 16, 18). This proportion was higher for property offences (PP, 1819, VIII, 128–31, cited by King, 2000, 231), giving rise to concerns that the grand jury was rejecting too many cases. In 1838 London grand juries were branded 'the hope of London thieves' (Bentley, 1998, 132). At that point a clerk started to attend grand jury meetings to offer advice. This gentle encouragement, and more importantly the passage of the Indictable Offences Act of 1848, which accorded magistrates greater powers to dismiss weak cases at an earlier stage in the process, led to a decline in the role of the grand jury in the nineteenth century, as it began to routinely approve virtually all cases brought before it (11 & 12 Vict. *c.* 42). Consequently in 1851 'not found' rates declined to 3.1 per cent in London and 5.3 per cent nationally; by the end of the century these figures were further reduced to 2.1 per cent in London and 3.2 per cent nationally (PP, 1852, vi, 21; PP, 1896, 67–70). Commenting on the 70.3 per cent decline in 'not found' verdicts nationally between 1836 and 1896, the *Judicial Statistics* credited the 1859 Vexatious Indictments Act, discussed below and in Chapter 3 (PP, 1896, 22). In 1885, Frederic Maitland observed that, owing to the ubiquity of magistrates' preliminary proceedings, 'for a grand jury to ignore a bill has become a rather rare event' (Maitland, 1885, 139). In 1933 grand juries were effectively abolished in England and Wales (23 & 24 Geo. 5, *c.*36).

Once approved by the grand jury, cases were ready for trial, but they could still be undermined by the failure of the victim to appear in court. As we have seen, victims were compelled to attend court by means of being required to enter into a recognizance, which meant that they could suffer a significant financial penalty if they failed to appear. Although this penalty was rarely imposed, only a small minority of prosecutions were dropped before trial. In Essex between 1775 and 1787, about 12.3 per cent of prosecutors, primarily the poor, failed to turn up (King, 2000, 43–5). In contrast, evidence from the Old Bailey suggests that only 2.7 per cent of all trials taking place between 1674 and 1913 failed owing to no evidence being presented or the victim's failure to appear; this was somewhat more likely when the victims were female or upper class (*Proceedings* dataset).

Some of the cases of 'no evidence presented' in the nineteenth-century Old Bailey nonetheless led to guilty verdicts. These cases appear to have involved plea bargaining, whereby before the case was tried the victim and defendant, or more likely lawyers acting on their behalf, with the tacit agreement of the judge, agreed on more lenient punishment in return for a reduced charge and a guilty plea (see Chapter 6). There are other reasons why victims may have chosen to drop a prosecution before trial. Many victims did not wish to testify in court, and were satisfied with having already forced the defendant to suffer, through the cost and ignominy of being charged, and probably having spent time in prison. As leading lawyer Sir James Fitzjames Stephen noted in 1863, the prosecution process inflicted 'cruel hardship on innocent persons who have the misfortune to be accused' (Stephens, 1863, 171). Taking advantage of this fact, some victims may have initiated prosecutions as a means of extorting money from defendants in return for dropping the case. As a result of the 1859 Vexatious Indictments Act, however, the proportion of cases where the prosecution was dropped declined nationally from 2.3 per cent to 0.1 per cent of indictments between 1836 and 1896 (22 & 23 Vict. *c.* 17; PP, 1896, 22).

A much higher proportion of misdemeanour cases failed to reach trial. Once a case was found to be a 'true bill', a trial was usually scheduled for the next sessions, when the victim would be expected to appear to testify. This extra delay for misdemeanour charges occurred because the defendant was normally not in prison, and had to be summoned and bound over to appear in court. For a variety of reasons, many such indictments (around a third in Middlesex between 1660 and 1725, for example) were not tried until two or more sessions after the indictment was approved. In the interim, many indictments were settled informally, or the victim simply dropped the case; a further sixth never reached a final verdict (Shoemaker, 1991, 134–9). As a consequence, victims had a greater influence over the outcome of misdemeanour indictments than they did for felonies.

In the nineteenth century, some restrictions were placed on the right of victims to prosecute. For certain crimes, according to J. Ll. J. Edwards, 'since the middle of the nineteenth century it has become increasingly common for parliament to restrict the right of a private citizen to initiate a criminal prosecution by requiring the consent of the Attorney General, Solicitor General, or Director of Public Prosecutions'. While the first restriction was introduced with the Roman Catholic Relief Act in 1829, they became more common with the establishment of the Director of Public Prosecutions (DPP) in 1879, and then further expanded at the close of the Second World War; by 1964 they applied to eighty offences. Edwards was not able to uncover 'any identifiable theme underlying the limitations', but they fundamentally derived from concerns about the illegitimate motives of some private prosecutors, who were thought to institute charges in order to extort money from the accused and the payment of costs by the state (Edwards, 1964, 237–42). The introduction of the Crown Prosecution Service (CPS) in 1986 (discussed in Chapter 4) introduced a further stage in the vetting of prosecutions before they were brought to trial, based on the perceived chances of, and public benefit from, securing a conviction.

Finally, victims and prosecutors of cases which actually made it to a jury trial faced the very real possibility that the jury would acquit the defendant. As discussed in Chapter 6, almost 20 per cent of Old Bailey prosecutions resulted in a verdict of not guilty, and in a further 10 per cent of cases the verdict was to convict the defendant of a lesser crime. While in the era of capital punishment many victims were often relieved, and even pleaded for, a partial verdict in order to avoid the possibility that the defendant would be hanged, a not guilty verdict was unlikely to be a satisfactory outcome from the victim's point of view. As noted in Chapter 6, these often unsatisfactory outcomes varied to some extent by the identity of the victim, with some minority ethnic and young victims less likely to obtain convictions. Once again, access to justice was more difficult for those who were socially disadvantaged in other ways.

When added to all the other reasons why victims chose not to prosecute crime or dropped prosecutions before a final verdict, rejected indictments, acquittals, and partial verdicts highlight just how difficult it was for victims and prosecutors to obtain full convictions. While some dropped prosecutions may have been advantageous for victims if the prosecution led to an informal resolution of the case, for many victims the fact that so many cases were unsuccessful must have been an additional reason why they often chose non-judicial means of responding to crime.

2.5 Sexual Crimes

All the obstacles to prosecution and conviction outlined here were—and remain—particularly strong in the case of sexual assaults, one of the least likely types of offence to be reported historically in England (and indeed in most other western countries) (Conley, 2014, 211). According to Louise Jackson, 'whilst the actual prevalence of child sexual abuse in the historical past is unknowable ... it is clear that it has always been significantly under-reported', with the number of prosecutions for the crime representing only 'the tip of an iceberg' (Jackson, 2015). In the eighteenth century the magistrate John Fielding complained that, owing to 'their necessities, or drowned by gin', mothers often accepted 'a trifle' as financial compensation from the culprits in exchange for not reporting rapes of their daughters, leading him to conclude that 'more of these offences are concealed from magistrates than brought to light' (Fielding, 1758, 45–6). While this section focuses largely on assaults on women, both children and adults, sexual assaults on men and boys were also significantly under-reported throughout this period, and for similar reasons (Jackson, 2000, 101–5; Bassanavar, 1921).

Victims of sexual assault, both female and male, young and adult, feared having their reputations undermined by public disclosure of their involvement in what were seen as shameful acts of sexual immorality, even when they had been forcibly attacked (D'Cruze and Jackson, 2009, 27; Clark, 1987, 50; Stevenson, 2005). Furthermore, as discussed below, they did not wish to be subject to the types of cross-examination about their own sexual past frequently experienced in trials for these offences. In a letter to *The Times* in 1788, 'Maria', a female correspondent, commented on the 'poor sufferers [of rape], who are unwilling to expose their misfortune in a Court of Justice, [and] are now lamenting their injury in silent sadness, rather than submitting to public shame' (*The Times*, 19 Sept. 1788; Clark, 1987, 50). Despite the increased support provided to female victims in the nineteenth century (discussed in Chapter 3), this reluctance continued, in part because of the increasing importance given to 'respectability' as a central component of personal reputation. Referring to a sexual assault carried out on a 'respectable married female' in public, *The Times* reported in 1836 that a Lambeth magistrate had observed that 'the more decent or respectable they [women] were, the more reluctant they were in coming forward to give public details of such gross outrages' (Simpson, 1986, 144; *The Times*, 1 Dec 1836; Clark, 1987, 63). Such reluctance was reduced, but not eliminated, in the case of child victims, owing to widespread public condemnation of the offence and the reduced salience of questions of consent; such prosecutions increased in the late nineteenth century (see Chapter 5).

Nonetheless, as noted above, there were particular obstacles to prosecuting crimes with child victims owing to the problematic status of child witnesses, and these were exacerbated when the crime was sexual. There was an enduring suspicion that children were corrupted by sin unless they had been properly religiously trained. Consequently, child victims were frequently examined about their understanding of Christian morality, in the process raising potential doubts about their credibility among members of the jury (Stevenson, 2017, 75–97). Furthermore, young victims needed to be able to describe the commission of the crime, while at the same time appearing sexually innocent, a difficult path to navigate (Jackson, 2000, 99; Cox, 2013).

Several studies have shown that at the first stage of the judicial process, the hearing before a magistrate, sexual assault cases were regularly dismissed. In the early 1750s Henry Fielding, an otherwise zealous prosecutor of crime, treated rape victims 'unsympathetically . . . of the eight cases of rape noted in the years 1752–4, he reported four in the most sceptical manner, claiming they were false accusations' (Clark, 1987, 51). Similarly, of seventeen cases of rape or attempted rape heard by magistrates at the Guildhall Justice Room in the City of London between 1752 and 1796, only two were forwarded on for trial. The other fifteen were tried summarily, despite the fact rape was a felony and attempted rape was viewed as so proximate an offence to a felony that magistrates were advised it should be tried by a jury (Simpson, 1986, 122; Shoemaker, 1991, 138–9). This pattern continued into the nineteenth and twentieth centuries. In Kent, between 1859 and 1880, only 21 per cent of men accused of rape actually stood trial, as magistrates 'clearly overstepp[ed] their authority' and 'dismissed the charges despite the presence of medical evidence, or reduced the charges and heard rape cases as common assaults'. This was a particularly likely outcome in cases where the victim was a working woman, owing to their perceived lack of respectability (Conley, 1986, 521, 531). Cases involving child victims, on the other hand, were more likely to lead to prosecutions (Jackson, 2000, 23, 90).

From the mid-nineteenth century, the police acted as an additional filter preventing many sexual crimes from going to trial. Nationally, between 1856 and 1914 almost a third (31.9 per cent) of sexual assault cases 'known to the police' failed to result in committals to trial (Gatrell, 1980, 288, Table VII). Similarly, in the twentieth century, despite significant increases in the number of cases of sexual assault reported, a growing proportion of cases were 'no crimed' by the police and not taken forward for prosecution (D'Cruze and Jackson, 2009, 28; Jackson 2015; Stevenson, 2000).

Grand juries threw out many of the cases which reached the indictment stage. Of the 276 cases of sexual assault which reached Kent grand juries between 1859 and 1880, 15 per cent were rejected, and 57 per cent were approved on reduced charges of attempted rape or indecent assault (which upon conviction led to much more lenient punishments). Grand juries never explained their verdicts, but it is surely telling that the charges were reduced in 81 per cent of the cases when the alleged perpetrator was above the rank of soldier or labourer. Conley argues that reduced charges 'were used when middle-class men were accused and the evidence was too serious for the case to be dismissed altogether' (Conley, 1986, 523).

As a result of this filtering of cases in the pre-trial process, the sexual assault cases which went to trial tended to fit a culturally acceptable model of a young, innocent woman (the ideal victim) charging a non-respectable male. Nonetheless, conviction rates were still low, owing to further obstacles victims encountered during trials. Across the whole span of the Old Bailey *Proceedings* (1674–1913), only 48.2 per cent of those accused of rape were convicted, compared to 69.0 per cent of all other defendants (*Proceedings* dataset). More strikingly, in Kent between 1859 and 1880 rape convictions were at 40 per cent, compared to 85 per cent for all other felonies, with only 4 per cent of men who could be described as respectable convicted (Conley, 1986, 521, 528). As discussed in Chapter 6, Old Bailey cases involving child victims (under sixteen) resulted in a higher rate of conviction. This pattern continued into the twentieth century, with the exception that female victims aged between thirteen and fifteen were the least likely to obtain conviction, owing to their indeterminate legal status and perceptions they were neither ideal victims nor entirely free of complicity in sex (Jackson, 2000, 90; Jackson, 2015).

To obtain conviction, prosecutors had to overcome a number of prejudices held by jurors and other male judicial officials, founded on the early modern belief, stated by Matthew Hale, that rape 'is an accusation easily to be made and hard to be proved, and harder to be defended by the party accused, though never so innocent' (Hale, 1736, I, 635). This fear of false prosecutions, combined with gendered notions of morality and sexual practices, led to high expected standards of proof, including expectations of corroborating evidence, specifically that the defendant acted with force and that the victim actively resisted. Prompted by the fact that women, or their male relatives, sometimes accepted financial compensation from their attackers on the promise that they would drop the prosecution, the 'blackmail myth' developed in the eighteenth century, that women made false accusations in order to extort money from wealthier men (Simpson, 1986). According to Shani D'Cruze and Louise Jackson, this myth was still evident 'within police culture' in the middle of the twentieth century (D'Cruze and Jackson, 2009, 28). To counter that suspicion, victims needed to prove that they were chaste, as any evidence of previous sexual activity outside marriage (which was thought to have awakened their sexual desire) was taken to imply consent (Clark, 1987, 72).

In this way, the familiar situation occurred in which rape trials put the victim under as much, if not more, scrutiny than the defendant. Despite legal changes which made it technically easier to prove rape (in 1828 the requirement to prove seminal emission was abolished), cultural changes and the growing use of expert witnesses in the nineteenth century made convictions more difficult (Clark, 1987, 60, 74). Owing to the 'desexualization' of sexual discourse in the nineteenth century, women lacked the respectable language necessary to describe the crime (Stevenson, 2005). Moreover, to counter the presumption of consent, women needed to be able to demonstrate injuries they sustained while resisting the attack, which were expected to be verified by expert medical witnesses. In this way, medical expertise on issues of consent and injury was used to 'articulat[e] wider social concerns to which other witnesses were not permitted to speak' (Bates, 2019, 117–51, at 134; Conley, 1986). Throughout the nineteenth and twentieth centuries, and despite legal reforms, these culturally rooted expectations that rape complainants must conform to the stereotype of the 'unequivocal victim' persisted (Stevenson, 2000, 343–66). Chapter 7 explores this in more detail in relation to the *Times*' coverage of twentieth-century sexual offence cases.

Given the difficulties of obtaining convictions, it is not surprising that throughout the period covered here, victims of sexual offences were particularly unwilling to report the crime, and that a high proportion of reported cases did not lead to formal prosecutions. Emblematic of the continuing difficulties faced in turning victims into prosecutors, rape victims feature very prominently in contemporary discussions of the limitations of victims' access to justice in the English courts (Brown and Walklate, 2011; Hohl and Stanko, 2015; Daly and Bouhours, 2010).

2.6 Conclusion

Any study of victims' historical experiences must take into account the very large proportion of crimes that were not reported or prosecuted. Failures to report crime and prosecute, and the use of alternative methods to formal prosecution, are endemic features of criminal justice in England. Another key characteristic is the failure of many prosecutions to proceed through all the stages of the judicial process to a formal resolution. Whether or not these outcomes constituted a failure of criminal justice is a separate issue, but for those unable to initiate or sustain prosecutions because of a lack of social capital or financial resources, the system appeared to fail. For those victims who were content with their choice not to report the crime and thus, at least in a legal sense, rejected the status of victimhood, the workings of the justice system may have been considered successful. But from the perspective of the public good, the failure to punish offending can be, and has been, seen as a dangerous violation of public order and a challenge to the state's authority.

Regardless of victim preferences, it was the public's manifest failure to prosecute sufficient crimes which lay behind the multifaceted initiatives by the state throughout this period, documented in the next two chapters, to encourage prosecutions and eventually introduce a public prosecution service. As we will demonstrate, these initiatives impacted patterns of prosecutions at the Old Bailey and transformed victims' experiences of justice over time. In the next chapter, we examine the various types of incentives and support offered to victims in order to encourage them to prosecute, and we consider how these altered the status of the victim over the three hundred years covered by this study.

3
From Prosecutors to Victims

As the previous chapter has shown, during the three centuries under review a formal legal proceeding was just one of several routes open to crime victims. Going to court could be a costly, time-consuming, and even a shameful means of seeking recompense. Aware of the unwillingness of many people to prosecute, the state introduced a patchwork of measures to induce victims to use the courts or to encourage others to bring cases on their behalf. While some commentators called for the state to take over the role of prosecutor, as was the case in Scotland and in continental Europe, this was fended off in England and Wales until the end of the twentieth century. Instead, national and local governments, judges, and voluntary associations introduced incremental changes that eventually resulted in major transformations of the victims' role in the judicial process. In effect, 'prosecutors' were transformed into 'witnesses' and then 'victims'.

This chapter outlines these changes and begins to investigate how they may have impacted victims' access to justice between the 1670s and the 1980s. While professionals assumed a greater role in the criminal justice system, thereby marginalizing victims, expanding state support for victims also facilitated prosecutions for more of the crimes they experienced. The first part of the chapter discusses early-modern English conceptualizations of victims as actors with legal obligations to prosecute, and shows how eighteenth- and early nineteenth-century efforts to encourage and support their prosecutorial efforts were innovative but limited in impact. It also assesses the increasingly substantial interventions by local and national government from the mid-nineteenth to the mid-twentieth century, noting the unevenness of provisions to encourage prosecutions and the continuing, if diminishing, role played by victims. The second and final part outlines the later twentieth-century creation of new forms of victim support—outside the prosecution process itself—to assist victims in dealing with the financial and emotional consequences of crime.

Victims and Criminal Justice. Pamela Cox, Robert Shoemaker, and Heather Shore,
Oxford University Press.
DOI: 10.1093/oso/9780192846488.003.0003

3.1 Supporting Victims as Prosecutors

A victim of crime in the seventeenth century moved in a legal landscape underpinned by distinct legal understandings of the nature of criminal justice. Since the middle ages, in English common law crimes were considered public wrongs against the king's peace (Godfrey, 2018, 15). As a consequence, there was no legal concept of the private 'victim'. As explained in Chapter 2, those who were harmed by, or witnessed, serious crimes had an obligation to prosecute those who committed such crimes, and were therefore identified as 'prosecutors'. When doing so, victims were acting on behalf of the monarch. As the eighteenth-century jurist William Blackstone put it, criminal prosecutions took place 'in the name of the king, but at the suit of any private prosecutor' (Blackstone, 1769, 1–2, 300). This duty to report and prosecute applied to both men and women (married and unmarried), but only to those above the age of criminal responsibility (Hale, 1736, I, 18–22, 48; Shore, 1999, 8–9, 69). Anyone not reporting a felony was, legally, committing the crime of 'misprision'.

In principle, therefore, all serious crimes should have been reported by victims or witnesses to the authorities and, where possible, the culprit should have been arrested. Of course, as we saw in Chapter 2, there were many reasons why this did not happen and, so far as records allow us to tell, the vast majority of victims did not fulfil their legal obligations to prosecute. They either did nothing or came to an informal settlement with the culprit. Those who came to an informal arrangement, such as agreeing not to report a felony in exchange for compensation or the return of stolen property, were committing the offence of 'compounding a felony' (a misdemeanour). Like 'misprision', this offence remained in place until 1967 (Criminal Law Act, 1967, *c.* 58). Compounding was a development of the medieval crime of 'theftbote' (bote meaning 'amends'), where a victim regained his or her goods in return for not prosecuting. A clause of the 1718 Transportation Act, passed in an attempt to control the activities of thief-takers (discussed below), increased the penalties for compounding and misprision, making it a felony to accept a reward for the return of stolen goods without attempting to prosecute the thief (4 Geo I *c.*11; Blackstone, 1769, 132–3). This offence was expanded in the 1861 Larceny Act, which stated that if someone were offered goods for sale or pawn and had reasonable cause to suspect the goods were stolen, they were required to arrest the party and bring them before a justice (24 & 25 Vic *c.* 96, s. 103; Maule, I, 298–9).

These legal obligations on private citizens to report and arrest felons, and not reach private accommodations with them, existed until 1967 but enforcement was extremely rare. There were only two prosecutions for misprision at the Old Bailey before 1800, both for misprision of treason (OBO, t16811017a-6, t16900717-1), and only two cases of compounding a felony (OBO, t17870418-118, t17980418-94). Similarly, Peter King's study of trials in Essex between 1740 and 1820 found that compounding was rarely brought to trial, even when it was practised openly (King, 2000, 24). The significance of these two offences lay not in their practical impact but rather in the legal principles they expressed, which identified prosecution as a key duty of victims.

Once a felony was reported to a justice of the peace and the JP determined there was sufficient evidence to support a prosecution, the victim was bound over by recognizance to appear at the next meeting of the relevant court. In law, victims were supposed to be supported in this process by a number of officials. In the early modern period, those officials were typically part-time or unpaid and the support they provided was limited. Parish watchmen and constables were available to help identify suspects and make arrests as part of their general responsibility to apprehend criminals, although research has shown that these officers typically acted only in response to requests from victims, witnesses, or JPs (Beattie, 1986, 35; King, 2000, 17; Bland, 2022, ch. 3, 50–73). JPs, appointed by the crown, were also unpaid, and, given their typical status as gentlemen, most were unwilling to spend much time on the role. In London and some other cities, the minority of JPs who actively made themselves available, labelled as 'trading justices', attracted suspicion and distrust on the grounds that they encouraged prosecutions in order to profit from the prison fees paid to gaolers and the fees and bribes paid by the parties in dispute (Landau, 1984, 184–203; Landau, 2002, 46–70; Shoemaker, 1991, 229–30).

Victims thus dominated the process of prosecuting crime in the eighteenth century, receiving only limited support from state officials. This partly explains why the term 'victim' rarely appears in the eighteenth-century trial accounts in the *Old Bailey Proceedings*. It was used only in sixty-two trials up to 1850, with the alternative terms 'prosecutor' and 'prosecutrix' used 764 times more often. This ratio declined to 126:1 between 1851 and 1900 and 34:1 between 1901 and 1913, but even in the early twentieth century 'victim' was used only about once a month. The alternative term 'complainant' was used only once in the entire eighteenth century, and only seventy-four times in the nineteenth century (0.06 per cent of trials) (OBO). In the mid-eighteenth century, Blackstone also preferred the term 'prosecutor', noting for example that 'on a conviction of larceny in particular, the prosecutor shall have restitution of his goods' (Blackstone, 1769, 355). This was also true for legal manuals throughout the eighteenth and nineteenth centuries and for parliamentary select committee reports on policing, which referred to the 'prosecutor' and 'complainant', not 'victim'. This changed to a degree with the 1856 Select Committee on Public Prosecutors report, in which the victim was referred to as the 'injured party' (PP, 1856).

There were certain offences, however, where there was no individual 'victim' and state agencies asserted responsibility for prosecution, even in the eighteenth century. As we will see in Chapter 4, the Treasury Solicitor, the Mint, the Post Office, and the Bank of England conducted a small number of prosecutions where the state's interests were at stake. Although in the early modern period these state prosecutions were used erratically and for only a narrow range of offences, we will argue that these practices were precursors of a future state role in prosecuting crime in place of the victim. A further category of prosecutions were those undertaken by voluntary organizations such as the NSPCC and the RSPCA. As we will see below, in the late nineteenth century the NSPCC were particularly important in shaping prosecution practices in sexual abuse cases and were increasingly supported by the state, working with police to bring successful prosecutions.

This pre-modern approach to the prosecution of crime gave the victim significant obligations, but also, as King states, 'immense freedom of manoeuvre'. As we saw in Chapter 2, victims often had considerable influence over the course of a case. Consequently, bearing in mind the high costs involved, 'formal prosecution was the exception' (King, 2000, 17, 22). While this approach may have suited many victims, by the late seventeenth century it was seen as inadequate by many commentators, public officials, and the wider public. Stimulated by the increasing volume of printed reports about crime in popular literature, the Old Bailey *Proceedings* (from 1674) and the rapidly growing number of newspapers (from the early 1700s), public concern about crime, particularly violent crime, grew (Shoemaker, 2017; Ward, 2016).

The actual severity of the periodic crime waves described in the late seventeenth century and subsequent media is impossible to determine, but with a growing population, an unstable economy, and inadequate poor relief (especially for a growing number of rural migrants), it is certainly plausible that crime did increase in the metropolis. Pressed by some MPs, the

City of London and voluntary societies, parliament, now meeting more regularly following the 'Glorious Revolution' of 1688, passed a series of statutes intended to defeat these early 'crime waves' (Innes, 2009, 33–40; Beattie, 2001, 314–38). These statutes combined deterrence, by adding new capital crimes to the large body of such offences known as the 'Bloody Code' and experimenting with new secondary punishments, with attempts to introduce more effective policing, by adopting measures to induce more victims to prosecute (Beattie, 2001, chs 7–8; Hitchcock and Shoemaker, 2015, 60–8).

Motivations for the new provisions to encourage prosecutions were plainly stated in the legislation itself. The 1692 'Act for Encouraging the Apprehending of Highwaymen', for example, noted that 'the Highways and Roads within the Kingdom of England and Dominion of Wales have been of late time more infested with Thieves and Robbers than formerly for want of due and sufficient encouragement given and means used for the discovery and apprehension of such Offenders' (4 Wm. & Mar. *c.* 8). The 1706 'Act for the Encouraging the Discovery and Apprehending of House-breakers' stated that burglary 'might be, in great measure prevented, if due encouragement be given to such as shall vigorously endeavour the discovery and apprehending of such malefactors' (6 Anne *c.* 31). And a 1719 Act mournfully observed that 'Laws in being have not proved effectual to the suppressing of Robbery, Burglary, and other Felonies ... some of the said Laws wanting to be amended and enforced' (6 Geo I, *c.* 23).

Rewards

To encourage victims, and others, to report and prosecute serious crimes, these and other acts and proclamations introduced a series of financial inducements. The first statute, in 1692, offered a £40 reward for the conviction of highway robbers and a second, in 1695, offered the same reward for prosecutors of coiners (counterfeiters). Further statutes offered rewards for convictions for burglary, housebreaking, sheep and cattle theft, and returning early from the punishment of transportation. In a significant escalation of incentives, a royal proclamation of 1720 offered £100 rewards, in addition to the statutory £40 reward, for 'the Discovery and Apprehending of Highwaymen and Robbers' in or near London (*London Gazette*, 5818, 19 January 1719/20). Some of these offences were crimes directly against the realm, although they also adversely affected many individual victims.

Highway robbery disrupted the state's communication networks, coining damaged confidence in the state's currency, while returning from transportation undermined a state-imposed criminal punishment. Even after the rewards were divided among several beneficiaries, these were substantial sums of money. A recent study has shown that 'the median value of the rewards was £8 for the £100 rewards and £3 15s for the £40 rewards (many rewardees received both)', sufficient to motivate even middle-class victims and witnesses, 'whose cost of living was between one and a few hundred pounds a year'. For an artisan family, whose annual living expenses were around £40, a reward 'could represent a considerable windfall' (Clayton and Shoemaker, 2022, 99).

The policy of offering rewards was successful in that the number of prosecutions for the specific offences concerned increased (see Chapter 5 and Clayton and Shoemaker, 2022). It also had unintended consequences, however. The large rewards encouraged the practice of 'thief-taking': capturing alleged offenders as a private business. By 1700, according to one estimate, there were between thirty and forty active thief-takers in the City of London (Beattie, 2001, 233). Although thief-taking had existed for some time, the size of the sums now on offer led to unscrupulous behaviour (Wales, 2000). Attracted by the substantial rewards and profiting from the reduced scrutiny given to prosecution evidence during periods of 'moral panic', some thief-takers became thief-makers. They used their influence over vulnerable individuals to stage crimes in which they conspired with the 'victim' to ensure that sufficient evidence was gathered to initiate a successful prosecution. The most famous thief-taker (and thief-maker), the self-styled 'Thief-Catcher General of Great Britain', Jonathan Wild, was responsible for between 100 and 150 cases at the Old Bailey between 1714 and 1724 (Howson, 1970, App. II). An unknown number led to the conviction and execution of innocent men and women. While Wild's energetic prosecution of crime in association with victims was initially praised, eventually both the public and the government lost patience with his corrupt practices and turned against him. He was executed in 1725 after accepting a reward from a victim in exchange for returning stolen goods and then failing to report the crime, a violation of the 1718 Transportation Act (OBO: t17250513-55; Hitchcock and Shoemaker, 2015, 87–8; Shore, 2015, 29–30, 46; Howson, 1970).

Despite the scandal which led to Wild's execution, and another surrounding the thief-making conspiracies of the McDaniel gang in 1754, thief-taking continued throughout the eighteenth century (Paley, 1989;

Hitchcock and Shoemaker, 2015, *passim*). Although the £100 proclamation rewards ended in 1752, the statutory rewards which nurtured thief-taking did not end until 1818, when, under Bennet's Act (discussed below) they were replaced by a system in which courts could award rewards at their discretion (Bentley, 1998, 7–8). Despite its drawbacks, thief-taking continued to be encouraged or condoned by governments and the legal system because the number of legitimate prosecutions it facilitated was seen as beneficial. Just as importantly, no better method for encouraging prosecutions had yet been found. The principle of offering a financial incentive to encourage criminal prosecutions was taken up by other bodies, such as local authorities, institutions, associations for the prosecution of felons (discussed below), and even victims themselves, who offered occasional additional ad hoc rewards (Hitchcock and Shoemaker, 2015, 62, 86, 183, 225).

Moreover, the rewards system, and thief-taking in particular, demonstrated the benefits of encouraging non-victims to get involved in the work of arresting and prosecuting criminals. In particular, it acted as an incentive for local constables and law enforcers to expend more energy on policing. While the vast majority of those who benefitted from rewards did so only once, a substantial number of those receiving rewards were policing agents and other men who started to act like them, apprehending, examining, and searching suspects, and even keeping them as prisoners until the victim was notified or they could be brought before a justice (Clayton and Shoemaker, 2022; Shore, 2015, ch. 2).

The idea that policing and detective work could be a way of earning a living was reflected in other innovations. In the early eighteenth century, the traditional system of (male) householders being required to serve both as night watchmen and parish constables by periodic rotation was replaced in parts of London by the appointment of salaried deputies (Beattie, 2001, chs 3–4; Reynolds, 1998). While the quasi-officials who served in these new roles were often of a lower status than the volunteers they replaced, the experience they acquired by repeated service made them more adept at detecting offenders, as was particularly the case with the 'informing constable' William Payne in the City of London in the 1760s and 1770s (Innes, 2009, ch. 7; see also Dodsworth, 2019, ch. 4). As discussed in Chapter 4, these salaried law enforcement officers formed the basis of the Bow Street Runners, a group of regularized thief-takers and former parish officers created by the reforming JP Henry Fielding in 1749. In 1792, the Middlesex Justices Act, which restricted the activities of JPs within the London area to a limited number of stipendiaries, built on the Bow Street model by creating seven 'rotation' offices, each with six constables who could be sent out to make arrests (32 Geo III, *c.* 53). All these 'runners' were dependent on statutory rewards for a substantial part of their income; in this sense the rewards system contributed to the growth of modern policing (Clayton and Shoemaker, 2022). In a period during which methods of information gathering about crime and criminality were still very rudimentary, the rewards offered significant encouragement to the detection of crime.

The creation of state-sponsored support for victims as prosecutors in the form of rewards and proactive policing marks the eighteenth century as a key period in the longer history of victim support. However, these innovations sat alongside others that remained firmly rooted in civil society and voluntarism. This is most clearly demonstrated by the mid-century rise of 'associations for the prosecution of felons'. These were voluntary societies, composed of propertied members who shared a common occupation or lived in the same area, formed to provide mutual assistance in the event any member was the victim of a crime. In return for the payment of regular dues, members acquired a sort of insurance policy which secured services including (depending on the association) patrols to prevent crime, detective work to apprehend those who committed crimes against them, reimbursement of costs if they needed to prosecute, and the provision of legal assistance in conducting prosecutions.

These associations were founded on the premise that the existing provisions offered by the state to support prosecutions were inadequate, and that victims needed further support and encouragement to carry out what was supposed to be their obligation. This is evident in the stated purpose of one of London's first such associations, the Society for the Prevention of Frauds and Felonies Committed on Tradesmen and Shopkeepers, founded in 1767: 'to pursue the most vigorous and effectual methods to bring such offenders to justice; as they frequently escape the punishment their crimes deserve, through the inability, timidity, avarice, or indolence of those they injure' (Trusler, 1786, 153; Shoemaker, 2004, 44). It is clear that the motive of the founders of this society, like the sponsors of earlier pieces of legislation, was not merely to support the victim per se but to mobilize the victim as a tool to improve public order. Some of the earliest prosecution associations in London were organized to protect the docks and warehouses along the River Thames (D'Sena, 1987), but the capital actually had relatively few associations when compared with the rest of the country. This suggests that the men living in central London who might have formed such associations were more likely to feel that they had sufficient access to policing and support for prosecutions. Prosecution associations were more prominent in less policed places on the urban periphery, such as Barnet, Enfield, Hammersmith, and Rotherhithe, which were notorious for highway robbers (Shoemaker, 2004, 45).

Outside the metropolis, large numbers of associations emerged in the late eighteenth and early nineteenth centuries, such that by the mid-nineteenth century there were approximately a thousand across the country (Hay, 1983; King, 1989; Philips, 1989). While significant in terms of what they can tell us about the perceived impediments to the prosecution of crime, the scale and impact of the associations should not be overstated. Their members were typically upper and middle-class men, and their focus was on serious property crimes. They played little role in policing other types of crime or in supporting non-elite victims. With the exception of promoting sociability among their members, most associations were also not very active. Surveying the evidence, Beattie concluded that, while they facilitated some 'prosecutions that would otherwise not have been undertaken', overall, the associations 'did not have a major effect on the number of offenders brought to trial before the quarter sessions and assizes' (Beattie, 1986, 50). King's research on Essex reached a similar conclusion (King, 2000, 55; for a contrasting assessment, see Philips, 1989, 144). Private initiatives could only go so far in increasing rates of prosecutions. In any case, with the advent of the 'new police' across the country from the 1830s, these types of prosecution associations declined (Philips, 1989, 150–1).

Significantly, however, they inspired the foundation of other kinds of prosecution societies in the nineteenth century, notably those aiming to 'use the law as best they could to protect women and children from violence, immorality and vice' (Stevenson, 2004, 98). These included the Associate Institution for Improving and Enforcing the Laws for the Protection of Women (founded in 1844), the Society for the Rescue of Young Women and Children (founded in 1853), and the National Society for the Prevention of Cruelty to Children (NSPCC, founded as the London Society in 1884; Behlmer, 1982, 110). As we will go on to discuss, these voluntary groups played a key part in bringing prosecutions in the Old Bailey and other courts.

Counsel

As we have seen, the rise of the professional thief-taker led to a series of scandals in which innocent people were convicted by sophisticated legal operators in search of rewards. Langbein's research on the early history of legal counsel at the Old Bailey has shown how certain judges became aware of these corrupt practices and moved to restore the balance of natural justice in the courtroom by allowing defendants access to legal advice, contravening a longstanding judicial ban on the practice (Langbein, 2003, 167–77). From the mid-1730s, defence counsel were admitted at the Old Bailey and the Surrey assizes with permission to examine and test the evidence being laid against the defendant, though they were not allowed to address the jury (Lemmings 2011, 119–20). This development altered the balance of power in the courtroom. Assisted by defence counsel, some suspects may have found it easier to escape conviction. It would not be until the twentieth century, and the Poor Prisoners Defence Act of 1930, that defendants had access to legal aid to fund counsel. Nevertheless, a surprisingly wide range of defendants, including some from lower-class backgrounds, were defended by counsel in the eighteenth century (Hitchcock and Shoemaker, 2015, *passim*).

Prosecutors had always had the right to counsel, but since legal experts and the courts viewed criminal cases as a straightforward (and low status) aspect of the law where specialist expertise was not needed, counsel rarely appeared in early modern criminal trials. This began to change in the early eighteenth century as the City of London and the government (in the form of the Treasury, Mint, and the Bank of England) began to use solicitors to assemble prosecution evidence in cases where convictions were deemed to be particularly in the public interest. From the 1710s, these solicitors, who were not allowed to appear in court, began to appoint barristers to present the evidence they had assembled (Langbein, 2003, 111–31, 145–6; May, 2003, 23–5, 38). However, most victims, even the small number who hired solicitors, continued without counsel: it was expensive (typically costing a guinea, or just over a pound, for the brief), and did not seem necessary. Traditionally, victims were supported in the courtroom by the judge, who guided them through their testimony and examined the defendant. Consequently, with the exception of state-backed prosecutions, very few complainants in the late seventeenth and early eighteenth centuries had counsel. But the emergence of defence counsel in the 1730s upset the balance in the courtroom and prompted more victim-prosecutors to appoint counsel as well.

It is difficult to measure the proportion of Old Bailey cases where counsel were present because the publishers of the *Proceedings*, who were much more interested in crime than the law, reported it erratically, and because the approaches and language used by different reporters varied over time. Information about counsel is not coded in the digitized Old Bailey trials, so our evidence comes from samples carried out manually (by John Beattie and Stephen Landsman for the eighteenth century, and our Trial Participants dataset for the nineteenth century) which demonstrate the increasing presence of counsel over the eighteenth and nineteenth centuries. While counsel for either side was very rare before the 1730s, by 1747 prosecution counsel was reported as present in 5.6 per cent of Old Bailey trials, and by the end of century that figure had almost quadrupled (20.8 per cent) (Landsman, 1990, 607; Beattie, 1991, 227; Hitchcock and Shoemaker, 2015, 188, 357). May concluded that 'by 1790, merchants, manufacturers and shopkeepers too were increasingly inclined to hire counsel to prosecute those who stole from them' (May, 2003, 35).

The number of trials with prosecution counsel does not appear to have changed significantly in the first half of the nineteenth century, although the data are limited by uneven reporting practices, owing to the City of London's decision in 1805 to delete counsel's arguments from the *Proceedings* (May, 2003, 98–9). Reporting resumed in the 1820s, and Figure 6.1 (in Chapter 6, section 6.1) shows that defence counsel were present more frequently than prosecution counsel (as they had been since the 1740s) until the middle of the nineteenth century, when the pattern dramatically shifted.

In 1836, the Prisoners' Counsel Act (6 & 7 Will. 4, *c.* 14) formally enabled the counsel employed by defendants in felony trials to address the jury (Griffiths, 2014). As with the initial decision in the 1730s to allow defence counsel to participate in trials, this new right altered the balance of power in the courtroom, and led to calls for prosecution counsel to play a greater role (May, 2003, 197, 242). One opponent of the new law, the barrister Charles Phillips, noted in 1834 that the Middlesex magistrates refused to grant the costs of employing counsel at the Old Bailey: 'In every other court in England the county in which it is held provides counsel to prosecute. The county of Middlesex refuses to do so and therefore in nineteen cases out of twenty there are no counsel employed for the prosecution'. He complained that it was being left to the trial judge 'to unwind the web of the defence and expose the guilt of the prisoner' (May, 2003, 193). With the judge having to act as prosecutor, the integrity of justice—in his view—was in jeopardy.

Over the next twenty years, however, the situation changed in the London courts. As demonstrated in Chapter 6, from the 1850s prosecution counsel became almost ubiquitous in Old Bailey trials and by 1891 they were required. Their initial impact, however, may have been limited. As R. M. Jackson wrote in 1942,

> In the middle of the last century it often happened that no preparation was made of a prosecution; the accused was committed for trial, and at the trial court the clerk simply handed a copy of the indictment and of the depositions to a barrister, who did the best he could on this last-minute instruction, or even in some cases no barrister appeared at all and the judge piloted the case from the depositions (109).

It is not clear who paid counsel's fees in such cases, and we have not been able to identify the precise cause of this dramatic shift towards the routine use of prosecution counsel (not previously identified by historians), but, as will be discussed in Chapter 4, it was probably caused by a growth in police-led prosecutions which involved counsel. In 1891, prosecution counsel became universal when an Old Bailey order stipulated that 'all cases committed for trial to this Court in which no Solicitor appears for the prosecution shall be prosecuted by Counsel to be instructed on behalf of the Court, and such counsel shall be selected from Members of the Central Criminal Court Bar Mess' (Crew, 1933, 50). This represented the culmination of the 160-year-long trend of increasing numbers of prosecution counsel at the Old Bailey. As discussed in Chapter 6, their presence had a major impact on victims, sidelining their role in criminal trials.

Prosecution costs and expenses

As we saw in Chapter 2, costs were a major factor in dissuading victims from prosecuting crime. During the second half of the eighteenth century, parliament addressed this issue by passing three statutes which allowed the courts to order prosecution costs to be reimbursed. This was a significant shift away from the culture of offering rewards, which had often been associated with corruption. The preambles to the laws made clear that, once again, the purpose of this public funding was to induce victims to bring cases to court. In 1752, in response to the crime wave which followed the end of the War of the Austrian Succession, 'An Act for the better preventing Thefts and Robberies' was introduced 'to encourage the bringing Offenders to Justice'. The law gave courts discretionary powers to reimburse the prosecution costs of victims in felony cases, including court fees and 'a reasonable allowance for [their] time and trouble therein' while 'taking his circumstances into account' (25 Geo II, *c.* 36). The Act only applied to cases where the defendant was convicted, and the benefits were discretionary, but this was the first time the state had intervened directly to address one of the biggest obstacles which prevented victims from prosecuting: the costs and time involved.

Two years later, the preamble to another Act noted that the 'Expence as well as Loss of Time in attending Courts of Justice, is a Discouragement to the poorer Sort to appear as Witnesses against Offenders, who thereby escape the publick Justice, and the Punishment due to their Crimes;' and gave the courts the power to pay the costs of 'poor persons' bound over to give evidence for the prosecution (27 Geo II, *c.* 3). A third act in 1778 claimed that the previous two laws 'have been a great Encouragement towards bringing Offenders to Justice' and extended the payment of 'expences' in felony cases to all prosecutors and witnesses and also in cases where the defendant was acquitted (18 Geo III, *c.* 19, ss. 7–8). The impact of these Acts on Old Bailey prosecutions is assessed in Chapter 5, but it matches evidence from areas outside London that their initial impact was limited. From his study of the Surrey assizes, Beattie found that, after initially interpreting the Acts 'strictly', judges became 'more generous', such that by the early 1790s they awarded costs in two-thirds of felony trials (Beattie, 1986, 42–5; see also King, 1984, 32–3). But he argues that the payment of costs was 'of marginal importance' in encouraging prosecutions. This was because the provisions did not cover all the costs incurred, including those involved in apprehending the accused, attendance at the preliminary hearing before a magistrate, legal advice, and the time spent attending court. Payment was also made in arrears (Beattie, 1986, 45–8; see also King, 2000, 49–51). Nonetheless, these three acts set important precedents, indicating the state's willingness to assume at least some of the costs of prosecution.

Further provisions came in the early nineteenth century, although these were subject to specific limits and some omissions. The text of the 1818 law known as 'Bennet's Act' acknowledged that 'many Persons are deterred from prosecuting Persons guilty of Felony upon account of the Expence and Loss of time attending such Prosecutions, whereby the Ends of Justice are frequently defeated' (58 Geo III *c.* 70). This Act may have been influenced by similar legislation relating to Ireland which had been passed three years earlier; the opening wording in the Ireland Act was almost identical (55 Geo III *c.* 91). Clearly, there was a broader push to support both prosecutors and witnesses financially. Moreover, parliament believed that public order was being undermined by the unwillingness of victims to pay the costs of prosecutions. The Act, named after the reforming M.P. Henry Grey Bennet, who chaired the Select Committee on the State of the Police of the Metropolis in 1817, allowed the expenses of victims and witnesses to be paid regardless of the verdict, not only for felony but also some cases of misdemeanour. As noted above, it also replaced the fixed statutory rewards system with one in which courts gained discretionary powers to authorize payment of a reward to individuals who assisted in the apprehension of persons accused of specified offences, whether or not the accused was convicted (58 Geo. 3 *c.* 70; Radzinowicz, 1956, II, 79–81). In addition, private individuals, with Home Office permission, remained able to offer pardons to accomplices of crimes in return for the identification of suspects, but this practice was discontinued by the later nineteenth century (Bentley, 1998, 252).

The innovations in Bennet's Act were further developed by the 1826 Criminal Law Act (7 Geo. IV *c.* 64) which extended the payment of expenses to cover attendance at pre-trial hearings in magistrates' courts. This enabled courts to pay an allowance for 'time and trouble' to prosecutors and witnesses in felony cases and in some misdemeanours, and to those active in the apprehension of any person accused of these offences (Smith, G. 2020, 57; Taylor, D., 1998, 110). A number of incremental changes thus widened the scope of support for victims of crime and witnesses, although costs still could only be claimed retrospectively. According to David Philips, these acts contributed to the increase in prosecutions between the 1810s and the 1840s (Philips, 1977, 135). In Chapter 5 we examine the impact of the most important of these acts on Old Bailey prosecutions.

From the mid-nineteenth century, there were further incremental changes to the costs that were allowed, which authority paid for them, and what they included. We suggest that these state-funded payments towards prosecution expenses were the equivalent of what would later become 'legal aid' for defendants. An 1836 parliamentary inquiry into local rates had resulted in an annual vote in parliament which determined that half of the reasonable expenses of prosecuting felonies might be recovered from the Exchequer (Chadwick, 1991, 203). A decade later, this provision was extended to cover the full costs, although there were still some excluded offences, including keeping disorderly houses and libel. While it is not entirely clear why some offences were excluded, according to the 1874 Judicature Committee (PP, 1874, vol. 24, 15) the costs of prosecution in such cases were borne by other individuals prosecuting or by special local funds. The costs covered comprised 'criminal prosecutions at assizes and quarter sessions in England, including adjudications under the Criminal Justice and the Juvenile Offenders Acts, sheriffs' expenses, salaries to clerks of assizes and other officers, and for compensation to clerks of the peace' (ibid., 22).

As the century progressed, the scope of cost-reimbursement was widened, although this varied regionally. In some parts of northern England, reimbursed costs were actually reduced (Churchill, 2017, 194). The 1851 Criminal Justice Administration Act further extended the provisions for the payment of costs of attendance before the examining justice (14 & 15 Vict. *c.* 55. ss. 2 and 3), and the 1866 Prosecution Expenses Act allowed for prosecutors to recover the costs of preliminary proceedings before a magistrate, even where the case was dismissed and the prisoner discharged (29 & 30 Vict. *c.* 52). The 1870 Forfeiture Act, which abolished the long disused practice of forfeiture of lands and goods by those convicted of treason and felony, gave courts the power to require any person convicted of felony not only to reimburse the victim for their lost goods (up to £100), but also to pay for the costs or expenses incurred in prosecution and conviction (33 & 34 Vict. *c.* 23). The 1908 Cost in Criminal Cases Act (8 Edw. VII *c.* 15) served largely to codify the scattered provisions relating to the costs of prosecution. Further amending acts in 1952 (15 & 16 Geo. 6 & 1 Eliz. 2 *c.* 48) and 1973 (*c.* 14) extended the provision of costs available for the conduct of the criminal trial, including payment of witnesses from central government funds.

Over time, the state's covering of prosecution costs and expenses contributed to an increase in the number of poorer victims who appeared before the Old Bailey (see Chapter 5). Parliamentary criminal statistics indicate that the vast majority of prosecutions at the Old Bailey in the second half of the nineteenth century were primarily funded by the state (while remaining, in legal terms, private prosecutions). In a sample of every fifth year between 1856 and 1890, the number of 'prosecutions' funded (which averaged 940.5) constituted 97.5 per cent of the total number of victim prosecutions (Parliamentary Papers and *Proceedings* datasets). The average sum paid out per trial increased from £5 3s in 1855 to £12 5s 6d in 1890.

While these are substantial sums, the commentary in the 1856 report noted that the averages were distorted by the very large sums paid out in a small number of 'expensive prosecutions for murder' (PP, 1856, xv).

The covering of prosecution costs did not mean that accessing the justice system became cost free, however. As the 1856 report went on to note:

> It must be borne in mind that these costs are the limited fixed allowances made to prosecutors and witnesses under approved scales, and in the majority of the cases proceeded against are far from representing the expenses which persons are out of pocket, who are compelled under their recognizances to prosecute (ibid).

Moreover, costs were awarded at the court's discretion and reimbursed only once the case was concluded. This meant, as Churchill (2017, 194) has observed, that 'time and expense remained formidable obstacles to victim participation'. These obstacles would have been particularly acute for working-class complainants with less disposable income. Nevertheless, the state's part-covering of these prosecution costs is a significant—and somewhat overlooked—aspect of the evolution of English public prosecution.

Another key aspect of this story is the apparent subsuming of the costs of hiring prosecution counsel within local authority and court budget lines. This meant that victims of all classes engaging in higher court trials gradually gained greater access to legal expertise, even if they had little say in how the court allocated that expertise to their case. These victims gained legal representation, if not pre-trial legal advice. In turn, this may help explain why crime victims did not feature very prominently in late nineteenth- and early twentieth-century debates about the need for what would come to be referred to as 'legal aid'—or access to free legal advice. To date, historians have shown that while there was a demand for such advice, particularly within working-class communities, this was likely to have been met in relation to criminal matters through the police courts (Davis, 1984) and in relation to civil matters—notably debt, housing, accidents, and divorce—through the work of the Poor Man's Lawyer Movement (Bradley, 2019). Up to now, they have not yet considered the extent to which this demand may have been partially met—for victims at least—through access to publicly subsidized prosecution counsel in the higher courts.

Later legal aid legislation would centre on defendants' continuing need for similarly subsidized legal advice and representation. The 1930 Poor Prisoners Defence Act made further provision for this, as did the much more comprehensive 1949 Legal Aid and Advice Act (Bradley, 2019; Leat, 1975). There was a hint that crime victims might also benefit from such a scheme in the latter's underpinning White Paper, which referred to a need 'to provide legal advice for those of slender means and resources, so that no one would be financially unable to prosecute a just and reasonable claim or defend a legal right; and to allow counsel and solicitors to be remunerated for their services' (cited in Brooke, 2017, 5; see also Cross, 2015). This angle was not pursued in the ensuing legislation. However, by this juncture, the state had been part-covering crime victims' costs for over two centuries, starting with the 1752 'Act for the better preventing Thefts and Robberies'. 'Legal aid' for victims thus arguably preceded 'legal aid' for defendants by some margin.

Legislation re-defining punishments, offences, and prosecution procedures

During the nineteenth century, among the many tactics that parliament used to encourage prosecutions was the passage of legislation which affected punishments, definitions of offences, and the procedures of prosecution. While all these reforms had the effect of facilitating prosecutions, in some ways they also diminished the victims' role in the judicial process.

Between 1808 and 1841 the scope of capital punishment (the 'Bloody Code') was dramatically curtailed, leaving only those convicted of the most serious offences (murder, wounding, violent theft, arson, sodomy) to be sentenced to death (though after 1835, of Old Bailey capital convicts, only murderers were actually executed). The complex mixture of motives behind this legislation has been much debated by historians but insufficient attention has been paid to the desire to encourage victims to prosecute who had previously been reluctant to do so owing to the severity of the punishment (Gatrell, 1994; Devereaux, 2017). The 1820s witnessed 'an increasingly pressing public distaste for capital punishment', particularly when the convicts were female or young (Devereaux, 2017, 43; Shoemaker, 2022). Consequently, the removal of the death penalty from the offences of pickpocketing in 1808 and shoplifting in 1823 led to an increase in prosecutions of juvenile offenders (King and Noel, 1993). Anecdotal evidence indicates that, prior to reform, some prosecutors were dissuaded from prosecuting capital offences both by their own objections to the punishment and by the fear of retribution from the community and the family and friends of the deceased if the convict was executed (PP, 1819, 27, 86–7, 113; McGowen, 1983, 112; Gatrell, 1994, 102; King, 2000, 31–2). As Thomas Buxton, an opponent to the death penalty, told the House of Commons in March 1818, public opposition had created a 'crisis' within the judicial system, since victims refused to prosecute capital offences: 'the public deny their assistance and are combined not for the law, but against it' (PP, HC Deb, 2 March 1819).

Regardless of whether these concerns were influential in securing the passage of this legislation, the restriction of capital punishment to a small number of the most serious offences may well have contributed to the sharp rise in prosecutions at the Old Bailey in the 1830s and 1840s documented in Figure 1.1 in Chapter 1, as prosecutors no longer needed to worry about the possibility that the accused would be hanged. Some victims likely gained from this reform in that they felt more able to bring prosecutions while others may have lamented the loss of the capital sanction, either for retributive purposes or owing to their influence over penal outcomes through the sentencing and pardoning process, which, up to the late 1830s, resulted in a high proportion of death sentences being commuted into lesser punishments. That victims took advantage of this possibility in selected cases can be seen by the fact that between 1730 and 1837 at least 746 Old Bailey victims recommended their defendants for mercy prior to the judge's sentencing at the end of the trial.[1] As further explored in Chapter 6, while punishments became less 'bloody' from the 1840s, they also became more certain, and less subject to victims' lobbying.

Along with the curtailing of the 'Bloody Code', nineteenth-century criminal legislation also attempted to consolidate and rationalize the vast body of statutes which defined criminal offences. In the process some crimes were defined more broadly in an attempt to facilitate prosecutions, particularly offences involving male violence, in part as a result of growing concerns to reform male behaviour and reduce violence against women (Wiener, 1998, 2004).

A series of statutes passed between 1803 and 1861 expanded the definition of non-fatal violent felonious assault and, from 1837, made them non-capital offences. In 1803 Lord Ellenborough's Act, which created a new capital offence of attempted murder, 'immediately generated a steady stream of prosecutions, convictions and executions' (43 Geo. III, *c.* 58; Handler, 2007, 183; Wiener, 2004, 22–3). Similarly, the 1828 Offences Against the

[1] Capital Convictions at the Old Bailey, https://hcmc.uvic.ca/project/oldbailey/search.php, accessed 12 May 2022.

Person Act (Lord Lansdowne's Act) expanded the range of offences incorporated within the 1803 Act by including the act of wounding; this too led to increased prosecutions at the Old Bailey and other assizes courts (9 Geo. IV, *c*. 31, ss. 11, 12; Wiener, 2004 23–4; Handler, 2007, 190). The 1837 Offences Against the Person Act, which removed the death penalty from felonious violence if it did not involve attempted murder or death, also expanded the definition of attempted murder and, crucially, enabled juries to convict an offender on a reduced charge of common assault, leading to an increase in partial verdicts and reduced sentences. (While this was a decision left to the jury, victims who sought such an outcome could tailor their evidence accordingly.) This was followed by the creation of the offence of unlawful wounding, with or without a weapon, as a misdemeanour in 1851. As Handler argues, 'the 1837 and 1851 Acts created a greater range of offences and prosecuting options' (1 Vict. *c*. 85; 14 & 15 Vict. *c*.19, ss. 4–5; Handler, 2007, 196–7). Finally, all these offences were consolidated in the 1861 Criminal Law Amendment Act (24 & 25 Vict. *c*. 100). While these acts resulted in increased numbers of prosecutions, it is important to note that, as documented in Chapter 6, their provisions were often 'nullified and mitigated' by 'judges, jurors, prosecutors and witnesses … according to their own conceptions of the bounds of acceptable violence' (Handler, 2007, 183).

Some of the same statutes contained specific provisions with respect to sexual violence, a matter of increasing concern in the nineteenth century. For example, the 1828 Offences Against the Person Act abolished the requirement to prove seminal emission in prosecutions for rape and related offences, because, the Act stated, 'offenders frequently escape by reason of the difficulty of the proof which has been required of the completion of those several crimes' (9 Geo. IV *c*. 31, s. 17). Noting that this Act reduced the necessity for more detailed courtroom testimony about the offence, Anna Clark has argued that this reform 'actually suppressed women's ability to speak out against rape', though many victims may have been grateful for the reduced evidentiary proof required for conviction (Clark, 1987, 60–3).

Further statutes clarified the laws on child sexual abuse, initially by providing a clear statutory basis for offences which were already offences at common law. The 1828 statute made the carnal knowledge of children under ten a capital offence (subsequently replaced by transportation; 4 & 5 Vict. *c*. 56, s. 3), while later acts, the result of pressure from social purity and feminist campaigners, progressively expanded and classified sexual offences against girls and young women by age. The 1861 Offences Against the

Person Act created a misdemeanour offence of 'carnally knowing a girl between ten and twelve years old' and this became a felony in 1875, when the carnal knowledge of girls aged twelve to thirteen became a misdemeanour (24 and 25 Vict. *c.* 100; 38 & 39 Vict. *c.* 94, ss 3–4; Jackson, 2001, 13). Finally, in 1885, the Criminal Law Amendment Act, 'An Act to make further provision for the Protection of Women and Girls, the suppression of brothels, and other purposes', made the carnal knowledge of a girl up to the age of thirteen a felony, and increased the age of consent for sexual intercourse to sixteen, making carnal knowledge of a child over thirteen and under sixteen a misdemeanour. The 1885 Act also made it possible for children to provide evidence in court while not under oath, thereby removing one of the obstacles to prosecuting child sexual abuse described in Chapter 2 (48 and 49 Vict. *c.* 69; Jackson, 2001, 13; Lamont and Cox, 2021).

Historians have noted that these acts facilitated increases in prosecutions for sexual offences against female children, a point we return to in Chapter 5 (Jackson, 2001, 18–21; Wiener, 1998, 206). A significant proportion of these cases were brought by voluntary organizations effectively acting as prosecution associations and thus playing a key role in 'the criminalization of sexual violence' in the Victorian period (Stevenson, 2004, 107). In the 1860s and 1870s, the Associate Institute for the Protection of Women and Children regularly prosecuted sexual abuse cases in the London courts, including the Old Bailey and the Middlesex Quarter Sessions. The society's officers also appeared hundreds of times in the police courts and petty sessions, both in order to prosecute specific cases and to 'offer assistance and support to unrepresented and deserving women and children' (Stevenson, 2004, 103). The professionalism of these organizations, with their prosecuting officers and experienced solicitors, meant that their prosecutions had a good chance of success. Louise Jackson found that in a sample of thirty-four cases prosecuted, 82 per cent resulted in convictions (Jackson, 2001, 59–60). On one occasion in 1870, the Associate Institute was directly praised by the judge at the Middlesex Sessions for its efforts in convicting a man of indecent assault on a girl:

> the society by whom the prosecution had been conducted were most beneficial in such cases, and very properly took them up where the parties themselves, from their poverty, were unable to employ counsel to lay the facts before the court; and but for them many cases might not be prosecuted at all, or if prosecuted, the facts would not be properly laid before the jury (*Daily Telegraph*, 15 March 1870, 6).

This mode of voluntary society prosecution of crimes against children including indecent assault and statutory rape was further expanded following the passage of the 1885 Criminal Law Amendment Act and the 1889 Prevention of Cruelty to, and Protection of, Children Act (52 & 53 Vict. *c.* 44), together with a series of repealing and amending Acts in 1894 (57 & 58 Vict. *c.* 41) and 1904 (4. Edw. VII *c.* 15). The newly established NSPCC became the key agency to make use of this new legislation, which also reformed the role of child witnesses and assigned payment of the costs of prosecution to the parish or union guardians (Jackson, 2001, 62–4). Between 1890 and 1910, around half the sexual abuse cases at the Old Bailey were NSPCC prosecutions, and in 1890, the NSPCC achieved convictions in 77 per cent of their cases. Cases were also prosecuted by their solicitors (including William Moreton Phillips and William Clarke Hall) across the London police courts. In 1897, the society claimed it had prosecuted some 4,000 cases of sexual assault on children over the previous decade (Jackson, 2001, 61–4). The NSPCC formed good working relationships with the police, who were keen to relinquish responsibility for such cases. In 1889, the Commissioner of the Metropolitan Police, James Monro, ordered that in all cases 'in which children are treated with cruelty' the police should notify the society and 'afford it every information and assistance within their power' (Behlmer, 1982, 218–29; *Times* 29 March 1889, 9).

While the statutes discussed in this section facilitated prosecutions for certain offences where it was deemed to be in the public interest, other legal provisions deliberately limited prosecutions for a small number of offences by specifying that they could only be undertaken with the consent of the Attorney General, or by specified officials. These included offences against the 1793 Lottery Act, the 1829 Roman Catholic Relief Act, and prosecutions for sedition, violations of the excise laws, and cases with 'sensitive domestic or international implications', where the government restricted the rights of private individuals in order to protect state interests (Hay, 1983, 178–89). Similarly, to reduce corruption, the 1859 Vexatious Indictments Act limited private prosecutions for certain offences including perjury, conspiracy, obtaining money by false pretences, keeping a gambling or disorderly house, and indecent assault (22 & 23 Vict. *c.* 17; Hay, 1983, 177–9). According to the 1896 edition of the *Judicial Statistics*, the Act contributed to a dramatic fall in the number of indictments which were rejected by the grand jury (PP, 1986, 22). While these restrictions on private prosecutions affected only a narrow range of offences, they demonstrate how statutory provisions to stimulate and control prosecutions could have the effect of constraining victim choices over the offences they prosecuted. They were also important forerunners of much wider restrictions introduced in the twentieth century.

Summary jurisdiction

Of more immediate importance was the use of statutes to encourage prosecutions by widening the range of offences which could be tried summarily. As we saw in Chapter 2, summary jurisdiction, in which criminal complaints were heard and determined by one or two justices acting on their own, was already extensively practised in the eighteenth century, particularly for petty thefts and accusations of assault (King, 2004, 126, 136–7). During the nineteenth century, motivated by concerns to reduce the costs of prosecution and the adverse consequences of defendants spending a long time in prison awaiting trial (Hanly, 2021b, 284, 301), a series of statutes, combined with an expansion and formalization of the courts which heard such cases, significantly increased the range of offences tried summarily, contributing to a substantial decline in the number of cases which came before the assizes courts, including the Old Bailey (see Chapter 1, Figure 1.1). While victims benefited from the greater ease of summary justice, the abbreviated procedures and lesser punishments may also have been seen as disadvantageous.

A number of statutes made a greater range of assaults subject to summary jurisdiction. The 1828 Offences Against the Person Act formalized existing practices by authorizing two JPs to determine assault cases, leading to a transfer of such cases from courts of quarter sessions to summary courts (9 Geo. IV *c.* 31; King, 1996, 61). In 1853, in an attempt to encourage more prosecutions of domestic violence, an act extended this statute by allowing summary prosecutions for those who committed aggravated assaults on women and children under the age of 14 (16 & 17 Vict. *c.* 30; Clark, 2000, 33).

Other statutes expanded summary jurisdiction for thefts. An 1847 statute enabled summary prosecutions of juvenile offenders, and the 1855 Criminal Justice Act significantly expanded the range of larcenies which could be tried summarily. It redefined larcenies under the value of five shillings as 'simple larcenies' which could be tried summarily, if the accused agreed. Those above that value could be dealt with summarily if the accused pleaded guilty (18 & 19 Vict. *c.* 126). In 1879, an Act further extended summary jurisdiction to embezzlement and cases involving the theft of goods up to forty shillings, regardless of the preferences of the victim. The Act also made all offences committed by juveniles under sixteen (except murder) triable in summary courts, subject to consent of the parents (up to age twelve) or the juvenile themself (for those aged twelve to fifteen) (42 & 43 Vict. *c.* 49, s. 10–13).

Concurrently, summary hearings were facilitated by the expansion of magistrates' courts, regular meetings of justices to which victims could bring their complaints. These could either be heard by the justices immediately or forwarded on to the higher courts. First established in the City of London and at Bow Street in Westminster in the eighteenth century, they were spread to other parts of London with the creation of stipendiary magistrates under the 1792 Middlesex Justices Act (Beattie, 2001, 108–13; 32 Geo. III *c.* 53). Following the formation of the Metropolitan Police in 1829, these courts came to be known as 'police courts' (whose practices were regularized and expanded by the 1839 Metropolitan Courts Act; 2 & 3 Vict. *c.* 71), which gave a single magistrate power to hear a broader range of offences and reduced the cost of a summons for complainants to two shillings (Auerbach, 2021, 79–80, 189). Despite the name, the police courts continued to be run by one or more magistrates.

The effect of the statutory expansion of summary jurisdiction was to divert increasing numbers of criminal cases away from the trial courts. Statistics on the number of cases tried summarily are only available from the 1850s. In 1855, thirteen police courts in London heard over 96,000 cases, of which the vast majority (77,000) were determined summarily. In contrast, only 1,232 defendants were tried that year at the Old Bailey (Davis, 1984, 313; OBO). The compiler of the 1856 *Judicial Statistics* observed that the 'unprecedented decrease' in the number of commitments for trial between 1855 and 1856 'must be largely, but not wholly, attributed to the extended powers of Justices to deal summarily in cases of larceny'. Similarly, the cause of a fall in commitments between 1880 and 1881 was 'to a certain extent' assigned to the 1879 Summary Jurisdiction Act (PP, 1856, vii–viii; 1881, xxv).

Summary jurisdiction increased over time as a proportion of all indictable offences tried in England and Wales. From 62.9 per cent of all commitments in 1857, this figure increased to 80.2 per cent in 1913, and then temporarily surged even higher during the First World War. Following the war, gradual growth resumed to a peak of 91.4 per cent of commitments on the eve of the Second World War before declining during the war and then levelling off to an average of 85.5 per cent in the post-war decades (Parliamentary Papers dataset; Gatrell, 1980).

Summary jurisdiction was somewhat less significant in London, however, since the quarter sessions courts and the Old Bailey met more frequently and potential prosecutors lived closer. In 1901, 80.5 per cent of indictable offences nationally were heard by summary jurisdiction, whereas in London the figure was just 67.8 per cent (PP. 1903b, 13). In less urban areas, magistrates' courts were more accessible than the higher courts. Following the passage of the 1855 Act, the total number of larceny cases tried in the Black Country doubled, suggesting that many potential victims had previously been deterred from prosecution by the costs and trouble involved (Philips, 1977, 49, 133). In all parts of the country, the easy availability of summary justice both increased the number of offences prosecuted and diverted many existing prosecutions from the higher courts. Because it was inexpensive and relatively informal, summary justice was particularly attractive to the poor, and to women (King, 2004, 140; Darby, 2015, 368, 372). Davis described the London police courts in the second half of the nineteenth century as a 'poor man's system of justice', owing to the ease of access and wide range of disputes heard (including marital violence and other domestic disputes); Auerbach recently amended that to 'a poor woman's court of justice' (2021, ch. 5). The poor brought a wide variety of criminal and non-criminal complaints before the courts, seeking justice, advice, or charity. At least one-fifth of all larceny charges under the Criminal Justice Act in these courts were brought by working-class prosecutors, who could afford the two-shilling cost of a summons. About half of these prosecutions involved charges against friends, relatives, or people who lived in the same house, often relating to the theft of clothes, food, or other belongings; in earlier times these complaints would have been settled informally (Davis, 1984, 318).

There is some evidence that prosecutors preferred summary trials: police magistrate John Hardwick reported in 1837 that in nineteen cases out of twenty they requested that larceny cases be tried summarily (cited by Hanly, 2021b, 285). But while summary jurisdiction undoubtedly made justice more accessible for victims, in some respects it also marginalized them; there are reasons to believe that some may have felt disadvantaged by this type of justice. The courts were more accessible and outcomes were quicker, but victims lost some control over the judicial process. The choice of whether a case was tried summarily or went to trial was not theirs, and we do not know how much they were able to testify in the summary courts, nor how much assistance they could receive there from lawyers. Moreover, the sanctions imposed on convicts were weaker, with the maximum penalty of a short spell of imprisonment, so those seeking substantial retribution for wrongs may have felt frustrated. But these outcomes suited some victims: wives bringing their husbands to court for abusive behaviour often sought a quick return to domestic coexistence (Davis, 1984, 322). For others, however, the short period of imprisonment was soon over and their antagonists were back on the streets, or at home, and able to repeat their abuse.

Through official and voluntary initiatives in the eighteenth and nineteenth centuries, therefore, victims were increasingly assisted in initiating and conducting prosecutions. While early efforts to stimulate prosecutions by the offer of rewards were eventually abandoned, the stimulus they gave to the development of both proactive policing and the use of counsel in trials was significant. Moreover, in an important change of tactics, the state began to reimburse legal costs. Victims were still recognized as prosecutors, but the state increasingly imagined them as social actors requiring mobilization through support.

But that support served to reduce victims' control over the prosecution process. Rewards were only available for certain capital offences, giving victims (and thief-takers) an incentive to define any crimes they experienced accordingly. Further, they were only payable upon full conviction of the accused, undermining victims' traditional discretionary preferences for informal settlements or partial convictions on lesser offences (Clayton and Shoemaker, 2022). Similarly, costs would only be paid for certain offences and were up to the judges' discretion, thus encouraging prosecutions of offences which met judges' expectations of the 'ideal' victim (Christie, 1986). Moreover, as will become apparent in the next chapter, both police and counsel did not just assist victims; they tended to take over the prosecutions they participated in and frame them according to their own understandings of crime and their priorities for enforcing the law. This supplanting or marginalization of victims within the prosecution process over time stimulated new calls for means of supporting them beyond that process. These calls gathered pace in the context of mid-twentieth century welfarism.

3.2 Supporting Victims beyond the Prosecution Process

The dramatic expansion of the state during the Second World War underpinned the post-war welfare state, and a new relationship between state and citizen. This new relationship was encapsulated in the work of economist and reformer William Beveridge, who believed that post-war reconstruction could not be achieved through pre-war means. His 1942 report, *Social Insurance and Allied Services*, called instead for a 'cradle to grave' social programme that could fight what he famously termed the 'five giants': 'idleness, ignorance, disease, squalor and want' (Beveridge, 1942). The needs of citizens were to be recognized in new ways through their emergent 'rights' to health, education, housing, and welfare, delivered by new services channelling unprecedented levels of state resource. That said, this was still very much a framework based on the obligations and duties of citizens. The worker was 'obliged' to accept work that was offered or risk losing access to welfare support; the child was 'obliged' to attend school or risk punishment; the social tenant was 'obliged' to keep an orderly home or risk eviction, and so on (Harris, 1992; Rose, 1999).

The impact of the post-war welfare state on the criminal justice system was in many ways less profound than on these other areas of social life. The pre-war prosecutorial collaboration of police, courts, counsel, and complainant continued within the mixed economy of criminal justice broadly established in the nineteenth century. However, the 1948 Criminal Justice Act (11 & 12 Geo. 6 *c.* 58) introduced sweeping changes to punishments, abolishing penal servitude, hard labour, and whipping. This liberalization had been gaining pace over decades but accelerated in the post-war moment (Radzinowicz and Turner, 1950; Emsley, 2013b; Godfrey and Lawrence, 2014). It contributed to a mid-century skirmish in a 'culture war' between those promoting penal reform and those resisting it. Rock's account (1990) of the different rhetorical positions adopted by these groups shows how both sides invoked the figure of the victim of crime to shore up their case.

Opposing the introduction of the 1948 Act, for example, MP Sir Thomas Ayr warned that, 'Children, inoffensive old people, and cripples were now ... the victims of the 20,000 vicious thugs and sadists scattered about the country' and that there were 'many people suffering from sloppy sentimentality, and the same pain should be inflicted on those brutal, greedy, sadistically-minded persons as they caused to others' (*The Times*, 15 April

1948, cited in Rock, 1990, 56). In a similar vein, Brigadier Raynes MP complained that, 'Henceforth the criminal who brutally robs an old man or woman will merely be relegated to the most complete form of social security—a not overcrowded house, with a bedroom to himself', noting that he himself 'had been beaten well in my time and I rather hoped that my children would go through the same useful discipline.' (*The Times*, 17 April 1948, cited in Rock, 1990, 56).

Some defenders of penal reform would come to neutralize these rhetorical attacks by arguing that they too were mindful of victims. In so doing, they opened up a new political space around the idea of the victim and their needs. They did not focus on encouraging greater access to the courts; rather, they focused on offering compensation to those injured by crime and later on creating new victim support services.

Criminal injuries compensation

In 1953, parliament debated a private member's bill introduced by Wing Commander Eric Bullus MP seeking to reverse the 1948 Criminal Justice Act (Rock, 1990, 60). Defenders of the Act included the Howard League for Penal Reform. One of the League's leaders, veteran campaigner and magistrate Margery Fry, urged its members to consider a new idea: that victims' suffering could be better assuaged through financial compensation rather than through the physical punishment of offenders (ibid, 60). The League considered but rejected Fry's proposal, preferring not to dilute its aim of building a progressive and rehabilitative justice system.

Fry continued to develop the idea over several years, enlisting the views of lawyers (notably those involved in the lobby group, Justice), social scientists, and journalists (ibid, 46–78). In July 1957, by then in her 80s, she wrote an article in *The Observer* newspaper entitled 'Justice for victims', calling for the establishment of a limited system of state compensation for victims of criminal violence (Fry, 1957, 8). Given her stature as a social commentator, the article attracted much political attention. It opened with a startling example:

> A man was blinded as the result of an assault in 1951, and awarded compensation of 11,500 pounds. His two assailants, now out of prison, have been ordered to pay 5 shillings a week each. The victim will need to live

> another 442 years to collect the last instalment. A bitter mockery! Have we no better help to offer to the victims of violent crime?

As a remedy, Fry proposed the introduction of state compensation for victims who had suffered criminal injuries, modelled on the industrial injuries compensation scheme. Such a scheme ought not to interfere 'with the present jurisdiction of the courts in awarding damages against the aggressor in cases of violent crime', but rather help to 'supplement' the 'meagre' sums available. It would extend the 'modern system of collective responsibility for sickness and injury' created by the post-war welfare state by offering 'equal benefits to the man who falls from a ladder at work and the man whose enemy pushes the ladder from under him at home' (Fry, 1957, 8) It would also, in effect, address the evident shortcomings of previous efforts to require the convicted to compensate those harmed.

Upon her death, less than a year after the article was published, supporters of Fry's idea propelled it further into the public domain, framing it as a fitting memorial to her life and work. Fry's proposal was featured in the 1959 White Paper, 'Penal Practice in a Changing Society'. It attracted cross-party support, and was first presented to parliament later that year as a private member's bill introduced by MP Reg Prentice, a former trade unionist and expert in industrial injury compensation and social insurance. After a further five years and much debate, although notably not one in which actual victims' views were sought, the new criminal compensation scheme was established in 1964, overseen by a new Criminal Injuries Compensation Board (CICB). This offered a sliding scale of payments, determined and administered by the CICB, based on the level of incapacity caused by a criminal injury and the character of the applicant (Miers, 1978, 2018; Mawby and Walklate, 1994). Not all victims who had suffered an injury were eligible. The fact that the state accepted responsibility without acknowledging legal liability meant that only *ex gratia* or discretionary payments were provided (Schafer, 1970).

The CICB scheme broke with historical practice in two important respects. It greatly extended the range of offences suitable for compensation, and it assigned responsibility for payment to the government, rather than the convict or the local community. Prior to this, under principles established by the thirteenth-century Statute of Winchester (13 Edw. I, 1285), the local community had a collective responsibility to compensate victims of robberies if they failed to apprehend wrongdoers. Later statutes extended victims' compensation to other offences. Under the 1715 Riot Act (1 Geo.

I st. 2 *c.* 5 s. 6), compensation from local funds was provided to those whose buildings were damaged by riots. This, for example, resulted in payouts to 110 victims of the week-long Gordon Riots in 1780 (Rudé, 1956, 99–100). Under the 1886 Riot (Damages) Act, the payment of this compensation was assigned to local police funds (Williams, 1959). By the 1826 Criminal Law Act, a criminal court could order the payment from public funds of compensation to the relatives of a person killed (but not those merely injured) in attempting to effect an arrest (7 Geo. IV *c.* 64, s. 30).

It is important to note that the new state CICB scheme sat alongside existing measures to make convicted offenders pay some kind of compensation. The scheme also had parallels with eighteenth-century informal settlements whereby culprits paid damages to complainants, as well as civil law compensation mechanisms, and it built on the 1914 Criminal Justice Administration Act, which had developed the principle of compensation by the defendant (Walklate, 2013, 109). This would be refined by the 1952 Costs in Criminal Cases Act, and further updated by the 1973 Powers of Criminal Courts Act, which created 'criminal compensation orders' and reconfigured offenders' responsibility to compensate victims for any personal injury, loss, or damage resulting from an offence. This renewed focus on the offenders' responsibilities was partly motivated by the sharply rising costs of the CICB. In 1964–5, it had awarded ex gratia compensation totalling £33,431, but by 1971–2 this sum had risen to £3,282,260 (PP, HC Deb, 9 Aug. 1972, v. 842, c480W).

Secondly, the 1964 state compensation scheme broke with the past by placing a new emphasis on the concept of victim satisfaction. Victims should be both able to access the justice process and also be satisfied with the outcome of that process. In proposing the scheme, Fry (1957, 8) had invoked Jeremy Bentham:

> It is old-fashioned now to quote Bentham, but on the tendency of criminal law to pay scant attention to the needs of the victim, he puts it well: 'Punishment, which, if it goes beyond the limit of necessity, is a pure evil, has been scattered with a prodigal hand. Satisfaction, which is purely a good, has been dealt out with evident parsimony'.

Bentham's utilitarian concept of satisfaction was linked to financial recompense, which he thought should be drawn from the offender's property, or 'if the offender is without property ... it ought to be furnished out of the public treasury, because it is an object of public good and the security of all is interested in it' (cited in Fry, 1957). But Fry looked beyond the materiality of money to the idea of recognition. As she did so, she helped to frame a new view of victims that would be very influential in the subsequent development of support for them. In contrast to Bentham, who was primarily concerned with property crime, Fry's focus was on interpersonal violence, recognizing that crime did not only cause financial damage to victims. For her, 'the value of the proposed compensation would not be economic alone':

> [The] State which forbids our going armed in self-defence cannot disown all responsibility for its occasional failure to protect... For the family of a murdered man, for the girl whose health has been permanently broken by brutal rape, for the skilled workman who can no longer follow his trade, the simple fact that their hardships had been specially recognized would help to assuage the bitterness of their lot (Fry, 1957, 8).

The criminal injuries compensation scheme opened a new chapter in the story of state support for victims. Rooted in efforts to defend penal reform and extend social securities, it did not seek to encourage victims to prosecute, or ease the cost of engaging in prosecutions, or extend access to legal advice. Rather, some victims become entitled to compensation payments. The scheme reframed the state's historic duty to protect its citizens by requiring the state to pay compensation to certain of its citizens when it failed in that duty—in particular when it failed to protect them from violent crime. Some supporters of the scheme also began to confer a new claim to emotional satisfaction on those victims who fell within its purview. This aspect of victimhood would be further developed by new support schemes, to which we now turn.

Victim support

England's first local support organization for victims of all types of crime was set up in 1974. Like the criminal compensation scheme, the Bristol Victim Support Scheme (BVSS) also had its origins in the post-war penal reform movement. It was set up and part-funded under the auspices of the National Association for the Care and Resettlement of Offenders (NACRO), a body created in 1966 to replace the old National Association of Discharged Prisoners' Aid Societies. NACRO's constitution committed it to 'involve members of the community in crime prevention' and in the (after)care of offenders (Rock, 1990, 93). Its newly established regional officers were encouraged to bring fresh thinking to this challenge. The south-west leads, based in Bristol, focused on the relationship between offenders and their victims, inspired by the work of Californian-based radical criminologists. Berkeley's Richard Korn, a social psychologist and prison therapist, encouraged unprecedented dialogue within the US criminal justice system as a means of forcing it to become more effective and humane. As Rock put it, '[p]olice and judges should listen to offenders, and offenders to citizens. Differences of power, rank and function should be ignored' (1990, 95). This invocation of the offender–citizen relationship in turn opened up a new space for imagining the offender–victim relationship and its political potential.

The Bristol team put this into tentative and historic practice, inviting victims along with ex-offenders and criminal justice professionals to their first meeting in February 1969. Like Margery Fry and Richard Korn, their primary motivation was to mobilize the figure of the victim to win public support for penal reform and the meeting was not badged as a form of 'victim support'. As one of them, Philip Priestley, wrote:

> A common reply to calls for a more humane penal system is that of 'What about the victim? This is where my sympathies lie' ... A collusion of silence, deliberate ignorance and indifference has prevailed in relation to victims for many centuries now ... In an attempt to explore some of these issues [we] set up a victims-offenders group. (Priestley, 1970, 1–2, cited in Rock, 1990, 99)

Local victims themselves were in fact reluctant to play their part, despite avid promotion by the local press of the opportunity for 'the good, the bad and the victim' to get together (Rock, 1990, 101). However, the few who did agree to attend occupy a particular place in the history of modern 'victim policy', in that their voices were among the first to be sought and heard by reformers. Listening to victims had a transformative effect on the Bristol group, convincing them that they should focus more directly on victims in their own right.

They quickly became divided, however, as to how best to do this. Priestley and another co-founder, Charles Irving, left NACRO to set up their own organization—the short-lived National Victims Association, which turned out to be national in name only (see Rock, 1990). Irving went on to become a Conservative MP and did much to raise the political and media profile of victims. Another co-founder, Chris Holtom, a lecturer in social work at Bristol University and former probation and prison officer, continued to work under the NACRO umbrella, going on to co-lead what would become the Bristol Victim Support Scheme (BVSS) in January 1974. Later that year, Holtom was invited to give the Howard League's annual lecture and chose the 'circumstances of victims' as his subject. He told his audience that 'the main emphasis of the British penal system [had] traditionally been upon the detection of crime and the punishment of the offender', that 'a more enlightened attitude' was emerging through efforts to 'support the offender' and 'prevent recidivism', but that 'very little attention [had] been paid by either voluntary or statutory bodies to assess the needs of the victims of crime'. Up to that point, 'the main role of the victim at law [had] been as a source of evidence to secure a conviction against the offender'. Criminal injuries compensation was only provided in 'cases of actual physical injury' to 'a small minority of victims'. The BVSS therefore sought to provide broader 'help [to] victims of crime' by identifying and starting to address their 'unmet needs' (Holtom, 1974, cited in Gay, Holtom, and Thomas, 1975, 263; see also Shapland, Willmore, and Duff, 1985; Rock, 1990; Mawby, 2022).

From the outset, the BVSS sought collaboration with, rather than challenge to, the police. It involved a team of volunteers including former and serving police and probation officers, lawyers, and psychologists. Their pilot location was south Bristol, an area described by the group as encompassing 'a cross-section of urban society—an old established residential area both publicly and privately owned, and two densely populated housing estates'. They initially aimed to 'visit every victim of crime' based on their 'theory . . . that any crime, however trivial, might have a devastating effect on its victim' (Gay, Holtom, and Thomas, 1975, 263). Their work relied on the willingness of the local police to share victims' personal details. Here, their links with local police inspector Ray Stone proved vital. Stone took the view that information routinely shared with local journalists ought to be available to the BVSS, and was instrumental in persuading his chief constable to approve this (BBC Bristol News, 2014). The re-purposing of this police victim data proved a turning point in the history of victims' relationship with the state, enabling them and their experiences to be codified and framed as newly visible subjects of governance. The Bristol group's subsequent tactics were described by them as follows:

> Every morning the project administrator contacted the police, and obtained details of all those against whom an offence had been

> committed in the previous 24-hour period (name, address, and briefly, the nature of the crime). The administrator then allocated the victims between the team of trained volunteers. The volunteers were ordinary members of the public coming from all walks of life. Initially, there were eight volunteers including students, housewives, a vicar and a tax inspector, but later, because of the volume of work, others were enlisted and trained (Gay, Holtom, and Thomas, 1975, 264).

In line with many criminal justice and social welfare practices of the period, the consent of those concerned does not appear to have been sought. Victims were to be made visible whether they liked it or not, presumably on the basis that, once known to the police, their details were in the public domain, regardless of whether they opted to proceed with any prosecution.

In the first three months, fourteen Bristol volunteers contacted hundreds of victims by phone, letter, or home visit. They were trained in 'crisis intervention, community resources, welfare rights, legal procedures, and police involvement'. They attended 'fortnightly case-work sessions, supervised by the Senior Probation Officer' to 'monitor their progress' and 'help with their difficulties'. They offered 'advice on insurance, information regarding the Criminal Injuries Compensation Board, guidance on legal matters, assistance in claiming any applicable State Benefits, or referral to the appropriate helping agencies', but their 'primary aim' was 'the provision of an emotional outlet for those unable to cope with their distress in a crisis' (Gay, Holtom, and Thomas, 1975, 264). Victim support, then, was based in part on the presumption of trauma and the projection of particular emotional responses to crime. This approach had been building up over time within pockets of the post-war justice and welfare systems. Therapeutic practice drawn from educational psychology, child guidance, and aspects of psychoanalysis had shaped social science degree content and practitioner training (Rose, 1999; Rock, 1996). While it shared space with traditional police and penal practice, it contributed to a significant shift in the post-war period wherein the inner emotional life of pupils, patients, offenders, and, latterly, victims, came to be seen as something that must be assessed, managed, and improved. The rise of this type of victim support occupies its own particular place, then, in the construction and consolidation of England's 'empire of trauma' (Fassin and Rechtman, 2009; Walklate, 2016).

Holtom and his colleagues calculated that a significant proportion of Bristol's crime victims experienced 'emotional disturbance'. Of the 926 individuals notified to them in their first six months, 446 were visited and 315 were 'successfully' contacted. The responses of these 315 were 'analysed in order to predict the more vulnerable categories of person'. The results indicated that 102 people had experienced 'maximum disturbance' or 'very severe upset' while 213 had experienced 'moderate disturbance' or 'slight or undetectable degree of upset', noting that only 2 per cent had experienced violent crime. The results were correlated to sex, age, social class, financial and relative value of loss, attitude to offender, social isolation (defined as living as single), previous experience of victimization, and attitude to the offer of help. A 'higher degree of severe disturbance' was found among women, those living alone, and those with 'the strongest feelings towards the offender, whether sympathetic or hostile'. There was a 'slight tendency' towards severe disturbance among older people and those who had been previously victimized, and 'no detectable' difference in responses based on social class (Gay, Holtom, and Thomas, 1975, 265–6).

The team used the results to finesse and target their future service, 'restricting visits to those groups most likely to be vulnerable' who were listed as:

1. Women rather than men.
2. In the older age groups.
3. Living alone.
4. Suffering the experience for a second time.
5. Experiencing moderate to severe financial loss.
6. Experiencing clear feelings towards the offender.

(Gay, Holtom, and Thomas, 1975, 267).

Thus, 'vulnerable' victims were distinguished from the wider victim pool and future 'mainstream' victim services and policy frameworks were created in their image. As Chapter 7 explores, other groups of post-war activists would fight for the recognition of the needs of victims whose vulnerabilities were bound up with very different forms of discrimination and inequality. It is notable that the Bristol volunteers were unable to make personal contact with two-thirds of those in the wider victim pool referred to them during their first six months. Many of these people had experienced theft from cars and were subsequently approached by letter only. From the outset of this new era of victim policy, a large number of victims preferred to remain less visible and to restrict their participation in schemes seeking to amplify their experience.

By 1978, at least thirty similar projects had been set up across the country as a result of dissemination work by the Bristol team and NACRO's reach. The following year, most agreed to group under what would become a new National Association of Victim Support Schemes (NAVSS), a body funded by charitable trusts and, in an historic move, by the Home Office. The funding enabled the employment of a national development officer, Helen Reeves, a former probation lead. She based herself in Brixton, one of London's most diverse communities at the time, in offices above a shop shared by the south London alcohol advisory committee of which she was also a member (Rock, 1990; British Library Sounds, 2010).

One of her first actions was to tour and take stock of these burgeoning but—as ever in English statecraft—highly varied local services run by different providers. She later recalled that those run by 'the Rotary Clubs and the police and some of the church schemes were doing repairs, mending windows, putting in new locks ... and providing basic grants when people hadn't been insured' whereas 'the probation- or psychiatric-based schemes were doing an awful lot of careful selection of volunteers, teaching listening skills and basic principles of counselling' (Rock, 1990, 199–200, interview with Reeves). In 1981, NAVSS introduced a national code of practice to encourage consistency and accountability.

Some of these local service leads were early enthusiasts for reparative justice, a concept emerging in the US and fast-capturing the UK penal reform imagination at the time. At its heart was the idea that structured forms of mediation and dispute resolution should stand as alternatives to full criminal trials, and that apologies and other acts of restitution should stand as alternatives to fines and imprisonment. Spurred by a growing sense of crisis in the US penal system, it was also an idea captured and furthered by Nils Christie's provocation that not only had the state 'stolen' conflict from its citizens (Christie, 1977), but it was now seriously failing to manage that conflict. Reparative pilot projects in both countries were winning the support of penal reformers on the political left who were calling for the dismantling of bureaucratic hierarchies as well as those on the right calling for more cost-effective justice systems that responsibilized offenders. Neither prioritized the views of victims but both sought to mobilize them for the reparative cause. Helen Reeves and NAVSS held firm, resisting efforts from the Home Office and the new All-Party Parliamentary Group on Penal Affairs to orient victim support schemes in this direction (Rock, 1990, 159–97).

In the early 1980s, this parliamentary group pressed for reparative schemes to help solve prison overcrowding and recidivism. Reeves, although one of their members, insisted that victim support could not be sublimated within the penal reform agenda: 'if they were going to talk about victims, they were going to have to talk about victims' needs as opposed to diverting offenders'. (Rock, 1990, 367, interview with Reeves). In this instance, then, this cross-party group was lobbying for the state to shift its mode of governing victims. In a development that echoed the mid-nineteenth century shift to summary justice, victims were still being encouraged to prosecute, but were now being told to accept swifter judicial processes and lesser punishments. The difference was that these proposed reforms were now being made, in part, in their name, in a tactical effort to use their projected needs for political ends. This struggle would continue into the 1990s and beyond as the reparative debate found new legal expression in the form of reparation orders, referral orders, and other restorative innovations. Criminological opinion on the extent to which victims have benefited from such measures has been divided (for summary see Daly, 2004; Shapland, Robinson, and Sorsby, 2011; Rossner, 2017). From an historical perspective, this in itself can be read as evidence of the shifting construction of victims' needs over time.

The political utility of victims would grow as the 1980s progressed. In 1986, the government decided to award NAVSS the very substantial sum of £9 million over three years. This time, statutory funding was to be used to directly fund local victim support services affiliated to NAVSS rather than just the operation of its central office. The announcement was made at the 1987 Conservative Party conference, in anticipation of the upcoming general election. Soon after, NAVSS became a charitable company and shortened its name to Victim Support. As the origins and impacts of this organization have been much studied, we do not seek to add another detailed account here (for overviews, see Rock, 1990; Simmonds, 2013; Mawby, 2022). Rock's argument that even the landmark 1986 funding award was the product of ad hoc pragmatism over any kind of 'directed programme' (Rock, 1990, 423) would fit the longer historical pattern that we have described in earlier chapters. A desire on the part of officials to respond to an influential study by Joanna Shapland of victims' experiences of criminal justice processes was also pivotal (Shapland, Willmore, and Duff, 1985). More widely, critical criminologists have argued that Victim Support caught the national imagination at a time when Thatcherite governments were both politicizing crime and encouraging community-led and charitable responses to a range of social challenges as part of wider ideological efforts to roll back the state. They also suggest that Victim Support was supported by these administrations because it offered a less confrontational response than that of, for example, feminist organizations addressing victims of domestic and sexual violence (Mawby, 2022; Walklate, 2016; see also Chapter 7).

Our aim here has been to situate the mid-to-late twentieth century history of compensation and support schemes into a much longer and much less familiar history of efforts by the state and others to imagine and mobilize victims. Fry, Holtom, Reeves, and those working alongside them set out to empower victims but did so through mechanisms that supported them outwith the prosecution process in their new capacity as supplanted participants in the justice system.

3.3 Conclusion

Over the course of the three centuries addressed here, the role of the victim in criminal proceedings changed dramatically, in ways not necessarily intended by those who pushed for change. In the late seventeenth century, the complainant was wholly responsible for conducting their own prosecution (as prosecutor or prosecutrix) of serious crime and expected to bear the cost of this. However, the state began to take the view that victims might better fulfil their obligations if some support or incentive was provided. Measures to encourage prosecutions took five main forms: the payment of rewards for successful convictions; the reimbursement of the costs incurred when prosecuting; the growing use of legal counsel in trials; new policing arrangements (discussed in the next chapter); and legislation governing definitions of offences, judicial procedures, and punishments.

By the mid- to late- nineteenth century, an expanded state had assumed responsibility for bearing much of the cost of prosecutions, and victims were being supported by the almost universal assistance of police and counsel, and in some cases the support of voluntary societies. Whereas the early-modern victim had a duty to the state to prosecute on the crown's behalf, by the mid-twentieth century the state had begun to take on a new duty to meet the victim's needs when it failed to protect them. These new duties were forged in part by penal reformers who came to believe that 'changes in the criminal justice system could be secured only if victims were first appeased' (Rock, 1990, 99). But the role of progressive activists and lobbying groups who were primarily focused on offenders and defendants, such as the Howard League, Justice, and NACRO, should not be overlooked. They played an important part in the leveraging, politicizing, and therefore, the broader governing of victims.

Overall, this chapter has shown how the victim's historically central role in the legal system came to be supplanted. These informed a new if fragmented language of victims' entitlements—to compensation, satisfaction, emotional recognition, and repair. New forms of support began to address the financial needs of those defined as deserving through a state-backed compensation scheme, and the emotional and practical needs of those defined as vulnerable, through a state-backed victim support network. Notably, these new forms of support no longer sought to incentivize direct victim participation in the prosecution process—in large part because the rise of the police-led and counsel-assisted prosecution over the previous century had created new forms of public prosecution that rendered this unnecessary. It is this rise of hybrid forms of public prosecution, culminating in the creation of the Crown Prosecution Service in 1986, that we turn to in the next chapter.

4
Public Prosecution

Over the course of three hundred years, from the late seventeenth century to the late twentieth century, the basis of prosecution in English and Welsh courts was transformed. At the start of the period, prosecution was the obligation of the private individual; in 1986 it was formally made an obligation of the state. As police and legal counsel, and then crown prosecutors, assumed control in the court system, the individual victim became marginalized. This chapter examines the uneven and ad hoc nature of this significant change, exploring how it developed on the ground, how it was framed in public debate and, where possible, how it affected victims.

The office of 'public prosecutor' came into existence in Scotland and continental Europe in the Middle Ages but was long resisted in England and Wales (Gilliéron, 2014, 39–61; Rock, 2019). Montesquieu described the role of a public prosecutor in his *Spirit of the Laws* in 1748 appreciatively, speaking of an official who 'watches for the safety of citizens; he proceeds in his office while they enjoy their quiet and ease' (Montesquieu, 1949, 81). This embodied a view of the state as a benign arbiter of justice that did gain some English admirers, but they remained firmly in the minority until well into the twentieth century. In the eighteenth century, many regarded the idea of a public prosecutor as politically oppressive. As Douglas Hay argues:

> The political elite of the eighteenth century were bred in a constitutional tradition that celebrated the recent humbling of tyrannical kings by Parliament. Many came from families in which executive tyranny under the Commonwealth or the Stuarts had caused much personal suffering, and the memory was still sharp. The Star Chamber had been abolished in 1641 and the monarchy restored and made beholden to Parliament in 1660 and 1688, and the gentlemen of England were not now going to be party to any increase in the power of the executive to set the criminal law in motion.... It was almost inconceivable that the Attorney-General

Victims and Criminal Justice. Pamela Cox, Robert Shoemaker, and Heather Shore, Oxford University Press. © Pamela Cox, Robert Shoemaker, and Heather Shore 2023.
DOI: 10.1093/oso/9780192846488.003.0004

should act as the protector of the ordinary citizen from oppressive prosecutions (Hay, 1983, 165).

There are only two uses of the term 'public prosecutor' in the Old Bailey *Proceedings* before the 1880s, if one excludes cases referring to public prosecutors in other countries. One is in 1841, the other occurred in a case of bigamy from January 1794. A witness testified that he had no relation to the parties in the case and, when asked if he is 'a sort of a public prosecutor', stated 'I did it merely for public justice' (OBO, t17941111-44). The questioner's implication was that being a 'public prosecutor' was an undesirable interference in English liberty. At that time, French public prosecutors were sending thousands to the guillotine in the post-Revolutionary 'terror'. The negative connotations of the French type of public prosecutor would endure in England for some considerable time.

In late seventeenth- and eighteenth-century England and Wales, direct prosecution by the state was limited to crimes against the state itself, such as treason, counterfeiting, and interfering with the mail. These offences were prosecuted by state agencies, notably the Treasury, the Mint, and the Post Office. This 'state prosecution' was distinct both from the idea of 'public prosecution' as a legal and constitutional principle, and from what would become 'police prosecution' as a practice. Moreover, 'police prosecution' was not a term used commonly in the past but rather one that we use here to capture the broad set of behaviours and relationships that brought together police, police clerks and solicitors, and counsel in the management of prosecutions during the nineteenth century. Over the course of two centuries, the use of police prosecution and state prosecution would expand, but in haphazard and piecemeal ways: a series of practical adaptations to particular circumstances. At the same time, arguments over the merits of public prosecution grew louder. They were, in a sense, debates between 'English' and 'continental' ways, between those who supported the 'old' obligation of individuals to plead their cases in court and those who called for a modernized framework in which the state would act on behalf of the individual.

These debates occurred repeatedly in parliament until the passage of the Prosecution of Offences Act in 1879 (42 & 43 Vict. *c.* 22). This established the office of the Director of Public Prosecutions (DPP), which had only limited impact in the courtroom, but was a milestone in the evolution of the criminal justice process. In this chapter we connect these debates with evidence from our Old Bailey and *Times* datasets, supplemented by relevant secondary material, to explore the expansion of state prosecution (managed for and on behalf of the state), police prosecution (managed by the police and other actors in the criminal justice process) and public prosecution (managed by state employees ostensibly for and on behalf of the public—and distinct from 'private' victim prosecutors), and consider the long-term implications of this for public access to justice. Untangling these processes is not something which has been much attempted by historians or criminologists, although Hay (1983), Rock (2004a) and Smith (2006), have provided some illumination. In large part this is due to the often undocumented nature of these changes. While, as we will show, legislation and other legal developments did have an impact on the ground, changes more frequently evolved at the level of everyday practice and are not always visible to the historian. As Smith notes, the lack of 'an official system of public prosecution until the latter half of the nineteenth century remains a historical puzzle' (2006, 31), but behind the scenes practices that preceded public prosecution became a substantial feature of criminal justice.

4.1 State Prosecution

As we saw in Chapter 3, prosecution in England and Wales was traditionally framed as an obligation of individual subjects rather than the state. The state only directly prosecuted some major cases of violence, riot, sedition, and treason through the Treasury Solicitor or the Solicitor General. In addition, the Post Office, a royal monopoly from 1609, brought prosecutions for theft of mail and mail-related frauds. A Solicitor to the Post Office was established in 1689 (Joyce, 1893, 6–7; Langbein, 2003, 113). The Mint and, after its foundation in 1694, the Bank of England, also prosecuted offences against the king's currency: coining, uttering (offering false coin in payment), and the forgery of banknotes. From the eighteenth century, these state or quasi-state agencies employed solicitors to prepare a small number of prosecution cases concerning particularly serious offences for trial (Langbein, 2003, 109–31). At first, these cases did not normally involve the use of counsel, but they began to do so from the 1730s (May, 2003, 23–4; Langbein, 2003, 113).

In 1842, the Treasury Solicitor was appointed solicitor to the Home Office, the Foreign Office, the Colonial Office, and the Privy Council Office. He was further appointed solicitor to the Office of Works in 1876, and to the War Office and Admiralty in 1877 (Howard, 1930, 15). Along with these expanded powers, the boundary between criminal prosecutions conducted on behalf of the state and those conducted on behalf of the public began to be blurred. As Howard would later observe, '[i]t soon became the invariable practice for the Home Office to direct the Treasury Solicitor to prosecute in cases of murder, manslaughter, vicious assault and other serious offenses arising in the Metropolitan Police District of Greater London' and, over time 'this practice was extended so as to include the conduct of important prosecutions of the same character in the country at large'. These were prosecutions where a private person, presumably the victim, or a police officer, had been bound over by a magistrate to prosecute and where the charges were sufficiently serious in nature for the matter to be referred to the Treasury Solicitor (Howard, 1930, 17).

At the same time, the Treasury Solicitor was also responsible for prosecutions brought directly on behalf of the state. From 1851, the office of the Mint Solicitor was moved to the Treasury, and all prosecutions of offences against the coinage became the responsibility of the Treasury Solicitor (Craig, 1953, 2011 edn, 320). However, this responsibility also expanded into other areas of monetary control: 'it was not long before fraudulent bankruptcy prosecutions grew to be an important phase of his work'. (Howard, 1930, 16). Yet, despite all this expansion in his responsibilities, the Treasury Solicitor's role was always limited. From 1856 the annual 'judicial statistics' in the parliamentary papers included the number of government-funded prosecutions for coining and for 'other' criminal offences. A sample of every fifth year between 1856 and 1871 shows that an average of only 315 coining cases were prosecuted by the Mint while the number of 'other' government-funded prosecutions gradually rose from a few dozen a year to 270 in 1880 (Parliamentary Papers dataset). Howard's research into prosecutions funded by the Treasury Solicitor's office from 1877 to 1879 indicates that these cases included an average of sixty-eight bankruptcy cases and 120 Home Office prosecutions a year (Howard, 1930, 18).

There were also local forms of 'state prosecution'. In the *Proceedings*, the phrase, 'City Solicitor' (acting on behalf of the City of London) appears in fifty-two trials from 1797, when there is a reference in a forgery trial to the 'City Solicitor's office, at Guildhall' (OBO, t17970920-4), through to 1913. These relate to a wide range of offences including both crimes against the state such as coining, perjury, and perverting justice, as well as crimes against the public such as wounding, simple larceny, bigamy, murder, manslaughter, fraud, and theft. Other cases concerned public nuisances. A case in 1854, for example, involved the unsafe storage of a large quantity of matches. One witness, Charles Pearson, introduced himself as 'the solicitor to the Corporation of London' who had been instructed to act by the Court of Aldermen following a public petition (OBO, t18540918-1039).[1]

Howard concluded that, in the mid-nineteenth century, '[t]he activities of both the Attorney-General and the Solicitor-General [had] always been confined in the main to representing the Crown in lawsuits and conducting a few outstanding prosecutions in which the government happen[ed] to be interested' (Howard, 1930, 15). This form of state prosecution was based on a much narrower conception of public prosecution than those operating in the continental and Scottish systems. Nonetheless, the line between prosecutions on behalf of the state and those on behalf of the public was already blurred. Holders of the posts of Attorney-General and Solicitor-General were members of the Government (and elected members of parliament). Reports in the *Proceedings* illustrate their combined role in both kinds of cases. Between 1840 and 1870, the term 'Attorney General' appears in reports of eighty-two Old Bailey trials some of which could be described as 'state prosecutions', such as mail theft, seditious words, and treason, and others as public prosecution, such as murder, fraud, forgery, and receiving stolen goods. The same is true for the term 'Solicitor General' which appears in reports of forty-five trials over the same period in connection with charges including mail theft, forgery, and murder (OBO).

As this chapter will demonstrate, parliamentary opinion on the expansion and governance of state prosecution remained divided throughout the nineteenth century. Yet official debates on the subject often lagged behind a changing reality in the courtroom, not only with respect to state officials acting as prosecutors, but even more clearly in the role of the police as prosecutors, and it is to this matter that we now turn.

4.2 Police Prosecution

A growing 'police' presence in court in the eighteenth century

Previous accounts of the changes in prosecution arrangements in England and Wales have tended to start with the creation of the 'new police' from

[1] Manuscript papers of the City Solicitor can be found at the London Metropolitan Archives (LMA): COL/CCS/SO/02/01/006b, 022.

the 1830s, followed by a slow move towards police-led prosecutions, which only became dominant in the late nineteenth or early twentieth centuries (Emsley, 1996, 235). Our research, however, suggests that forms of prosecution involving policing agents were widely practised prior to this.

Our data suggests that there was a growing police presence in criminal trials at the Old Bailey in the decades *before* the introduction of the new police (which began with the creation of the Metropolitan Police in 1829). While we are not able to measure directly the extent to which that police presence contributed to the prosecution process, we can chart the changing presence of the police as witnesses in trials. Figure 4.1, based on machine reading of the text, tracks the proportion of prosecutions in which a policing agent was mentioned in the *Old Bailey Proceedings*. The term 'policing agent' includes a wide range of officers whose duties were to make arrests and enforce the law. These include individuals labelled as constables, headboroughs, watchmen, officers, marshalsmen, patrols, detectives, and various types of policemen. The data are limited by the fact that the trial reports in the *Proceedings* are not full transcripts, the thoroughness of the reporting varied over time, and the fact a policing agent was mentioned does not necessarily mean that they were present in court. It both undercounts

Figure 4.1: Old Bailey Trials in which Policing Agents are Mentioned, 1674–1913
Source: Proceedings dataset

the number of trials where the police were involved, but also overcounts them, since it includes these words in contexts which may not have indicated meaningful police participation. However, while the resulting data is thus subject to degrees of error, the trends are clear.

The first half of the eighteenth century witnessed a significant increase in the police presence in Old Bailey trials, largely by men identified as constables and watchmen. Even before the creation of the 'Bow Street Runners' in 1749 (discussed below), some form of policing agent was already present in over 30 per cent of trials. This was probably related to changes in the recruitment of constables and watchmen in the first half of the century, as offices filled by householders serving by rotation for a year were replaced by salaried men who served for longer periods, creating a more experienced body of police (Reynolds, 1998; Beattie, 2001, chs 3–4).

The foundation of the Bow Street Runners propelled a growth in the police presence at court from the 1750s to the early 1800s (dips in the graph in the 1770s and 1780s are probably due to changes in the level of details provided in the *Proceedings*.) The *Proceedings* contain increasing references to agents described as 'police', 'patrol', and (unidentified) 'officers' at this time. The wider vocabulary reflects innovations in policing, and a growing recognition of policing as an important law enforcement activity (Harris, 2004). Overall, between 1791 and 1828, policing agents were present in more than half (58.1 per cent) of trials. Specific references to 'police officers' are found as early as the 1790s, although the first reference to 'policeman' did not appear until December 1829, when two police witnesses giving evidence stated, 'I am a police-man' (OBO, t18291203-27). Even before the introduction of the Metropolitan Police, 'police' already had a substantial presence in the courtroom. Unsurprisingly, the vocabulary changed after 1829 and policing agents were now predominantly called 'police', 'policeman', and 'police constable' in the *Proceedings*. Their presence in the courtroom increased yet further, although the graph in Figure 4.1 indicates a levelling off after 1844. This may be due to the fact court reporters used a different terminology during this period, often referring to police officers by their badge number only. In the early twentieth century references to 'police' resumed.

Between 1791 and 1913 policing agents were most likely to testify in trials for property offences (by far the most common offences tried in the court). Proportionally, however, they were most often present in some of the more serious cases: property offences involving violence and threats to the person (where the police were present in 84.9 per cent of cases) and acts intending to or actually causing harm to the person (68.6 per cent). In contrast, they were proportionately less likely to appear in cases of forgery and fraud, where the harm caused to the individual victim may have been perceived as far more significant than the harm to the wider public. Complex trials often involved newly established detectives rather than, or along with, regular police officers (Shore, 2015).

A key development which advanced the role of policing agents in the criminal trial was the creation of the 'Bow Street Runners' in 1749 by justice of the peace Henry Fielding, who was soon joined (and then supplanted on his death in 1754) by his half-brother John Fielding. This initiative was built on existing practices of thief-taking and employing experienced policing agents (both discussed in Chapter 3), while attempting to make the former a respectable activity. The Fieldings hired several men by retainer (including former constables and thief-takers) to create a small police force. Operating out of their home in Bow Street in Westminster, the Fieldings sent the Runners out to detect criminals whenever they received reports of a serious crime. In addition to their retainers, they received additional remuneration from the rewards then paid by the government for successful convictions. The potential for corruption inherent in thief-taking remained but, by overseeing the processes of arrest and prosecution, the Fieldings hoped to keep the Runners' reputations clean (Beattie, 2012).

The Runners, and their principal employer Justice John Fielding, had a major impact on the prosecution of crime in London. With Fielding acting as a 'prosecuting magistrate' and the Runners as 'prosecuting policemen', the Bow Street office was responsible for a significant proportion of Old Bailey trials and successful convictions. Beattie (2012, 95) calculated that the Bow Street office accounted for almost half of all commitments for trial at the Old Bailey between 1767 and 1773. While the Runners did not testify in all these cases, Beattie's data suggests that their impact extended beyond their arrests to include the role that they, together with Fielding, played in organizing prosecutions.

Fielding used his magistrate's office to conduct 're-examinations', which vetted the arguments against the accused and sometimes sought further evidence, gathered by the Runners, before committing defendants for trial (Beattie, 2007b). The practice was illegal, in that it subverted the role of juries by conducting what was essentially a preliminary trial by a magistrate, and it was eventually curtailed. In the short term, however, it was successful in the sense that those tried at the Old Bailey when the Runners testified against them were about a third more likely to be convicted (78.5

per cent were found guilty vs 58.8 per cent when no Runners were present). As Beattie observes, evidence presented by the Bow Street Runners 'undoubtedly strengthened the prosecution cases in which they testified, in a decisive way in some; juries appear to have found them credible witnesses' (Beattie, 2012, 87–103; 2007a, 5; 2007b). Two of the most active runners were Charles Jealous and Thomas Carpmeal, who between them gave evidence in 284 trials in the years 1775 to 1800 (Beattie, 2012, 113). Their evidence often took the reported form of just one or two sentences, describing their search of the prisoner or of a property, or offering identification of a defendant. They were thus presented as witnesses rather than prosecutors in the trial, although we know, from Beattie's evidence, that their role was much greater. In effect, the Runners took over a large part of the role of the prosecutor from the victim, although at this stage victims continued to provide the lead testimony in the Old Bailey courtroom (Beattie, 2012, 87, 120).

In the years after Sir John Fielding's death in 1780, and following the creation of similar 'rotation offices' run by JPs after the 1792 Middlesex Justices Act, the Runners' role expanded to address issues of national security, including protecting the royal family and suppressing radicalism. They also became, in effect, a national anti–counterfeiting force, heavily involved in the prosecution of coining and uttering of false coin. In cases of the making of counterfeit coins the 'victim' was in effect, the state, and specialist expertise was vital (Beattie, 2012, chs 5–8; Cox, 2010). This new focus reduced the Runners' role in London. It is clear, however, that during the three decades between 1750 and 1780 the Fieldings' Runners created the foundations of future approaches to policing and prosecution. Their activities in detecting crime, gathering evidence, and testifying in court represented a key step in not merely supporting but, eventually, supplanting the role of the victim in prosecuting crime.

As noted, one crime the Runners were particularly effective at prosecuting was coining, where the Runner John Clarke became an expert in identifying bad coins, and the equipment and materials used to produce them. Acting as a 'prosecuting policeman', he was involved in at least 106 Old Bailey cases of coining and uttering between 1770 and 1793. In many cases he acted as the principal expert witness against the accused (Beattie, 2012, 120–5). When banknotes replaced coins during the period of the suspension of payments in specie from 1797 to 1821, Clarke's practices may well have inspired the campaign initiated by the Bank of England to suppress the forgery of £1 and £2 bank notes. Acting as a quasi-state or 'institutional' prosecutor, the Bank spent considerable sums on payments and rewards for inspectors, constables, and other policing agents to encourage them to gather evidence and make arrests, as well as on solicitors who managed the cases for prosecution. In 1819–20 the Bank prosecuted 557 forgers across the country (McGowen, 2005, 92). The scale of this organized activity was unprecedented. Innovation was underway in the English legal system, driven both by JPs and policing agents in their day-to-day law enforcement activities and by the state's response to offences directly affecting its interests and related agencies.

Early nineteenth-century police prosecution

Whilst the previous section demonstrated how policing agents were increasingly visible at the Old Bailey, clarity about their specific role in the prosecution process in the later eighteenth and early nineteenth centuries remains elusive. Formally the police could only prosecute as private citizens, so they were not public prosecutors in the Scottish or continental sense (Stephen, 1863, 493; Barrie, 2008, 42). Hay argues that 'when the modern police were invented in the second quarter of the [nineteenth] century it was certainly not envisaged that they should come to control the prosecutorial process' (Hay, 1983, 173). Nevertheless, the evidence suggests that they came to play an important role in the management of prosecutions, working with police clerks, solicitors, and magistrates. However, actually documenting such practices is far from easy.

A sense of the processes and practices on the ground can be gleaned from contemporary select committee evidence. In evidence about the City of London police, Patrick Colquhoun used the broader term the 'criminal police' to refer to both magistrates in the City and the policing agents who assisted with gathering evidence and making arrests (PP, 1797–8, 361). Much in the way that the Fieldings had operated in previous decades, magistrates and policing agents were integral to the 'police system' or 'Police Establishment' as Colquhoun refers to it (1797–8, 14–16). He was speaking here in the wake of the 1792 Middlesex Justices Act, which established rotation offices and a stipendiary magistracy—formalizing the model which John Fielding had developed (Paley, 1983).

This cooperation between the police and magistrates was particularly effective in cases heard by summary jurisdiction. As Bruce Smith argues, facilitated by statutes which authorized policing agents to search and arrest individuals suspected of carrying stolen goods and empowered magistrates to convict such offenders summarily (Smith, 2007, 162–3), 'public officials' in the lower courts in London between the 1790s and 1850s created 'an important and distinctive mode of public prosecution':

> In the 'police offices' of the metropolis, established throughout London in 1792, persons suspected of petty theft were, in fact, *routinely* arrested, prosecuted, tried, convicted, and sentenced in ways that dispensed with the involvement of private victims altogether. In many such cases, public officials rather than private victims carried out the essential investigative and forensic tasks of criminal prosecution (2006, 32, 58).

In this period before and after the passage of the Metropolitan Police Act the separation of functions between police and magistrates was far from clear and both operated a system which at times amounted to one of public prosecution. Colquhoun, drawing on his experience of the Scottish system, would be an early advocate for a form of office of public prosecutor (see below). Despite this, it would not be until mid-century that the debate about public prosecution would gain momentum, when, as Rock notes, the 1855 Select Committee on Public Prosecutions was a 'critically important' intervention (2004a, 337). The early nineteenth century, then, remains both opaque and crucial to our understanding of the evolution of the role of the police as agents of the state in developing practices of public prosecution.

Evidence of police involvement in forms of public prosecution can be found in the period leading up to the passage of the Metropolitan Police Act. In the 1810s, a number of parliamentary select committees examined policing in the metropolis and their evidence provides examples of the relationship between the magistrates and policing agents, and the central role of the 'police office' in this period. Seven offices were established under the 1792 Middlesex Justices Act for the management of crimes and prosecutions. In 1816, giving evidence, Sir Nathanial Conant (magistrate and one of the architects of the 1792 Act) was asked how common it was for officers to be joined with the prosecutor in the prosecution. Conant responded, 'The party aggrieved is generally the person bound over to prosecute; but, in the Police Offices, if no other person is ostensible for that object, we always bind over one of the Police officers, or a constable, to do it' (PP, 1816, 8). Conant's evidence suggests that police officers were bound over to prosecute in cases where either there was no prosecutor, or where the 'aggrieved party' could not be found or declined to prosecute. Bentley describes police officers as being 'pressed into service' in these cases (1998, 73). Conant notes that police officers are 'not bound over to prosecute, if, on the commitment of the offenders, we find the person aggrieved' (1816, 8). This Committee also provides evidence from magistrates that police clerks were significantly involved in prosecution, underlining the crucial role of the 'Police Office' in this period (Hay, 1983, 176). For instance, the magistrate Robert Reynsford notes that his clerk, John Shearman, was involved in the prosecution of Eliza Fenning in 1815, although he is not named in the trial proceedings (OBO, t18150405-18). In 1818, a select committee witness, Benjamin Linsey, described as a constable of one of the divisions in Shoreditch, referred to his 'Expenses and refreshments in attending seven days at the Sessions House, with Bryerly, the watchman, both being bound over to prosecute John Field for a robbery in High-street, Shoreditch; the prosecutors being sea-faring men did not attend' (PP, 1818, 134).

In 1834, a further select committee investigated the role of police in prosecutions. Asked whether magistrates bound over police constables to prosecute, John Wray, Charles Rowan, and Richard Mayne (Receiver and two Commissioners of Police), answered that police constables were not bound over to prosecute when 'ordinary prosecutors can be found' (PP, 1834, 83), suggesting that this may have been used as a special measure when a prosecutor did not appear. This needs to be considered in the light of other evidence which suggests that there were concerns (related to both justice and costs) about the non-prosecution of offenders, and about prosecutors who dropped out of the process. John Hardwick, a magistrate at the Lambeth Police Office, suggested to the same 1834 committee that 'I see no reason at this moment why the Superintending Officer of each district might not on occasion act as a sort of public prosecutor' (PP, 1834, 153).

There were also cases where the police desired a prosecution, but no individual victim could be identified. Wray, Rowan, and Mayne provide the following example:

> there was a family of the name of Guest; both the father and the son are now convicted as receivers of stolen goods; the second son is now in custody for a felony; after a great deal of difficulty the police got cases against both father and son as receivers, on which they were ultimately convicted; there were no parties to prosecute in those cases, and I believe the cases would have entirely failed had not the police taken them up and borne the expense of prosecution (PP, 1834, 83).

Further evidence from this, and later, select committees, suggests some early police involvement, presumably with the encouragement of the magistrates, in leading prosecutions. In the *Report from the Select Committee on Metropolis Police Offices* (PP, 1837–8, 83), evidence from Rowan and Mayne explicitly stated that, in the case of summary jurisdiction, police officers took the role of what was, in effect, a public prosecutor. As Mayne noted, it had also become the practice for magistrates to bind over inspectors of the police to prosecute.

In summary, evidence from magistrates and police officers in London demonstrates the important functions of police, magistrates, and police offices both in the period leading up to 1829 and also in the subsequent period when the new police were being implemented across England and Wales. While the police were not routinely bound over to prosecute, it is clear that in some cases of misdemeanours at the lower courts, and more generally in cases where a prosecutor was not available, the police took a proactive role (Bland, 2021; Smith 2006). This police involvement in prosecutions intensified with the establishment of the new police. From the 1840s, the police were present in 80 per cent or more of Old Bailey trials (Trial Participants dataset); and in some cases the police were clearly instrumental in obtaining all the key evidence for the prosecution.

What is clear is that while the terms 'prosecutor' and 'the prosecution' could refer to specific individuals and cases, 'prosecution', in the context of police action, also referred to a process in which the police did not necessarily manage the whole case, but in which they played key roles, such as observing suspicious individuals to detect crime, gathering evidence, searching the premises of the accused, identifying individuals (both the accused and witnesses), and, at trial, presenting evidence and, where relevant, providing certificates that a defendant had been previously convicted. As Bland notes, 'proactive policing was a significant part of the policing role for some police officers and ... their policing activities impacted patterns of arrest and prosecution' (2022, 74). From 1829, the powers that enabled them to undertake these duties—as part of the broader arrest and prosecution process—were significantly strengthened.

The impact of the new police on prosecutions

In the decades after 1829, police involvement incrementally eroded the role of the victim in the prosecution process. Although 1829 is often seen as the decisive point in the creation of the police force, it represented an evolution, rather than a revolution, in policing (Churchill, 2017; Emsley, 1991; Reiner, 1985). In London, much of the architecture was already in place before 1829 (Reynolds, 1998) and this would be replicated in other regions and jurisdictions, particularly urban areas such as Liverpool (where the new police were established in 1836), Leeds (1836), Birmingham (1839), and Manchester (1839), where demands for more effective and systematic policing (and by extension, prosecution) led to early innovation. The Municipal Corporations Act of 1835 allowed towns to make changes which, in practice, were likely already taking place (Churchill, 2017, 34). Liverpool and Leeds became reformed boroughs under the Act in 1836. This meant that policing in these boroughs moved under unified control (Joyce, 1993). These changes were then implemented in other towns, although the move to incorporation was not always smooth. Conflicts between the parliamentary boroughs created by the 1832 Reform Act and the municipal boroughs created by the 1836 Act meant that the transition from 'old' to 'new' police was often confused, with a proliferation of police forces in one area (Joyce, 1993, 204–7).

Liverpool and Leeds benefitted from their early incorporation, and established a system of local public management of prosecutions, which was controlled by the municipal borough. In Liverpool, the Chief Constable was bound over by magistrates to prosecute cases, although Langford notes the 'binding over' merely marked the transference of the case to the town clerk, who would then manage the prosecution (Langford, 1993, 109). Leeds was still using this system in the 1850s. At the Common Law (Judicial) Commission in 1857, a witness was asked about the binding over of the Chief Constable by the Leeds magistrates. The witness, Sir John Bayley (Clerk of the Assize on the Northern Circuit), responded: 'They took the opinion of counsel some years ago, as to whether they could not appoint a public prosecutor, and they were advised that they could not, but they could attain the same object in another way, which was to bind over the Chief Constable in every case, and make him employ an attorney of their own naming' (PP, 1857, session 2, 21). As in London, it seems that in some provincial cities the early integration of police, magistrates, and the prosecution process can be dated to the years after 1829. We see the same shift in other regions. From the 1830s, the Staffordshire County force saw themselves 'explicitly as filling the gap caused by the absence of any form of public prosecutor'. Staffordshire police had handled almost 30 per cent of prosecutions as early as 1830, and by the mid-century it amounted to many more (Phillips, 1977, 130). This changing relationship between the police and prosecution, and the subsequent (if unintended) marginalization of the victim-prosecutor, was not simply a metropolitan shift.

Evidence from the Old Bailey shows that a key aspect of this new form of prosecution involved the developing relationship between the police, solicitors, and prosecuting counsel. In a theft case from 1845, solicitor Thomas Wontner described how he had authorized City police constable George Wardle to pay an informant, 'just sufficient to support himself' (OBO, 18450707-1539). Wontner and Sons subsequently acted for the Commissioner of Police, as well as handling difficult police cases at the City of London and Middlesex Sessions, until a solicitors' department was set up at New Scotland Yard in 1935 (Jackson, 1940, 2015 edn, 125). We have evidence from London which demonstrates close connections between police and legal agents in earlier nineteenth-century prosecutions. For example, there are a number of cases prepared by the City of London Solicitor for counsel prior to the 1850s, where police officers were embedded in the prosecution because there was a strong interest in achieving a conviction.[2] One example is a case of attempted murder by shooting of a police officer, tried by City barristers Ryland and Laurie in 1849. The victim, City policeman Frederick Shipton, was the first to take the stand and provided a full account of the event (OBO, t18490917-1734). While the accused was allowed to cross-examine, the witnesses, led by questioning from counsel, worked strongly in the favour of the victim/police officer. In a case of pickpocketing from 1849, also with Ryland and Laurie prosecuting, the police testified first (OBO, t18491029-1870). In this case, the accused had been under plain clothes surveillance by Michael Haydon, the police officer, who, along with a colleague, followed the accused and watched until the commission of the crime. At the trial the victim only testified third, following the two police officers. Unsurprisingly, the accused were found guilty.

One crime where proactive policing involved a particularly close relationship between police, counsel, and institutional prosecutors was counterfeiting currency, both coining and uttering. Echoing the earlier activities of the Bow Street Runners, the police worked closely with Inspectors of the Mint from the early nineteenth century, particularly with John Field between 1825 and 1847, and William Webster and his son, William John Webster, from 1849 to 1910. These two men gave evidence in over 3,000

[2] LMA, Solicitors Papers: COL/CCS/SO/02/01/006b.

Old Bailey trials for coining between 1849 and 1910. They were closely connected with the Metropolitan Police, whose officers undertook surveillance as part of coordinated efforts to clamp down on coiners and utterers of bad coin. The most prolific of these was Inspector James Brannan, who first appeared in a Mint case in 1837 (OBO, t18371023-2309), and noted in a case in 1847 that he 'received information from the Solicitor of the Mint', adding, 'I am often employed by them—I very frequently go on expeditions to break into rooms—I get additional pay from the Mint on those occasions, more than in a case of larceny' (OBO, t18470301-685; see also Shore, 2015, 124–5).

A further significant development in policing which influenced proactive policing and prosecution was the establishment of the Detective Branch of the Metropolitan Police in 1842. Initially consisting of two inspectors, six sergeants, and some constables, it gradually expanded in the mid-nineteenth century. Investigation of crime, as opposed to the enforcement of law and order, was not a new feature of policing in 1842, as we have seen from the activities of the Bow Street Runners from the mid-eighteenth century (Smith, G., 2020; Beattie, 2012; Cox, 2010, 225). However, with the formalization of the detective function, especially after the mid-nineteenth century when the new police were fully established, the figure of the detective would become ubiquitous at Old Bailey trials. The term 'detective' occurs less than a dozen times a year in the *Proceedings* before 1855 but after this time appears regularly either as the main police witness or alongside uniformed police. An early reference is in August 1844, when Stephen Thornton gave evidence, describing himself as 'one of the detective force' (OBO, 18440819-2181). Detectives most often gave evidence in cases of theft, financial crime, and deception.

As discussed below, after the mid-century the police role in the prosecution process became more widespread, and accepted—although not without some uneasiness and expressions of distrust of the police as prosecutors. In his testimony to a parliamentary committee in 1855, Attorney General Alexander Cockburn complained about a 'subordinate officer … clothing himself with the function of a public prosecutor' (Hay, 1983, 175). His remarks combined some class prejudice with wider concerns about the potential for police corruption.

In summary, during the early nineteenth century the police encroached into the prosecution process. In London particularly, the growth of the stipendiary magistracy, the setting up of the police offices, the introduction of proactive policing agents both before and after the creation of the new police in 1829, and the establishment of the Detective Branch, all made police more central. This more significant role for police in prosecutions was not introduced as a formal process, but was part of an emerging agenda around proactive policing and more systematic law enforcement. Moreover, this growing connection between the various forces of law and order came to sideline the victim-prosecutor, but not without controversy.

Prosecutions involving police and counsel

The growing relationship between the police and counsel was one of the mid-nineteenth-century concerns leading to attempts to pass a public prosecutors bill, led by the barrister MP, John George Phillimore. A solicitor from Stafford who gave evidence at the 1855 Select Committee on Public Prosecutions referred to

> prosecutions being either improper in themselves, or improperly got up; and in the case of Stafford, to the police being under pecuniary inducements to bring forward charges on insufficient grounds. It is notorious that policemen are there found to act in league with low attorneys, and that prosecutions depend very much on a conspiracy between them (PP, 1854–5: v).

In London, apparent collusion between police and counsel was also seen to be a problem. When the barrister William Henry Bodkin was asked about this, he argued that 'the duties of the police constable and the attorney ought to be kept perfectly distinct' (PP, 1855, 9). Whilst these accusations of corruption did not, in the 1850s, provide sufficient impetus for a public prosecutor, they do reveal the interconnectedness of the relationship between police and legal agents, as this section will explore in more detail.

Our data suggests that from around 1855 trials in which the police participated involved disproportionately high levels of prosecution counsel. Evidence from our Trial Participants dataset covering the period 1855–70 shows that in trials where counsel was present, 84.4 per cent also had a police presence. When counsel was not present, on the other hand, only 17.2 per cent of trials had a police presence. The difference is even more stark when viewing the data the other way around. If police were involved in a trial, they were accompanied by prosecution counsel in 91.5 per cent of cases. When police were not present, only 30.3 per cent of prosecutions involved counsel. This practice became universal: cases with counsel that involved the police increased from 33.3 per cent in 1840 to 100.0 per cent in 1870, and cases with police that involved counsel increased from 3.3 per cent in 1840 to 100.0 per cent in 1870.

It seems likely, although we have not been able to prove this, that these counsel were publicly funded, possibly through the discretionary allocation of costs allowed for mounting the prosecution. Thus the growth in the presence of prosecution counsel, which had previously been largely (but not exclusively) driven by private prosecutors, was now being driven by the state. This expansion of prosecution counsel was piecemeal, and was not driven by any statute or overarching government policy. Nor was it, however, mere coincidence. The main impetus was a desire to support the police in prosecutions perceived as directly promoting the interests of the state, and once this relationship was established, it was extended to a much wider range of prosecutions. In effect, the 1840s and 1850s were key decades for the emergence of a form of public prosecution of serious crime, in practice, if not in name (for similar findings on summary justice in an earlier period, see Smith, 2006).

More evidence for a connection between the rise of police prosecution and the use of prosecution counsel can be found in the repeated use of particular counsel in police cases. The dataset, as demonstrated in the examples given in Table 4.1, shows that certain barristers were particularly likely to have police testify in the trials where they conducted the prosecution, and that they did so much more often than in the general pattern of Old Bailey trials.

It is notable that the majority of the cases conducted by Bodkin in 1855 (fifteen of twenty-one) involved coining offences and that he was a formally appointed Counsel to the Treasury (May, 2003, 248). Similarly nine of Orridge's thirty cases in 1860 involved coining, but of his twenty-one non-coining trials, 87.5 per cent involved police. Clearly there was an overlap in the use of counsel for both 'crimes against the state' (such as coining) and other police prosecutions (see also Shore, 2015, 117–40).

Once counsel was expected in Old Bailey cases, given the limited nature of the provisions for reimbursing legal costs (which were only paid at the minimum rate) victims had an incentive to leave prosecutions to the police. As R. M. Jackson wrote in 1942, 'unless it appears that the complainant is both able and willing to run a prosecution, it falls to the police to do this, and some police officer becomes the nominal prosecutor'. He labelled these prosecutions 'police prosecutions', despite the fact 'there is in general no

Table 4.1: Old Bailey Trials with Legal Counsel and Police: 1855 and 1860

Year	Prominent counsel	Cases involving police
1855		
Total cases with both police and prosecution counsel		251 of 974 cases (25.8%)
Of which, cases with particular named counsel	Bodkin Lilley	19 of 21 cases (90.5%) 18 of 22 cases (81.8%)
1860		
Total cases with both police and prosecution counsel		289 of 914 cases (31.6%)
Of which, cases with particular named counsel	Orridge Metcalfe	27 of 30 cases (90%) 19 of 25 cases (76%)

Source: OBO; Trial Participants dataset

legal distinction between a private prosecution and a police prosecution'. He described the process as follows:

> At the Old Bailey the simpler police prosecutions used to be carried out without the services of a solicitor. When an accused person is committed for trial the magistrate's clerk sends all the papers to the clerk of the Central Criminal Court, and the police officer in charge also sends his report on the case. The clerk of the Central Criminal Court then instructs a barrister ... Counsel so briefed usually confer directly with the police, and if further work on the case is needed it can be done by the police (Jackson, 1942, 107–10).

By the late nineteenth century, therefore, prosecution counsel and the police, often working in tandem, were virtually universal in Old Bailey trials, with profound consequences for victims' experiences of justice. This will be explored in Chapter 6.

Thus far, this chapter has set out the parameters of state-led prosecutions largely prior to the creation of the DPP, and it has summarized the complex expansion of the involvement of policing agents and counsel in prosecutions: the role of the police in detecting and arresting criminals, finding evidence and working with solicitors and counsel to build a case, and finally, testifying in court. This increasing involvement of the police and counsel, and particularly their more visible contributions in court, amounted to a de facto system of 'police prosecution'. This led to the inevitable but unintended de-centring of the victim from their historical prosecutorial role. The next part of the chapter explores political debates around the possibilities of the adoption of a formal system of public prosecution, many of which were driven by these ground-level changes in criminal justice practice.

4.3 Towards a Public Prosecutor

Debates about whether a formal office of public prosecutor should be established had a long ancestry. In 1798, the magistrate Patrick Colquhoun gave evidence to the Parliamentary Select Committee on Finance, which was examining the costs of policing and the convict establishment six years after legislation established the seven 'rotation' offices for magistrates and police in London described above. Colquhoun pointed out that the high numbers of accused who were discharged at every gaol delivery sessions,

> partly from the carelessness or inattentiveness of prosecutors, who are either unable or unwilling to sustain the expense of Counsel to oppose the arguments and objections which will be offered on behalf of the prisoner, afford another reason why a prosecutor for the Crown appears to be necessary (PP, 1797–8, 361).

Colquhoun was pointing to three problems with the late eighteenth-century prosecution system: the expense (and the corresponding cost to individual prosecutors), the lack of prosecution counsel due to this financial burden (giving an advantage to defendants who could afford counsel); and the lack of a crown (or public) prosecutor.

He went on to detail his remedy, which was to place the prosecution of what he termed 'public offences' under the charge of an officer of the crown (Smith, 2007, 159). Colquhoun saw this as not only cost-effective but also efficient in terms of preventing crime and achieving justice. He envisaged a 'deputation' of counsels, led by the Attorney General: 'Such a system, while it counteracted the tricks and devices of old thieves, and placed them on the same footing as the novices in crimes, would protect real innocents, as the public prosecutor in that case would never fail to move an acquittal' (PP, 1797–8, 361–2). He also raised the issue of offenders who escaped justice, referring to:

> cases where its being administered depends upon the party injured, who is frequently prevented, by the dread of expense, from coming forward at all for the purpose of disclosing the loss he has sustained, or intimidated by the threats of the culprit or his friends, or brought off by corrupt means, extending also to the witnesses, who are too often open to seduction when under no control (PP, 1797–8, 361).

This was not the first time Colquhoun had raised these issues. He had discussed them in one of the chapters of his *A Treatise on the Police of the Metropolis* published in 1796, and he would warm to the theme in later editions (1796, 31, 35–6, 249, 253–7; 1806, 21–6, 421–33). But Colquhoun's exhortations seem to have largely fallen on deaf ears (Barrie, 2008, 59; Emsley, 1996, 22). However, many other magistrates, including William Fielding, the son of Henry Fielding, repeatedly made the same case to parliamentary inquiries (for other arguments in favour of a public prosecutor before 1836, see May, 2003, 194–7, 238). Nevertheless, despite a significant attempt in the mid-nineteenth century to introduce a more formal system of public prosecution, as we will see below, the debate about introducing such a system in England and Wales would not be resolved for almost two centuries.

There were three main arguments against the introduction of public prosecutors: cost, liberty, and local autonomy. Bennet's Act had been passed in 1818, enabling the payment of expenses of victims and witnesses regardless of the verdict, but not all offences were covered and the law still required victims to pay costs before being reimbursed. In the early nineteenth-century select committees, supporters of public prosecution emphasized that their system would remove a financial burden from the victim. Their opponents countered this with the prospect of a much more expensive system imposed on local rate-payers. And moreover, as we have seen in Chapter 3, incremental legislation expanding the payment of costs during the early nineteenth century may also have undermined the argument in favour of a public prosecutor.

Others had more principled arguments against creating a state-funded prosecution service: the defence of English liberty. James Fitzjames Stephen, at the time Recorder of Newark, wrote in 1860:

> The fault, if there is one at all, lies in the passion of the English people for personal freedom, and in their intolerance of personal restraint or interference for any purpose whatever. This is the real obstacle which

> has always prevented the appointment of any permanent officer with inquisitorial powers specially charged with the detection of offences and so long as we choose to enjoy an exemption from the abuses to which the existence of such officials would or might lead, we must be content to pay the price in the form of the occasional impunity of offenders (Stephen, 1863, 697).

Two decades later, he continued to assert individual rights over a state-led process:

> No stronger or more effectual guarantee can be provided for the due observance of the law of the land, by all persons under all circumstances, than is given by the power, conceded to everyone by the English system, of testing the legality of any conduct of which he disapproves, either on private or on public grounds, by a criminal prosecution (Stephen, 1883, 496).

The third set of arguments were between local authorities and central government over the control of the courts and judicial appointments. Some of this was a principled defence of local autonomy. There was also opposition from those who would expect to pay for it. In a debate on 16 February 1872, the MP for York, George Leeman, argued that the role of public prosecutor should be limited to the Old Bailey, 'if the people of London wished it, let them not force it upon the provincial counties and boroughs, which, to use a Yorkshire phrase, had no more use for it than a cow had for a watch pocket' (PP, HC Deb, 16 February 1872. v. 209, c. 593). There were also suspicions that some opposition was motivated by the desire to maintain local arrangements in which officials were able to 'farm' the system for their personal incomes, particularly police officers, clerks, and solicitors (Kurland and Waters, 1959).

Parliamentary debates

The legislative story of efforts between 1854 and 1879 to establish public prosecution in England and Wales has been well told (Kurland and Waters, 1959; Rock, 2004a). While earlier discussions, including those in parliamentary select committees, had often considered the specific role of police as prosecutors, the debate in the second half of the century focused on the need for a more formal role of public prosecutor. This was, in part, a response to the growing intervention of the new police into the prosecution process.

In 1854, John George Phillimore sponsored a bill to establish a public prosecutor. He criticized the court system's reliance on individual victims, arguing that 'Under the present neglected state of our law, after the proceedings before the magistrate closed, it was left often to the ability or zeal of a private prosecutor whether the greatest criminal should be brought to justice, or whether he should, as was too frequently the case, escape with impunity'. He also addressed the question of cost, arguing that the developing system of police prosecution was encouraging

> frivolous prosecutions … by which expenses were multiplied exceedingly. Arrangements of the most scandalous kind were frequently made between the attorney who had charge of the prosecution, and the policeman who was bound to prosecute, and it constantly happened that the policeman did not discharge his duty, and was induced to overlook some material part of the evidence, and the criminal was thereby suffered to escape (PP, HC Deb, 14 February 1854, v. 130, cc. 665–72).

As this speech demonstrates, Phillimore intended his bill to resolve one of the consequences of the expansion of police prosecution. As Langford has noted, Phillimore's contemporaries were particularly concerned about 'an excessive and uncontrolled exercise of prosecutorial discretion and power', particularly in relation to police powers. Once again, the issue was cost, and the awareness of corrupt relationships between police who would deliver cases to what were described as 'low' attorneys in return for payments (Langford, 1993, 109). Phillimore's bill also attracted opposition from country magistrates and solicitors, who were opposed to central government interference in local matters, and it failed (Kurland and Waters, 1959, 505).

Langford has argued that while the Bill was not passed, 'Its collapse had placed the issue directly on the terrain of Parliamentary concerns' (Langford, 1993, 117). Public prosecution would increasingly be framed as a political issue, leading to the establishment of a Select Committee on Public Prosecutors to investigate the issue the following year, with Phillimore as its chair (Morris, 2001, 122). While this Committee remains important in understanding the slow evolution of public prosecution, it is notable that no new bill arose from it. As Rock notes, 'The Select Committee on Public

Prosecutors, a weighty body that included a former Attorney-General of Ireland and the Lord Advocate of Scotland (jurisdictions where systems of public prosecution already existed), considered the matter … but the Bills that followed after a long lapse of 14 years in 1870, 1871 and 1872 failed, as did another such Bill in 1873' (2004a, 336).

While police magistrates seemed to be broadly in support of the call for a public prosecutor, opponents were also vocal in pointing to the potential for bribery, nepotism, political factionalism, and the protection of the powerful from charges (Hay and Snyder, 1989, 44; Rock, 2004a, 341). This distrust arose in part from accusations about the corruption already found in police prosecutions, noted above. As Phillimore stated in the Commons in 1855:

> The Crown, indeed, was the nominal prosecutor, but the consequence was that we gave to policemen, to a class amongst whom were to be found some of the most hardened and profligate of mankind, and over whom the most incessant vigilance was requisite to prevent flagrant and cruel abuses of their authority, we gave to these men an unlimited power of pardon and connivance; and we intrusted [sic] them with an authority which in every country but England was regulated with as much anxiety as the functions of the Judge himself (PP, HC Deb, 20 February, 1855, v. 336, cc. 1631–1713).

Eventually, these concerns about corruption and abuse of authority reached those at the head of the legal profession. Lord Cockburn, the Lord Chief Justice, wrote to the Judicature Commission in 1874, 'It seems to me that both in theory and in practice every prosecution, however small the offence, should be subject to the control, and, if necessary, to the action, of a public officer or officers appointed by and responsible to the State' (PP, 1874, xix). Cockburn argued that the trial should not remain in the hands of the police: 'The police are in a great many cases important witnesses, and when a prosecutor is also a witness, there is a risk of his becoming biased in his testimony' (PP, 1874, xv). In other evidence to the Commission, Judge Baron (Anthony) Cleasby stated his concern that the police were 'over-anxious' in how they constructed charges: 'I have known of many cases in which a quarrel and fight in the street has been made the subject of a charge for highway robbery; and also many in which an indecent assault by lads has been the subject of a charge for rape'. However, he could not see how a public prosecutor would be able to deal with this 'mischief', which he felt was a result of the police desire for successful prosecutions (PP, 1874, First Appendix, 5). For these officials, there was clearly a tension between the apparent desire for a more formal public prosecutorial function involving the police and the need to reign in the over-reach of their growing powers (see also Petrow, 1994).

At the beginning of the nineteenth century, calls for a public prosecutor had been framed by supporters such as Colquhoun and William Fielding as a means to relieve victims of crime from the burdens, financial and otherwise, of conducting a prosecution. By the late 1870s, the matter of costs had been largely resolved (although payment remained retrospective), and the burdens of seeking evidence, compelling witnesses, and managing trials had largely been assumed by the police, through arrangements which differed in each local authority. That had created opportunities for (quasi) corrupt payments and the imposition of what were perceived as excessive costs on local rate-payers.

The sponsors of the bills and parliamentary committee reports of the 1850s and 1870s had sought to create a national machine of public prosecution (Langford, 1993, 136). Resistance to that system resulted, instead, in a series of piecemeal reforms to the legal system. Kurland and Waters provide a useful list of the statutes which were passed in this period, which taken together, demonstrate the evolution of low-level governance of prosecution in this period, if not directly dealing with public prosecution (1959, 561, fn. 292). These ranged from attempts to speed up the process of claiming costs, in the 1855 Criminal Justice Act (18 & 19 Vict. *c.* 126); the 1859 Vexatious Indictments Act (22 & 23 Vict. *c.* 17); and a number of acts which amended the process of dealing with fees to witnesses in criminal proceedings and payments to clerks. Their purpose was to improve the efficiency and speed of the system while leaving the fundamentally 'English' character of the legal system intact; they avoided the creation of 'continental' state prosecutors, while reducing costs, corruption, and delay.

By 1879, the desire for a comprehensive reshaping of the English legal system had been worn down by a combination of philosophical principle and the dogged resistance of those who stood to lose the most: those who would pay for it and those whose jobs would be threatened, primarily the clerks of the courts. When the Prosecution of Offences Act (42 & 43 Vict. *c.* 22) finally received royal assent on 3 July 1879, it was little more than a legal recognition of what was already the reality in English and Welsh courtrooms (Lamont, 2022). The Act created a Director of Public Prosecutions (DPP) 'under the superintendence of the Attorney General, to institute, undertake, and carry on criminal proceedings and give such advice and assistance to chief officers of police, clerks to justices, and other persons, whether officers or not, respecting the conduct of such proceedings' (Howard, 1930, 23).

When the first DPP, Sir John Maule, was appointed in December 1879, *The Times*, which had long supported the cause of more far-reaching legal reform, was downbeat:

> The great fault of our existing system is that while it is everybody's right to prosecute, it is nobody's business to do so ... There are few persons who have the courage or the means to bring to justice the guilty authors of a complicated commercial fraud ... None but a fool or a rogue, it has been said, will prosecute in an English court of justice; and it is notorious that those who have done so once rarely repeat their example of public spirit ... The public little knows of the degree to which the criminal law is perverted into an instrument of petty extortion ... Honest men are worried with prosecutions which ought never to have been begun; and the sorry compensation is that proceedings against undoubted criminals are abruptly terminated in circumstances which make it morally certain that the prosecution has been bought off or tampered with (*The Times*, 24 December 1879, 9, col. 4).

As far as *The Times* was concerned, victims did not trust the courts to provide fair access to justice; and despite the rumbling of debate over previous decades, and the passage of incremental legislation, the creation of the office of the Director of Public Prosecutions would fail to resolve this issue.

The impact of the Director of Public Prosecutions

The 1879 law specified that the Director of Public Prosecutions would be a solicitor or barrister with at least ten years' experience, and would be provided with up to six assistants (Rock, 2004a, 342). Regulations approved in 1880 stipulated that the cases which should be the duty of the DPP to institute were those 'Where it appears to the Director that the offence or circumstances of its commission is or are of such a character that a prosecution in respect thereof is required in the public interest, and that owing to the importance or the difficulty of the case or to other circumstances the action of the Director of Public Prosecutions is necessary to procure the due prosecution of the offender' (*Law Times*, 16 March 1886, 341). The first part of the formulation meant the DPP merely took over the criminal portion of the Treasury Solicitor's existing powers. The second part was aimed at encouraging intervention in exceptional cases where, for example, individual victims refused or failed to prosecute: a new attempt to resolve a problem dating back to at least the early modern period. The right of private citizens to institute prosecutions was explicitly retained by Section 3 of the Act.

In its first three years, the DPP's office took up only 809 out of the 2,324 cases referred to it (Bentley, 1998, 86–7). These were referred by justices of the peace, the police, and in some cases, by the Attorney General. As the first DPP, Maule, noted in 1884, his role was 'to give advice in cases of importance and difficulty to justices of the peace, and to Chief Officers of Police, who may apply for his advice in such cases, and to other persons in his discretion, subject to any special instructions which he may receive from the Attorney-General' (PP, 1884, XXII, 317; cited by Langford, 1993, 140). The majority of cases were very quickly passed over to the Treasury Solicitor for prosecution, so at this early stage the involvement of the DPP was limited and the police and Treasury Solicitor remained as the primary bodies to pursue prosecution if the victim was unwilling or unavailable (Lamont, 2022).

The similarity in the roles of the DPP and the Treasury Solicitor was confirmed by a further Prosecution of Offences Act in 1884 (47 & 48 Vict. *c.* 58) which merged their two offices. As a result, Sir John Maule stepped down as DPP, and Augustus Stephenson (KCB, QC) took up a combined role of both DPP and Treasury Solicitor (Hetherington, 1989, 15; Howard, 1930, 26–7; also *The Standard*, 7th June 1884). The two offices would be divided again by the Prosecution of Offences Act of 1908 (8 Edw. VII *c.* 3). This was due to changes brought about by the Criminal Appeal Act of 1907, which imposed the duty of prosecuting appeals at the newly established Court of Criminal Appeal on the DPP (7 Edw. VII *c.* 23). As Langford notes, 'Practically it led to the re-division of Treasury Solicitor and Director of Public Prosecutions into separate roles undertaken by separate persons who would conduct civil and criminal business respectively' (Langford, 1993, 145). Serious criminal prosecutions were now to be conducted by the office of the DPP. Moreover, the Act also made it obligatory for police chief officers to make periodic returns to the Director (Bentley, 1998, 87).

By 1900, however, the office was still handling only four to five hundred cases per year. Evidence from the criminal statistics in the Parliamentary Papers shows the limited involvement of the DPP in criminal prosecutions. Our sample evidence (approximately every fifth year of the *Judicial Statistics*) indicates that, as a proportion of all indictable offences nationally, the DPP conducted between only 2.7 and 6.6 per cent of all prosecutions on indictment. As a sign of its limited powers, the activities of the office did not consistently increase over time. They peaked in 1922 at 6.6 per cent (559 indictments). As the number of indictable offences increased after World War II, the DPP was responsible for decreasing proportions of them: falling to 2.8 per cent (1,325 indictments) in 1971 (Parliamentary Papers dataset).

Actual references to the DPP appear in the *Proceedings* from 1882, but only in eighty-five cases up to 1913. These cases overwhelmingly fell into one of three categories: financial crimes and crimes of deception (including fraud, forgery, and perjury); murder; and breaking the peace (including wounding, libel, riot, and threatening behaviour). It is easy to see why some of these offences would fall into the remit of the DPP. In the later nineteenth century, fraud was becoming a more significant problem. These were often complicated cases involving multiple victims and, sometimes, multiple accused. The issue of public interest could perhaps similarly be applied to murder and sexual offences, where the focus was also on particularly difficult and sensitive cases. In the case of murder, eight of the thirteen DPP cases found in the Old Bailey Online involve either a verdict of insanity, or some attempt to claim an insanity defence during the trial. In one case from 1901 the accused was an anarchist (OBO, t19011021-764), suggesting a politically significant crime. Three other cases were extremely high profile: Hawley Harvey Crippen for the murder of Cora Crippen in 1910; Stinie Morrison for the murder of Leon Beron in 1911; and Frederick Henry Seddon for the murder of Elizabeth Mary Barrow in 1912 (OBO, t19101011-74; t19110228-43; t19120227-48).

This limited and specific involvement of the Director of Public Prosecutions is also a feature of our *Times* data. We only found 252 trial reports mentioning the DPP in the *Times* years sampled (accounting for just 4.9 per cent of victims), although it is possible that their involvement was underreported. Moreover, only 11.9 per cent of these DPP cases were located in the later period (1960–75). From this limited evidence, it appears that DPP involvement continued previous patterns of being confined to offences relating to death and fraud. There is no direct evidence of the office assisting in drug and sexual offence prosecutions, although evidence from the Law Reports suggests that the DPP did address sexual offences where the offence was linked to a killing, or intention to kill or similar

(*DPP vs Beard* [1920] AC 479). The murder trials may have involved some in which the insanity defence was presented, but in only five cases was a 'guilty but insane' verdict given, and four of these cases were in 1910 (Ernest Partridge, for the murder of his wife; Harry William Ball for the murder of his employer; Stanley Dennis and Ernest Arthur Martin Royle, both for the murder of their child). While broadly the patterns of DPP prosecutions followed those of the nineteenth century, there were a number of twentieth-century cases which involved acts against public order and provisions of the state (5.5 per cent), and against public safety and security (10.4 per cent). These included cases involving espionage and contravening the Defence of the Realm Act (known as DORA), which was passed in 1914 (Emsley, 2013b, 30–2). In most of these cases the victim was an institution, the state. Almost half the *Times'* cases prosecuted by the DPP involved either institutional or unknown victims. Finally, perhaps owing to the complexity of the cases he was involved in, the presence of the DPP did not necessarily lead to a higher conviction rate—in fact the rate was slightly lower (62.7 per cent guilty vs 63.8 per cent in all other cases, excluding unknown verdicts). In cases of offences leading to death, for example, 64.8 per cent of cases involving the DPP led to a conviction, compared to 67.3 per cent of all other cases. In fraud cases the figures were 56.1 per cent with the DPP, compared to 66.1 per cent.

For much of the twentieth century, then, the role of the DPP remained limited. By the 1950s, as Rock has noted, their duties had become more clearly defined: 'he was not an investigator or examiner of witnesses, he was to be independent of government, his role was not to control but to advise the police, he should take decisions in cases referred to him, and the right of private prosecution was to be preserved' (2004, 343). The Director eventually became the 'prosecutor of last resort'. The police were required to inform the DPP about details of every indictable offence in their district, indicating those cases where DPP action was necessary to ensure efficient prosecution. The DPP could instruct police to oversee the case under supervision or entrust it to a local solicitor acting under DPP authority. In practice, this affected very few cases, only those regarded as high profile, legally complex, or raising particular points of law (Lamont, 2022).

Towards a Crown Prosecution Service

The creation of a national DPP did not lead to a national system of prosecution in England and Wales. The nineteenth-century patchwork of local solutions to the problem of managing relations between victim, police, counsel, and court continued for most of the twentieth century. Although the crimes of 'misprision' and 'compounding' were formally abolished in 1967 (Criminal Law Act, *c.* 58), the fundamental basis of the system remained: the right of the private individual to bring a prosecution against their malefactor. In theory, the police and the prosecutors were merely facilitating and expediting this right. As R.M. Jackson explained the system in his 1964 book *The Machinery of Justice in England*,

> The basic principle of prosecutions in England is that it is open to any member of the public to institute criminal proceedings, there being no need for such a person to have any interest whatsoever in the subject of the charge . . . When 'the police' prosecute, the correct analysis is that some individual has instituted proceedings, and the fact that this individual is a police officer does not alter the nature of the prosecution (Jackson, 1964, 120).

The right of an individual to bring their own case thus endured. In Jackson's description, if the police did not pursue a case, an injured party could go before a magistrate and make an allegation. The magistrate would issue a summons, served by a police officer, both parties would attend a hearing and the magistrate would either issue a ruling or refer the case to a higher court. In essence the procedure remained the same as in the eighteenth century and similar obstacles to prosecution of cost, time, and trouble endured (Jackson, 1942, 121). As a result, this method of private prosecution was of course seldom pursued by victims of crime. Most victims who suffered a crime and reported it to the police allowed the 'machinery of justice' to take responsibility for it.

By the 1970s, however, there was increasing public concern about the machinery's failings. The system was fundamentally uneven and the experience of the victim could vary in different parts of the country. This patchwork provision resulted in calls for these inconsistencies to be addressed. Partly, these calls focused on failures to systematically consider the damage—physical, financial, and emotional—done to victims of crime, as discussed in the previous chapter. A greater part concerned the fairness of the system for defendants. In 1970, the campaigning organization 'Justice', the British section of the International Commission of Jurists, published a critical report on 'The prosecution process in England and Wales'. Referring to the 'patchwork' of prosecution practices, it noted that 'The machinery for the initiation and conduct of prosecutions in England and Wales presents a surprisingly complex and confusing picture'. It observed that 'abuses do occur and the system ... produces disquieting anomalies and variations which have, from time to time, resulted in errors and miscarriages of justice, sometimes of a very serious nature'. It called, therefore, for a 'fundamental reappraisal of both principle and practice' (Justice, 1970, 1). It spoke admiringly of the Scottish system of public prosecution and recommended the establishment of a 'Department of Public Prosecutions to be responsible both for the decision to prosecute and for the conduct of the prosecutions' (Justice, 1970, 13).

The report triggered considerable discussion but no action by the government. It was, however, referred to in Sir Henry Fisher's 1977 report into a high-profile miscarriage of justice: the wrongful conviction of three boys, aged between fourteen and eighteen, for the murder of transsexual Maxwell Confait (known as Michelle) in Catford in south London in 1972. The case against the accused was itself suspect from the outset, involving the unorthodox interrogation of minors and of a youth with learning difficulties, contested confessions and allegations of police maltreatment (McConville, Sanders, and Leng, 1991; Robins, 2019; Rock 2019). The young men's subsequent exoneration led to the then Home Secretary, Roy Jenkins of the Labour Party, ordering Fisher's inquiry, which reported in December 1977. A key objective for Jenkins was for Fisher to make recommendations about the 'Judges' Rules' which stipulated how police should treat suspects. The inquiry found that police had breached interviewing rules, that they were unaware of certain rules, and that some rules (such as police being able to interview suspects without a lawyer present) were unfair. Like the Justice report, it compared aspects of the English system unfavourably to the Scottish system and found 'A change to a system like the Scottish, for the investigation and prosecution of serious crimes, might be expected to achieve a number of beneficial effects' (Fisher, 1977, 26).

Although Fisher's report stopped short of calling for a change in the English and Welsh prosecutorial system, the government immediately announced a Royal Commission, 'so that those suggestions which raise fundamental issues affecting police investigation and criminal procedure can receive the close examination which they warrant' (PP, HC Deb, 13

December 1977, v. 941, *c.* 122). At the time, parliament was considering a Criminal Law Bill and MPs had proposed amendments to create a Scottish-style public prosecutor for England and Wales (PP, HC Deb, 3 May 1977, v. 931, *c.* 269). The Labour MP and barrister Alex Lyon later claimed that 'It seemed clear that by agreement with the Opposition of that time those amendments might have been carried' (PP, HC Deb, 20 November 1981, v. 13, *c.* 554). But these amendments were dropped because of the Royal Commission announcement, with the effect that reform took a further decade (see Rock, 2019, chapters 7 and 8 for more details).

The Royal Commission on Criminal Procedure chaired by Professor Sir Cyril Philips was formally established in February 1978 and published its report in January 1981 under the new Conservative government. Its response was influenced by the Brixton riots of April 1981 and Lord Scarman's subsequent investigation (published the following November) which criticized many aspects of policing in London (Scarman, 1982, 78). Between those two dates, the government published a consultation document (in August) and then a formal response (in November). The Home Secretary, Willie Whitelaw, summarized Philips' recommendations on the prosecution process as:

> a partial, but not total, divorce of the police from the prosecution process. Under its proposals, the original decision to prosecute would remain with the chief officer, but, in every police area, there would be an independent Crown prosecutor who, although working in close consultation and partnership with the chief constable, would have an independent role in the handling of prosecutions once the original decision to prosecute had been made. He, and not the chief officer, would decide what, if any, charges should be pressed, and would be wholly responsible for seeing that there was adequate evidence to support them. Each Crown prosecutor would be responsible to a new police and prosecutions authority, which would be based on the present system of police authorities. The Commission reached no conclusion on whether the responsible Minister would be the Attorney-General or myself (PP, HC Deb, 20 November, 1981, v. 13, c. 527).

Consideration of the Royal Commission's report continued with an interdepartmental Working Party on Prosecution Arrangements which examined three possible models for the service. By the time a White Paper was issued in 1983, the government had opted for a national prosecution service under the supervision of the DPP (and the Attorney-General) (Khan, 1986, 298; Rock, 2019, 411–13). The earlier Philips' Commission recommendation that the new public prosecutors should be accountable locally was rejected on the grounds that 'it would not be appropriate for local authorities to have control over the conduct of prosecutions under the general criminal law' (Khan, 1986, 299).

While many of the findings of the Fisher Report and the Royal Commission were addressed in the Police and Criminal Evidence Act of 1984, the question of prosecutorial authority was resolved in the Prosecution of Offences Act 1985 (1984 *c.* 60; 1985 c, 23). It mandated the creation of a new Crown Prosecution Service (CPS), managed by the DPP, which commenced operation in 1986. England and Wales were divided into thirty-one areas, distinct from the countries' forty-two police forces, with responsibility for prosecutions within those areas given to a Chief Crown Prosecutor (Khan, 1986, 298; Adams, 1998, 223). For the first time, England and Wales possessed a formal system of public prosecution.

Even this innovation did not end the principle of private prosecution, however. Section 6 of the 1985 Act still allowed anyone who believed they had been a victim of crime to instigate a private prosecution against the alleged perpetrator. In some cases the DPP was obliged to take over the case, in others they could choose whether to allow the case to continue or to take it over and drop it. Initially the DPP took the view that cases could continue unless there was 'clearly no case to answer' or because the case would be against the public interest. In 2009, however, the DPP adopted a policy requiring that a case must have a 'realistic prospect' of conviction to go forward. A UK Supreme Court ruling upheld the legality of this rule, causing a dissenting judge, Lady Hale, to remark that this had 'effectively removed' the right to private prosecution (Stark, 2013, 8).

Nonetheless, private prosecutions continued, with voluntary organizations such as the RSPCA, the NSPCC, and other private individuals bringing cases. Most notably, in April 1995, Doreen and Neville Lawrence, the parents of murdered teenager Stephen Lawrence, attempted a private prosecution against three men whom they believed were responsible for his killing (see Chapter 7). In 2016, the Cyclists' Defence Fund (CDF) brought a private prosecution at the Old Bailey against a woman accused of causing the death by dangerous driving of a cyclist on Regent Street in London. The Metropolitan Police had declined to refer the case to the CPS so the CDF gathered funds from the public to pursue it. The trial judge refused applications to dismiss the case although the accused was eventually found not guilty (Jones, 2017). Quasi-state institutions, such as the Post Office, could also act as a private prosecutor. These types of prosecution have caused significant controversy with the wrongful civil and criminal prosecutions of sub-postmasters for fraud, theft, and false accounting. What are now seen as the extensive misuse of powers has resulted in overturning the prosecutions as miscarriages of justice, and subsequently an ongoing appeals process (Brooks and Wallis, 2020; Post Office, 2022).

4.4 Conclusion

This chapter has shown how gradual changes in police and public prosecution de-centred the victim within court proceedings. There is ample evidence to suggest that the same process was happening both at the Old Bailey and in trial courts beyond the capital, and also in the summary courts, although victims retained more of a voice in the latter (Davis, 1984; Godfrey, Cox, and Farrall, 2007), at least until the 1920s when the 'bureaucratization and professionalization' of these courts 'drastically reduced . . . the ability of local clientele to employ the arena for their own purposes' (Auerbach, 2021, 41). Overall, victims' participation in court was shrinking; a point we will further explore in Chapter 6.

By charting the interplay of key factors leading to the erosion of victim-led prosecution in England and Wales, we have shown that this long-term process was far from linear, was often driven by changes at the local level, and that practice was uneven across different regions and police forces and in different courtrooms. It also varied according to the type of offence (Godfrey, 2008). The police presence in prosecution cases, for example, was most visible in the case of serious crimes tried at the Old Bailey, and presumably at other higher courts. Nonetheless, the establishment of the DPP in 1879 did not result in a wholesale shift of higher court offences to its remit.

Until 1986, in England and Wales there was no public prosecution system of the kind that operated in Scotland and continental European states with state-funded public prosecutors. By the mid-nineteenth century, however, a *form* of public prosecution had developed in the sense that the local state-funded police forces initiated legal proceedings working with counsel, purportedly in the public interest and funded from the public purse. Despite the creation of the DPP in 1879, it was not until the 1980s that this role would involve more than a minority of cases, following the establishment of the CPS in 1986 (Ashworth, 2000, 259). The DPP became the head of the CPS, appointed by, and responsible, to the Attorney General.

Yet despite the creation of the CPS, as Ashworth notes, and while the CPS has the duty to take over all criminal prosecutions instituted on behalf of a police force (other than some minor offences), 'there is still a right of private prosecution in England and Wales—the power of a private individual, or company, to bring criminal proceedings by applying to a court and presenting credible evidence' (Ashworth, 2000, 262). Nonetheless, that power was (and is) limited in that private prosecutors still need to obtain some form of approval, from the Attorney General or the DPP, before they can proceed with their case (CPS, 2019). This remains a vestige of a medieval obligation, demonstrating the piecemeal evolution of the English legal system. In practice, private prosecution in the modern criminal justice system in England and Wales is mainly the preserve of companies and voluntary organizations. In summary, through the office of the DPP, England and Wales finally acquired a public prosecutor, but that role was limited, and remained limited until 1986, and even to some extent thereafter.

By the time the Prosecution of Offences Act was passed in 1985, eighteenth-century concerns about the potential of a state prosecutor to become an agent of state tyranny had fully abated. Instead, concern about the abuses of the state's powers had become focused on the police, who had assumed significant powers over the course of the nineteenth century. The response of England's legal and political elite was not to re-empower individual citizens to direct the prosecutorial system but to create another state agency, the CPS, to act as a check on the first. What had changed in the interim were views of the respective roles of the individual and the state in society, a recognition that by the late twentieth century the individual was poorly positioned to champion their rights alone, and an acceptance that the state could be trusted to act as the individual's protector. Arguably, the individual complainant was now seen as a 'victim' who suffered and needed state welfare, rather than an active and able agent capable of pursuing their interests. In the process, and without any explicit policy or legal choice, the 'victim' had been marginalized.

The next chapters investigate the impact of these major changes. Did they result in a democratization of justice by expanding access to a greater range of complainants? Did a justice system catering to the needs of the propertied become more responsive to the needs of working-class communities and to women across classes? If it did, why did so many victims, campaigners, and criminologists feel that, by the 1980s, the system was archaic, broken, and unable to meet the needs of victims or defendants?

5
Victims at the Old Bailey

In previous chapters we have described the ways the state tried to encourage and manage the number of prosecutions through the use of rewards, reimbursements of costs, and the provision of legal and police support to victims of crime. In the following two chapters we examine evidence from the Old Bailey, the most important criminal court in England, to see what effect, if any, these measures had upon patterns of prosecution and the outcomes of trials.

We make use of the unique records of trial participants and outcomes recorded in the contemporaneously published Old Bailey *Proceedings* and subsequently digitized in the Old Bailey Online. To this we add a sample of reports of Old Bailey trials published in *The Times* in the twentieth century. Together, this allows us to examine patterns of victim participation at this court over three centuries, from the 1670s to the 1970s. In the current chapter, we look at overall trends in prosecutions by type of offence and consider the extent to which marginalized groups, particularly working-class victims, female victims, young and elderly victims, and minority ethnic victims, prosecuted cases. In the following chapter we look at victims' changing role within the criminal trial and the outcomes of those trials as measures of whether prosecutions might be deemed 'successful' by victims.

5.1 The Data and Their Limits

Throughout this section of the book, we are attentive to the influence that the changing mix of offences tried at the Old Bailey had on the numbers and types of victims involved in prosecutions during the three centuries under review. As we outlined in Chapter 1, the Old Bailey heard cases involving felonies, the most serious violations of the criminal law. Over time, however, minor felonies were diverted into lower courts (quarter sessions) or

Victims and Criminal Justice. Pamela Cox, Robert Shoemaker, and Heather Shore, Oxford University Press.
DOI: 10.1093/oso/9780192846488.003.0005

summary jurisdiction (as we discussed in Chapter 3). However, a core of major offences, including murder, rape, robbery, burglary, and fraud, were tried at the Old Bailey throughout the period.

The 230,646 victim-prosecutions recorded in the Old Bailey *Proceedings* dataset provide an unprecedented window into the experiences of victims at one criminal court over 240 years, from 1674 to 1913. (A reminder here that each criminal charge linked to a victim is counted separately and referred to as a prosecution, regardless of whether the actual victim was responsible for the prosecution). Nonetheless, the dataset does have some limitations, which must be acknowledged (see the Appendix for a full account). Trial reports in the early years were often brief and incomplete. One-third of the editions of the *Proceedings* covering Old Bailey sessions in the forty years between 1674 and 1714 have not survived. More importantly, the identities of a significant minority of victims (26,521 over the whole period, or 11.4 per cent) were either not reported, or not captured in the tagging process used to create the Old Bailey Online, and thus cannot be analysed statistically. The majority of these (79.3 per cent of the missing victims) relate to trials occurring between November 1834 and April 1913.[1] Since most of these cases were in the 'deception' category of offence, we have chosen to omit this category from our analysis of victim gender and class.[2]

As also outlined in Chapter 1, the City of London stopped publishing the *Proceedings* in April 1913 for reasons of cost. We were therefore obliged to use a different source to capture Old Bailey prosecutions in the twentieth century. We chose *The Times* newspaper for this purpose, owing to its reputation as an authoritative source and its practice of regularly reporting Old Bailey trials. As manual collection of newspaper evidence is time intensive, we opted to create two samples of *Times* reports, for the periods 1910–25 and 1960–75. The first three years duplicate the period covered by the final issues of the *Proceedings*, which allowed us to compare the court reporting of the two publications. Beyond that, we sought to include both a period which captured the early twentieth century when, among other factors, the office of the Director of Public Prosecutions was still in its infancy, and a period in the later twentieth century when several important statutory

[1] Trials occurring between November 1834 and April 1913 were digitized during the second phase of the Old Bailey digitization project when the project used a more economical manual tagging process which did not capture victim names unless they featured in the first paragraph of trial reports.

[2] Owing to the limited evidence available, however, we chose to include deception cases in our analysis of victim ages and ethnicity.

provisions were introduced for victims (introducing criminal injuries compensation, and anonymity for rape victims, for example), and when calls for new ways of recognizing victims' experiences began to emerge.

In line with more general patterns of newspaper crime reporting, *The Times* featured only a selection of Old Bailey trials, focusing on those which were deemed most newsworthy (Rowbotham, Stevenson, and Pegg, 2013; Crone, 2012; Reiner, Livingstone, and Allen, 2003). Our datasets show that only 14.4 per cent of the prosecutions documented in the *Proceedings* in the three years between 1910 and 1912 (which can be considered a reasonably full record of the Old Bailey's business) were reported in *The Times*. Furthermore, as explained in Chapter 1, these reports were more likely to focus on murders and other crimes which led to the death of the victim (13.1 per cent in *The Times* vs 4.3 per cent in the *Proceedings* for the period 1910–12), crimes which disproportionately affected female victims. *The Times* was also prone to report other acts involving violence (to the person and involving property appropriation), and financial crime, particularly fraud (see also Shore, 2015). On the other hand, *The Times* was much less likely to report more mundane property and public order offences. These distortions and omissions, along with the fact that these reports varied in detail, should be kept in mind when interpreting this data. As a result, the following discussion makes greater use of the earlier and more comprehensive Old Bailey *Proceedings* data.

Offences over time

To analyse the types of crimes prosecuted at the Old Bailey we used eleven general categories derived from United Nations classifications (UNODC, 2015; see the Appendix for an explanation of our application of these categories). As explained in Chapters 1 and 3, the composition of offences heard at the court changed dramatically in the middle of the nineteenth century, primarily owing to the transfer of many crimes to summary jurisdiction. Non-violent property offences, which had accounted for over three-quarters of all prosecutions up to 1850, declined by half after this date, while the proportion of prosecutions involving fraud and deception and violent offences increased.

In Figure 5.1 the data have been divided into four periods: an early period of relative stability (between 1674 and 1850) when Old Bailey business was dominated by property crime; the remainder of the *Proceedings*

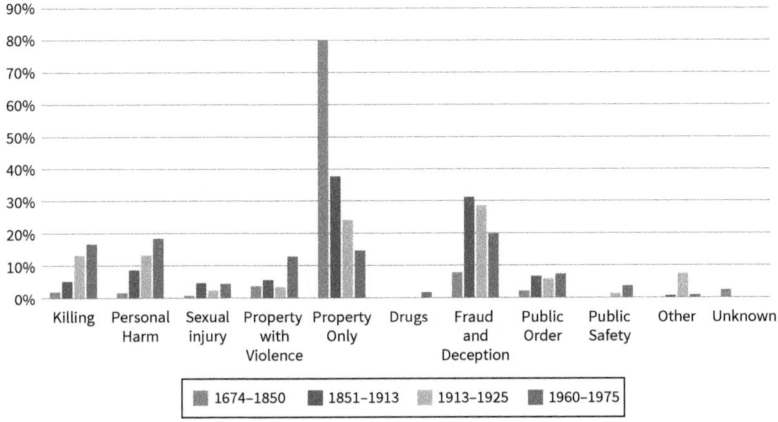

Figure 5.1: Crime Categories Over Time: Per Cent of Old Bailey Cases by UNODC Categories, 1674–1975

Source: Proceedings (1674–1913) and *Times* (1913–25, 1960–75) Datasets

period up to 1913; *Times* reports between 1910 and 1925; and *Times* reports between 1960 and 1975. There are some clear long-term trends. Non-violent property offences declined as a proportion of Old Bailey court business while offences leading to death or involving personal harm, property crimes involving violence to the person, drugs offences, public order offences, and acts against public safety and security all rose (although numbers for the latter categories are very low). A sharp increase in cases of fraud and deception (including forgery, acting under false pretences, and corruption) in the 1851 to 1913 period appears to have been followed by a decline in the twentieth century. This, however, may be because *The Times* was less interested in reporting such cases (as well as non-violent property offences).

Our data on one type of crime, offences involving sexual injury, follows a more erratic trajectory. While a reluctance to discuss the details of such crimes is evident in the *Proceedings* of the late eighteenth and nineteenth centuries, the basic facts of the cases were at least reported (Emsley, Hitchcock, and Shoemaker, 2018c). In the early twentieth century, however, *The Times* reported relatively few Old Bailey trials involving sexual offences, perhaps owing to lingering Victorian sensibilities about sex. Then, in the period from 1960 to 1975 when attitudes towards sex and sexuality were changing, it gave them far more coverage. As noted in Chapter 2, however, this type of crime was one of the least likely to be reported to the authorities and prosecuted in the first place.

While a diverse range of offences was tried at the Old Bailey, the vast majority were property offences, offences involving violence to the person, or both. Across the three centuries under review, there was a broad shift from property offences to those involving violence. These changes affected the composition of the victims whose cases appeared before the court, as we discuss below.

Conclusions should not be drawn from these trends about patterns of actual victimization: the increasing proportion of crimes involving violence to the person most likely reflects a growing sensitivity to such crimes and the resulting propensity to prosecute, not an increase in actual violence in society (which historians have argued was declining for most of the period [Gatrell, 1980; Emsley, 2005]), while the decrease in property prosecutions reflects the diversion of those offences into summary jurisdiction, not a decrease in thefts, which continued to be prosecuted in the magistrates' courts. In contrast, cases of fraud and deception (including forgery, counterfeiting, embezzlement, handling stolen goods, and corruption), which had been increasing from the 1780s, reached a peak in the second half of the nineteenth century. In the second half of the twentieth century *The Times* reported fewer of them, but there is no evidence that such crimes actually declined.

Our analysis of Old Bailey victims examines how access to justice at this London court varied between social groups across time. First, we examine the two characteristics for which we have significant quantitative evidence: class and gender. Then we look at the more limited evidence available for victims' age and ethnicity. To those familiar with the literature, it will come as no surprise that, across the whole period, we find that victim-prosecutors were overwhelmingly male, middle-class, white adults. However, we identify significant increases over time in the proportions of lower class, female, minority ethnic, young, and elderly victims appearing at the Old Bailey.

5.2 Social Class

Were victims with money and status more likely to bring prosecutions? Did this change over time? Previous historical studies of victims in the English legal system have found that 'middling sort' (King, 1984) and middle-class 'non-elite' (Langbein, 1983) prosecutors predominated in the eighteenth and nineteenth centuries. These works challenged previous assertions by Hay and others (1975) that access to justice was dominated by elite groups. The work of King and Langbein suggested that this broad access to justice was driven by widespread public recognition that the courts, even if they could at times be oppressive, provided a useful tool for victims to bring criminals to account. To date, however, no study has looked at the impact of incentivization on prosecution patterns nor has any looked systematically at nineteenth- or earlier twentieth-century developments in use of the courts by working class, female, or child victims or those acting on their behalf. Unlike previous studies, we use large and comprehensive datasets to explore the impact of specific measures that were intended to alter the possibilities of participation in the justice system, notably rewards, reimbursements, legal support, and changing definitions of offences.

To assess the social status of victim-prosecutors at the Old Bailey we used the occupational labels provided in trial reports by the *Proceedings* and *The Times*. This analysis was not without its difficulties since information on victims' occupations was not consistently provided in either source, nor was it consistently tagged by the Old Bailey Online project. Moreover, interpretation of the large number of diverse occupational labels and their conversion into categories indicating social class is far from straightforward. In the following analysis, we exclude institutional victims and, for the *Proceedings*, prosecutions for deception owing to the large number of missing victim names.

Occupations were only recorded for 27.7 per cent of victim-prosecutors in the *Proceedings* dataset (excluding children under seventeen), but this still amounts to 62,082 victims, enough to justify statistical analysis. Victims' occupations were less likely to be reported in *The Times*, but when they were, they were manually recorded in our dataset, with 15.3 per cent of victims (493) so identified. As is often the case with historical occupational evidence, female occupations were particularly underreported. Where women were mentioned at all, they were typically assigned a marital status rather than an occupation. Thus, in the *Proceedings*, we have occupational labels for only 12.7 per cent of female victims, compared to 34.9 per cent of men. Similarly, in *The Times*, the proportion of occupations reported was 9.7 per cent for women and 23.6 per cent for men.

To categorize occupations, we adapted the HISCO (Historical International Classification of Occupations) classification scheme, devised by the History of Work project.[3] These categories not only make it possible to undertake meaningful analysis of thousands of occupations and compare them to other evidence internationally and historically, but also allow us to group together these categories into broader groupings according to social class. As explained in the Appendix, the thousands of occupations recorded were placed into fifteen broad categories, ranging from aristocrats and gentlemen to unskilled manual work. Clearly these classifications are open to dispute, but we use them on the basis that they are the only available internationally agreed system, and our goal is to determine a rough social hierarchy and assess how it changed over time. From these categories, we created three larger social class groups, broadly reflecting nineteenth-century definitions of the upper, middle, and lower classes. Class is, of course, a complicated and multi-dimensional social and cultural concept, in which perceptions vary according to perspective and the criteria used, and the class position of occupations can change over time. While the occupational data analysed here cannot capture these nuances, it does provide valuable evidence of the place of victims within recognized social hierarchies based on status, skills, and responsibilities. The 'upper class' category includes aristocrats and gentlemen, and higher managers and professionals; the 'middle class' includes medium and lower skilled managers and professionals, clerical and sales personnel, foremen, small manufacturers, and artisans; and 'lower class' includes medium-skilled workers, farmers and fishermen, lower-skilled workers, unskilled workers, and unspecified workers.

After excluding the substantial amount of missing data, Figure 5.2 summarizes the available occupational information by class; the *Proceedings* data has been divided into periods which correspond with the dates of available estimates of the overall class structure. Although we have relatively few occupations for women, the class distributions of male and female victims are similar. Overall, contrary to the view that victims were overwhelmingly middle and upper class (Rudé, 1985, 117), the evidence shows that the vast majority of victims were from the broadly framed lower and middle classes. However, both the upper and middle classes were significantly overrepresented among Old Bailey victims compared to estimates of the class composition of the overall population. The presence of lower-class victims, nonetheless, did gradually increase, both as a

[3] 'History of Work Information System', https://historyofwork.iisg.nl/detail_page.php?act_id=35200 (accessed 13 May 2022).

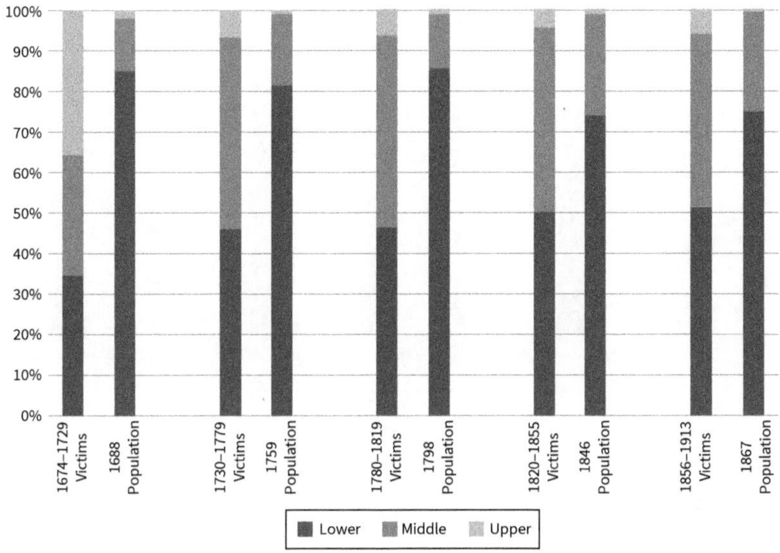

Figure 5.2: Victim Class in the *Proceedings* Compared to Estimates of Overall Class Structure
Source: Proceedings Dataset, and for overall population: Allen, 2019.

proportion of Old Bailey victims and in relation to their composition in the overall population. It is significant that the large growth in summary jurisdiction in the second half of the nineteenth century (discussed in Chapter 3) did not diminish lower-class representation at the Old Bailey. In the twentieth-century *Times* reports, the distribution of victims was much more skewed towards the higher classes, with 27.7 per cent upper class, 50.5 per cent middle class, and only 21.8 per cent lower class. This, however, seems to reflect journalistic reporting practices and the interests of the newspaper's readership more than the class composition of the victims appearing at the Old Bailey at this time (Reiner, 2001, 5; Reiner, Livingstone, and Allen, 2003, 22).

There were significant differences in the class composition of victim-prosecutors across different types of crimes (Figure 5.3). This reflects both the types of crime that members of different classes experienced and the types of crimes they were particularly concerned to prosecute. Crimes involving death were disproportionately likely to be prosecuted by members of the upper class (on their behalf). Crimes involving public order (libel, perjury, and the perversion of justice) and fraud and deception were

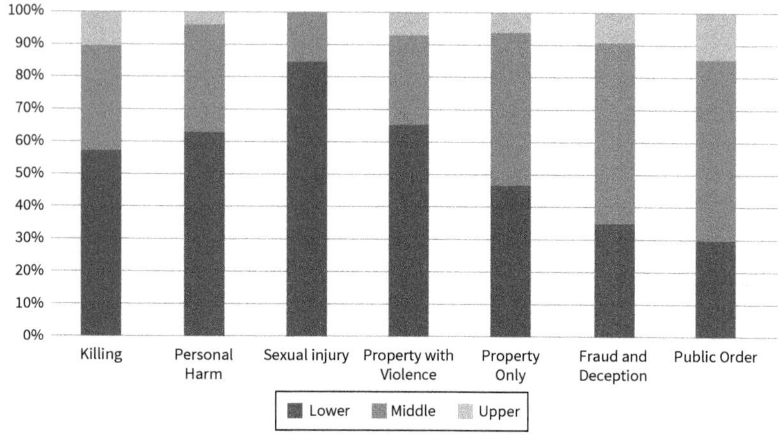

Figure 5.3: Distribution of Crimes by Victim Social Class
Source: Proceedings Dataset ('other' offences and those with low number of identified victim occupations excluded)

more likely to be prosecuted by both upper- and middle-class victims. Property offences were most likely to be prosecuted by middle-class victims. By contrast, lower-class prosecutors were more likely to bring cases of violence, involving both sexual injury and other forms of assault, and violent property offences, particularly in the second half of the nineteenth century. By the 1870s, acts causing personal harm and property offences involving violence accounted for half of their prosecutions. There are three possible explanations for these figures. First, while higher-class victims may have used the law to protect their status, property, and the public order, lower-class victims were particularly concerned about personal harm. Second, the introduction of the new police may have created more interest in prosecuting interpersonal violence and harm among poorer communities (Inwood, 1990; Reiner, 1985). Third, there was a greater interest at the end of the nineteenth century in prosecuting male violence (Wiener, 1998, 2004).

The uneven distribution of crimes prosecuted by members of different classes helps to explain the changing social composition of Old Bailey victims over time, evident in Figure 5.4 (information is provided by decade owing to low case numbers in certain years). The high proportion of upper-class victims in the first decades of the *Proceedings*, 1670s–1720s, reflects elite involvement in violent disputes, including duels and affrays. These

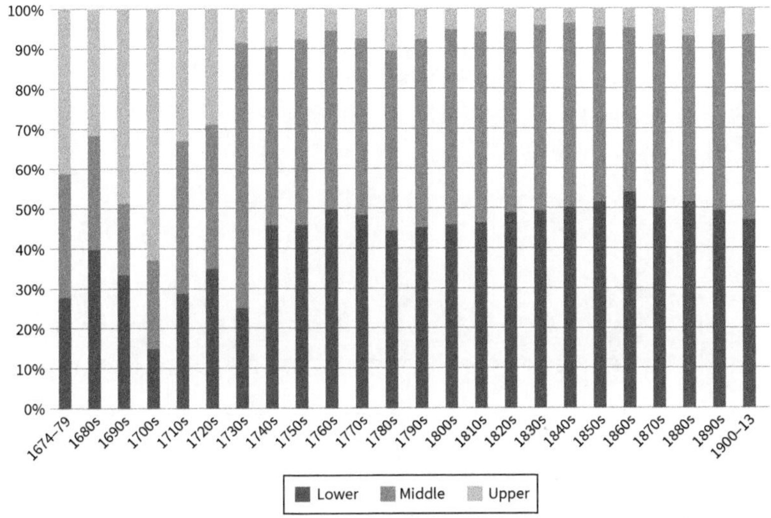

Figure 5.4: Victim Social Class in the *Proceedings* by Decade
Source: Proceedings Dataset

declined after the 1720s because of changing expectations of appropriate elite conduct (Shoemaker, 2001). From 1750 to 1913, the upper class constituted just 5.9 per cent of victims. By contrast, 21.8 per cent of *The Times* reports involved upper-class victims but this probably is more a reflection of its readership's interest in crimes against members of the upper classes than it is of the proportion of actual prosecutions.

These data give us our first evidence for the impact of the substantial efforts made by the state to ease the financial costs of prosecution, as discussed in Chapter 3. We can see increases in the proportion of lower-class victims between the 1700s and 1720s, then a fall, another rise in the 1740s, and a slow rise from the 1780s to the 1860s. In Figure 5.5, we confine our analysis to the poorest group of occupations where the changes were most marked: unskilled workers (HISCLASS codes 11 and 12).[4]

As a proportion of all victims with identifiable occupations, unskilled workers initially peaked at 11.0 per cent in the 1730s, declined to the 1770s, and then rose significantly during the 'long' nineteenth century to a fifth of

[4] While HISCO labels define such workers as 'unskilled', it would be more accurate to consider them as 'less skilled' than the 'lower skilled' manual workers ranked above them in the occupational hierarchy.

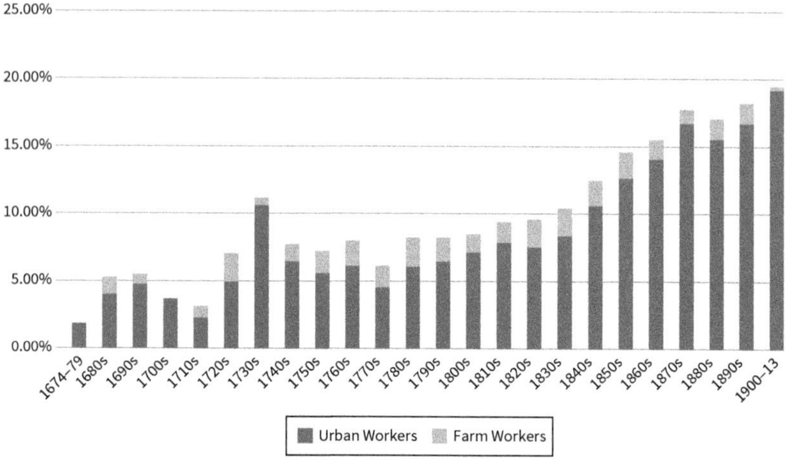

Figure 5.5: Unskilled Workers as a Proportion of all Victims with Identified Occupations in the *Proceedings*
Source: Proceedings Dataset

all victims (19.3 per cent) in the early twentieth century. A small and relatively steady proportion of these victim-prosecutors were farm labourers but, as befits the urban jurisdiction of the Old Bailey, most worked in street vending, transport, warehouses, and workshop-based manufacture (for businesses such as leather curriers and trunk makers). In addition, many worked as sailors. In the later twentieth century, our *Times* data shows many fewer cases involving unskilled workers: just 5.3 per cent of all identified occupations. However, this may be more of a reflection of reporting choices rather than actual prosecutions.

Some of this rise reflects a growth in the relative proportion of this section of the working population owing to industrial and commercial growth, but it also appears to reflect the impact of the provision of financial support for victims to encourage prosecutions. These measures, outlined in Chapter 3, initially took the form of government rewards for successful convictions for the most serious offences, and then of statutes enabling the reimbursement of costs to prosecutors. Substantial rewards were introduced after 1692 for some of the most serious crimes, notably highway robbery, and virtually all those responsible for convictions for the specified crimes received rewards. Our data shows that levels of prosecutions during the periods when the rewards were available were higher than at other times. In the first half of the eighteenth century, for example, the number of defendants accused of highway robbery during periods when the £100 proclamation reward was available was 68.4 per cent higher than during periods when the proclamations lapsed (Clayton and Shoemaker, 2022).

The low number of victim occupations recorded in these years makes it difficult to establish whether it was poor victims who benefited most from these rewards. The evidence, however, is suggestive. In the 1730s, a decade when many rewards were paid out, eighteen of the eighty prosecutions by unskilled workers (22.5 per cent) were for rewardable offences (robbery, burglary, and coining). As a proportion of all prosecutions for these offences, the unskilled were also overrepresented. They accounted for 10.9 per cent of all prosecutions in this decade (where the victim occupation is known) but for 14.0 per cent of the 129 prosecutions for rewardable offences. The rewards system was not intended to support the poor (in fact it distributed a large amount of funding to wealthier victims, including thief-takers), but it did benefit some of the lowest-skilled workers, and seems to have encouraged their prosecutions. The fact that this pattern did not continue, and that the number of unskilled workers bringing prosecutions in the ensuing years declined, may be due to the fact that thief-takers began to play a greater role in bringing, and benefiting from, such prosecutions (Clayton and Shoemaker, 2022).

As explained in Chapter 3, however, there were considerable unintended consequences to the rewards system, primarily its facilitation of perjury and corruption. From the mid-eighteenth century, the state took a different approach to addressing the major disincentive to victims initiating prosecutions. Between 1752 and 1826 a series of statutes provided for the reimbursement to victims of their fees, witness costs, and even trouble and time. Table 5.1 outlines the key provisions of these statutes. Further statutes passed in the second half of the nineteenth century refined, expanded, and consolidated these provisions, but since by this point the government already part-funded the vast majority of prosecutions, their impact was likely to be minimal (for a fuller discussion of the payment of costs, see Chapter 3).

Figure 5.6 assesses the impact of these statutes. We have divided up the analysis by social class, and included separate bars for unskilled workers, a subset of the lower class. Since the number of victims in each group varied significantly, it helps to present this data in the form of the changes in the proportion of all prosecutors coming from each class. This graph thus provides evidence to show which groups, relative to the others, benefited most

Table 5.1: Statutes Providing Financial Assistance to Victims and Prosecutors 1752–1826

1752	Reimburse victims' costs including legal expenses and 'time and trouble' at court's discretion (25 Geo. II c. 36)
1754	Reimburse poor persons bound over to give evidence for the prosecution (27 Geo. II c. 3)
1778	1754 Act widened to include acquittals (18 Geo. III c. 19, ss. 7–8)
1818	Pay expenses regardless of verdict (Bennet's Act, 58 Geo. III c. 70)
1826	Costs of prosecutor and witnesses to be paid out of local funds, fixed fees for counsel and solicitors at county level (7 Geo. 4 c. 64)

from each statute. The results are varied, but the overall pattern is that the lower classes as a whole failed to benefit from the eighteenth-century statutes. This was probably because the benefits, which were subject to the judges' discretion and paid in arrears, were not yet sufficiently generous to offset the full costs of prosecutions for poorer victims. This changed in later periods, however. Lower-class victims did benefit from the 1818 statute, and unskilled workers from the 1778 and 1826 statutes. This may help explain the growth, evident in Figure 5.5 above, in prosecutions brought by or on behalf of unskilled victims which started in the 1780s and accelerated from the 1820s.

However, the statutes do not fully explain the long-term gradual increase in prosecutions by unskilled workers. It is likely that the new laws were accompanied by equally important cultural changes affecting judicial officers, who may have awarded costs more frequently and more generously as the idea that the state should encourage prosecutions by reducing disincentives took hold. In addition, lower-class victims may have come to see the courts as more affordable and accessible.

The particularly marked increase in the presence of unskilled victims at the Old Bailey in the 1840s and 1850s (Figure 5.5) came at a time when the vast majority of prosecutions were at least part-funded by the government (Chapter 3), and it corresponds with a period when the use of counsel increased. Unfortunately, the number of victim-prosecutors with identified occupations in our Trial Participants dataset was too low to categorically state that unskilled victims benefited from counsel, but the coincidence is suggestive. With increased funding available, poorer victims may have felt able to hire counsel to support their prosecutions (or counsel may have

Figure 5.6: Ten-year Impact of Selected Statutes on Victim Prosecutions: Changes in Percentage of Victims by Social Class
Source: Proceedings Dataset

been assigned by the court). It also appears that lower-class victims were disproportionately supported by the police. During the nineteenth century, the presence of police in cases involving lower-class victims rose from 63.5 per cent between 1790 and 1829 to 96.3 per cent between 1900 and 1913. By contrast the proportion of the total number of cases involving the police gradually fell over the same period.

In summary, working people made up the majority of London's population throughout the period considered here, and were likely the primary victims of criminal offences. As summary jurisdiction expanded in the nineteenth century (Auerbach, 2021), these offences, if reported and pursued, were increasingly likely to have been prosecuted within the capital's magistrates' courts rather than referred up to the Old Bailey. Nonetheless, by the early twentieth century prosecutions initiated by or on behalf of lower-class victims accounted for 47.1 per cent of Old Bailey business. Poor complainants were not being excluded from the higher courts, though they remained underrepresented compared to their proportion of the overall population. Our *Proceedings* data suggests that this increase was linked to specific measures to reduce the personal financial costs involved and ad hoc measures to facilitate prosecution through the rise of counsel-assisted police prosecution. Our *Times* data, although much more limited, suggests that these factors continued in the twentieth century.

Unfortunately, we do not have sufficient evidence to measure lower-class victims' access to the Old Bailey in the twentieth century, when debates about enhancing public access to justice in the interwar period were focused on establishing legal aid for poorer defendants in criminal cases or for poorer parties in civil cases, particularly divorce (Chapter 3; Bradley, 2019). There was very little debate at that time around the ability of poorer complainants to be able to access the criminal justice system if they so chose, most likely because so many were clearly able to do this. In the period after the Second World War, new debates around complainants and class emerged around criminal injuries compensation. The effects of this measure on prosecution patterns are difficult to determine from our *Times* data but would repay further investigation. The rapid increase in the level of compensation paid in the 1960s and 1970s may, for example, have stimulated an uplift in reporting of relevant offences. Overall, the increase in poorer victims at the Old Bailey over our long time span resulted from a combination of specific statutory provisions, changing judicial practices, and wider cultural changes. As we shall see in the next section, something similar happened with female victims.

5.3 Gender

The Old Bailey, like other parts of the English criminal justice system, was a masculine arena. Until the early twentieth century, only men could serve as judges, magistrates, court clerks, policing agents, legal counsel, and jury members. In most cases, men meted out justice to other men. As outlined in Chapter 2, this changed to a degree during the twentieth century, with the appointment of female magistrates and police officers, crown court judges, and jury members (Logan, 2008). Women were, however, always active participants in the justice system historically—as victims, prosecutors, witnesses, and defendants. Their experience as defendants has been much studied but their experience in these other capacities much less so.

Female victims were, nonetheless, always outnumbered by men. From the 1670s through to the 1970s, adult men accounted for the majority of victim-prosecutors in Old Bailey trials. The *Proceedings* dataset (1674–1913) indicates that 79.9 per cent of victim-prosecutors were men while 14.4 per cent were women. In 5.7 per cent of cases the victim's gender was unidentified (noting that we excluded cases of deception and cases involving

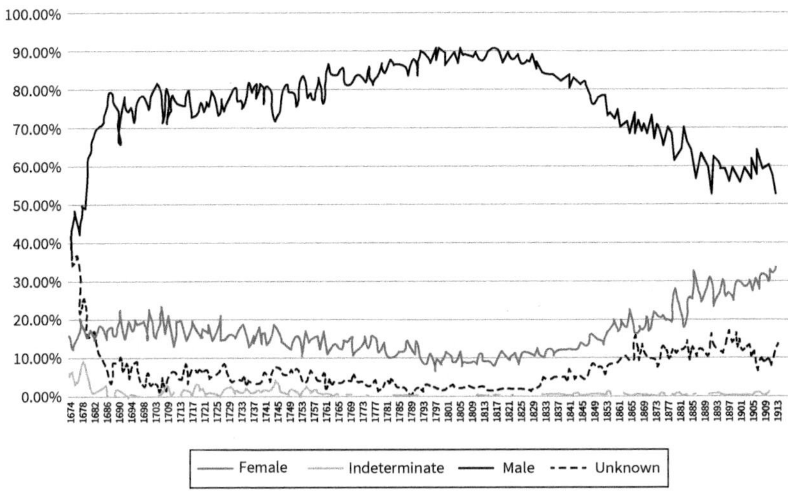

Figure 5.7: Victim Genders at the Old Bailey, 1674–1913 (1701, 1705–06 excluded for lack of evidence)
Source: Proceedings Dataset

institutional victims).[5] This changed significantly over time. As Figure 5.7 shows, the proportion of female victim-prosecutors in the Old Bailey declined between the early eighteenth century and the early nineteenth century, but then rose quite markedly. By the early twentieth century, women accounted for a third of all Old Bailey victims. Possible explanations for this greater prominence of female victims are explored below. This trend of increasing female participation appears to have stalled in the twentieth century, as women continued to account for about the same proportion of victims in *Times* reports in both of our sample periods: 32.9 per cent in 1910–25 and 31.3 per cent in 1960–75.

Figure 5.8 compares this pattern to the proportion of female defendants over the same period (significant fluctuations in the period up to 1715 reflect low case numbers). In total, female defendants were more common than female victims (21.0 per cent vs. 14.4 per cent), but the trends differ significantly. The long-term decline in the proportion and numbers of female defendants at the Old Bailey has been the subject of historical

[5] The 'unidentified' category includes cases where the trial reports did not include the name of a victim, where that name was not captured in the digitization tagging process, or the first name of that victim could not readily be connected to a specific gender.

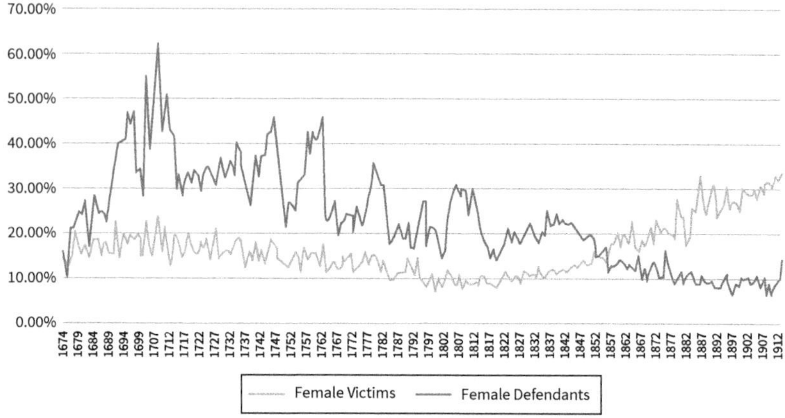

Figure 5.8: Female Victims Compared to Female Defendants in the *Proceedings* (1701, 1705–06 excluded for lack of evidence)
Source: Proceedings Dataset

controversy over whether it reflects a real decline in female crime or simply the transfer of cases involving women to lower courts (including summary jurisdiction) or non-judicial resolutions. Nonetheless, the decline is clear (Feeley and Little, 1991; King 2006). Whereas in the early years of the eighteenth century female defendants equalled or even outnumbered male defendants (a rare phenomenon in the history of crime), by the first decade of the twentieth, women accounted for fewer than 10 per cent of defendants.

Until around 1820, the proportions of female defendants and victims declined in broad parallel, although the decline was more substantial among defendants. It is likely that the explanations for both the peaks in the early eighteenth century and subsequent declines are similar. An influx of young, single women into the metropolis in search of work such as domestic service around the turn of the eighteenth century led to large numbers of women falling into hard times owing to low pay, job insecurity, and lack of family and parochial support. At the same time, growing concerns about prostitution, and the serious crime it was thought to be linked to, led the authorities and other prosecutors to clamp down on female deviance (Beattie, 2001, 63–71; Shoemaker, 2010, 75–6; Shore, 2009). Correspondingly, it is likely that it was the same independence of such women which led to the large number of prosecutions they initiated, as they were vulnerable to theft and attack, and often lacked access to informal means of resolving disputes.

The subsequent decline in the proportions of female victims to the 1810s, and of defendants to the end of the nineteenth century, may reflect changing expectations of women, as the rise of the ideology of domesticity may have encouraged them to resolve their disputes in the less public summary courts, or more private venues, but this cultural change is a subject which needs further research (see Davis 1984; Auerbach, 2021; Turner, 2019; for this argument with respect to female defendants, see Feeley and Little, 1991, 740–9; Davis, 1984, 1989).

When, from the early 1820s, female prosecutions began to rise while female defendants continued to decline, it was concerns about male, rather than female, criminality which stimulated prosecutions. Instead of prosecuting roughly equal proportions of male and female defendants, female prosecutors now overwhelmingly prosecuted men. During the period when the proportions of female victims and defendants were both high, from 1693 to 1762, the defendants in cases with female victims were almost equally male and female. But when female victims became more frequent in the late nineteenth century, they were much more likely to prosecute men. Between 1864 and 1913, 86.1 per cent of the defendants in cases with female victims were men, and this continued in the twentieth-century crime reports (79.9 per cent in 1910–25 and 91.6 per cent in 1960–75).

This was accompanied by a shift in the crimes where women were victims: whereas 81.0 per cent of prosecutions with female victims in 1693–1762 were for property offences, from 1864 to 1913 this proportion fell to 26.1 per cent, and there were more prosecutions for crimes often carried out by men on women, particularly those involving sexual injury (27.3 per cent of female prosecutions), harm to the person (18.8 per cent), and killing (11.8 per cent). Figure 5.9 demonstrates the growth of prosecutions of violence against women over the whole period, showing that prosecutions of acts involving sexual injury increased most dramatically. The considerable year-to-year fluctuations are the result of relatively low numbers of prosecutions, but the overall trend is clear.

While some statutes, particularly those concerning sexual offences against young women (discussed in the next section), facilitated some of the increase in cases involving female victims, these increases occurred over a long period starting in the 1840s, suggesting that broader forces were at play. The reasons for this increase merit further study but we suggest three possible factors. Firstly, it might reflect a growing sense of urban women's vulnerabilities and a sense of mission on the part of lawmakers and female activists to protect them, particularly from violence. Secondly, and closely

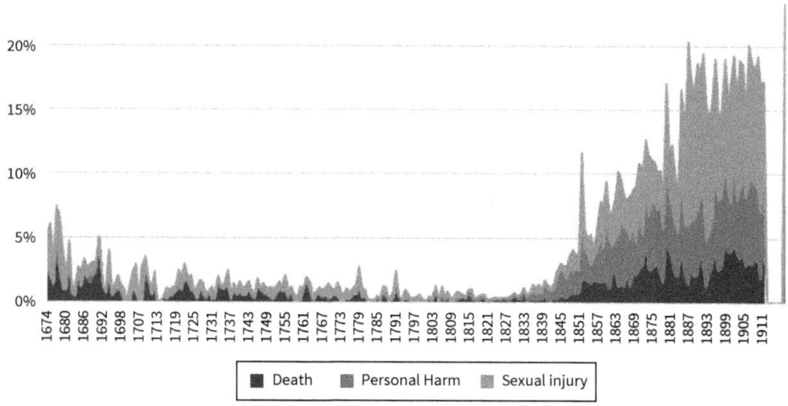

Figure 5.9: Female Victims of Violence, as Per Cent of All Known Victims, 1674–1912
Source: Proceedings Dataset

connected to the previous factor, it may reflect the mid-nineteenth-century activities of police, counsel, and voluntary organizations bringing cases on behalf of women and girls. Finally, it could be a reflection of the increasing assertion and recognition of women's capabilities in public life in Victorian England. To explore this in more detail, we examine the prosecution of violent, sexual, and property offences committed against them.

Female victims of violent, sexual, and property offences

As crime historians have shown, political and public attitudes towards violence shifted considerably from the mid-eighteenth century. A growing intolerance of male violence, particularly in urban settings, found expression in the condemnation of many male behaviours, from duelling to bare knuckle boxing (Weiner, 2004; Shoemaker, 2004; Wood, 2004). This shift was closely linked to the growing division between 'rough' and 'respectable' cultures, a division marked by the physical withdrawal of elites from previously mixed urban communities (Garrard, 1995; Huggins, 2015). The new police were introduced in part to act as 'domestic missionaries' to enforce these new standards of order (Storch, 1976). Drawing on the concept of the 'civilising process' (Elias, 1939), Liddle (1996) characterizes this as a long-running battle between 'brutish men' and 'bourgeois men', although Wiener (1998, 2004) reminds us that this was also a battle fought between elite men. This effort had long involved moral reformers, particularly those from evangelical Christian groups, but from the mid-nineteenth century onwards it also involved a broader range of women political activists demanding not just female suffrage but an end to prostitution, rape, and, in the parlance of the time, wife-beating (Gillis, 1985; Clark A., 1987, 1995; Tomes, 1978; Williams and Walklate, 2020). These activists mobilized new discourses of female victimization in the name of claims to female citizenship—an approach adopted and adapted by subsequent waves of feminist campaigners, as explored in Chapter 7.

These cultural changes underpinned legal changes which triggered increases in the prosecution of sexual offences, particularly those involving girls and young women. As outlined in Chapter 3, two statutes were key. The 1861 Offences Against the Person Act created a statutory, as opposed to a common law, basis for rape, and created a new felony offence of 'carnally knowing a girl under ten years old', and a misdemeanour offence of 'carnally knowing a girl between ten and twelve years old' (24 & 25 Vict. *c.* 100; Jackson, 2001, 13). The 1885 Criminal Law Amendment Act made the 'carnal knowledge of a girl up to the age of 13' a felony and increased the age of consent for sexual intercourse to 16, making carnal knowledge of a child over thirteen and under sixteen a misdemeanour. It also made it possible for children to provide evidence in court while not under oath (48 & 49 Vict. *c.*69; Jackson, 2001, 13). To a certain extent, these statutes codified offences concerning sexual assault which were already offences at common law. However, the extension of the offence of carnal knowledge with children (first introduced in 1576) to include girls up to the age of sixteen did expand the scope of prosecutions since, prior to 1861, there were few prosecutions for sexual offences against girls aged thirteen and over (Gillespie and Ost, 2016, 162). In any case, it is likely that the publicity associated with the campaigns against child prostitution and 'white slavery', and for the passage of these acts, contributed to the increase in prosecutions documented below (Walkowitz, 1982, 1992; Bibbings, 2018). Many such prosecutions were brought by the Associate Institute for the Protection of Women and Children and later by the NSPCC.

To measure the impact of these statutes, we compared the number of prosecutions for sexual injury during the ten years before the passage of each statute with the ten years after passage (Figure 5.10). This is, of course, a crude measure of impact since many factors can cause changes to levels

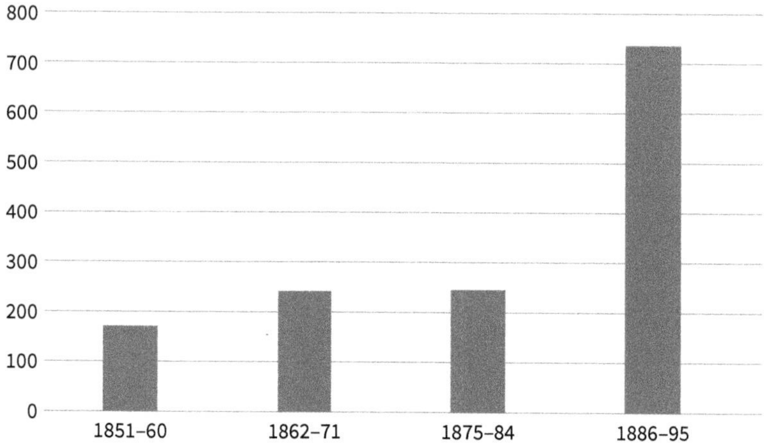

Figure 5.10: Acts involving Sexual Injury, Selected Periods, 1851–1895
Source: Proceedings Dataset

of prosecution. The figures are, however, dramatic. In the decade after the 1861 Act there was a 42.9 per cent increase in prosecutions, mostly for rape, while in the decade after the 1885 Act prosecutions more than tripled.

Some of these 'extra' prosecutions involved very young female victims. In general, as discussed below, victims' ages were infrequently reported in the *Proceedings*, but child victims were an exception. This was particularly true for statutory offences which were defined by the age of the victim but also because sexual offences against children were viewed as particularly egregious. Despite the judicial distrust of child victim testimonies described in Chapter 2, a significant number of child victims did appear at the Old Bailey, particularly in sexual offence cases, and the 1861 and 1885 Acts led to increases in the number of cases in which they were involved.

Figure 5.11 shows that the number of victims aged one to nine rose by over a quarter following the 1861 Act, which specifically created a felony of carnally knowing a girl under ten years old. Prosecutions for offences against girls aged ten to sixteen declined, but the number of prosecutions for sexual offences where the age was not reported increased by two-thirds. Following the 1885 Act, on the other hand, prosecutions increased for offences against all three age groups of girls, most significantly for age groups one to nine and thirteen to sixteen. In the case of the latter group, there had been no prosecutions reported in the ten years prior to the passage of the Act. One impact of the Act must have been to make the courts more

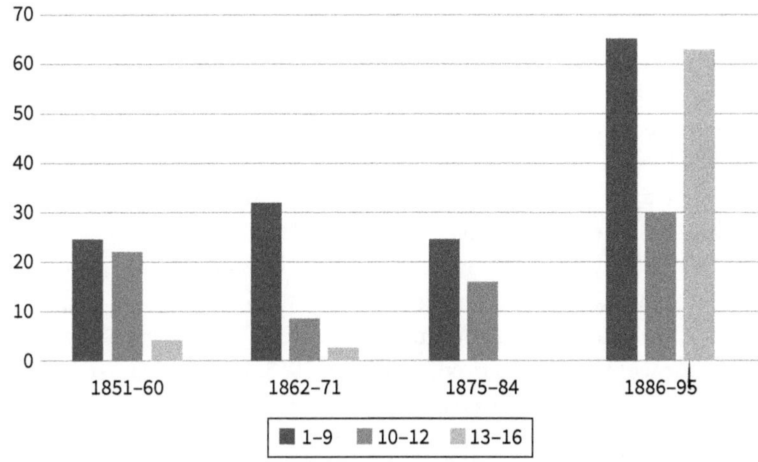

Figure 5.11: Number of Child Victims of Sexual Injury by Age, Selected Periods, 1851–1895
Source: Proceedings Dataset

likely to record such ages, so it is impossible to determine how many female victims between the ages of thirteen and sixteen had previously been before the courts. Overall, however, we can conclude that the expanded definitions of the crimes covered by the two Acts led to significant increases in prosecutions involving female victims in all age groups up to sixteen. But it is worth noting that the increase in prosecutions for female victims of violence, including sexual violence, predated these statutes (Figure 5.9). It seems likely that the same socio-cultural forces which led to increases in prosecutions in the 1840s and 1850s also led to the passage of the 1861 and 1885 statutes. These statutes also led to an increase in the number of adult (age seventeen and above) female complainants in cases of sexual injury. Assuming (as is likely) that females who were not given an age were adults, the annual number of such cases increased from an average of 11.7 per year between 1851 and 1860 to 58.7 between 1886 and 1895.

In addition to age, our Old Bailey data offers further illuminating insights into the social circumstances of the women and girls involved as victims in prosecutions for violent offences (sexual injury, killing, and personal harm). Applying HISCO class codes (discussed above), we see that most cases involved working-class victims. Although these crimes were no doubt distributed widely across the London population, the cases that reached the Old Bailey overwhelmingly involved working-class victims, with 77.2 per cent lower class, 19.8 per cent middle class, and only 3.0 per cent upper class; these proportions did not change significantly over time. The proportion of lower-class victims was highest for cases of sexual injury (86.5 per cent), no doubt reflecting a reluctance on the part of upper and middle-class victims to place their reputation at risk by testifying in court, given that 'a woman who brought a charge of sexual assault was making a public issue of her loss of virtue' (Conley, 1991, 95).

While, as discussed above, *The Times* was disinclined to report sexual crimes in the early twentieth century, there was a significant number of child sex cases at the Old Bailey in the 1960s and 1970s, mirroring national trends (Rowbotham, Stevenson, and Pegg, 2013, 197–200; Jackson, 2015). Prosecutions may have been encouraged by the 1908 Punishment of Incest Act (8 Edw. VII, c 45), 1956 Sexual Offences Act (4 & 5 Eliz II, c 69) and 1960 Indecency with Children Act, which expanded the range of offences which could be prosecuted (8 & 9 Eliz. II c 33). Sexual assault (predominantly rape) accounts for 17.5 per cent of female victims in *The Times* between 1960 and 1975. Male victims of sexual assault (the rape of men did not become a criminal offence until 1994) were rare, accounting for just 2.7 per cent of male victims in 1960–75. While underreporting of sexual assaults remained widespread during the twentieth century, trials for these offences did receive attention in *The Times* between 1960 and 1975.

Overall, the rise in the prosecution of sexual offences was a key element of the increase in the proportion of Old Bailey prosecutions involving female victims towards the end of the nineteenth century. Between 1900 and 1913, sexual injury accounted for 24.2 per cent of all cases involving female victims, and 45.8 per cent of all crimes against women involving violence. There was, however, also a modest increase in prosecutions involving female victims of property offences (including those with violence). Across the whole period 1674 to 1913, men were the victims of 86.2 per cent of property crimes prosecuted in the Old Bailey but Figure 5.12 shows that over the course of the nineteenth century this proportion decreased, while the proportions of female victims and unknowns gradually increased. Whereas women accounted for 8.2 per cent of such cases between 1800 and 1819, by the last two decades of the century they accounted for 11.3 per cent, rising to 14.1 per cent between 1900 and 1913. Even as the number of property cases tried at the Old Bailey halved in the late nineteenth century, owing to the increase in summary jurisdiction for non-violent property crimes (which, as we saw in Chapter 3, often involved female victims), women accounted for a higher proportion of the theft cases tried at the Old Bailey, many of which involved violence.

In part, the growth of female prosecutions for property cases was the result of the Married Women's Property Act of 1882, which allowed married women to own property in their own right (45 & 46 Vict. *c*.75). As documented in Chapter 2, this act contributed to a significant rise in prosecutions by women for property offences and fraud and deception. But Figure 5.12 demonstrates that the increase in female-led prosecutions for property offences was a long-term, gradual, but not entirely linear change, suggesting that there were more important socio-cultural reasons behind the increasing participation of female victims at England's highest criminal court.

A further key factor driving the increasing proportion of female victims at the Old Bailey may have been that women took more advantage of the increasing support available to complainants, including the increased availability of financial support. While it is impossible to measure whether women benefited more than men from the payment of prosecution costs, women, particularly those who were not married, were paid less than men and tended to be poorer, so it seems likely. Women certainly seemed to have benefited from the increasing support offered to victims by counsel (discussed in Chapters 3, 4, and 6). According to our Trial Participants dataset, female victims were more than twice as likely as male victims to have prosecution counsel in the nineteenth century (as reported in the *Proceedings*). In the first

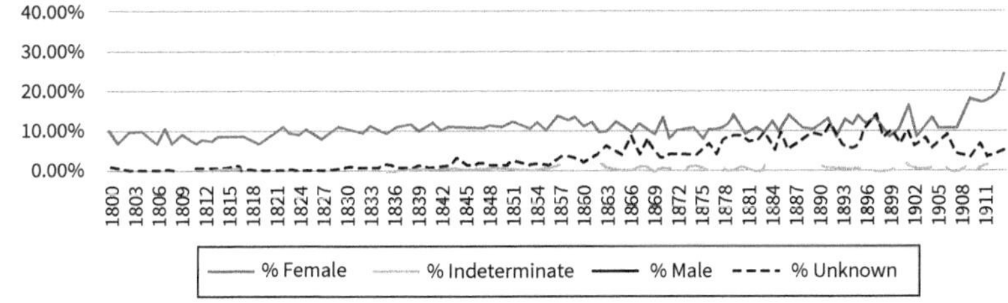

Figure 5.12: Victim Gender, 1800–1913, Property Offences (Including with Violence)

Source: Proceedings Dataset

half of the nineteenth century, 10.2 per cent of cases involving male victims had prosecution counsel, compared to 26.1 per cent of female victims. In the second half of the century, when prosecution counsel became almost universal, women were still more likely to have counsel (96.3 vs 92.0 per cent).

In part, this is related to the different mixture of prosecutions for each gender, as the offences disproportionately involving female victims (assault, bigamy, and coining) were among the offences most likely to have prosecution counsel present. But even if we confine the analysis to property offences, women were still more likely than men to have prosecution counsel present. Across the whole nineteenth century, 31.6 per cent of female victims and 18.2 per cent of male victims of these offences were represented by counsel. Given the possible hesitancy of female victims to prosecute, discussed in Chapter 2, we suggest the increased presence of prosecution counsel in their trials was a further reason why the proportion of female victims increased in the late nineteenth century. On the other hand, it appears that women did not benefit disproportionately from the growing role of the police in prosecutions (discussed in Chapter 4). Between 1850 and 1913, police were reported as present at 58.0 per cent of trials involving male victims, but only 43.4 per cent of those involving women. Nor, except with killing offences, did they benefit from significant involvement from the Director of Public Prosecution. There are only four DPP cases with female victims not involving killing offences in the *Proceedings* and nineteen in *The Times*. Half of these involved cases of fraud or deception; except with respect to technical legal issues such as the admissibility of evidence (not reported in these sources), the DPP was rarely involved in cases of sexual injury and personal harm short of death.

In summary, the increased presence of female victims at the Old Bailey likely resulted from the combined impacts of legislative reform that introduced new prosecutorial possibilities around sexual and property offences and new measures to reduce costs; the increased role of counsel in certain kinds of prosecutions; increased female participation in public life; and a new cultural focus on urban female vulnerabilities.

5.4 Age

Evidence on the ages of victims who appeared at the Old Bailey is extremely limited, but it suggests that while most victims were adults between the ages of twenty and fifty-nine, the number of both younger and older victims changed significantly over time. No consistent victim age evidence is available from the Old Bailey Online data before November 1834, and after that date only 0.7 per cent of victims were assigned an age in the trial reports in the *Proceedings* dataset. In *The Times*, 17.5 per cent of victims were assigned ages by the newspaper reporters. Overall, age only seems to have been regularly reported when it increased the severity of the offence, notably in the case of sexual assaults on children.

Nonetheless, the 728 victim ages reported in the *Proceedings* and 621 in *The Times* provide sufficient evidence from which to suggest that some important changes in the age composition of Old Bailey victim-prosecutors took place over time, particularly of those under twenty, who were primarily female and victims of sexual offences. Figure 5.13 traces patterns in reported ages across the period from 1835 to 1975, divided into four periods. As discussed earlier, the number of victims aged under thirteen increased as result of the 1861 and 1885 statutes which expanded the definitions of sexual offences against children, leading to a small but significant increase in the presence of young victims in court. Whereas those aged sixteen or below comprised 0.3 per cent of all victims (including those of unknown ages) between 1835 and 1860, this figure tripled to 1.0 per cent between 1890 and 1913. In particular, compared to the period between 1835 and 1860, the number of victims aged thirteen to sixteen increased dramatically following the 1885 Act. Since *The Times* largely failed to report sexual offences between 1910 and 1925, fewer young victims appeared in their reports. Between 1960 and 1975, however, there was a modest increase in young victims, particularly those aged between seventeen and nineteen, as well significant increases in the number of victims aged twenty to fifty-nine and above sixty.

To make sense of the increased number of young teenage victims in the nineteenth century, it is necessary to examine the distribution of offences. Figure 5.14 shows that those under 16 in the *Proceedings* were predominantly victims of sexual offences and other forms of personal harm, while the small number of victims who were identified as being twenty or above were victims of offences leading to or intending to cause death and property offences. There were many fewer victims of sexual offences under thirteen in *The Times*, and those aged thirteen to sixteen were the most frequent victims of sexual offences reported (Figure 5.15). These victims, as well as those aged seventeen to nineteen, also frequently appear in the related category of public order offences, particularly charges of procuring young girls

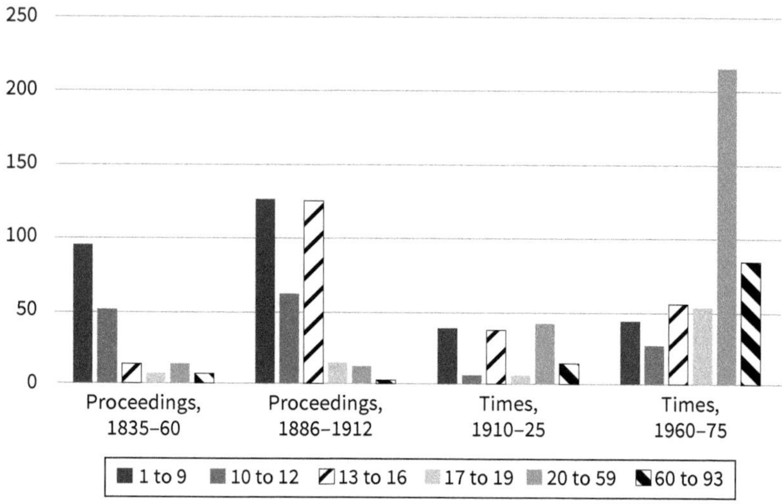

Figure 5.13: Victim Ages in Old Bailey Trials, 1835–1975 (Unknowns Excluded)
Source: Proceedings and *Times* Datasets

for prostitution, buggery, and the lesser offences of indecency and improper conduct: offences which occur relatively rarely in the *Proceedings*.

It may be that concerns about the reliability of young witnesses, discussed in Chapter 2, led to a decline in prosecutions of sexual offences against young children in the twentieth-century *Times* reports, and a change towards more easily provable offences, such as procuring, where the issue of consent did not arise. Despite legal efforts to protect child witnesses and the prosecutorial work of voluntary organizations such as the National Society for the Prevention of Cruelty to Children (NSPCC), children and young people's access to justice in the highest criminal courts arguably declined. As discussed in Chapter 2, statutes passed between 1885 and 1933 intending to encourage prosecutions of offences against children by allowing unsworn testimony to be admitted in court may have had the unintended consequence of making it more difficult to secure a conviction in such cases. This was because children's unsworn evidence was deemed unsafe without corroboration and the accused could not be convicted without such corroboration. It was only after 1988 that statutory provisions began to enable children under fourteen to testify unsworn, and without corroboration (Lamont and Cox, 2021).

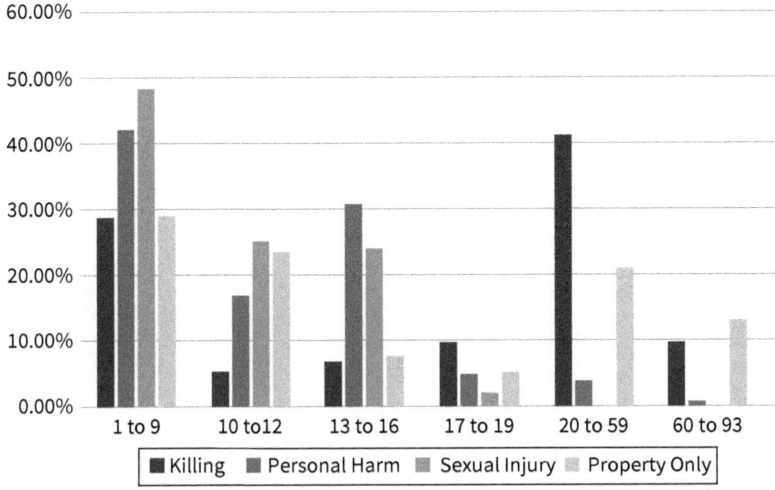

Figure 5.14: Age Groups of Victims at the Old Bailey by Offence Categories in the *Proceedings:* Per Cent of Offence Category in Each Age Group (Categories excluded owing to the low number of offences: property with violence, fraud and deception, and public order offences)
Source: Proceedings Dataset

Nineteenth-century thinking about age and vulnerability to crime was overwhelmingly focused on youth, with little attention paid to adults and the elderly. In contrast to the frequent reporting of juvenile ages in the *Proceedings* (as well as *The Times*), ages of victims above nineteen were rarely reported in the *Proceedings*, accounting for only 8.4 per cent of all recorded ages. The vast majority of victims whose ages were unknown, therefore, must have been adults. In contrast, in the period between 1960 and 1975 *The Times* more routinely reported adult ages. As Figure 5.13 attests, adults (twenty to fifty-nine) and the elderly (sixty and above) were the most common victims whose ages were reported. Adults whose ages were reported who appeared before the Old Bailey in the twentieth century were most frequently the victims of killing, personal harm, or property offences involving violence (Figure 5.15).

Historians have not previously considered the role of elderly victims (here defined broadly as those sixty and over), but the evidence presented here suggests that they represented a small but distinct minority of victims which became more visible in the court over time (Reiner, Livingstone, and Allen, 2003, 22). Whereas those sixty and over constitute only 2.3 per cent of

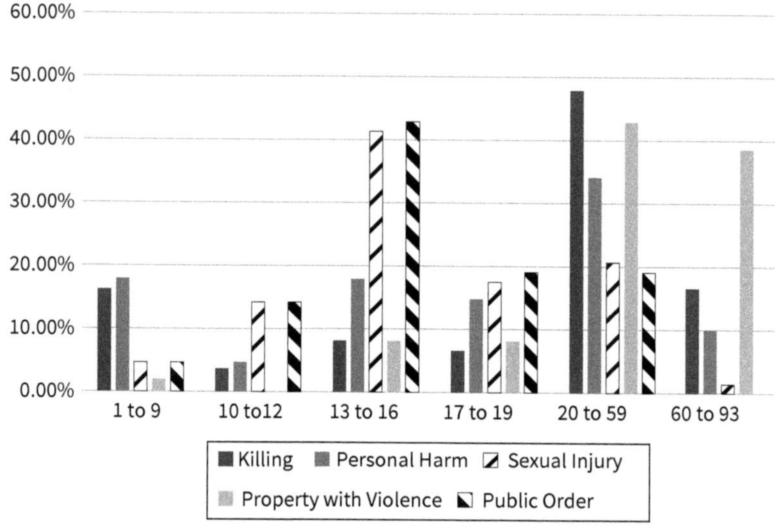

Figure 5.15: Age Groups by Offence Categories in *The Times*: Per Cent of Offence Category in Each Age Group
(Offence categories excluded owing the low numbers: property only, fraud and deception, and public safety)
Source: Times Dataset

the victims with identified ages in the *Proceedings* between 1835 and 1913, they account for 17.4 per cent of victims of cases reported in *The Times* between 1960 and 1975, cases which primarily concerned violent crimes or fraud. This may reflect not only greater interest in reporting adult ages and the changing composition of offences tried at the Old Bailey, but also some combination of greater press interest in reporting offences against the elderly and greater societal concern for their welfare, also evident in the formation of charities to support older people at the time, such as the 'Old People's Welfare Committee' during and after the second world war (Thane, 2000). The increase in reported offences against this age group, documented in Figure 5.13 in the period from 1960 to 1975 compared to the period from 1910 to 1925, may thus reflect *The Times*' response to greater public interest in elderly victims (see Shore and Williams, 2022). Some of these victims could be seen as a type of 'ideal' victim, characterized by criminologist Nils Christie (1986) as those deemed most deserving of public sympathy due to their innocence, frailty, or moral rectitude.

5.5 Ethnicity

Evidence of the ethnicity of victims at the Old Bailey is extremely limited, since it was only mentioned rarely by the court reporters, and this information has not been tagged in the *Proceedings* dataset. Perhaps reflecting growing perceptions of its importance, reports in *The Times* in the twentieth century contain more frequent references to ethnic minorities, and these are included in our dataset, but they still apply to only 0.9 per cent of all victims, increasing from 0.5 per cent in 1910 to 1925 to 1.5 per cent in 1960 to 1975. How regularly such information was reported, however, is impossible to say.

Despite the limited evidence, crime historians have become increasingly interested in the experience of ethnic groups in the courts, as they consider how both access to the courts and the treatment of defendants and victims was affected by ethnic identity. More attention has been paid to defendants but some work has also addressed victims. In particular, Adam Crymble and Emma Azid have studied the evidence of Black people in the *Proceedings*, while Crymble, Peter King, and John Carter Wood have looked at the (white) Irish. Through systematic keyword searches, Crymble and Azid identified 639 possible references to Black people in the *Proceedings* between 1720 and 1841, some of which have low degrees of confidence attached. Of these, 328 were defendants and 75 were victims (Crymble and Azid, 2021; see also King and Wood, 2015, 104). These represent tiny fractions of the 137,072 defendants and 123,027 victims recorded in those years (OBO), but Crymble and Azid established an important point, rarely recognized previously, that Black people could appear as victims as well as defendants in court in this period. Given the proportionally much larger presence of Black people in the overall population of London throughout the period, it is very likely that many Black people who appeared in the courtroom were not actually referred to as such (Chater 2011; Myers, 1996; Olusoga, 2021). For much of the eighteenth and nineteenth centuries, it is likely that race was not an aspect of identity that trial reporters thought worth noting consistently. It has been argued that, in eighteenth-century London, 'race was an object of peripheral vision rather than of central focus', although by the mid-nineteenth century emerging essentialist beliefs about racial difference had hardened into scientific racism (Wahrman, 2004, 87; King and Wood, 2015, 101–03). This was also probably true of ethnicity more generally. In a study of (white) Irish participants in Old Bailey trials between 1750 and 1825, King found that only 0.2 per cent of victims were Irish, basing his evidence on labels attached to victims by the court reporters (King, 2013, 395–7). Crymble has shown, however, based on surname analysis of Irish names from the 1841 census, that there were far more Irish participants in Old Bailey trials, though his focus was on defendants rather than victims (Crymble, 2015). The inconsistent use of perceived race and ethnicity as noteworthy categories of individual identity in the eighteenth and early nineteenth centuries, and the growing attention to these categories over the remainder of our period make systematic analysis of the race and ethnicity of Old Bailey victims over time impossible.

With caution, however, we can analyse the labelled ethnicity of Old Bailey victims recorded in *The Times* in the twentieth century, when these categories of difference appear to have been more consistently applied. Any relevant information has been identified and included in our dataset. This includes twenty-three Black victims (including those labelled as 'coloured' and those identified as being from the West Indies or sub-Saharan Africa),[6] 24 Asian victims (from China, India, and Pakistan), and six Jewish victims. No doubt reflecting increased post-war immigration, references to both Asian and Black people in the Old Bailey were higher in *Times* reports in our 1960–75 sample than in our 1910–25 sample. We address their experience in more detail in Chapter 7.

Minority ethnic victims prosecuted a somewhat different range of offences to other victims. They were more likely to appear in prosecutions involving violence, including killing offences and those involving personal harm, crimes which were perhaps linked to their identity. These two categories account for 72.3 per cent of Black and Asian victims in *The Times*, compared to 30.4 per cent of all other victims. Blacks and Asians were less likely to prosecute offences in the most frequent categories of crime tried at the Old Bailey: fraud and property offences not involving violence. The small number of victims identified as Jewish means that little can be gained by any breakdown by offence prosecuted by this group. While it is tempting to conclude that these patterns reflect the actual patterns of offences suffered by these communities, the limited number of cases and the unsystematic nature of the trial reporting means that other explanations cannot be ruled out. It is possible, for example,

[6] Some of the 'coloured' victims may have actually been South Asian.

that these labels were more likely to be used when referring to certain offences conforming to stereotypes, such as racially motivated assaults. In addition, these offences were, of course, the ones that such victims chose to report, and/or were supported by the police in taking them to trial, while other offences went unprosecuted or unreported.

While this analysis raises more questions than it can answer, perhaps the most important finding here is the simple fact that the visibility of non-white victims at the Old Bailey appears to have increased over time, and was at its highest between 1960 and 1975.

5.6 Institutions

Alongside the increased presence of victims from underprivileged groups at the Old Bailey was an increased number of institutional prosecutors. Up to this point the discussion has focused on individual victim-prosecutors and those representing them, but a significant and growing number of Old Bailey cases were brought by both public and private institutions. In their position as representatives of either official bodies or, often powerful, commercial organizations, these prosecutors behaved differently from private victims, as will become evident when we examine defendant pleas in the next chapter.

Only 2.8 per cent of all victim prosecutions recorded in the 240 years of the *Proceedings* involved institutions, but they were heavily concentrated towards the end of the period (Figure 5.16). In the late seventeenth and eighteenth centuries, a small number of prosecutions, primarily for coining, banknote forgery, and public order offences, were conducted by the Mint, the Bank of England, the Treasury Solicitor, and the Solicitor General (as discussed in Chapter 4). It was only in the second half of the nineteenth century that institutional prosecutions increased dramatically, reaching 16.9 per cent of all cases in the 1910s. The largest number of these cases were prosecuted by government bodies, particularly the Bank of England and Postmaster-General, but increasing numbers came from private companies such as the railways and the East India Company. We found over two thousand separate organizations which acted as prosecutors up to 1913. Unsurprisingly, the offences that institutional prosecutors were most concerned with involved property and fraud and deception, which accounted for 97.4 per cent of their prosecutions.

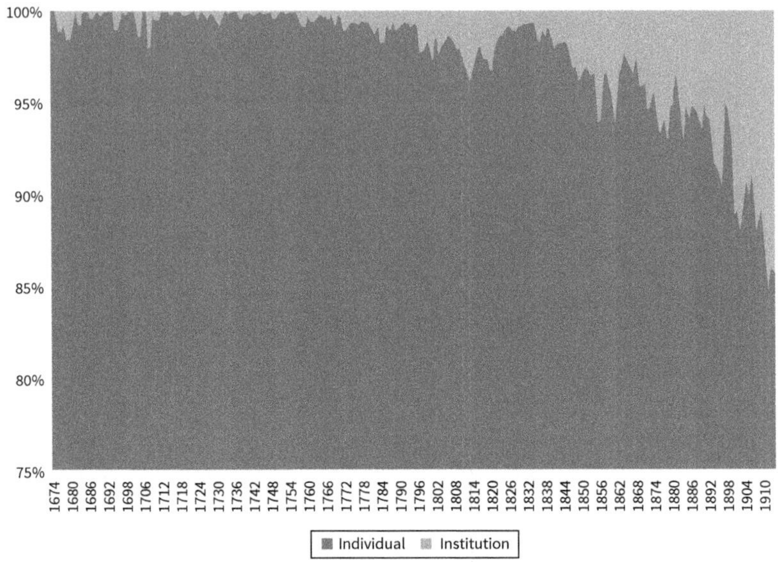

Figure 5.16: Individual vs Institutional Prosecutors in the Proceedings, 1674–1913
Source: Proceedings Dataset

There was an even greater proportion of institutional prosecutions reported in *The Times*. These accounted for 36.8 per cent of prosecution reports (with similar figures in each sample period). Since as noted earlier *The Times* was more prone to report fraud offences, this figure may be exaggerated, but it is clear that institutional prosecutors were a major presence at the Old Bailey in the twentieth century. The composition of this group further broadened, with a wide range of private companies and societies, including banks, hotels, and trade organizations prosecuting small numbers of cases, supplementing the continuing activities of major state institutions (which now included several state departments including war, pensions and the HMRC). Once again, fraud and property offences dominated.

Not only were institutional prosecutors more powerful than individual victims, they did not have a personal relationship with the defendants they prosecuted, unlike many individual victims. Consequently, their goals in terms of trial outcomes were likely to be different. These differences, in terms of pleas, verdicts, and sentences, will be discussed in the next chapter.

5.7 Conclusion

As we saw in Chapter 2, a victim's accusation needed to pass through a number of filters before it could reach the Old Bailey. These processes were designed to reject weak or unfounded allegations and divert less serious complaints into other methods of resolving disputes, both formal and informal. Over the course of the period under review, one of these filters—summary jurisdiction—expanded significantly, which helped cause a dramatic fall in Old Bailey cases from the mid nineteenth century. Despite this, the range of victims whose cases were referred there widened, as some of the key barriers to prosecution, namely cost and access to legal and police support, were reduced.

Our data shows that, as might be expected, white, middle- or upper-class, adult men continued to be the dominant group of victim-prosecutors at the Old Bailey into the twentieth century. However, it also shows that this dominance was substantially eroded by the growth in cases involving female and lower-class victims. In 1912–13, the last sixteen months of the *Proceedings*' publication, women made up a third of the complainants appearing in court. While prosecutions of sexual and violent offences increased the most, even property cases involving female victims increased relative to the number prosecuted by men. This major change was the result of a combination of changing statutory definitions of offences and increased victim support, as well as broader cultural changes affecting the social position of women.

Something similar took place with lower-class victims. By 1913, our evidence suggests that working-class complainants made up just under half of all those bringing prosecutions and, of these, unskilled workers accounted for a fifth. Again, this seems to have been the result of specific measures intended to reduce the costs involved in bringing prosecutions combined with the rise of state-funded, counsel-assisted police prosecution. Evidence for minority ethnic group participation at the Old Bailey is very limited, but the rise in the number of black and Asian victims in the 1960s and 1970s suggests that during the second half of the twentieth century the court became accessible to a more diverse range of victims (or, at least there was growing awareness of such victims by court reporters).

Evidence for changes in access to justice for younger victims and the elderly is also limited, and more complex. The one area where we can see clear expansion is for those aged between ten and sixteen, primarily girls who were victims of sexual offences, where the relative number of such victims increased in the late nineteenth and early twentieth centuries. Data from *The Times* indicates, however, that they fell back somewhat after World War II. There is some evidence that the number of elderly victims appearing at the Old Bailey increased in the post-war period. At the very least, towards the end of our period such victims were more likely to be identified as such, and their visibility in the courtroom increased.

The causes of these important changes are manifold, including changing patterns of actual offences and the demographics of victims, cultural changes, and official and ad hoc efforts to encourage the successful prosecution of crime. With the evidence in our datasets, we have only been able to consider the last of these, by evaluating the impact of these interventions. They include changes to the legal definitions of offences and efforts to support victims through the reimbursement of their costs and the increased presence of prosecution counsel. We have seen that statutes which clarified and expanded definitions of rape and sexual assault appear to have contributed to increases of young victims and women in court in the late nineteenth century, and those which provided for the payment of victim costs contributed to the increasing number of lower-class victims from earlier in the century. As we have seen, however, for the most part these statutes reinforced and accelerated trends that were already in process, which suggests that campaigns for reform and wider cultural changes played a significant role in stimulating increased prosecutions. With respect to the rise in the number of female victims, we should acknowledge the significance of nineteenth-century developments including the increasing condemnation of male violence against women and sexual violence against children as well as the growing acceptance of women in public life. There also appears to have been a recognition in elite circles of the importance of encouraging lower-class victims to prosecute. This recognition appears to have expanded in the second half of the twentieth century to include new groups of victims: the elderly and those from minority ethnic groups.

This chapter has examined trends in the bringing of cases to court. In the following chapter we turn to the practices and procedures of the court itself, looking in particular at the impact of legal counsel, plea bargaining and sentencing, and examining the success or otherwise of different groups of victims in prosecuting their cases. This will allow us to draw some conclusions about what effects the gradual sidelining of the victim in court had upon their overall access to justice.

6
Trials and Outcomes

This chapter examines what happened to prosecutions brought by or on behalf of victims to the Old Bailey. We saw in Chapter 5 that an increasingly diverse range of victims appeared before the court, but in order to understand the full extent of their access to justice we need to determine how their cases were tried, and the verdicts and sentences handed out to the accused. Changes in court practice in this period, notably the rise of legal counsel, the development of plea bargaining and changes in sentencing practices had the potential to marginalize victims. Their experiences of trial were shaped by the opportunities that they were given (or not given) to testify, and by the presence or absence of legal and policing agents who could support (but also potentially control) their prosecutions. Paradoxically, just as broader victim access to the courts was accompanied by the sidelining of their role in the prosecution process, changes in court practice led to improved trial outcomes for many at the expense of further marginalizing their role in court. In the same way that state action, motivated by a desire to increase prosecutions, was crucial to ensuring greater access to the courts, achieving better outcomes, driven by the perceived need for higher conviction rates, was dependent on control of the prosecution process by legal officers and the police; individual victims lacked the resources to effect such changes.

For most victims, we presume that the most important measure of their access to justice was the extent to which they achieved their presumed goal of convicting those who wronged them and were satisfied by the sentences that the guilty party received (though, as noted in Chapter 2, for some prosecutors merely taking a case to court put sufficient pressure on their defendants). For all cases that went to trial at the Old Bailey, we have virtually complete evidence of the ensuing verdicts and sentences, although we cannot know why those decisions were reached by jurors and judges, how victims perceived them, or if they were successfully appealed. We can, however, investigate whether sentences might be considered robust by

Victims and Criminal Justice. Pamela Cox, Robert Shoemaker, and Heather Shore,
Oxford University Press.
DOI: 10.1093/oso/9780192846488.003.0006

the standards of the day. Our research demonstrates that these outcomes changed significantly over time, and there were significant differences in trial outcomes by social group. A study of these patterns is an essential component of any understanding of victims' experiences at the Old Bailey.

The *Proceedings* contains detailed evidence of the conduct of trials although, as already noted, much of what was said in court was not reported. Victims' testimony was, however, the most likely to be included (Shoemaker, 2008b; Emsley, Hitchcock, and Shoemaker, 2018c). Analysing the 134 million words in the 197,745 trial accounts in the *Proceedings* demands quantitative analysis and sampling to identify significant patterns. In addition to our core *Proceedings* dataset, the following analysis relies on data extracted from the *Proceedings* in the Trial Participants and Old Bailey Corpus datasets (see the Appendix). Unfortunately, trial reports in *The Times* newspaper provide insufficient evidence to permit comparable analysis, but they do provide valuable evidence on verdicts and sentences. In any case, our research has identified the nineteenth century as the crucial period of change in victims' courtroom experiences.

6.1 The Impact of Counsel

The first important change to trial procedures was the introduction of counsel. The availability of counsel is now regarded as a key measure of access to justice, a necessary form of assistance in the complex environment of the courtroom. Hired initially at the behest of victims, counsel clearly had the potential to present the case for the prosecution more effectively than inexperienced victims, but they could also reframe the prosecution in different ways, and reduce victims' own opportunities for speaking in court.

Before the 1730s, as we saw in Chapter 3, counsel were very rarely present in Old Bailey trials since individual victims prosecuted their own cases. Over the next 150 years, however, counsel (for both defence and prosecution) gradually became more common. Measuring their participation is problematic, because there was no requirement for trial reporters to mention them, and a crucial deficiency of the *Proceedings* is that they rarely reported words spoken by counsel. However, their presence was normally noted. From the Trial Participants dataset we can see that there were more defence than prosecution counsel present in the first half of the nineteenth century, but that after 1850 the pattern flipped, and prosecution counsel became almost universal, while defence counsel was only reported as being present in about half of cases (Figure 6.1).

As explained in Chapters 3 and 4, there were two important causes of this remarkable shift. First, the passage of the Prisoners' Counsel Act of 1836 led to an increase in defence counsel in the 1840s, and this may have stimulated victims to employ their own lawyers. More importantly, the emergence of police prosecutions involving apparently publicly funded counsel from the 1850s greatly increased the presence of prosecution counsel. By the early twentieth century, counsel for the prosecution were present in the vast majority of Old Bailey trials, and this appears to have continued through the remainder of our period. While information about counsel was not systematically reported in *The Times*, in 94 per cent of cases where the presence or absence of counsel was reported, prosecution counsel was present. The dramatic increase in the proportion of victims who benefited from counsel over the course of the nineteenth century represents a major shift in victims' experiences of Old Bailey trials. As demonstrated below, the police witnesses who often appeared in cases with counsel (and in some other cases) also significantly affected the presentation of prosecution cases.

Despite the fact that the appointment of prosecution counsel in the eighteenth century was initially made by victims, once present in the courtroom, counsel, often working with the police in the nineteenth century, took over the presentation of the prosecution, effectively de-centring the

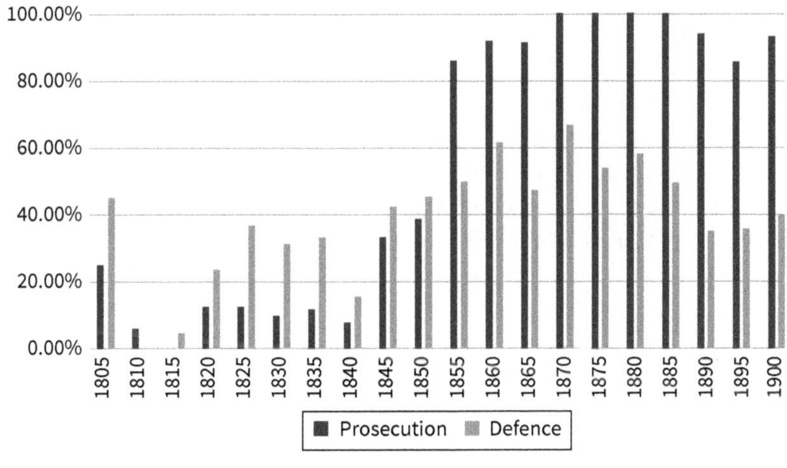

Figure 6.1: Prosecution and Defence Counsel in Old Bailey Trials, 1805–1900
Source: Trial Participants dataset

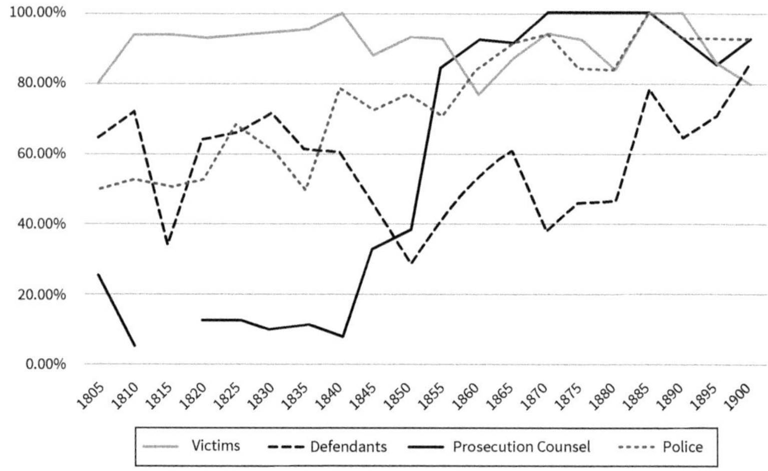

Figure 6.2: Participation in Old Bailey Trials, 1805–1900
Source: Trial Participants Dataset

victim. In his study of defence counsel at the Old Bailey, Langbein argued that their presence 'silenced' defendants, who no longer needed to speak in their own defence, and the principle of the defendant's right to remain silent developed (2003, 258–84). The impact on victims was somewhat different because they were still expected to testify, but the presence of counsel nonetheless contributed to a decline in their role in the courtroom. It was now counsel who opened the prosecution and conducted the cross-examination of witnesses.

The increasing roles played by the police and prosecution counsel in Old Bailey trials can be seen in Figure 6.2, which charts the proportion of trials where prosecution counsel was present against the proportions in which victims, defendants, and police witnesses testified.[1] While the proportion of trials involving testimony from the victim remained between 80 and 100 per cent throughout the nineteenth century, the participation of police and, particularly, prosecution counsel was low at the beginning but increased significantly from the late 1830s.

As a result, while victims continued to testify, many lost influence over how their cases were presented in court. We can demonstrate this

[1] Since the Trial Participants Dataset is made up of a relatively small sample of Old Bailey trials (see the Appendix), year-to-year fluctuations are to be expected.

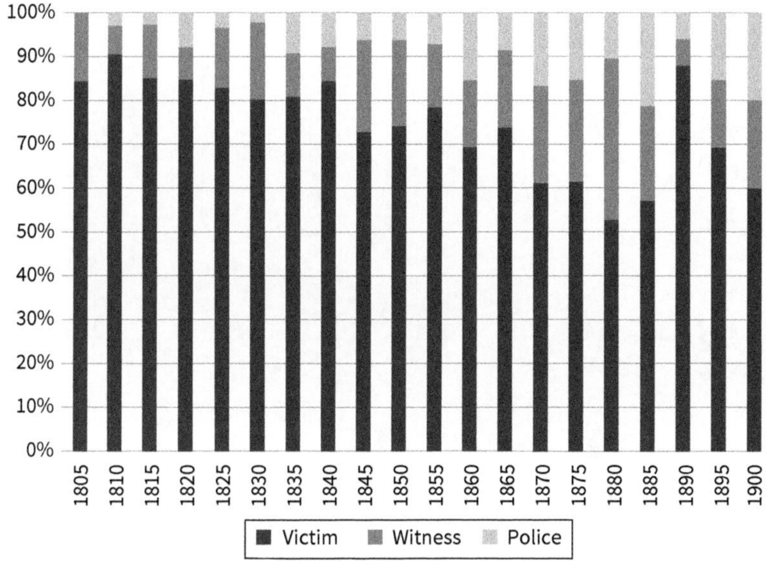

Figure 6.3: First Speakers in Trials, 1805–1900
Source: Trial Participants Dataset

by examining the trial accounts to determine the order in which witnesses testified and the length at which they spoke. Traditionally, victim-prosecutors were the first persons to testify at trials, after any opening statements by counsel (which were not reported in the *Proceedings*). In the early nineteenth century, victims spoke first in 84.5 per cent of trials, but this declined to 64.5 per cent by the end of the century (1880–1900; Figure 6.3). In some of these cases, the victim only spoke to testify to their ownership of the stolen property; it was the police who had detected the crime and recovered the property. The number of cases in which the police spoke first increased from 4.5 per cent to 13.9 per cent, and opening testimony by other witnesses rose from 10.7 per cent to 20.3 per cent (these statistics do not include counsel, whose statements, other than questions, were rarely reported in the *Proceedings*). By the end of the century, the police were one of the first two persons to speak in more than a third of all trials, and one of the first three persons to speak in over half (Trial Participants dataset). Victims were slowly being marginalized in the courtroom. While not entirely sidelined, in many cases their role was pushed to later in the trial proceedings.

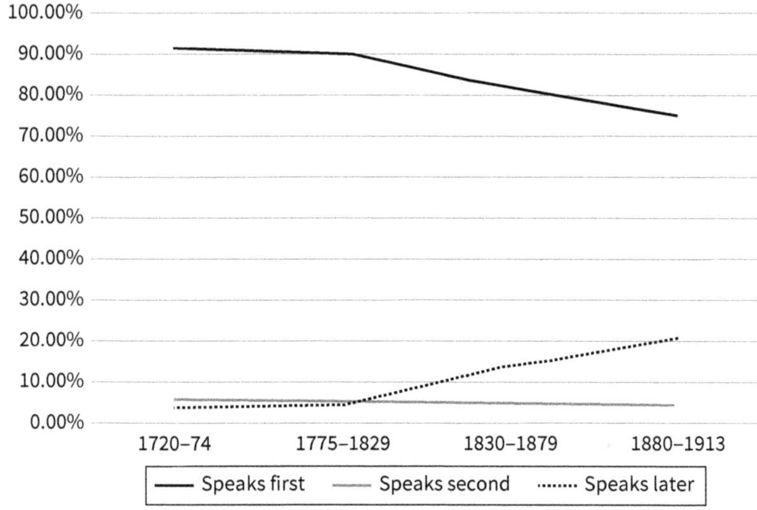

Figure 6.4: Proportion of Victims Speaking by Order of Appearance, 1720–1913
Source: Old Bailey Corpus Dataset (n = 18,161 trials)

Data extracted from the Old Bailey Corpus allows us to examine this phenomenon over a longer period, revealing that the change began around the turn of the nineteenth century (Figure 6.4). While throughout this period victims continued to speak first more often than other trial participants, the proportion of trials where they were the third speaker or later increased from 4.5 per cent between 1775 and 1829 to 20.5 per cent of trials from 1880 to 1913, as witnesses and the police more frequently provided the first or second testimonies in trials.

These changes led to an overall reduction in the amount that victims spoke in the courtroom (Figure 6.5). Data extracted from the Old Bailey Corpus of words spoken in court (a database derived from the *Proceedings* developed by linguistics scholars; Huber, Nissel, and Puga, 2016) shows that from a peak of just over a quarter (26.3 per cent) of the words spoken in trials in the 1820s, victims' speech fell to half that figure by the 1910s (13.5 per cent), as more words were spoken by defendants and other witnesses, including the police; the proportion of words spoken by judges also declined. By the early twentieth century, after almost two hundred years trailing far behind victims in the number of spoken words reported, defendants were speaking more in court than their accusers. It is important

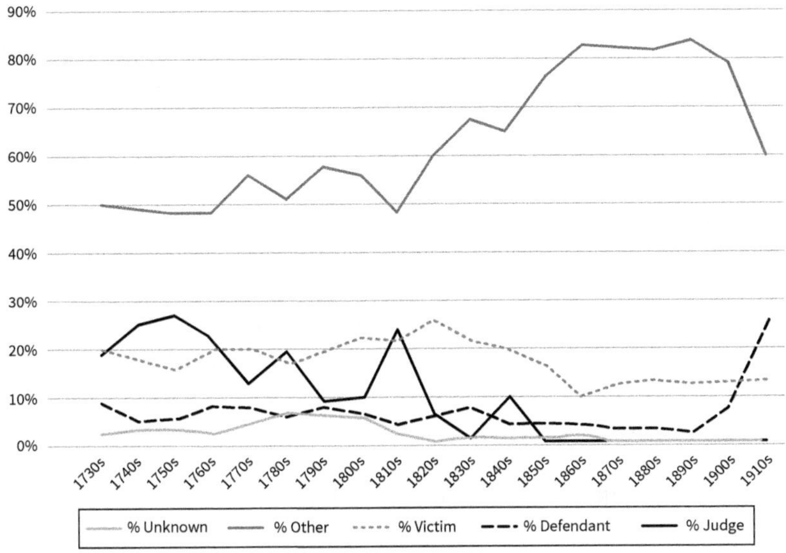

Figure 6.5: Proportions of Words Spoken by Trial Participants by Decade, 1730–1909
Source: Old Bailey Corpus Dataset (n = 585 sessions)

to note that this graph is based on the reports (not transcripts) of criminal trials in the *Proceedings*, and is affected by the limitations of that source.

Of course, these quantitative measures do not indicate how influential victims' speech was, but they strongly suggest that it was slowly being eclipsed by other trial participants. During the nineteenth century, although victims continued to be described as 'prosecutors', the labour of prosecution in the courtroom was actually carried out by a mixture of prosecution counsel, police witnesses, and victims, with the boundaries between their roles hard to detect. Over time, victims played a decreasing role and the police and prosecution counsel became the primary actors. Although victims still had the right to represent themselves and not engage counsel, few did.

Class and gender

These overall patterns varied by victims' class and gender, compounding existing inequalities. Victim-prosecutors from lower social classes generally spoke less than those from the middle and upper classes.

Figure 6.6 shows that, with the exception of the 1775–1829 period, upper-class victims were consistently recorded as speaking more than victims from other social classes. As the length of the overall reports was consistently higher from 1855, these differences between social classes increased (Hitchcock and Turkel, 2016, 938).

On average across the whole of our research period, female and male victims spoke the same number of words (132) per trial (OBC). However, perhaps as a result of women's higher use of prosecution counsel (discussed in Chapter 5), female victims were less likely than male victims to testify at all. At Old Bailey trials in the nineteenth century, 94.5 per cent of male victims gave testimony, whereas only 84.9 per cent of female victims did so. Moreover they tended to speak later in trials, as can be seen in the declining percentage of female victims speaking first, from 91.0 per cent in 1775–1829 to 73.5 per cent in 1880–1913 (OBC). This seems to reflect continuing misogynistic attitudes towards female participation in public life, despite the increasing proportion of female victims at the Old Bailey. An essay in the *Pall Mall Gazette* in 1865 advocated 'keeping ladies out of the law' and female witnesses out of the courtroom, complaining about the 'peculiar tortuousness and intricacy about female cases, arising either from a hopeless confusion of facts, or from an absence of facts altogether' (7 February 1865,

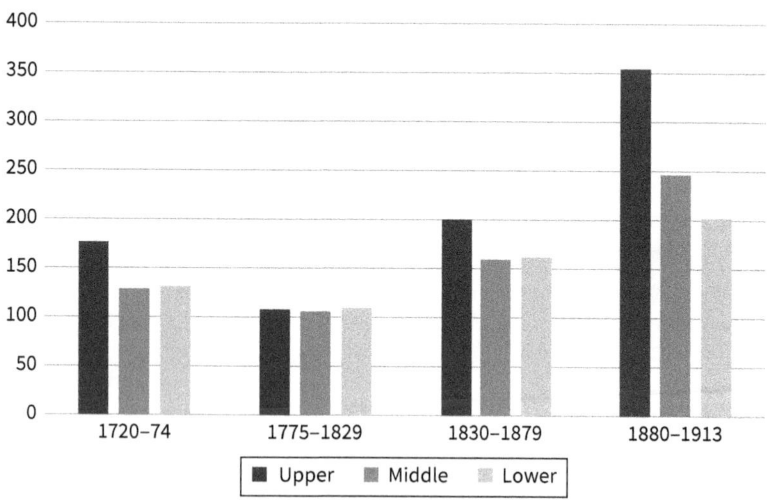

Figure 6.6: Mean Count of Words Spoken by Victim Social Class, 1720–1913
Source: Old Bailey Corpus Dataset

7). Similarly, Henry Waddy, a London stipendiary magistrate, confessed in 1925 that he had 'an unfavourable opinion of female witnesses … as a class I find them more malicious, more untruthful, and much more clever [devious] than men' (Waddy, 1925, 61). Such attitudes may have led prosecution counsel to play a greater role in cases involving female victims. Female victims certainly spoke in court, even at somewhat greater length than men in the last years of the *Proceedings* (averaging 233 words per trial vs 225 for male victims between 1880 and 1913), but they did so in fewer trials and at a later point in the trial.

In sum, compared to other Old Bailey trial participants, the role of victims in the courtroom declined over time, most likely as a result of the increasing roles played by the police and counsel in organizing prosecutions. Paradoxically, despite their increasing access to the courts, female and lower-class victims were most affected by these changes. These findings merit further research into the actual language of courtroom testimonies. Linguistic analysis of the patterns of speech of victims and their interlocutors over time could shed further light on changing victim roles and experiences of the courtroom. This type of analysis, however, is beyond the scope of this book.

6.2 Defendants' Pleas

Counsel also likely facilitated a further major change in victims' experiences of the Old Bailey: the increasing proportion of defendants who pleaded guilty in the nineteenth century. This important change meant victims, who may or may not have been party to any 'plea bargaining' which led to such outcomes, would not have to testify and the accused would almost certainly be punished, but these outcomes eliminated victims' role in court and they may not have suited all victims.

Once a grand jury had approved the charges (before grand juries were abolished in 1933), defendants were required to enter a plea at the start of their trial. During the era when capital punishment was a real possibility for a wide range of offences (until the 1830s), defendants were positively discouraged from pleading guilty (regardless of any willingness to confess) because the judges wanted a trial to take place, since it would allow them to determine the severity of the crime and any mitigating circumstances, and thus determine whether the charge merited the death penalty or whether they should subsequently recommend the convict for a pardon. This was even the case in prosecutions where the defendant's guilt was not in doubt (Beattie, 1986, 446–7). Following the reform of the 'Bloody Code', however, guilty pleas became much more common.

Figure 6.7 charts this important change. The relatively high number of guilty pleas recorded in the period up to 1715 is likely an anomaly, probably the result of the very brief trial reports of the time, which failed to distinguish initial guilty pleas from trials during which the defendant confessed the crime. The existence of the 'mixed' category, a combination of one or more guilty and not guilty pleas, results from our counting all data in this chapter by the victim. Some victims prosecuted more than one defendant for the same crime, each of whom could enter different pleas and have different verdicts and sentences.

From the 1830s the number of guilty pleas increased rapidly, particularly between 1832 and 1854, at the time when prosecution counsel began to play a greater role. By the early twentieth century, they accounted for almost half of all defendant pleas (45.2 per cent between 1900 and 1913). Guilty pleas were less likely to be reported in *The Times* (where they account for just 19.0 per cent of pleas), probably because there were no trial proceedings to report.

The significant nineteenth-century increase in guilty pleas, following the curtailing of capital punishment and the growth of prosecution counsel, was likely due to the introduction of various forms of plea bargaining (Langbein, 1978). While plea bargaining was not a formally accepted

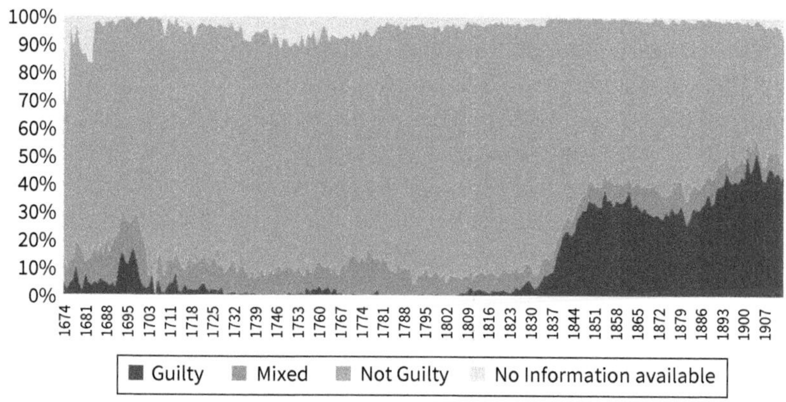

Figure 6.7: Defendant Pleas in the *Proceedings*, 1674–1913
Source: Proceedings dataset

judicial practice at the time and we are not aware of any explicit legal or policy change which encouraged it, it was clearly happening in practice. Facilitated by 'the lawyerization of the [judicial] process', agreements were reached that if defendants pleaded guilty, possibly to a reduced charge, they would receive a lesser sentence than if they were convicted following a full trial (Feeley, 1997, 219; Hitchcock and Turkel, 2016). Experience indicated that defendants had good reason to expect a lower sentence if they pleaded guilty: those convicted of simple larceny, for example, were more likely to be sentenced to imprisonment if they pleaded guilty (79.8 per cent vs 60.0 per cent for those pleading not guilty) and less likely to be transported (15.1 per cent vs 32.8 per cent). It is difficult to find direct evidence of such private settlements, although as early as 1833 Thomas Wontner, then governor of Newgate Prison, claimed there were cases where defendants knew their sentence before they even entered the court (Wontner, 1833, 56, 103). Unfortunately, it is not possible to ascertain how frequently Old Bailey pleas were negotiated by counsel, as the trial reports in these cases do not provide any evidence on the participation of counsel.

Institutional victims, such as the Postmaster-General and dock and railway companies, appear to have led the way in the use of plea bargaining, since guilty pleas in their prosecutions were more common, and occurred earlier, than cases involving individual victims. Overall, in the period when plea bargains were frequent (from 1831 to the end of the *Proceedings* in 1913), defendants pleaded guilty in 46.6 per cent of institutional prosecutions, compared to only 27.6 per cent of the cases with individual victims. It is likely that solicitors and barristers acting on behalf of institutions were particularly active in encouraging such outcomes, perhaps seeking to reduce costs and the publicity of a public trial.

The advantages of plea bargaining for the courts, defendants, and victims were clear in terms of the reduction of costs by avoiding a trial. On the other hand, victims achieved less retribution against those who had harmed them and they were denied their 'day in court': their opportunity to publicly present their narrative of the crime and the suffering it may have caused. By the early twentieth century, they experienced a trial in little more than half the cases scheduled to be heard at the Old Bailey. Whether victims considered this an advantage because they did not have to spend time in court, or they felt aggrieved by losing their opportunity to speak and seeing a lesser sentence meted to the defendant cannot be known.

There do not appear to be significant differences in plea bargaining between cases with male and female victims. However, upper-class, young, and elderly victims were considerably more likely to have their defendants plead guilty. Focusing on records from the period when guilty pleas became common (1831–1913), defendants in cases with upper-class victims pleaded guilty in 5.0 per cent of cases, but only in 1.7 per cent of cases with lower-class victims. The equivalent figures for cases reported in *The Times* are 12.0 and 6.6 per cent. Like institutions, it is likely that high-status victims had more sustained access to the legal expertise which could facilitate satisfactory plea bargains.

For probably different reasons, there were proportionally more plea bargains in cases involving young victims, 12.4 per cent of pleas, than in cases with victims aged between 20 and 59, just 2.3 per cent. The equivalent figure for young victims in *The Times* is 25.8, compared to 20.7 of adults aged twenty to fifty-nine. There is sufficient evidence in *The Times* to provide a separate figure for the elderly, who were particularly prone to plea bargains, at 31.6 per cent. In the case of the young and old, the courts or their legal representatives may have wished to keep potentially vulnerable and possibly unreliable victims (in terms of their testimony) from having to appear in court.

The advent of plea bargaining thus had a significant but mixed and uncertain effect on victims. Those who had access to counsel probably had the best chances of securing this outcome, but whether it was seen as favourable or not is impossible to determine.

6.3 Verdicts

Whether victims achieved justice in the courtroom depended most obviously, from their point of view, on whether the accused was convicted (unless all they wanted was to compel the defendant to appear in court). Despite the waning influence of victims in the courtroom, guilty verdicts predominated, but the likelihood of such a verdict depended on the nature of the offence and the identity of the victim, thereby potentially influencing whether victims chose to report crimes and prosecute them in the first place, as well as considerations about whether to seek or accept a plea bargain. We can also assess whether assistance from the police or the Director of Public Prosecutions enhanced the chance of a guilty verdict.[2]

[2] Unfortunately, the evidence in our datasets does not permit us to assess the impact of prosecution counsel. This is because the *Proceedings* dataset does not distinguish between prosecution and defence counsel, and the Trial Participants dataset does not include verdicts.

Jurors chose, in essence, between three possible verdicts: guilty, part guilty (guilty of a lesser offence), or not guilty, although there were various permutations of these and also the possibility of special verdicts, where no verdict was given or the verdict was deferred, pending consultation with senior judges over legal issues. Jurors who wished to reduce the punishment received by defendants often issued partial verdicts by convicting them of a lesser offence, but there was not a partial verdict available for every offence. For these and other reasons, patterns of verdicts differed according to offence and the personal characteristics of the victim. The first part of the following analysis includes defendants who pleaded both guilty and not guilty, as the key point of investigation is the overall result of the prosecution for victims. Overall, most prosecutions in the *Proceedings* dataset resulted in guilty verdicts: 62.3 per cent full guilty, 9.3 per cent part guilty, and 5.8 per cent mixed verdicts (in trials with multiple defendants). Only 17.3 per cent of verdicts were not guilty, and 5.3 per cent were classified as miscellaneous, special, or unknown.

Figure 6.8 charts the changing pattern of these verdicts in the *Proceedings*. Despite the growth of summary jurisdiction (which removed many larceny cases in which the defendant chose to plead guilty), victims' chances of obtaining a guilty verdict, either full or partial, increased over

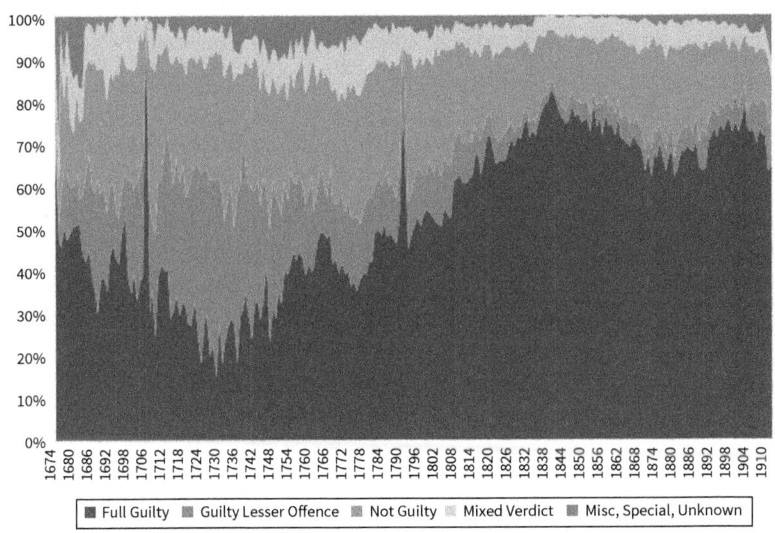

Figure 6.8: Verdicts in the *Proceedings*
Source: Proceedings Dataset

time. Whereas around 60 per cent of their cases resulted in convictions up to 1800, this rose to around 80 per cent in the 1830s, before declining somewhat in the late nineteenth century and then returning to the 80 per cent level at the end of the period. The growth in guilty verdicts is likely due to the increased pre-trial vetting conducted by police, magistrates, and the grand jury (see Chapter 2). Correspondingly, acquittals declined in the nineteenth century.

Of the guilty verdicts, convictions on a lesser offence were particularly common at the start of the period, reaching 40 per cent of all verdicts in the 1720s, but from the 1730s they started to decline rapidly towards a nadir of only a few per cent in the mid-nineteenth century, followed by a modest recovery to around 10 per cent of verdicts in the early twentieth century. This late increase in partial verdicts occurred in cases of wounding, where it is likely that juries undermined attempts to punish this offence more severely (Handler, 2007). Guilty verdicts resulting from guilty pleas increased to over half of all convictions by the end of the period. Overall, by the early twentieth century the prospect of a full conviction in Old Bailey cases, whether or not the case went to trial, had increased markedly, perhaps serving as an incentive for victims to prosecute.

A key factor shaping the pattern of part-guilty verdicts was the availability and actual use of the death penalty, and for this reason in the eighteenth century victims may have been satisfied with such verdicts. As discussed in Chapter 2, both prosecutors and jurors were often reluctant to see defendants hanged. Consequently, some victims refused to prosecute on capital charges or charged the culprit with a non-capital offence, and when capital cases went to trial, some even asked the court to exercise mercy. For the same reason, jurors often convicted on a lesser charge (King, 2000, 240–2, 315–16; Shoemaker, 2022). These behaviours started to decline in the eighteenth century, particularly after 1790, as execution rates fell significantly and prosecutors and jurors could become more sanguine about the possibility of a convict escaping the noose (Shoemaker, 2022). By 1840, when the capital code had been significantly restricted to a narrow range of offences, this process was complete. Consequently, full guilty verdicts peaked at this time and partial verdicts were largely restricted to murder cases. Similarly, in the twentieth-century *Times* reports, verdicts of guilty of a lesser offence account for only 2.4 per cent of verdicts.

The pattern of verdicts in the twentieth century fluctuated. For unknown reasons, the overall proportion of guilty verdicts in *The Times* reports from 1910 to 1925 was lower (64.0 per cent) than in the later nineteenth century,

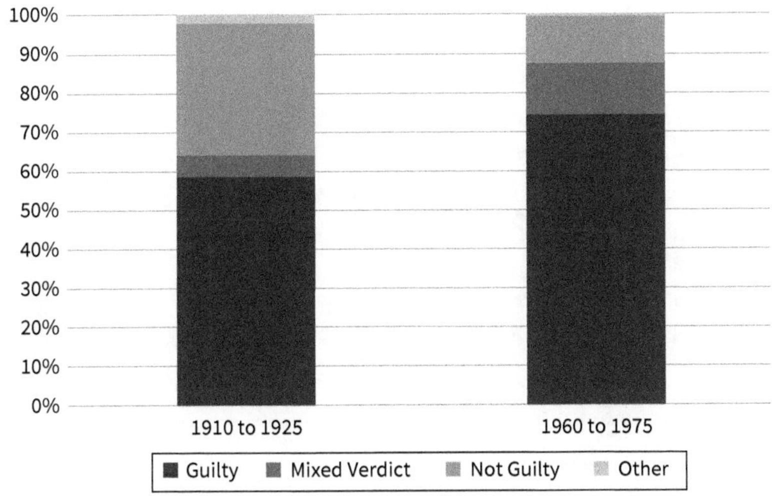

Figure 6.9: Verdicts in *The Times* (Excludes Unknown Verdicts)
Source: Times Dataset

but it was considerably higher between 1960 and 1975 (87.0 per cent; Figure 6.9). It is likely that the latter figure reflects wider concerns about the threat posed by crime resulting from the dramatic post-war increase, in which national commitments for crimes heard at the quarter sessions and assizes courts almost doubled from 17,497 in 1946 to 34,324 in 1960, and doubled again to 67,975 in 1976 (Parliamentary Papers dataset; Bottoms and Stevenson, 2016, 2; Emsley, 2013b). Those victims whose cases went to court in the 1960s and 1970s had a strong chance of a guilty verdict, and thus, if they were aware of this, a greater incentive to report the crime.

Verdicts varied considerably based on the offence charged, the nature of the potential sentence, and contemporary perceptions of the severity of the offence. Figure 6.10 shows that acts against property only, fraud and deception, and personal harm, were most likely to result in convictions. Conversely, those charged with serious crimes involving violence, which at the start of period could lead to the death penalty, were least likely to involve guilty verdicts. These offences include killing, sexual injury, and property with violence (though the high rate of mixed verdicts in this category increases the conviction rate). In murder cases, it is likely that the certainty of a death sentence following a full conviction was in jurors' minds, which

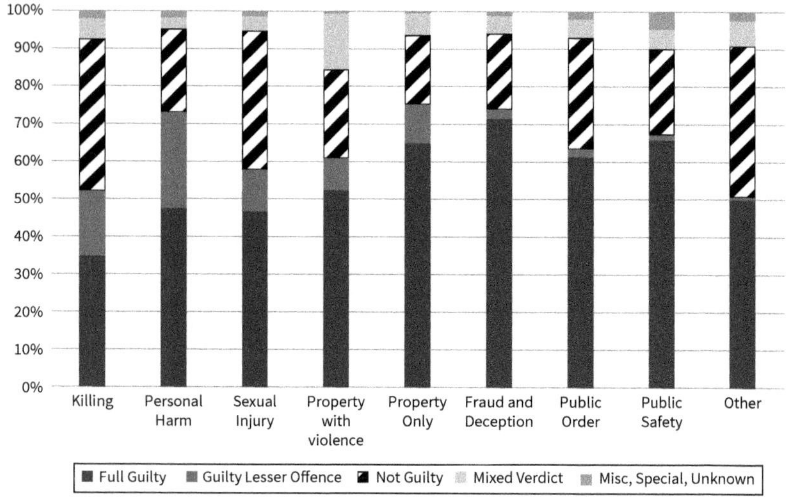

Figure 6.10: Verdicts by Offence Category in the *Proceedings*
Source: Proceedings Dataset

also explains the relatively high level of convictions for a lesser offence (manslaughter).

With respect to sexual injury, the particularly high acquittal rate (and also the relatively high rate of partial verdicts) must have served as a further disincentive to report offences and prosecute, as discussed in Chapter 2 (see also Jackson, 2000, 3). The highest level of partial verdicts was for offences involving harm to the person, particularly wounding, which was frequently prosecuted from the 1830s through to the end of the period. Despite Victorian concerns about violence, juror perceptions of mitigating circumstances such as provocation and drunkenness meant that such charges were frequently reduced to the misdemeanour charges of unlawful wounding or assault (Handler, 2007, 196–202). Full guilty verdicts were most common for fraud and deception offences (where the opportunity for conviction on a reduced charge rarely arose) and offences against property only, for which the absence of aggravating circumstances meant that the possibility of a death sentence rarely arose. Once again, the prospect of the likely punishment influenced the patterns of verdicts determined by juries.

Reflecting changes in the penal system, this pattern is much less evident in the twentieth-century *Times* reports (Figure 6.11), where conviction rates appear to more consistently reflect considerations of the severity of the

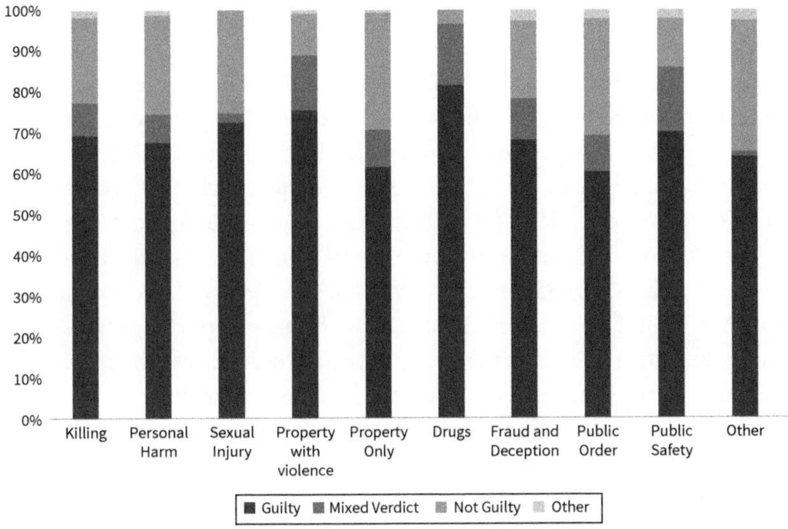

Figure 6.11: Verdicts by Offence Category in *The Times* (Unknown verdicts excluded, n = 4,912)
Source: Times Dataset

offence (as perceived by the courts). The highest conviction rate (including mixed verdicts), 97.7 per cent, was for drugs offences (primarily prosecuted in the 1970s), followed by property with violence (86.5 per cent), and acts against public safety (including sedition, treason, and possession of unlawful weapons or explosives, 86.1 per cent). Other offences with above average conviction rates include fraud and deception (76.3 per cent) and killing (74.9). In contrast, acts with the highest acquittal rates were, once again, sexual injury (33.3 per cent), property only (32.0 per cent), and public order offences (30.7 per cent, primarily indecency and conspiring to pervert the course of justice). These high acquittal cases had the potential to dissuade victims from reporting crimes and cooperating with prosecutors, a phenomenon frequently reported in studies of the prosecution of sexual assault (Brown and Walklate, 2011).

Significantly, the chance of a guilty verdict was substantially increased if the police were involved. When the police were mentioned as participating in trials in reports in the *Proceedings* (this evidence could not be obtained from the *Times* reports), 65.6 per cent of prosecutions resulted in a full guilty verdict, compared to only 43.0 per cent in cases where there was no reported police presence. Apparently, the police made compelling witnesses, which helps explain the prominence they were given when they testified. The presence of the police helps explain the higher conviction rates in the *Proceedings* for fraud and deception, property offences, and acts against public safety and security. On the other hand, the presence of the police made much less difference in cases of sexual injury, where 48.6 per cent of verdicts were full guilty, compared to 39.3 per cent when the police were not present. Even before the twentieth century, the actions of the police were only marginally likely to have inspired victims of sexual offences to seek their assistance in court. With this exception, victims had a strong incentive to include the police in their prosecutions (when they had a choice), as the chances of a guilty verdict were much higher.

Other official prosecutors could also make a difference: when William Webster and William John Webster (discussed in Chapter 4) were involved in coining cases as Inspectors of the Mint, the conviction rate was 83.1 per cent (OBO). Having the Bank of England involved in a prosecution, on the other hand (2,701 cases), made little difference to the conviction rate (67.4 per cent vs 65.0 per cent when they were not involved), probably because the offence they were most concerned with, forgery, was capital during the period when most of these prosecutions took place. Prosecutions involving the Director of Public Prosecutions (as reported in *The Times*), on the other hand, resulted in fewer guilty verdicts than when they were not present (54.9 vs 73.2 per cent), perhaps because these were, by design, some of the most difficult cases. Overall, institutional prosecutors (both state and private) were more likely to achieve guilty verdicts than individuals (75.9 per cent vs 61.9 per cent in the *Proceedings*, 60.4 per cent vs 57.5 per cent in *The Times*), in part because institutions obtained more guilty pleas than individual victims and probably because they were more likely to have assistance from counsel. As with individual victims whose prosecutions involved the police, institutional prosecutors were incentivized to prosecute by the higher chance of securing a guilty verdict.

Verdicts by class, gender, ethnicity, and age

An examination of verdicts according to the personal characteristics of victims suggests that jurors' decisions were occasionally influenced by prejudices for or against particular types of victims. The following analysis excludes cases where the defendant pleaded guilty so as to focus on decisions made by trial juries. While we cannot take into account the strength of the evidence in individual cases, and thus the likely actual guilt or innocence of victims, the results suggest subjective factors did sometimes influence jury decision-making. Excluding cases of sexual injury (where, as we have already seen, conviction rates were lower), the gender of the victim does not appear to have influenced verdicts reported in the *Proceedings*. In cases reported by *The Times*, however, women achieved a higher conviction rate (64.6 per cent vs 56.6 per cent for men).

With respect to social class, middle-class victims had a marginally higher conviction rate in the *Proceedings*, while upper-class victims were most likely to obtain convictions in twentieth-century cases reported by *The Times* (65.8 per cent guilty, compared to 56.8 per cent for middle and lower-class victims). Whether this is statistical fluke based on the relatively small number of upper-class victims (114) and large number of unidentified occupations in *The Times* reports, the selection policy of the paper in terms of which crimes to report, or actual class prejudice in which upper-class testimony was more trusted, is impossible to determine. But this evidence raises the possibility that in the twentieth century female and higher-status victims made the most convincing victims at the Old Bailey.

Except in the case of Irish victims, verdicts do not appear to have been shaped by the ethnic identity of the victim. A study of Irish prosecutors at the Old Bailey between 1750 and 1825 found that Irish prosecutors 'laboured under considerable disadvantages', owing to negative stereotypes. Only 50 per cent of 129 cases with Irish victims resulted in convictions, compared to 65 per cent of all victims (King, 2013, 397). Unfortunately, it has not been possible to identify a sufficiently large number of Irish prosecutors in *The Times* to draw any comparable conclusions for the twentieth century. In contrast, a study of Black prosecutors at the Old Bailey between 1725 and 1825 found that, despite concerns about the reliability of testimony by non-Christians (many Black people in this study were of other faiths, so rendering the required oath meaningless in the eye of the court), Black people's testimony was 'generally accepted' and prosecutors were 'relatively successful', achieving a higher conviction rate, 74 per cent, compared to 67 per cent of all prosecutors in those years (King and Wood, 2015, 108–10). In the eighteenth century, as noted in the previous chapter, ethnicity was a less important category of difference than it became in the following centuries. Unfortunately, we cannot measure the success of Black (or Asian) prosecutors in the twentieth century owing to the low number of *Times* cases with sufficient evidence. Overall, with the exception of eighteenth-century Irish victims, our evidence suggests that, in judging the veracity of prosecutors, jurors did not make judgements based on ethnic stereotypes (though of course minority ethnic prosecutors may have found it more difficult to prosecute cases in the first place).

Victims' ages had a more significant impact on verdicts, with young victims in different age groups achieving distinctive outcomes (Figure 6.12). Despite doubts over the reliability of child testimony (discussed in Chapter 2), particularly in the large number of offences concerning sexual injury (the most frequently tried offence in these age groups), children twelve and under had slightly higher percentages of convictions than the overall average in the *Proceedings*. In the twentieth-century *Times*, perhaps as a result of reforms to the treatment of child witnesses and the support of voluntary organizations such as the NSPCC, such victims had significantly higher than average chances of conviction (although, as noted in the previous chapter, the number of such prosecutions declined). A further contrast is with victims aged thirteen to sixteen, who had the lowest chances of conviction in both datasets, particularly in contrast to those aged both ten to twelve and seventeen to nineteen. As evident in Figures 5.14 and 5.15 (Chapter 5), those aged thirteen to sixteen were frequently the female complainants in sexual offences (other than rape). In such cases, the conviction

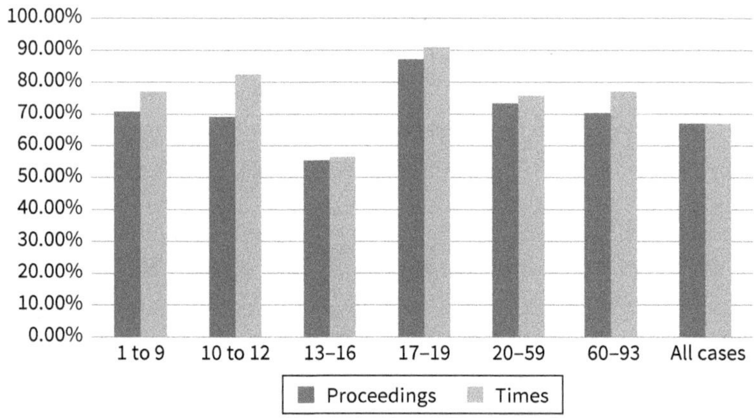

Figure 6.12: Proportion of Guilty Verdicts (including for lesser offences and mixed verdicts) by Age Group in the *Proceedings* (n = 629) and *The Times* (n = 371)
(Guilty pleas and unknown verdicts excluded)
Source: Proceedings and *Times* Datasets

rate for this age group was only 53.6 per cent in the *Proceedings* and 53.0 per cent in *The Times*, much lower than other age groups under twenty and the overall conviction rate of 67.0 per cent. Despite the fact the 1885 Criminal Law Amendment Act raised the age of consent to sixteen, it is possible that some jurors continued to believe that those between thirteen and sixteen were old enough to be complicit in sexual activity (indeed, the age of consent had only been raised to thirteen in 1875 under the Offences Against the Person Act [38 & 39 Vict. *c.* 94]; Jackson, 2001, 13). These relatively poor outcomes must have discouraged prosecutions involving victims in this age group. In contrast, those aged seventeen to nineteen, for whom virtually the only sexual offence prosecuted was rape, achieved higher levels of convictions.

Since most adult ages were not provided, it is difficult to draw specific conclusions about the twenty to fifty-nine age group, though the totals for all prosecutions (the last bars in the graph, including unknowns) are more reflective of this group than the small number of victims given ages in this range. Attitudes towards the elderly (sixty and above) appear to have changed over time, with such victims achieving a higher conviction rate in the twentieth century, perhaps reflecting greater trust in their testimony or concern for their welfare. This complements the higher proportion of victims in this age group reported in 1960–75, discussed in Chapter 5. While we should bear in mind the limited number of cases for which we have sufficient evidence, it seems clear that victim age had a significant effect on courtroom verdicts.

Victims whose decisions about reporting and prosecuting crime were influenced by likelihood of a guilty verdict encountered mixed results at the Old Bailey. The high proportion of guilty verdicts achieved overall may have encouraged prosecutions, particularly as this proportion increased over time, and with the increase in guilty pleas by defendants. As we have seen, some victims, particularly upper class, female, and elderly victims in the twentieth century, were most likely to be successful. The higher number of guilty verdicts achieved in cases which had support from police and official and institutional prosecutors may have encouraged their participation in prosecutions. For those cases which went to trial, most of the evidence suggests that verdicts did not vary substantially according to victim gender, class, ethnicity, and age, but there are some significant exceptions to this conclusion, particularly with respect to eighteenth-century Irish prosecutors and nineteenth- and twentieth-century young teenage victims of sexual assault, where wider cultural prejudices may have influenced juror decision-making. For these victims, the significantly lower conviction rates may have dissuaded some, or those who acted on their behalf, from bringing forward a prosecution.

6.4 Punishment Sentences

For trials resulting in convictions, it seems self-evident that victims had an interest in the resulting punishments. But beyond the fact that many victims were reluctant to see those they prosecuted hanged, we have little evidence about what victims wanted. Most victims probably desired a substantial punishment for their antagonists, as confirmation of the legitimacy of their complaint, a form of retribution, and perhaps as a means of excluding the offender from their lives. In this respect, transportation overseas in the eighteenth and nineteenth centuries could be seen as the 'ideal' punishment, while imprisonment for a long period was, in effect, another form of exile (Shore, 1999, 110–15; Shore, 2002; Watkins, 2020). Others, however, favoured mercy, hoping to see the offender reintegrated quickly into the community. Despite the potential variability of victim attitudes, it is useful to ascertain the punishments which resulted from prosecutions, and to consider whether victims had any influence over those outcomes. Once again, there are important variations according to the victims' personal characteristics.

Since our data comes from reports of criminal trials, we can only consider the sentences meted out in court, and it is important to recognize that the actual punishments convicts received may have been more lenient. A significant and increasing proportion of convicts sentenced to death were pardoned, and between a quarter and a third of convicts sentenced to be transported to Australia never left England. Even those sentenced to a period of imprisonment, by far the most common punishment in the last century of our study, often had their sentences cut short or the conditions of imprisonment mitigated (Shoemaker, 2020, 2022; Shaw, 1977, 150). Consequently, victims could only know for certain the original sentences given to their defendants, not what would actually be imposed.

The landscape of punishment sentences changed dramatically from the late seventeenth century to the early twentieth century (Figure 6.13). While death was the dominant sentence in the early years, after 1718 transportation to America was most common, with death sentences continuing at a lower level. As a result of the suspension of transportation during the

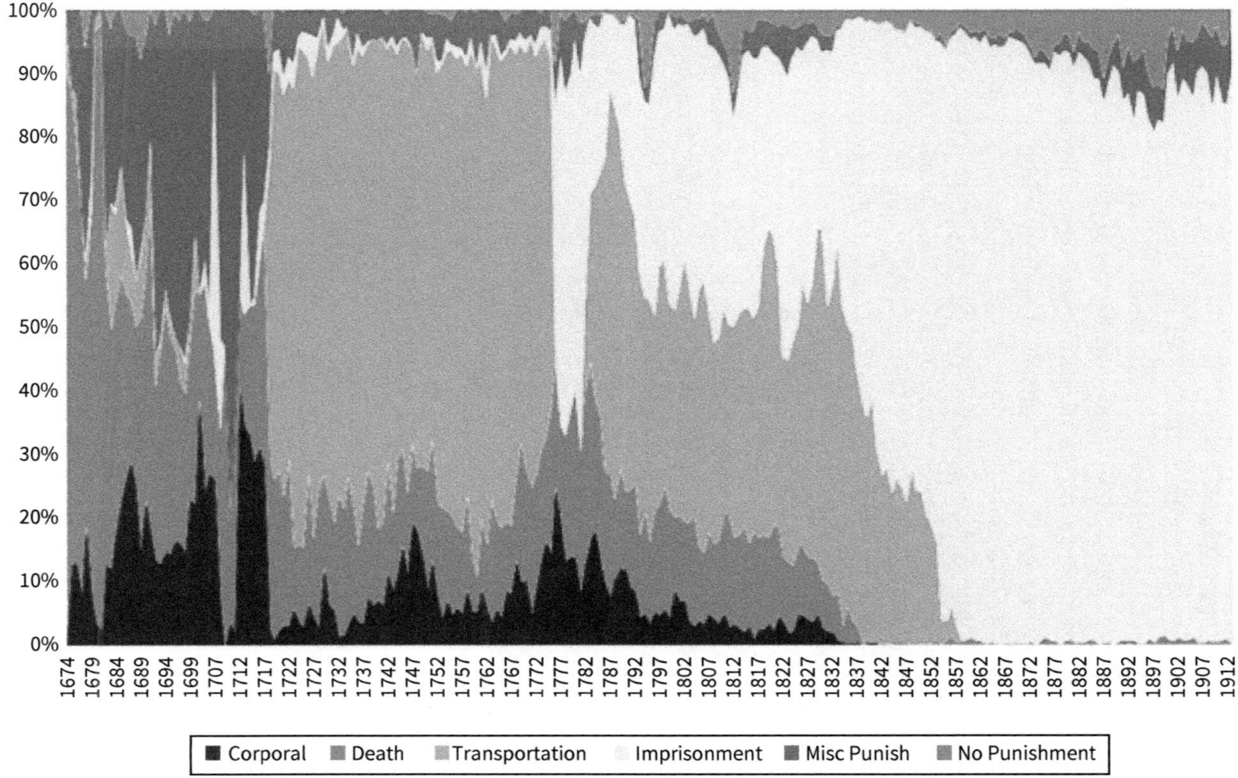

Figure 6.13: Punishment Sentences in the *Proceedings*
(1701, 1705–06 excluded for lack of evidence)

Source: Proceedings Dataset

American War of 1776–83, imprisonment rose for a decade until Australia was opened for transported convicts in 1786. Transportation then resumed its place as a major punishment, though it was increasingly supplemented by imprisonment. Following the curtailing of the 'Bloody Code' in the 1820s and 1830s and the abolition of transportation as a sentence in 1853 (and its replacement by penal servitude, which often involved transportation) followed by its abolition as a punishment in 1868, imprisonment dominated in the second half of the nineteenth century. From the 1870s, however, fines and a requirement to find sureties for good behaviour (in the 'miscellaneous punishment' category) began to replace imprisonment in a small proportion of cases. The twentieth century saw less dramatic changes, as imprisonment continued to dominate (Figure 6.14). Nonetheless death sentences disappeared after 1965, court orders declined, and two types of non-custodial punishments grew in importance: financial and community penalties.

Punishments were determined by statute for most offences, so judges had limited flexibility when it came to choosing sentences. To examine whether this flexibility could have been shaped by the personal characteristics of the victim, it is necessary to focus on specific offence types rather

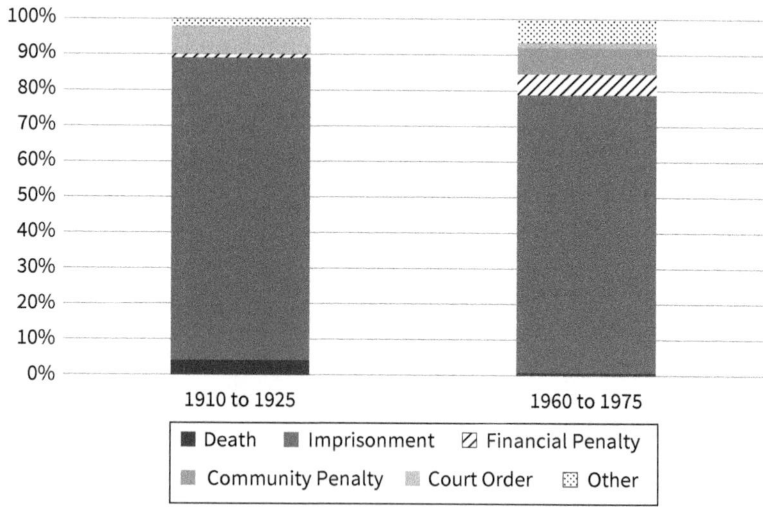

Figure 6.14: Punishment Sentences in *The Times*
(Unknown cases excluded; n = 3127)
Source: Times Dataset

than general offence categories in order to reduce (though it is impossible to eliminate) the possibility that differences in sentencing were due to differences in the nature of the offence tried. The following analysis examines six specific crimes which constitute some of the most serious and/or frequently prosecuted specific offences at the Old Bailey over the period of our study: murder, wounding, rape (female victims only), robbery, pickpocketing, and fraud. To reduce the possible influence of lesser verdicts (where the defendant would receive a different sentence), only cases where the defendant was found fully guilty of the offence are included. In the following analysis we rank the severity of the punishment, from highest to lowest, as: death, transportation, imprisonment, other (corporal, financial, court order, community penalty), and consider whether certain types of victims could expect those who were convicted on their behalf to receive harsher sentences than others.

Just as jurors were more likely to convict when the police were involved in trials reported in the *Proceedings*, judges were more likely to impose harsher sentences. The following analysis is restricted to the period from 1840 to 1913, when the police were most frequently present in trials, and following the reform of the 'Bloody Code'. Whereas 31.4 per cent of those convicted of murder in trials when the police were present were sentenced to death, that figure falls to 4.4 per cent when there was no police presence. Where the death penalty was no longer available and transportation was the most serious punishment, it was used more often than imprisonment when the police were present at the trial. Focusing on the period from 1840 to end of transportation in 1868, this was true of wounding (16.7 per cent when police were present vs 9.1 per cent when they were not), robbery (23.4 vs 13.8 per cent), and pickpocketing (30.6 vs 17.3 per cent). For fraud, an offence for which transportation was rarely used, defendants were more likely to be imprisoned when the police were present (88.0 vs 79.2 per cent in the period between 1840 and 1913). While police presence did not invariably lead to a harsher sentence, judges were certainly more likely to choose the most serious punishment available.

This type of analysis cannot be performed for the period covered by reports in *The Times*, but these reports show that judges awarded more serious punishments in offences with institutional victims.[3] We have seen that

[3] It was not possible to ascertain the impact of having the Director of Public Prosecutions involved in a case, since for the relevant offences (primarily murder, fraud, forgery and counterfeiting, and acts against the judicial system), there were not enough other cases where the DPP was not present to establish a valid comparison.

the evidence from the *Proceedings* shows that juries were more favourable towards institutional victims. Evidence from *The Times* suggests institutional prosecutions were more likely to result in prison sentences for those convicted for property-only offences (82.8 per cent vs 72.0 per cent for individual victims), and fraud (88.0 per cent vs 79.2 per cent). It may be that frauds prosecuted by institutional victims were more substantial, but we cannot determine this. For other offences, significant differences between the two types of prosecutors were not detectable.

Sentencing class, gender, ethnicity, and age

This pattern of the judges meting out more serious punishments in prosecutions involving the powerful (the police and institutions) can also occasionally be seen with respect to individual victims. Defendants prosecuted by upper-class victims were more likely to receive harsher punishments (death and transportation) for three offences—wounding, robbery, and pickpocketing—than defendants of victims from lower social groups. Figure 6.15 provides evidence from the *Proceedings*; there was insufficient

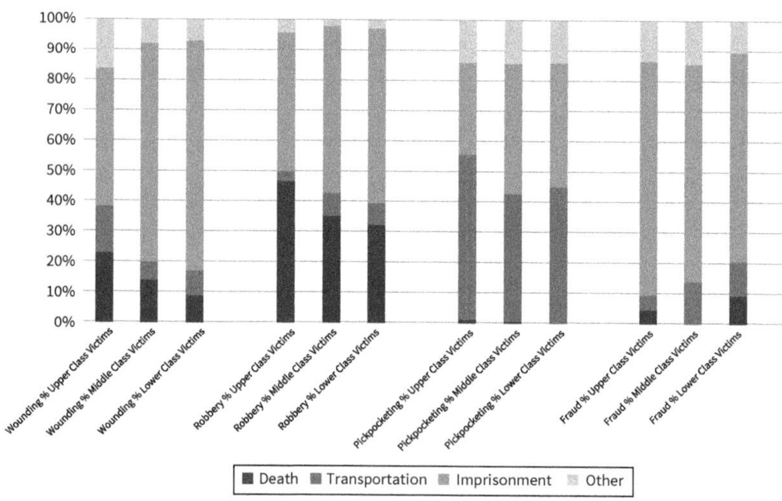

Figure 6.15: Class Differences by Victim in Sentencing for Selected Crimes in the *Proceedings*
(n = 584 wounding, 1,322 robbery, 17,295 pickpocketing, 817 fraud)
Source: Proceedings Dataset

evidence to conduct this analysis on *The Times* reports. For most categories of crime, lower-class victims were most likely to obtain the least harsh punishment, imprisonment (excluding the small number of cases with 'other' sentences). Middle-class victim-prosecutors obtained stronger punishments than poorer victims, but weaker ones than richer victims. This suggests that cases involving upper-class victims were seen as more serious offences by the judges, meriting harsher punishments. The one exception is in cases of fraud, where, for unknown reasons, lower-class victims were more likely to see their defendants sentenced to death or transportation than their social bettors.

On the other hand, judges were more sympathetic towards what was perceived as the weaker sex. Figure 6.16 focuses on sentences by victim gender for four specific crimes, though for two (robbery and pickpocketing) there were insufficient cases in *The Times* to permit analysis. In one crime, fraud,

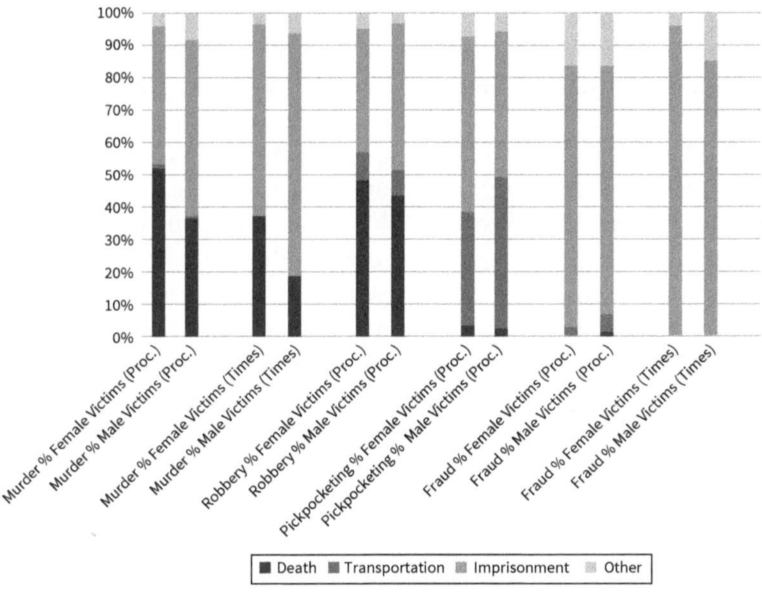

Figure 6.16: Gender Differences by Victim in Sentencing for Selected Crimes, 1674–1979
(n in *Proceedings* = 1565 murder, 5052 robbery, 10362 pickpocketing, 4391 fraud)
(n in *Times* = 227 murder, 95 fraud, unknown sentences excluded)
Source: Proceedings and *Times* Datasets

there were no significant differences in the *Proceedings*. In general, cases involving female victims in the *Proceedings* were more likely to result in a death sentence rather than imprisonment, particularly in the case of murder (also in *The Times*) and robbery, albeit to a smaller extent. These differences probably reflect the perceived seriousness of the offences, with women seen as weaker and more vulnerable victims, and male on male violence seen as more acceptable (Handler, 2007, 200). The same might apply to female victims of fraud reported in *The Times*, where cases were likely to result in imprisonment, as opposed to a court order, fine, or community penalty. By contrast, in other property cases not involving violence such as pickpocketing, it was defendants facing male victims who received the more serious punishment, perhaps because transportation was deemed a more suitable offence for the young men frequently convicted of this offence (see Shore, 1999, 110–15).

While we have seen that the evidence on age is very limited, it is possible to draw some conclusions in cases of sexual offences and victims aged sixteen and under recorded in the *Proceedings*. There are some important differences in the punishments awarded, as shown in Figure 6.17. Perhaps reflecting worries about the reliability of evidence from young victims, no one convicted of the rape of a girl under the age of seventeen was sentenced to death in the *Proceedings* although, overall, this sentence was awarded in 11.1 per cent of all convictions for this offence. Instead, a significant proportion of convicts were sentenced to transportation, though most commonly for victims aged one to nine, reflecting the perceived greater severity of this offence. The vast majority, particularly those charged with crimes against victims aged thirteen to sixteen, received the lighter sentence of imprisonment, further evidence of the ambivalent attitudes towards victims of that age. Similarly, in the twentieth-century *Times* reports, at a time when imprisonment was the severest punishment available for sexual offences, rape cases involving victims aged thirteen to sixteen were less likely to result in imprisonment (60.0 per cent vs 75.0 per cent overall) and more likely to result in a fine (15.0 vs 3.8 per cent). While these figures are based on low numbers of cases (twenty victims aged thirteen to sixteen and eighty victims overall) and *The Times* reporting may have been selective, this reinforces other evidence that suggests that victims aged thirteen to sixteen achieved some of the least satisfactory outcomes. Although the age of consent was increased to sixteen in 1885, the courts nonetheless often treated this age group as proto-adults who were somehow complicit in these crimes.

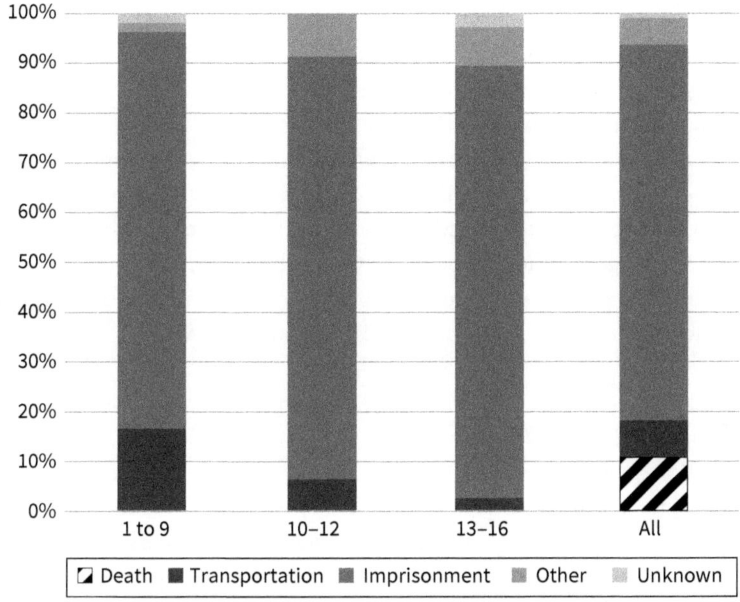

Figure 6.17: Sentences for Rape Victims Aged 16 and Under in the *Proceedings*, Compared to all Old Bailey Rape Sentences
Source: Proceedings Dataset

In sum, patterns of verdicts and punishments suggest that the identity of the victim and prosecutor shaped trial outcomes, although a lack of evidence for the thinking of jurors and judges means we cannot establish causal links. It is also possible that there were variations in the nature of the offences charged, not captured in our datasets, which explain the differences we have identified. Nonetheless, it is important to recognize that, despite the fact that prosecutions from marginalized groups increased over time, certain types of non-elite, minority ethnic, and young victims, and those acting on their behalf, received less favourable outcomes. Potential victim-prosecutors may have noticed that in some circumstances (particularly with sexual offences) trial outcomes could be less favourable for these groups than for the majority of victims, and this may have shaped decisions about whether to bring cases to trial in the first place. Certainly, this contributed to the disinclination to prosecute sexual offences discussed in Chapter 2. Conversely, prosecutions which involved powerful actors such as the police and institutions could result in more favourable outcomes.

By contrast, despite their marginalized status, female victims of some types of crime achieved more frequent convictions, and in certain circumstances their defendants were awarded harsher punishments, than male victims. We suggest that it is likely that it was women's perceived status as the weaker and more vulnerable sex which led to these outcomes. Overall, however, we must recognize that the differences identified in this section were often relatively minor, and that verdicts and sentences were influenced by a wide range of other factors which cannot be included in this analysis, including the precise nature of the offence and its contemporary context, and the individual predilections of the decision-makers.

6.5 Conclusion

For victims, criminal justice depends not only on access to the courts, but also the conduct of trials and successful trial outcomes. We have seen that, despite the increasing support offered to victims, the growing presence of police and counsel in trials led to a decline of the victims' voice in the courtroom, as they appeared less often, testified later, and spoke fewer words in trials. Despite this, cases involving the police and institutional prosecutors were more likely to secure a guilty verdict, and the likelihood of such a verdict increased substantially over time, partly owing to plea bargaining, such that victims could increasingly believe they had a good chance that the prosecution would result in a guilty verdict. The resulting punishment sentences changed considerably over the course of the period, with the broad shift from death to transportation to imprisonment no doubt welcomed by some and opposed by others; but one thing the changes achieved was greater certainty over the likely punishment for those convicted. By the twentieth century victims at the Old Bailey could expect that not only the most likely sentence, but also the most likely actual punishment, would be imprisonment. What was lost in this process was the influence some victims had previously achieved through the pardoning process, through which they could, in particular cases, ask both jurors and the courts to exercise 'mercy'. Until the 1830s, such requests contributed to the large number of partial verdicts and, for defendants found fully guilty, a significant proportion of death sentences commuted into lesser punishments (Shoemaker, 2022). This type of influence has returned in some respects in recent years, with victims' input into offender management.

Verdicts and punishments sometimes appear to have been shaped by juror and judge biases based on the presence of powerful prosecutors, and the social position of the victim. Cases in which the police and institutions were involved achieved more convictions and harsher punishments, while lower-class and Irish victims achieved fewer convictions and lower-class victims achieved lighter punishments. On the other hand, with the important exception of sexual offences, female victims achieved higher levels of convictions and harsher punishments, perhaps owing to their perceived weakness. The most striking discrepancy in these patterns concerns girls up to the age of sixteen who were victims of sexual offences. Here the general public revulsion against the offence, particularly when it was committed against those under the age of ten, conflicted with concerns over the reliability of their evidence in court, leading to the absence of death sentences for rape. Cases involving girls aged thirteen to sixteen appear to have attracted a particularly high level of scepticism, apparently owing to longstanding attitudes towards consent and worries about victim complicity in the offence. All these less favourable outcomes for socially disadvantaged victims had the potential to discourage prosecutions.

The changing patterns of prosecution and trial outcomes discussed in this chapter, shaped by the decisions of victims and legal officials, were the result of a growing recognition over the three centuries studied of the importance of encouraging victims to report crimes and the need to support (or supplant) their efforts to prosecute. While in many respects victims' access to justice improved, patterns of discrimination continued, and change came at the price of a decline of victim participation in, and influence over, criminal justice practices, a loss which disproportionately affected female victims. In some ways, these changes led to the identification of weak and vulnerable 'ideal victims' such as women and children, whose loss of courtroom agency was not always balanced by improved outcomes (Gorham, 1978). Ultimately, that loss had serious consequences for many victims in marginalized circumstances, as we will explore in the next chapter.

7

Post-war Victims and the Pains of Prosecution

In previous chapters we have shown how the ad hoc institutionalization of police-led, counsel-assisted and state-funded prosecution resulted in the gradual marginalization of victims in the courtroom. This was not the result of any grand plan but of incremental measures introduced over time, each intended to create a more efficient prosecution system. By the mid-twentieth century, the complainant's role as 'prosecutor' had been largely taken over by professionals, with the complainant relegated to the status of 'witness'. In this context, it became more possible to conceptualize the complainant as a 'victim', as a passive participant within the criminal justice process, and as the recipient of services offered by the state. In the final section of Chapter 3, we showed how the figure of the 'victim' emerged thereafter in public debate. A key trigger was Margery Fry's 1957 call for 'justice for victims'—a call made in the context of post-war welfarism that led to new forms of state-funded compensation and support for those deemed to have been physically and mentally harmed by crime. Through these measures, certain groups of victims began to gain a new visibility as deserving subjects of governance. In time, that visibility would give them a powerful political currency.

We suggest that a key motivation of the state's periodic interventions throughout these three centuries was the defence of the legal system's popular legitimacy. When the late seventeenth-century state was seen to be failing to control crime, it introduced rewards to encourage prosecutions. When the rewards scheme was criticized for tilting the scales of justice, the judges allowed defence counsel, and when the state was thought to be succumbing to growing crime and disorder in the 1820s, parliament created the new police. In the previous two chapters we have shown how social pressures in the nineteenth century forced changes in law and legal practice that ultimately enabled greater access to justice for women and children.

Victims and Criminal Justice. Pamela Cox, Robert Shoemaker, and Heather Shore, Oxford University Press.
DOI: 10.1093/oso/9780192846488.003.0007

These shifts were fought-over, drawn-out, and usually partial responses to public criticism of the legal system's failings but they did, ultimately, have measurable effects. New groups of victims were able to make greater use of the legal system, albeit sometimes with poorer outcomes. This was a process that continued into the post-war period, and continues today.

The chapter seeks to extend key criminological work on the emergence of the post-war politics of victimization (Shapland, Willmore, and Duff, 1985; Mawby, and Walklate, 1994; Zedner, 2002; Rock 2004b; Goodey, 2005; Walklate, 2007; Tapley and Davies, 2020; Mawby, 2022) and on the 'politics of pain' within victim movements (Barker, 2007). Drawing on *Times* coverage of Old Bailey trials and public commentary of the time (see also Shore and Williams, 2022), it offers empirical evidence to frame a new historically-inflected reading of the emergence of distinct aspects of post-war victim policy, with a particular focus on the impact of prosecutorial practice on socially marginal victims. The chapter quotes from materials that use terminologies of the period, now rightly contested in many instances.

As the founders of Victim Support had discovered through their early 1970s field research, many victims experienced trauma as a result of the offence committed against them, and many felt sidelined within the criminal justice process. As an organization, Victim Support sought to find new ways to meet those needs and deployed their own tactics of governance in the process (see Chapter 3). They worked with the police to reach victims who had typically already engaged with the criminal justice system and drew on volunteer expertise to guide them through that system. Over time, if not by design, this form of support came to focus on those who would be more readily identified as ideal victims or as deserving of protection. As a result, they came to be more readily incorporated into the emergent 'victim policy' terrain.

In this chapter we examine how, in the later twentieth century, groups of more socially marginal victims who had experienced particular forms of violence—of a sexual, domestic, homophobic, or racial nature—pressed to be treated more justly in the prosecutorial system. That system was now inseparable from the work of police forces, with the police leading on both the investigation and prosecution of crime, assisted by specialist and often embedded teams of solicitors. Victims of all kinds were chiefly viewed as witnesses to the crimes they had experienced. In short, all victims had become 'marginal' players in court but some were more marginal than others. We explore here how they and their advocates sought to make themselves visible as more troublesome subjects of governance through protest and pressure. The particularly troublesome status of these victims was rooted in long-held historical perceptions of their quasi-culpability for the violence they experienced. To draw on Christie's familiar characterization, this made them 'divergent' rather than 'ideal' or blameless victims (Christie, 1986). That divergent status was reinforced in the adversarial courtroom, where defence and prosecution counsel battled to persuade the jury of their case. Counsel's pejorative characterizations of victims (and sometimes defendants), along with judges' remarks and summations, were crucial to trial outcomes but often caused fresh harms.

Building on the civil rights movements of the 1960s and early 1970s, activists involved in feminist, anti-racist, and gay liberation work challenged those characterizations in new and powerful ways, criticizing prejudicial prosecution procedures and calling for new forms of support. The state responded by recognizing that some legal innovation was necessary to facilitate greater, and more effective, participation by some of these excluded groups, as a means of shoring-up its own legitimacy. However, many of the historic barriers to their participation remained unresolved because they were (and are) structural features of the adversarial system. The effect of these barriers was to inflict what we term here the 'pains of prosecution', experienced in particular (but not exclusively) by divergent victims. While these were clearly distinct from the emotional 'pains of imprisonment' experienced by incarcerated offenders (Sykes, 1958; Ignatieff, 1978; Crewe, 2011), they and their history highlight some of the inherent, and ongoing, limitations of the adversarial criminal trial from the victims' perspective.

7.1 Rape and Sexual Assault

The early 1970s saw an outpouring of anger about the status of women in society and under the law. Through liberation conferences, protests, and writings, feminist movements of the era mobilized networks of campaigning women and their supporters to demand a range of women's rights. One of the injustices around which activists organized was the judicial treatment of rape cases. They were particularly outraged by decisions taken by some of the judges of the period. In April 1974, William Regan was convicted at the Old Bailey of raping a nineteen-year-old woman previously unknown to him. Despite labelling him a 'dangerous and violent man', the judge nevertheless remarked that, 'I make allowances for the fact that girls who take lifts from strangers are asking for trouble' (*The Times*, 9th April 1974). Regan received a sentence of just four years' imprisonment. This and other similar damning judgements on female victims' characters and motivations exacerbated the already poor judicial outcomes received by rape victims (Bourke, 2008).

As this example, and the data presented in Chapter 6, have shown, many men were prosecuted and punished at the Old Bailey for rape and other sexual offences, but conviction rates and sentencing patterns were profoundly uneven. Women and girls' victimization was, in many cases, recognized and their criminal complaints upheld. However, the narrative framing of their victimhood within the adversarial trial setting and beyond was often highly problematic. Such framing, and the attendant shaming, contributed to poorer court outcomes for women, and to their historic reluctance to seek full access to justice by actively pursuing the prosecution of their attackers (as discussed in Chapter 2). This meant, in turn, that 'support' for female victims of sexual offences, particularly from the late nineteenth century, was often connected with efforts to secure their 'moral reform'. The rape crisis activists of the mid-1970s roundly rejected this narrative.

A year after the William Regan trial, in April 1975, campaigners were enraged and energized by an appeal court ruling of the House of Lords. In the case of *DPP v Morgan & Others*, the Law Lords ruled that a man might be acquitted of rape if he honestly believed his victim was consenting, regardless of whether that belief was 'reasonable' or not. The ruling was described as a 'rapists charter' by one critic, and the Home Secretary, Roy Jenkins, responded to public anger by announcing a review, 'to give urgent consideration to the law of rape in the light of recent public concern' (Baird, 1999). He established an 'Advisory Group on the Law of Rape', chaired by the first woman to become a High Court judge, Rose Heilbron.

The Advisory Group reported in December 1975. It noted that, 'Much of the criticism we have received is directed not so much against the substantive law of rape or the particular decision in Morgan as against the practice and procedure followed in rape cases' (quoted in Baird, 1999, 199). It made recommendations in three areas: the definition of rape, the type of evidence that could be used, and on anonymity for complainants. In the view of Heilbron and her colleagues, prosecutions of rapists were being prevented by victims' fears of the shame that would accompany the bringing of charges. 'Public knowledge of the indignity which [the complainant] has suffered in being raped may be extremely distressing and even positively harmful, and the risk of such public knowledge can operate as a severe deterrent to bringing proceedings' (quoted in McGlynn and Downes, 2018, 2).

After the report, the government moved quickly to turn many of the Advisory Group's recommendations into law. The Labour MP Robin Corbett introduced his Sexual Offences (Amendment) Bill into parliament on 13 February 1976 with a speech highlighting the number of women who suffer rape but do not press charges for fear of the shame that a court appearance would entail (HC Deb, 13 Feb 1976, v. 905, cc.799–857, 799). The Act received Royal Assent the following November (1976 *c.* 82). As a result, it became an offence to publish the name of either the victim or the defendant in a rape trial outside court. If the defendant was convicted, then his anonymity would be revoked. But the law allowed these protections to be waived in special circumstances.[1] In 1978, an Old Bailey judge ruled that one victim's anonymity should be waived in order to allow the defence a higher chance of tracing witnesses. As a result, seventeen-year-old Lorraine Brown was named in the press and identified as a prostitute—an accusation that she denied. Meanwhile, the defendant, a 'wealthy company director', continued to be 'protected from publicity by the Act and was referred to as Mr X' (*The Times*, 7 February 1978). In open court the judge speculated that Brown might have reservations about seeing her name 'plastered all over the national dailies', to which defence counsel responded that 'It could be argued that it might boost her trade' (ibid).

The Heilbron report also criticized a frequent tactic of defence lawyers in rape trials: cross-examination about the victim's sexual history. It argued that 'A woman's sexual experience with partners of her own choice are neither indicative of untruthfulness nor of a general willingness to consent' (para 131, quoted in Adler, 1982, 664). The Sexual Offences (Amendment) Act 1976 gave the judge complete discretion whether or not to admit evidence of the complainant's sexual experience but failed to lay down guidelines for its exercise, or considerations for exclusion or inclusion of such evidence at trial.

In 1978–9, Zsuzsanna Adler studied the impact of the Act on the workings of the Old Bailey by examining conduct in fifty rape trials where the plea was not guilty and thirty where the plea was guilty—85 per cent of the total rape trials held during that period. She found that the Act failed to

[1] This provision was later repealed for defendants by the 1988 Criminal Justice Act following a Criminal Law Revision Committee report in 1984 (https://www.parliament.uk/business/publications/research/key-issues-parliament-2015/justice/anonymity-for-defendants/).

protect the victim's anonymity in a significant minority of cases. In 40 per cent of the contested trials, lawyers for the defendants applied for leave to introduce evidence of the complainant's previous sexual experience and in three-quarters of those, the application was wholly or partly successful. Adler found that judges differed widely in their interpretation of this point of the new law. Some even performed their own cross-examination of the victim about their sexual history, apparently in contravention of its stipulations. Overall, the 1976 Act may have spared some rape victims the indignity of cross-examination about their sexual history and given them anonymity in the media but it seems to have failed in its sponsors' main hope of encouraging more women to report sexual assaults. According to Adler, writing in 1982, 'the number of offences known to the police has remained remarkably constant since 1976' (Adler, 1982, 45).

While the Sexual Offences (Amendment) Bill was going through parliament, in March 1976 the UK's first rape crisis centre opened in north London. As reported by the feminist magazine, *Spare Rib*, it aimed to offer 'sympathetic non-judgemental support, advice and information on police and legal procedures for those women who chose to report' and 'to help raped women regain their strength as individuals' (Green, 1976, 17). Inspired by a New York initiative, it was run by a women's collective and offered a 24-hour telephone line, face-to-face support and medical referrals, and also engaged in research, campaigning, and training (Diduck, 2019). Over the following decades, similar centres were opened in many other towns and cities. Along with women's refuges (discussed below), they opened up new spaces for women to speak about their experiences of violence and offered new forms of victim support outwith the criminal justice system. A vital element of this voicing of violation was that it rejected dominant narratives around rape that, like narratives around domestic violence, blamed or punished women for their victimization. In this respect, the rape crisis movement was distinct from its historical predecessors.

While nineteenth-century voluntary movements, many involving women, had certainly challenged male sexual and domestic violence and succeeded in securing changes to prosecution procedures, they had taken highly ambiguous positions towards its female victims. Their 'support' for them was often inseparable from efforts to secure their 'moral reform' and to prevent them 'contaminating' others. Those under sixteen could find themselves removed from their families for their own protection and then placed in a network of rescue homes (Jackson, 2000a, 2000b; Cox, 2013). From the 1860s, the emergent juvenile justice system developed new summary proceedings, further refined by the 1908 and 1933 Children Acts, to ensure the 'care and protection' of children. Girls who were found, or believed, to have experienced sexual assault formed a significant contingent of these proceedings up to the 1960s and beyond. These girls were among those sent to juvenile reform institutions—the industrial and reformatory schools that operated up to the 1930s and the approved schools that replaced them (Cox, 2013). For those who ran these institutions, the victims posed a threat to the integrity and welfare of those with whom they were incarcerated because they had 'knowledge of evil' or 'moral contamination' which could be spread to others (ibid).

The assertion that young women were complicit in their own sexual victimization was frequently made in court and it seems likely that it contributed to the poor trial outcomes documented in Chapter 6. Two Old Bailey cases serve to illustrate this. In September 1956, sixty-two-year-old General Sir Frank Messervy, a renowned war veteran, pleaded guilty to indecently assaulting a thirteen-year-old girl. He had a previous conviction for indecent exposure, referred to in court as 'similar troubles'. The victim was described by the prosecution as 'sub-normal, dishonest and of abnormal sex tendencies'. Messervy was bound over for three years, and in passing this lenient sentence, the judge stated that he considered 'the evidence showed clearly that he was not the instigator of the offence' against his child victim (*The Times*, 11 September 1956; *Daily Telegraph*, 11 September 1956; see also Davies, 2007, 2017 edn). In November 1960, twenty-eight-year-old Frederick Stewart, of Jamaican origin, was convicted of having unlawful carnal knowledge of a girl under sixteen. For this serious sexual offence, he was sentenced to just six months imprisonment. However, Stewart appealed and within two months his sentence was reduced to a £50 fine. The appeal did not seek to prove that he was innocent of the offence but to provide mitigation in the hope of overturning the sentence. Handling the appeal, the Lord Chief Justice noted that Stewart was 'of previously good character' that the offence was committed 'with a no-good girl of 15½ who slept with black men quite promiscuously, [and who] the morning after the offence … was found in bed with another Jamaican'. He concluded that 'this man had been led astray by the girl and as he had been released on bail, it would not seem right to take him away from work and bring him back to prison' (*The Times*, 23 November 1960).

Rape crisis and feminist movements challenged these framings of female victimization (Toner, 1977; Bourke, 2008, 2018). Another means of doing this was via a renewed emphasis on encouraging victims to report cases and on the implementation of measures to protect them from further harm (or secondary victimization) within the prosecution process itself. In 1986, the Home Office issued guidance recommending the provision of dedicated suites for the examination of rape victims (Temkin, 1998, 822). Measures to protect victims' anonymity were enhanced by the Youth Justice and Criminal Evidence Act 1999 (1999 *c.* 23), which provided a range of special measures, including giving evidence from behind a screen or via live videolink, in order to assist 'vulnerable and intimidated' witnesses to give their best evidence in court (Charles, 2012, 6). This followed measures in the Criminal Justice Act 1988 (1988 *c.* 33), which afforded the same options to witnesses under the age of fourteen years in cases of violence or cruelty, and under seventeen years in respect of sex offences (Applegate, 2006, 182).

However, these innovations failed to secure a transformative uplift in reports, prosecutions, and convictions. Official data jointly published by the Ministry of Justice, the Home Office and the National Office for Statistics in 2013 found that, 'Whereas 24 per cent of complaints resulted in a conviction in 1985, only 12 per cent did so in 1995, and conviction rates have remained at around a low 7 per cent since 2000' (Hohl and Stanko, 2015, 326). It may be that the introduction of the Crown Prosecution Service (CPS) in 1986 unintentionally created significant barriers to justice for victims of rape and sexual assault (see Brown, 2011). The nature of these barriers requires further research that would, in turn, rely on access to historical CPS data. A comprehensive history of the impact of the CPS has yet to be written and is beyond the scope of this book (see Spencer, 2011). The key point here is that, despite reforms to the handling of rape cases and the efforts of support groups, the pains of prosecution progressed, largely unchecked.

7.2 Domestic Violence

In 1971, England's first women's refuge opened in Chiswick in southwest London. Founded by the activist Erin Pizzey, it started as a drop-in women's centre but soon began to offer emergency accommodation for women and children fleeing domestic violence. A derelict house—which became Chiswick Women's Aid—was leased by the local council to Pizzey for a 'peppercorn' rent and made habitable via a £300 bank loan (Pizzey, 1974, 10). Its rooms were rarely empty but the refuge offered more than accommodation. Like the rape crisis centres that would follow, it offered a new space—outwith the legal system—for public recognition of this very particular form of victimization. Pizzey's work inspired others to follow suit. By 1975, women's refuges had been set up in thirty towns and cities with a further forty in preparation (Pizzey, 1975, 298), many of them joining a new national federation that eventually became known as Women's Aid. The legal reforms sparked by this kind of activism would, however, purposefully focus more on civil law rather than criminal justice options. Our discussion opens with a review of the latter and their problematic history.

As with the rape law reforms, domestic violence activists were re-fighting earlier campaigns against 'wife beating'. Nineteenth-century reformers had secured measures to limit lawful levels of 'reasonable chastisement' of wives by their husbands; encourage prosecution (with or without a wife's consent) where this was unreasonable; and enable stiffer sentences for those convicted (Williams and Walklate, 2020; Edwards, 2005; Tomes, 1978). In 1891, the right to use corporal punishment on a wife was removed (Williamson, 2017). Further, as discussed in Chapter 3, the expansion of summary jurisdiction in the second half of the nineteenth century had given women victims of domestic violence and other offences greater access to more immediate and less protracted justice (Davis, 1984; Auerbach, 2021). In higher courts, such as the Old Bailey, violence against women by husbands and other men known to them was prosecuted as serious assault, wounding, grievous bodily harm, manslaughter, or murder. Victims of significant violence thus had a potential route to the courts and a long-standing ability to initiate a prosecution. However, the evolving structure of the adversarial trial, now including counsel for both parties ready to undertake testing cross-examination, meant that many suffered as a consequence. *Times* reports of Old Bailey trials from the post-war period show how, even in an era of increasing women's rights, defence counsel continued to present women as being part-culpable for their own victimization and how this, in turn, contributed to the more lenient sentencing of perpetrators. In the era before the abolition of the death penalty for murder in 1965 (Seal, 2014) this quest for leniency was particularly urgent for defence counsel.

Doris Harrison died from multiple skull fractures inflicted by her husband in 1957. A statement from the accused read out in court claimed that she had been 'nagging [him] about money' (*The Times*, 6 July 1957). In his summing-up, the judge told the jury that she was 'a difficult woman, a nagging woman who drove her husband to desperation' but that this was not what the jury needed to consider. Rather, they had to weigh the husband's defence that he suffered from an 'hysterical personality' which should reduce his offence to manslaughter on the grounds of diminished responsibility. In the end, the jury rejected this plea and found the husband guilty of murder. He was sentenced to life imprisonment (*The Times*, 19 September 1957). Given that at this time the death penalty was still extant, it is likely that the judge's remarks were intended as mitigations that would enable the court to avoid applying it.

The death sentence was given in sixty-five of our *Times* dataset cases for the period 1910–25 and for nine in the period 1960–65, including four for murder in 1965. It was only actually carried out—via a prison-based hanging—in a small number of these cases, all of them occurring in our earlier sample. The framing of mitigating courtroom narratives in the period up to 1965 in all death penalty cases would repay further study. These narratives, which had been part of courtroom culture for centuries, became more powerful in the context of campaigns to abolish the death penalty. They contributed to a culture of strategic victim-blaming as part of wider resistance to the use of that penalty. In the Doris Harrison case and others like it, these narratives also indicate that the threat posed by domestic violence continued to be minimized within the adversarial trial process.

In cases of non-lethal domestic violence, the need to save an accused husband from the death penalty was not a factor. However, the same mitigation narratives were routinely used in these Old Bailey cases. In March 1958 Miriam Donald survived her husband's attempt to electrocute her. His QC noted in his defence that 'Whenever there were quarrels [she] taunted him with the fact that he was illegitimate and he decided to teach her a lesson'. Her husband, John Donald, pleaded guilty to 'unlawfully and maliciously administering an electric shock to his wife with intent to annoy her'. This plea to a reduced charge, rather than to attempted murder, was accepted by the court and he was convicted and jailed for twelve months. (*The Times*, 9 May 1958). In a parallel case in 1971, Jacqueline Silverton was tortured for ten days by her boyfriend because he believed she had allowed her employer to kiss her. His plea to reduced charges of actual bodily harm and attempted grievous bodily harm was accepted by the court and he was jailed for four years (*The Times*, 2 March 1971).

This brief discussion of the post-war prosecution of domestic and intimate partner violence has shown that the choice to prosecute could cost surviving victims dear in terms of emotional harm and misrecognition (failure to recognize harms caused) whilst doing little to ensure their future safety. This helps to explain the greater appeal of civil law actions addressed below. Again, these had historical roots in late nineteenth- and early twentieth-century legislation giving wives greater access to divorce and to property and custody of children following a divorce (Williams and Walklate, 2020; Burton, 2008). Measures introduced in the 1970s similarly sought to enable victims and their children to escape violence through the use of civil law orders rather than more effectively preventing or prosecuting it.

The publication of Pizzey's account of the work of Chiswick Women's Aid in 1974 prompted the Secretary of State for Health and Social Security, Barbara Castle, to call for an investigation into family violence. The timing coincided with public anxiety following the killing of seven-year-old Maria Colwell by her stepfather in January 1973. This led to the convening of a Parliamentary Select Committee on Violence in Marriage in February 1975, which reported in July. The following February a new Select Committee on Violence in the Family was convened. In May 1976 it produced a report entitled 'Battered Wives', an important milestone in reframing narratives of domestic violence. As one observer noted, 'the Select Committee seemed to accept the view of the women's aid organizations and of the victims themselves that there was nothing problematic or unusual about domestic assault, except that it took place in circumstances where the victim suffered from social and legal disadvantage' (McCabe, 1977, 282). The Committee 'made no bones about the extent of the prejudice that had stood in the way of a proper redress for women victims and indicated that this prejudice was to be found even among Government ministers, civil servants, and the police' (ibid).

In response, a significant increase in the power of the civil courts was obtained by the passing of a Private Members' bill, sponsored by the Labour MP Jo Richardson, which became the Domestic Violence and Matrimonial Proceedings Act of 1976 (1976 *c.* 50). The Act enabled a woman to seek a civil injunction against an abusive husband without divorce or separation proceedings and, in certain cases where such an injunction was breached, to secure possession of the matrimonial home (McCabe, 1977, 283).

Such measures were significant, not least because they gave victims more autonomy in framing their own response to the violence they faced, but these injunctions could be very difficult to obtain in court and women and children still needed safe spaces (Morgan, 1988). To that end, the 1975 Select Committee also recommended an expansion of the number of family places in the emergent national refuge network. Those who fled to refuges did so as a last resort. As citizens, they could not rely on the state to protect them from the serious harms they faced in their homes. For these victims, securing a public conviction against their abuser was less pressing than securing personal safety and shelter for themselves and their children. Over time, Women's Aid developed legal advice services but remained highly sceptical about the prosecution process (Harwin, 2006; Harwin and Barron, 2000).

Police practice was clearly a contributing factor here. *The Times* crime reporter Peter Evans drew on the 1985 Islington Crime Survey (ICS) and a Metropolitan Police working party on domestic violence to highlight the 'inadequacy of police recording practices' and argued that the police were 'more likely to side with wife-beater than battered woman' (*The Times*, 4 Dec 1986). A study of police prosecutorial decision-making between 1986 and 1988 found evidence that the police typically used their discretion to downplay the seriousness of domestic violence and to actively discourage its escalation to prosecution (McConville, Sanders, and Leng, 1991). Those making the decision were doubtless aware of the difficulties of securing a conviction in court and this may have been a key factor in their thinking.

These decisions, and the scale of domestic violence, became much more visible through the new tool of the community crime survey. As discussed in Chapter 2, these surveys shed unprecedented light on everyday experiences of (un)reported crime. For the first time, residents of a local area were given the opportunity to submit an anonymous record of harms they had experienced, typically in the previous twelve months, and the actions that had followed. One of the earliest, the 1985 ICS, found a 'high frequency of sexual assault and domestic violence' (Jones, MacLean, and Young, 1986, 158). It offered ground-breaking insight into these offences, including details of where and when they took place, and the emotional and physical injuries inflicted. The interviewers captured shocking details of women being 'grabbed/punched', 'punched/slapped' or 'kicked' as well as examples of 'other' forms of violence including 'strangulation, cigarette burns, pinched and bitten, stabbed in the face with a cigarette, spat at, hair pulled and head-butted' (ibid, 172). The resulting injuries included 'broken bones' as well as 'sprained ankle, sprained wrist, sore breast, loss of hair, burns, bite marks, dizziness, bloody nose, tooth knocked out, bruised vocal chords, damaged back, broken vein in ear, bumps on head, "internal damage", concussion and partial loss of hearing' (ibid, 172–3). Perhaps surprisingly, the survey also showed that a 'full two-thirds' of respondents who disclosed their experience of domestic violence to these interviewers 'expressed some satisfaction with police response' (ibid, 175). In noting this, however, the data analysts warned that this aspect of their results should be 'interpreted with extreme caution' as they 'probably over-estimate[d] the serious cases of domestic violence in relation to the less serious ones'. As they put it, 'women reporting the less serious cases' in the survey tended to be 'less willing to report' to the police (ibid, 175). Although clearly open to interpretation, the ICS results, along with those of other crime and victimization surveys of this era, opened a new chapter in the governance of victims linked to a new quest for evidence-driven policy in this field.

An Old Bailey case that took place in the same year as the ICS served as a stark reminder of the challenges. The court heard how a woman named Christabel Boyce had been murdered, dismembered, and roasted by her husband, Nicholas Boyce, who was described by his lawyer as 'an exceptionally calm, patient and kind man who finally snapped and lost control' due to her 'constant nagging' and 'remorseless grinding down and provocation' (*The Times*, 3 October 1985). Boyce, an economics graduate, was sentenced to just six years imprisonment but released after three. Divergent victim narratives clearly retained their power in the adversarial court.

They were beginning to be challenged at the frontline policing level, however, with the introduction in the 1990s of new evidence-based initiatives: 'domestic violence units' within police forces offering specialized support to women victims, and new multi-agency 'crime and disorder reduction partnerships' which sought to share information to reduce risk (Harwin, 2006, 562–3). These innovations would be followed by the creation of 'Specialist Domestic Violence Courts' in 2005, aiming to reduce the pains of prosecution by fast-tracking proceedings and better supporting victims before, during, and after those proceedings (ibid). Some of that support was offered by newly created 'Independent Domestic Violence Advocates' as a new legal mechanism 'to improve the victim journey' through the criminal justice system' (Taylor-Dunn and Erol, 2021, 115). The CPS also sought to drive up prosecutions in this period through its domestic violence guidelines and mandatory training for prosecutors (Burton, 2008; Porter, 2019).

These new measures were forged through a new politics of multi-agency partnership, but they represented a return to an established mode of governing victims—one that encouraged them to prosecute. However, this encouragement to access justice continued to have its critics. In 1977, McCabe observed that 'for an unknown but probably sizeable number of women victims of assault there is, in practice, no redress in criminal law' (McCabe, 1977, 281). Little had changed by 2000, when Nicola Harwin, the Director of the Women's Aid Federation England, could write 'For the majority of women, the options provided by the civil legislation—however inadequate—may be more appropriate to their needs than the criminal process' (Harwin and Barron, 2000, 213). From the 1970s to the 2010s, a scepticism towards the value of criminal law as a mode of dealing with perpetrators has prevailed among feminist campaigners against domestic violence. Nonetheless, prosecutions continued. The fact that the CPS began to encourage prosecutions in the many cases where victims withdrew their complaint stands as a controversial testament to the ongoing pains of prosecution in these cases (Ellison, 2002; Porter, 2019).

7.3 'Homosexual' Victims

In October 1970, Bob Mellors and Aubrey Walter, both students at the London School of Economics, set up the Gay Liberation Front (GLF). From the start, they were driven by their demand that gay men's experiences as victims be recognized and challenged. The group was formed after the 'Stonewall riot' in New York, triggered by a protest against a police raid on the Stonewall bar. In this example, gay men were victimized by the police. In other examples, their victimization at the hands of others was not taken seriously by the police or the courts. In both instances, they experienced particular 'pains of prosecution' as a result. Social activists sought to challenge the double disadvantages that homosexual men experienced when they came to prosecute as victims.

One of the GLF's first interventions, the month after their formation, was to hold a protest against the arrest of Louis Eakes, former chair of the Young Liberals, for alleged 'gross indecency' with another man in Hyde Park. He was later fined £100 (*Daily Telegraph*, 20 April 1971, 2). Coverage of the protest by the GLF's journal *Gay International News* included the comment that 'attitudes against homosexuality have allowed the pigs to frame someone who happens to be heterosexual. Everyday, people who happen to be gay are threatened and busted under those same laws' (*Gay International News*, 1970, 11; see also Robinson, 2007). The GLF and their successor organizations discussed below continued to campaign against the harassment of gay men, their mistreatment by police officers, and the related wider misrecognition of their experiences of victimization.

The Times coverage of Old Bailey trials involving gay male victims from the 1960s to the 1990s reveals the repeated use of narratives of divergent victimhood, in which the victim was portrayed as bearing some share of the blame, even where assailants were prosecuted and punished.

That blame was inseparable from the long-term historical criminalization of male homosexuality. Certain homosexual criminal acts had been re-codified by the Labouchere Amendment (Section 11) to the 1885 Criminal Law Amendment Act (48 & 49 Vict. *c.* 69), which allowed a charge of 'gross indecency' to be made whether or not sodomy could be proven. Between 1885 and 1913 there were fifty-five Old Bailey trials of males for indecent assault against other males, and a further six for assault with sodomitical intent, more than double the number prosecuted during the equivalent period before the Act's passage (1857 to 1884) when there were only twenty-four and one respectively (OBO). The 1885 measure was initially repealed and re-enacted by the 1956 Sexual Offences Act (1956 *c.* 69), but the move first towards full re-enactment and then de-criminalization was dealt with as part of the 1957 Wolfenden Committee's wider reform of the laws relating to homosexual offences and prostitution (Weeks, 1981; Lewis, 2016). As we will go on to show, while the 1967 Criminal Law Act (1967 *c.* 58) decriminalized homosexual acts in Britain, defence counsel, prosecutors, and judges continued to invoke and promote a social intolerance of homosexuality. As a result, gay men's access to justice was seriously diminished, regardless of their class or social position.

The trial of Thomas Somers for the murder of George Brinham began in November 1962. It illustrates how, prior to its decriminalization, characterizations of homosexuality distorted prosecution practices and trial outcomes. Brinham, aged 46, a former chair of the national Labour Party, had been found dead at his Pimlico flat with multiple head wounds. Within weeks, sixteen-year-old Thomas Somers was charged with his murder. He admitted that the two had met, shared drinks, and gone to the cinema together. That evening, Somers had accompanied Brinham back to his flat. Once inside, Somers alleged that Brinham, 'put his arms around him and said "Give us a kiss"' at which point Somers bludgeoned Brinham to death with a decanter. Brinham tried to escape during the assault, running to the front door, but collapsed before he could leave (*The Times*, 22 January 1963). Somers dragged him back into the room and left him on the floor, ransacking the flat to make the scene appear as a burglary. Brinham's body was found five days later. A short way into the trial, the judge directed the jury to ignore the charge of murder—which would have carried the death penalty—and proceed with that of manslaughter instead, declaring that:

> I cannot see how any jury properly directed on the evidence can fail to find there was provocation. There is the statement of the lad which

> shows quite clearly that this man attempted to make homosexual advances, and that in consequence Somers picked up the decanter and hit him on the head. I should think that is about as clear a case of provocation as it is possible to have (ibid).

Reading material uncovered at Brinham's flat was labelled by the defence 'the literature of a male pervert' (ibid). The police testified as to previous complaints by other young men about the victim's conduct. Somers was found not guilty of manslaughter and released. His counsel had stated, 'I shall submit that one is entitled to kill a man if he commits a forcible and atrocious crime against you' (ibid). If this statement was reported accurately by *The Times*, it was extremely contentious. While self-defence was a legitimate justification for killing, in this case there was no allegation of physical assault by Brinham, only a suggestion that he had propositioned the witness, asking for a kiss. The tacit acceptance of his 'deviant' moral character on account of his homosexuality was enough, in the eyes of defence counsel, judge, and jury to explain, if not justify, the killing.

In February 1970, twenty-four-year-old Jeremy Wingfield, from a prominent political family, was found dead in Earls Court having suffered a single stab wound (*The Times*, 23 February 1970). A nineteen-year-old van driver, Thomas Baxter, with no former connection to Wingfield, was charged with murder. The men had apparently met for a short period the night before the body was found. At his Old Bailey trial, Baxter pleaded not guilty, contending that on identifying Wingfield as a homosexual he had drawn a dagger to protect himself and that Wingfield had tripped and fallen on it (*The Times*, 16 May 1970). Significantly, Baxter was found guilty on the reduced charge of manslaughter, for which he was sentenced to four years imprisonment. The judge pronounced that he 'accept[ed] the jury's verdict in this case that you were provoked' (*The Times*, 16 May 1970). In the eyes of the defence, jury, and judge in this case, the 'deviant' sexuality of the defendant, despite the decriminalization of homosexuality, was deemed threatening enough to warrant a defence of provocation, and a mitigated verdict of manslaughter.

Similarly, when thirty-six-year-old theatre director Edwin Thornley was robbed and murdered in December 1974, his sexuality played a central role in both the prosecution case and the reporting of the proceedings. Prosecution counsel told the court that Thornley had been 'lured from Piccadilly Circus, the haunt of male prostitutes, to Hungerford Bridge' where he was attacked (*The Times*, 3 December 1974). Although gay, there was no evidence to suggest that Thornley had been engaging prostitutes. Moreover, the prosecution highlighted the victim's regular frequenting of the Piccadilly area, and told the court that Thornley was 'A victim of a gang of queer-rollers who rob homosexuals hoping they will not go to the police for fear that their weakness may become known to the world' (*The Times,* 3 December 1974). Of the three youths tried, one was found guilty of murder and ordered to be detained at Her Majesty's pleasure, and two were found guilty of the reduced charge of manslaughter and sentenced to five and six years each (*Gay News*, December 19, 1974–January 15, 1975, 7).

The following year, Barry Humphries, a twenty-seven-year-old manservant, was convicted of a 'frenzied knife attack' on his employer, forty-seven-year-old Peter Sugden. Humphries, noted by *The Times* report as being married with two children (thus signalling his apparent heterosexuality), had beaten his 'wealthy Homosexual' employer with an iron bar and stabbed him four times (*The Times,* 21 March 1975). The attack had taken place on board the victim's boat, shortly after he had made a will leaving Humphries 'much of his wealth'. Despite clear evidence of motive for murder, Humphries' plea of manslaughter based on sexual advances from his employer was accepted, and he was sentenced to just four years in prison (ibid).

The fact that guilty verdicts were returned in all these cases shows that the prosecution process delivered a form of justice for these gay victims. However, in pronouncing reduced verdicts and passing reduced sentences, Old Bailey juries and judges in effect undermined the right of those victims to equal protection under the law.

It was cases like these that motivated the GLF and others to highlight continuing gay victimization and to demand changes in the criminal justice system. Their victimization, like that experienced by female victims of rape, sexual assault, and domestic violence, was often brutal. In the majority of prosecuted cases involving extreme violence, it was perpetrated by (apparently heterosexual) men. In this sense, the efforts of all the campaigners highlighted here were akin to the historical efforts of others to challenge male violence, the unequal power relations that fuelled it, and the apparent impossibility of effectively policing and prosecuting it.

In May 1990, a new activist group, OutRage!, set out to combat ongoing violence. Led by Peter Tatchell and others, it was created following the murder of actor Michael Boothe outside public toilets in Elthorne Park in Hanwell, west London (Lucas, 1998). Boothe joined a grim list, previously published in the *Gay Times*, of twenty-eight gay men murdered in the capital between 1986 and 1989 (Cook, Mills, Trumbach, and Cocks, 2007, 205). No trial took place as this was, and remains, an unsolved killing. A later Metropolitan police review of the case said that Boothe's lifestyle was 'destined to bring him into contact with his murderers' (Muir, 2007). In June 1990, OutRage! held a rally outside Hyde Park's public toilets protesting against the murder and against Metropolitan police entrapment operations. It was followed by an organized 'mass kiss-in by same-sex couples' at Piccadilly Circus 'in protest at arrests for public displays of affection' (*Guardian*, 10 May 2020). For OutRage! and their supporters, police homophobia was continuing to both criminalize the gay community and to impede the effective prosecution of crimes against them. Research undertaken by these campaigners suggested that the clear-up rate for killings of gay men was 55 per cent compared to 92 per cent for all murders at the time (Cook, Mills, Trumbach, and Cocks, 2007, 205). Police mishandling of the murders of four young gay men by Stephen Port in east London between 2014 and 2015 demonstrates the continuing impact of 'police failings' in this regard (BBC, 10 Dec 2021). Members of OutRage! were among those who would come to lobby for the introduction of 'hate crime' (discussed below) as a new means of prosecuting existing criminal acts that were compounded or motivated by proven hatred or intolerance of certain groups.

Other efforts to improve this community's access to justice in this period included the creation of the Lesbian and Gay Police Association in 1990 (Burke, 1993), followed by the National LGBT + Police Network in 2014. Overall, however, it can be argued that fewer reforms were enacted to encourage the prosecution of offences against the gay community relative to the modest reforms enacted to tackle rape and domestic violence against women. Campaigns to curb male violence against women could perhaps more readily present women—rather than men—as 'ideal victims' or mobilize them as 'survivors', while also drawing on historical statutory precedents to protect women (see Newburn and Stanko, 1994).

7.4 Racially Aggravated Victimization

Thus far, this chapter has shown how an animating dynamic of grass-roots social movements of the 1970s and their successors constituted an effort to uncover hidden victimization caused, in part, by the police's failure to protect the groups concerned and compounded by the criminal justice system's misrepresentation of them in court. We now turn to consider the actions and arguments of groups who galvanized in the same period to fight for racial equality.

In 1970, a group of young black activists were tried at the Old Bailey for inciting a riot in Notting Hill. Once again, a marginalized group was experiencing double disadvantage. The activists had led a protest against persistent police harassment of a West Indian restaurant, *The Mangrove*, owned by one of the defendants, Frank Crichlow. The case ended with a landmark acquittal of all defendants on the main charge, although some of them were convicted on lesser charges (Bunce and Field, 2013, 119–37). The trial of the Mangrove Nine was notable for many reasons. The case had initially been dismissed by the local magistrate but was reactivated by the Director of Public Prosecutions. Two of the defendants, Darcus Howe and Altheia Jones-Lecointe, opted to defend themselves rather than being represented by defence counsel. They also requested that the all-white jury be replaced by an all-black one on the grounds that the Magna Carta enshrined the right to be tried by peers. In the event, two black jurors were recruited. The trial also led, via Judge Clarke's closing remarks that 'racial hatred' had been displayed 'by both sides', to a watershed moment: the acknowledgement of racial prejudice in the Metropolitan Police (Hillel and Iglikowski-Broad, 2015).

Although racial prejudice was a feature of the British criminal justice system, it did not put justice completely out of reach for members of the black community. As some of the data we analysed in Chapter 6, together with the case of Michelle Confait discussed in Chapter 4, demonstrates, it was possible for black victims of white violence to receive justice in the court system. In November 1961, for example, three white youths were sentenced at the Old Bailey to between eighteen months and six years imprisonment, having been found guilty of seriously assaulting two young black men: Cecil Coates and Easton Tarrant. The prosecution counsel made a point of stressing the racist nature of this and related attacks by the group: 'They ... attacked individual passers-by for one reason only—the colour of their skins. There was not a shred of evidence ... that any of the coloured persons attacked or gave offence by so much as a word or the flicker of a gesture' (*The Times*, 1 November 1961). In his sentencing remarks, the judge described the attacks as a 'despicable outrage' (*The Times*, 11th November 1961). The successful prosecution of this case shows that the pains of prosecution are uneven and must be historicized with care; justice is not always denied.

Nonetheless, the racial prejudice acknowledged by Judge Clarke in the Mangrove Nine case often had devastating impacts for London's minority ethnic communities. Crime surveys like the ICS would later indicate that they were much less likely than white victims to report their experiences of crime to the police (Jones, MacLean, and Young, 1986). Other studies highlighted the extent of the extreme end of that victimization. Research for the Runnymede Trust completed in the mid-1980s listed sixty-two murders committed between 1970 and 1985 which were believed to be 'racially motivated' (Gordon, 1986).

One of these was the murder in April 1970 of Tausir Aly (also spelled Tosir Ali), a fifty-year-old Pakistani kitchen porter, who was stabbed at the entrance to his block of flats in Bow (*The Times*, 8 April 1970). Two eighteen-year-old white men were found respectively not guilty and guilty of manslaughter on the grounds of diminished responsibility (owing to medical confirmation of his 'mental abnormality'). Reporting of the ensuing Old Bailey case suggested both racist and homophobic motives. Prosecution counsel said that Ali had invited the young men to his flat and this had been taken by the accused to suggest 'some immoral purpose, but there was no evidence he was an homosexual', adding that '[I]t was also right for the jury to bear in mind that some young men went in for the past-time known as paki-bashing'. This was one of the first uses of this phrase in an Old Bailey case or the wider media but it referred to longer-standing hostilities experienced by the East End Pakistani and Bangladeshi communities (*The Times*, 17 July 1970, 4). Some local reports suggested that the accused were skinheads (*Daily Mail*, 9 April 1970, 12).

The case attracted high profile attention from the outset. Two days after the murder, *The Times* reported (9 April 1970) that Mr. Salman Ali, the Pakistani High Commissioner, had visited the community and also raised the issue with the Commonwealth Relations Office. In the weeks following Ali's death, *The Times* reported (20 April 1970), under the headline 'Protection groups to be formed by Pakistanis', that '[a] noisy meeting of nearly 1,000 Pakistanis decided in London yesterday that self-defence groups should be formed in the Pakistan community to protect them from attacks'. The meeting had been 'organized by the Pakistani Workers' Union' and was held at the Grand Palais Hall on Commercial Road, with 'an overflow hall around the corner'. According to the report, 'both halls are in the centre of the area in which about 4,000 Pakistanis live and where attacks by white gangs have been increasing, culminating in the death on April 7 of Mr. Tosir Ali'. This community mobilization bore some similarities to

Jewish self-defence groups created during and after the Second World War seeking to protect their communities from anti-Semitism: the 43 Group, the 62 Group and the Association of Jewish Ex-Servicemen (Whine, 2011, 113). These actions on the part of minority ethnic communities clearly signalled their lack of faith in the police and wider criminal justice system's ability to ensure their safety.

A further incident that gave rise to major protest among the Asian and West Indian community was the murder, in June 1976, of eighteen-year-old Indian student, Gurdip Singh Chaggar. The murder occurred in Southall in west London, another area experiencing high levels of racial tension. A group of five white youths banged hard on the window of an Indian restaurant 'no doubt to provoke the customers whom they expected to be Asians' in the words of the trial prosecution counsel. In the resulting confrontation Singh Chaggar was stabbed (*Daily Telegraph*, 21 April 1977, 17). *The Times* reported, 'The murder charges came last night after more than two thousand Asians and West Indians had marched through the streets of Southall demanding justice' (*The Times*, 8 June 1976). Asian community leaders had attempted to defuse the situation but complained of little support from the government. They 'appealed to the Prime Minister and Mrs Thatcher to make a statement denouncing the killing … and all racial violence' (ibid). By the time the trial started in April 1977, the events were being described in the press as a conflict between gangs of black and white youths, rather than a racially aggravated murder (*The Times*, 21 April 1977). This was something that was criticized by other legal commentators (*The Times*, 12 May 1977, 19). In May, two of the white youths, seventeen-year-old Jody Hill and eighteen-year-old Robert Hackman, changed their plea from not guilty to murder to guilty of manslaughter. They were jailed for four years, with the judge saying the sentence would have been longer if the two had been older. Notably, the judge commented that he was 'quite satisfied that neither of you were activated by feelings of racial prejudice' (*The Times*, 3 May 1977).

The parallels between the murder of Gurdip Singh Chaggar in 1976 and that of Stephen Lawrence in 1993 are striking. The circumstances in which both teenagers died were horribly similar. However, the criminal justice system's response to each was quite different. Singh Chaggar's assailants were prosecuted and put on trial, even if they were convicted on reduced charges, whereas those who attacked and killed Lawrence were not, at least initially. As a result of failures in the police investigation the CPS decided not to bring charges against the suspects. The Lawrence family subsequently brought one of the most famous private prosecutions of the twentieth century. It, too, failed after the trial judge ordered that key evidence could not be admitted, but this resulted in a major inquiry, conducted by Lord Macpherson, 'to identify the lessons to be learned for the investigation and prosecution of racially motivated crimes' (Macpherson, 1999, 2.8). The inquiry led to a change in the law (the 2003 Criminal Justice Act; 2003 *c.* 44) which allowed suspects to be tried a second time where new evidence emerged, thereby eventually resulting in the conviction of Gary Dobson and David Norris and their sentencing to minimum terms of 15 years and 4 years respectively. As in the Chaggar case, the judge said the sentences would have been longer had they been adults at the time of the murder (*R v Dobson & Norris*, 4 January 2012). This change in the law was described as the overturning of an 800-year-old principle—that no-one should be tried twice for the same offence—and thus constituted a key change in prosecutorial procedure (see Shore, 2020).

The Lawrence case also contributed to the Blair government's introduction of the concept of racially-aggravated offences under the 1998 Crime and Disorder Act (1998 *c.* 37), which carried an additional penalty if proven in recognition of the additional harm caused to both the victim and the wider public (Iganski, 1999, 386). These new offences paved the way for later hate crime legislation that would extend these harsher penalties for those convicted of crimes involving hostility on the basis of a victim's race, religion, disability, or sexual orientation via the 2001 Anti-terrorism, Crime and Security Act, the 2003 Criminal Justice Act, and the 2006 Racial and Religious Hatred Act (Law Commission, 2021, 14; Mason-Bish, 2010, 59; Duggan, 2015, 87).

In parallel to these developments, the New Labour government and official bodies encouraged measures that would reduce some of the 'pains of prosecution' for members of black communities. Prompted by criticism from the Commission for Racial Equality (CRE), the CPS and CRE initiated the Denman Inquiry in 2000, which found evidence of racial discrimination within the CPS and 'unwarranted complacency about the possibility of discrimination in the prosecution process in areas such as the handling of racist crimes' (Taylor, 2008, 67). In 2003, the CPS took this a step further with its Diversity Monitoring Project, 'a comprehensive race impact assessment of the prosecution process' (ibid, 69). These measures were judged sufficiently effective by the CRE that in 2007 it ended its monitoring of the CPS (ibid, 69).

At the same time, the Home Office encouraged reform inside the police. By 2004, Black Police Associations had been founded in thirty-five of the forty-three constabularies of England and Wales. The Home Office had begun providing financial support to the National Black Police Association and, as a matter of course, inviting the association's representatives to take part in its working groups and committees (Holdaway and O'Neill, 2004, 854) These steps amounted to a concerted effort to develop trust in the policing and prosecution systems within a community that had long felt violated by it.

Through these measures, and in line with the longer story told in this book, state agencies sought to strengthen the criminal justice system, to encourage the public to use the law with confidence and thereby to reinforce the rule of law and their own legitimacy. For all this, minority ethnic victims continued to experience multi-dimensional disadvantage in the criminal justice system (Kalunta-Crumpton, 2005; Webster, 2017; Long, 2018).

7.5 Conclusion

This chapter has offered a new historically-inflected account of post-war campaigns on behalf of marginalized victims, drawing on cases reported in *The Times*. It has shown how these influenced prosecutorial debate and practice and highlighted what we have termed the 'pains of prosecution' experienced by those who were positioned as divergent victims. While acknowledging that all victims came to be sidelined in criminal justice proceedings over time, it suggests that for some groups these pains were quite distinct and exacerbated.

While Chapter 3 traced the rise of the Victim Support movement from the 1970s onwards, this chapter has traced the rise of other forms of support that were forged, at the same time, by other kinds of activists in the fire of their respective fights against social and legal injustice. For the ICS survey pioneers, good evidence was vital, not just to build effective victim support, but to challenge the interlocking economic, ethnic, and gendered inequalities that caused crime in the first place. Campaigners against these inequalities and against the sexual, domestic, homophobic, and racial violence they created often worked in separate domains but they shared a common motivation to combat prejudice in the criminal justice system. For all their diversity, those they championed shared a common experience: they had typically been failed by a state that did not protect them from harms, and specifically from harms frequently rooted in male violence.

This chapter has moved beyond merely documenting that failure. Rather, and in line with the wider argument of this book, it has sought to document how that same state sought to adjust its criminal justice practices as a result. Forced to confront these pains of prosecution, the post-war state responded—in part to demonstrate its care for these victims but more specifically to uphold the rule of law, and thereby to shore up its role as a guarantor of equal access to the law. This flexing of the state in response to social pressure is thus an important part of our story, but was itself selective and variable. We have suggested here that social campaigns challenging rape and domestic violence achieved more prominent—albeit still limited—reforms from the 1960s to the 1990s than those challenging homophobic and racist violence. The differential level of flex was, in turn, linked to varying perceptions of the victims concerned, as well as to the uneven political influence of those campaigning on their behalf and their ability to frame harms in ways that both achieved political recognition and prompted political action.

Epilogue

This book has offered a new historical account of victims' encounters with the criminal justice system across three centuries: how they exercised their agency by reporting and prosecuting crime (or by choosing not to), and how the state attempted to manage what they did. Victims' agency could only be exercised within the available prosecution mechanisms of the day but their choices also helped to change those mechanisms. Our analysis of these changes offers new insights into the governance of prosecution and the changing relationship between the state and its citizens. The historic right of the 'freeborn Englishman' to have his day in court depended upon the recognition, exercise, and protection of that right. Victims' labour and practice was necessarily enacted alongside that of others involved in the prosecution process, notably magistrates, policing agents, counsel, and public prosecutors. This critical history of victims and criminal justice is necessarily, therefore, a crucial part of the history of these other actors in the justice system. More broadly, the history of the state's approach to the governance of victims can be read as part of the history of governance itself.

In the previous chapters we have offered new insights into the governance of prosecution, the mobilization of victims, and shifts in access to justice over time. We explored the origins and impacts of key legal, procedural, and institutional changes introduced in order to encourage, finance, and manage the prosecution of serious crimes. We have explored five processes in particular: reporting an offence; initiating a prosecution; presenting evidence as a prosecution witness; recouping costs arising from prosecutions; and influencing sentences. This Epilogue draws our investigation to a close, and summarizes the value of historicizing victims' participation, entitlements, and support.

From the outset, we have acknowledged that the vast majority of those who suffered from criminal offences were either unwilling or unable to report and prosecute offences against them. Chapter 2 outlined the varied reasons for this, drawing parallels between historic and more recent

Victims and Criminal Justice. Pamela Cox, Robert Shoemaker, and Heather Shore,
Oxford University Press.
DOI: 10.1093/oso/9780192846488.003.0008

examples. We argued that for those victims who were content with their choice not to report the crime and who thus, in a sense, rejected the legal status of victimhood, the justice system may not have appeared to fail. From the perspective of the public good, however, the failure to prosecute and punish could subvert public order and undermine the state's authority. Chapters 3 and 4 examined measures to incentivize and facilitate prosecution and the historical contexts in which they were introduced and revised. Chapter 3 showed that the eighteenth century was a key period in the history of 'victim support', broadly defined, with the provision, for the first time, of support in the forms of rewards, proactive policing, the reimbursement of costs, and the growing presence of prosecution counsel. It showed how these provisions developed through the nineteenth century and were formalized during the twentieth century. Partly because that process sidelined victims' influence as prosecutors, it prompted the need for the post-second world war mechanisms which offered broader forms of state and community support. Chapter 4 showed that the nineteenth century was a key period in the creation of public prosecution mechanisms, particularly through the involvement of the new police and state-funded counsel. We argued that these reforms were not introduced primarily to support the victim per se but to mobilize the victim as a tool to uphold law and order.

Analysing what victims *did* in the past sheds new light on who victims *were*, at least in the sense of showing us which social groups of victims became visible through their engagement in the criminal justice system. Chapters 5 and 6 identified key changes that emerged in the courtroom as prosecution practices changed over time, drawing on data gathered from over 200,000 Old Bailey trials. Our analysis showed that these changes did have an effect, in that access to certain forms of justice broadened during the nineteenth century. Greater victim support and the professionalization of prosecution facilitated greater access to justice for poorer, female, and child victims. By the early twentieth century, working-class complainants made up just under half of all those bringing prosecutions at the Old Bailey, unskilled workers comprised a fifth of the total and women brought around a third. The corollary of this process, however, was that the victim-prosecutor became marginalized or supplanted within the actual prosecution process. While we acknowledge the view that through the professionalization of prosecution the state 'stole' community responses to crime (Christie, 1977), we challenge it by demonstrating how, rather than 'stealing' conflict, the state socialized its resolution. We suggest this largely served the public interest, whilst fully acknowledging the injustices generated along the way, many of which continue to blight the justice system today.

Together, these chapters have allowed us to offer, for the first time, an historical measurement of victims' access to justice. In contrast to previous historical studies (see Chapter 1), we provide a comprehensive treatment of each stage of the criminal justice process, and a systematic examination of the business of a single important criminal court over 300 years. Unlike more contemporary studies of justice metrics (Gramatikov, 2010), our measures take account of the impact of informal practices, such as the rise of plea-bargaining and the increase in state-funded counsel, as well as the impact of formal requirements such as legislation to encourage specific kinds of prosecution. A key finding of our study is that such changes within prosecution mechanisms often had unintended consequences that, in turn, generated iterative mitigations. Our discussion of the secondary effects of the introduction of rewards is a powerful example of this. Over time, these efforts to make the prosecution system more efficient led to the procedural marginalization of the 'complainant' and their reframing as the 'victim'.

The twentieth century saw, first, a consolidation of public control over prosecutions, and then a reconceptualization of the victim as someone the state should take care of: as the recipient of compensation for the damage received, and more recently as the possessor of specific 'victim's rights' which the judicial system should respect. The control of the prosecution process by state agencies, and the consequent de-centring of the victim within judicial processes, left some feeling voiceless and discriminated against. This was particularly true for 'divergent' victims who were ignored, discriminated against, or even persecuted by the judicial system (Christie, 1986). Chapter 7 focused on efforts from the mid- and late-twentieth century to improve the access of these groups to the prosecutorial process. We showed how campaigning by 'outsider' groups that challenged the legitimacy of the criminal justice system led to efforts to recognize these groups' victimhood in prosecution practice through changes in both legislation and policy, a process which continues to this day. Our core study closes in the late-twentieth century—the chronological point at which many criminological accounts of victim policy and experience typically begin.

Historicizing 'Victim Policy'

This book has shown that what we would now call 'victim policy', broadly defined, has a long history, albeit not one expressed in these terms until the 1980s. Over the past three centuries, different measures have been introduced—with very different outcomes—to incentivize victims to report, prosecute, and testify. These measures both made and mobilized complainants as subjects of governance, first as prosecutors and then as victims.

A key driver of post-second world war initiatives for victims has been the perceived need to address problems arising from the emergence of the state as the primary prosecutor of crime. As Kirchengast (2016) suggests, the resulting sidelining of the victim has led to new efforts to create and secure their rights and interests in adversarial systems around the world. As statutory agencies—first the police and then the Director of Public Prosecutions and the Crown Prosecution Service—came to act on behalf of the crime victim in England and Wales, key decisions and choices came to be made by those agencies, sometimes to the disadvantage of the persons victimized. The resulting sense of disenfranchisement opened up a political space for the mobilization of certain types of 'ideal' and 'divergent' victims (Christie, 1986) as both political actors in their own right and as objects of political rhetoric. The final stage in the professionalization of prosecution, the creation of the CPS in 1986 was followed by a rise in public discussion of the newly recognized needs of victims. With 'ideal victims' in mind, efforts to address these needs, with their origins in the 1960s, had focused on compensation for physical harm and counselling for emotional hurt. By the end of the century, an influential segment of public and political opinion deemed them inadequate.

From the 1990s onwards, a series of political initiatives have sought to address that disenfranchisement. Rather than fundamentally altering the configuration of the prosecution process, they have aimed at imposing enforceable obligations on state agencies within existing procedures. The first Victims' Charter was introduced by David Waddington, the last Conservative Home Secretary to be appointed by Margaret Thatcher, on the day designated by Victim Support Europe as the first 'European Day for Victims of Crime', 22 February 1990. Waddington commended the Charter to MPs as an instrument 'which set out for the first time how victims of crime should be treated' (PP, HC Deb, 22 February 1990) although in fact it echoed many of the guidelines that had been espoused by the British organization Victim Support for a decade.

The Charter functioned as a set of service standards, calling for victims to be kept informed of case developments and assisted to apply for compensation. It was revised in 1996 and then more substantially reframed by the New Labour government in 2004 to become the Code of Practice for Victims of Crime in England and Wales (Rock, 2004b). The Victims'

Code extended existing entitlements by, for example, allowing victims to give a 'victim personal statement' in court, making information available about restorative justice options (greatly expanded by the 1998 Crime and Disorder Act) and clarifying complaints procedures. The enforceability of the Code and its successors remains a major challenge, however, given that twenty-eight different criminal justice agencies (at the time of writing) have some responsibilities relating to victims (Cox, Lamont, and Sunkin, 2020). Governing victims today requires metagovernance tactics (ibid, 11–12), given the highly fragmented nature of their entitlements (Kirchengast, 2016).

Notably, the legislation that established a statutory basis for the Victims' Code—the 2004 Domestic Violence, Crime and Victims Act (2004 *c.* 28)—redefined a 'victim' as 'a victim of an offence, or a victim of anti-social behaviour', noting that it was 'immaterial that no complaint has been made about the offence, or that no person has been charged with or convicted of the offence'.[1] This broader definition sealed an historic transition, prioritizing 'victims' (who had experienced an alleged offence) over 'complainants' (who had engaged with the criminal justice system as a result). This book's primary task has been to trace the history of measures impacting on complainants, in particular those who went on to have their complaints prosecuted in the Old Bailey. It has also, however, explored the history of measures affecting the recognition of victims more broadly defined, especially those which attempted to turn more victims into complainants. At the time of writing, these measures are finding new expression in the form of a draft parliamentary Victims Bill which, if passed, would transform aspects of the existing Code into a more binding victims law. In a notable early response to the Bill, the president of the Law Society recorded her organization's support for 'measures that are designed to improve the experience of victims in the criminal justice system and improve the way agencies within the system interact and communicate with them', with a significant caveat, 'as long as such measures do not impact on a defendant's right to a fair trial' (Fouzder, 2021).

[1] This new definition was influenced by the 2001 European Union Framework Directive on the standing of victims in criminal proceedings, which had defined a 'victim' (in Article 1a) as a 'natural person who has suffered harm, including physical or mental injury, emotional suffering or economic loss, directly caused by acts or omissions that are in violation of the criminal law of a Member State' (EU Framework Directive, 2001).

Historicizing Victim Participation

As we have shown, in the past, a victim of a serious crime (a felony) in England and Wales had an obligation to prosecute. If the peace of the crown had been disturbed, the victim had a duty to play their part in restoring it—particularly prior to the creation of the new police. That obligation may have been rarely enforced but it was, nevertheless, the foundation of the rule of law and the 'social contract' between ruler and ruled. Some victims obliged. Most did not. Our book has sought to understand which kinds of victims were more likely to make use of the law to pursue their offenders and, of these, which were most likely to see their case tried in a higher court and what kind of outcomes they might expect. By understanding how the state and other agencies sought to govern victims by encouraging, yet also managing, their participation in the justice system, our historical account of (un)conscious and (un)intended 'victim policy' becomes a wider historical account of state (trans)formation.

We have traced what the state *did*, but also traced battles for what the state *was*, by highlighting the power struggles between its different components and separated powers. Its evolution has been extensively studied by constitutional historians, legal scholars, and political theorists but somewhat overlooked by governmentality theorists, who tend to treat 'the state' as a monolithic entity. A critical history of victims is thus also a critical history of the shifting relationship between the branches of 'mixed government' in England and Wales, crown, parliament, and judiciary, set against the increasingly embedded and quotidian power of local government. As this book has shown, as well as by statute, Old Bailey practices were shaped by local policing, local court arrangements, and local contributions to their funding. In other words, local state initiatives often drove change at the national level.

In the context of nineteenth-century liberalism, calls for a fully public prosecution system were ultimately rejected because no consensus could be reached between local and central government. Liberal logic that combined a desire for personal freedom and localism with a belief in the public interest continued to shape the governance of, and participation within, prosecution. The post-second world war social democratic settlement altered this by extending the central state's duties towards victims of crime. While the judiciary continued to shape victims' formal participation as complainants and witnesses, parliament took on a much greater role in relation to addressing victims' experiences of, and confidence in, those processes. As Chapter 7 showed, statutory and policy measures to make the justice system more accessible—to all victims, and to divergent victims—meant that criminal justice had to flex again.

When a victim initiates a prosecution, they perform a symbolic if tactical show of faith in the legal apparatus of the day. Today, many justice activists argue that those involved in criminal proceedings (both victims and defendants) should (again) be active participants in the prosecution system (Doak, 2005; 2008; Jacobson and Cooper, 2020; Gordon and Gordon, 2020; Baird, 2020). This view is derived from post-war human rights discourses which hold that in order to enjoy rights, citizens must be able to participate in their society. It is also informed by procedural justice theory which holds that if people are treated fairly within a given system, they will have higher levels of trust in it (Rawls, 1971; Tyler, 2003).

However, the notion of greater victim participation has been fiercely criticized in other quarters. David Garland's work stands for many here, arguing that victim policy in the UK and the US since the 1980s has been a key plank of a politicized, populist, illiberal law and order agenda, of late modernity's particular 'culture of control':

> The new political imperative is that victims must be protected, their voices must be heard, their memory honoured, their anger expressed, and their fears addressed. The rhetoric of penal debate routinely invokes the figure of the victim ... as a righteous figure whose suffering must be expressed and whose security must henceforth be guaranteed (Garland, 2001, 11).

Garland points to a resulting carceral drift, arguing that the 'interests and feelings of victims – actual victims, victims' families, potential victims, the projected figure of the victim—are now routinely invoked at the expense of those convicted of crime in support of the measures of punitive segregation' (2001, 11). These concerns have been echoed more recently by others (for overview and critique, see Pemberton, 2012). From a different perspective, some prosecutors argue that victims should not play a more active role in criminal justice proceedings because it would disrupt the public accountability of the justice system (see Holder, 2018a and b). For these critics, victim-complainants' interests are subsumed within those of the wider public and, by extension, those of the state. Because they cannot be separated from the public interest, they cannot be separately represented. To do so would convert the victim-complainant's interests into private interests.

Historicizing the Pains of Prosecution

Scholars thus stand divided on the matter of victim participation today. Few, however, have investigated its history. The main aim of this book has been to identify and contextualize factors affecting public participation in the justice system across a broad time period. We have endeavoured to bring together two bodies of work that have hitherto existed in separate worlds: historical accounts of crime and prosecution in the eighteenth and nineteenth centuries, and criminological accounts of the politicization of victims in the twentieth and twenty-first centuries. Up to now, crime history has tended to ignore victims and victimology has tended to ignore history. We have sought to write a social history of prosecution and a political history of victims.

Since the 1980s, scholars have commonly framed the issue of victims' rights in terms of its importance to victims themselves and to populist politicians. However, as we have shown, securing this participation in its broadest sense has been a governmental concern for centuries, albeit participation on limited terms. As we have shown, these efforts often had unintended consequences. In the post-war period, the cause of 'victims' rights' also became an activist-led project focusing attention on deep social injustices and resulting justice gaps around gender, sexuality, and ethnicity. As Chapter 7 showed, divergent victims have experienced particular 'pains of prosecution' arising from both their exclusion from the process and their problematic inclusion within it. They experience these alongside and in addition to the 'pains' experienced by many victims as a result of their historic sidelining within the criminal justice process. Given that all these pains continue to be perpetuated and debated today, it seems more than reasonable for scholars to consider how victim participation might be progressed in more equitable ways.

Prosecution practices matter because they are central to historical cultures of control and the social production of justice. The eighteenth- and nineteenth-century state ultimately sought to encourage victims to prosecute in order to control crime through the conviction of offenders. Those involved in developing these measures did not seek to create rights for victims in particular, but to preserve the right of all citizens to access the law, because such private access served the public good as determined by the state. Citizen-led prosecution, pursued within a statutory framework with the assistance of a police force and private legal counsel, was preferred over a system led by continental or Scottish-style state prosecutors.

The marginalization of citizen-led prosecution—from the 1830s—by police and counsel-led prosecution was an unintended consequence of two linked processes: the socialization of prosecution (through the gradual consolidation of police powers and payment of prosecution expenses) and the juridification of prosecution (through the expansion of the legal profession).

As we have seen, this resulted in the squeezing of victim participation. Although victims continued to initiate the majority of crime reports, their interests came to be represented by others during subsequent proceedings. Another result was that the practices of the adversarial trial—the means by which a fair trial was ensured—changed. Standards of admissible evidence, for example, became more exacting. This is an obvious but significant point. The adversarial trial, which only emerged in the eighteenth century, is a social as well as a legal practice and, as such, is subject to change in response to legal and social pressures. If methods of determining guilt and innocence have changed in the past, they can change in the future.

Historically, the state did not *care* explicitly about victims. It cared about the peace of the realm and it cared that victims took action to enforce it. Victims were displaced within the higher courts as a result of efforts to construct a more effective English criminal justice system to maintain that peace. They were brought back into view as a result of four political changes after the mid-twentieth century. Firstly, through the welfarism of the 1950s, which gave some victims a right to state compensation. Secondly, through the emergent politics of recognition, first articulated by Margery Fry in 1957, that prioritized the recognition of trauma and harm over other aspects of victimization. Thirdly, through the new welfarism of the 1980s and 90s—with victims as objects of increasingly targeted interventions led by powerful third sector agencies such as Victim Support. In this model, the state was responsible less for the delivery of services and more for the funding and regulation of increasingly outsourced services, and victims were increasingly seen as individualized consumers of criminal justice services. And fourthly, from the 1990s, through a European Union-required codification process leading to a statutory Victims' Code, a Victims' Commissioner, and a set of largely unenforceable entitlements.

A victim's ability to participate in the legal process—as an independent citizen—has long been governed by a range of subtle and overlapping legal frameworks which sit within a pluralistic regulatory regime (Kirchengast, 2016; Holder and Kirchengast, 2021). It has also been unavoidably shaped by the changing impacts of gender, class, ethnicity, and age, and associated inequalities of economic, social, and cultural capital. Any effort to further amend those statutory frameworks—through the introduction of new laws or by other means—needs to be very alert to these complex forces. It also needs to guard against the introduction of measures that shore up our current culture of (carceral) control in the name of victim rights, and which are more likely to meet the demands of a populist media and electorate rather than meeting the evidence-based needs of victims—difficult as these are to determine.

Today, however, influential segments of British public opinion demand that the state *must* care, and be seen to care. As a result, the state has taken on legal duties in relation to victims and must also be seen to *perform* that care to the public. The political price of apparent indifference is too high. Victim groups, and indeed other constituencies, who can mobilize around the claim that the state 'doesn't care' have a powerful card to play in today's political arena. One way the state can respond is through spending. In 2021, the Ministry of Justice spent £150 million on victim and witness support services, and other parts of the UK government spent a further £150 million (MoJ, 2021, 38). These sums would have appeared extraordinary half a century ago but they are a sign of how political imperatives have changed. But within the adversarial trial and its historic delegation of powers to police, counsel, and public prosecutors, there are clear limits to what can be achieved through wider policy measures—simply because the trial cannot prioritize the interests of victims. In this sense, the victims' rights agenda is incompatible with adversarialism as currently framed. Rather than implying that it is possible to restore aspects of victims' historically central role in the prosecution process, the state needs to develop a more explicit narrative to justify why any efforts to further expand victims' rights within the criminal justice system would not serve the current public interest.

Those charged with balancing the rights of victims and defendants in court have an unenviable task—but one that might be eased with a better and more critical grasp of the history of how we came to be here. We hope that our efforts to trace victim participation in criminal trials have placed current policy debates in a much-needed critical historical context.

APPENDIX

Datasets

This study of the experience of millions of victims in the criminal courts of England and Wales over the three centuries covered by this study required analysis of large bodies of quantitative data. As explained in the Introduction, owing to the depth of the information available we focused on the prosecution of the most serious crimes and on London, in particular on cases heard at London's principal criminal court, the Old Bailey, also known (from 1834) as the Central Criminal Court. Detailed evidence from the published *Proceedings* of that court, contained in 134 million words of text describing 197,745 trials from 1674 to 1913, formed our most important dataset, which has been supplemented by two further datasets containing selected additional data from both the *Proceedings*, as well as twentieth-century trial reports in *The Times* newspaper. To place the Old Bailey data in a wider perspective, we also compiled a dataset of national statistics. With the exception of the Old Bailey Corpus, which is already publicly available, the datasets have been deposited with the UK Data Service (SN 9082, https://beta.ukdataservice.ac.uk/datacatalogue/studies/study?id=9082), and the DHI Data Service (University of Sheffield, https://www.dhi.ac.uk/data/victimsproject), from which they are freely available for non-commercial reuse. In this Appendix, we describe the source of each dataset, explain its parameters, and provide details about how the information was collected and coded. Analysis of the data was primarily carried out using SPSS, with the results exported to Excel for the creation of graphs.

These five datasets were constructed over three years of research on the ESRC Project, 'Victims' Access to Justice through the English Criminal Courts, 1675 to the present' (ESRC ES/R006962/1). The first contains personal details of all 230,646 victim prosecutions recorded in the *Proceedings* of the Old Bailey between 1674 and 1913, together with details about their trials and outcomes. (Each criminal charge made by or on behalf of a victim is counted as a 'victim prosecution'.) The second contains details from all Old Bailey trials (5,618 victim prosecutions) reported in *The Times* newspaper in two time periods: 1910–25 (3,104 cases) and 1960–75 (2,514 cases). The third is comprised of a sample of victim prosecutions in the nineteenth-century *Proceedings* for which we have manually collected additional details about the participants in their trials. The fourth contains data derived from a separate but related dataset, the Old Bailey Corpus of words spoken during trials. Finally, the fifth comprises statistical evidence extracted from annual reports published in the Parliamentary Papers concerning the number of criminal prosecutions in England and Wales between 1805 and 1979.

In addition to guilty verdicts, all datasets include cases where the defendant was acquitted or no verdict was reached for various reasons, or the verdict is unknown. Our analysis therefore incorporates data on people whose criminal complaints were deemed worthy of a formal prosecution, and were thus regarded by prosecutors as victims of crime, even if the trial jury or judge did not agree.

1. *Proceedings* Dataset (1674–1913)

This dataset is derived from the published *Proceedings* of the Old Bailey during the entire period of their publication. Reports in the *Proceedings* were not transcripts, although they typically include, at a minimum, the key facts of each case: the offence charged, names of victims and defendants, verdicts, and punishment sentences. Although reports in the early years were often brief, they normally include some account of the testimony by victims, witnesses, and defendants, and over time they lengthened and included, from the 1720s, increasing amounts of verbatim testimony. Inexpensive, and targeted initially at a popular audience, the *Proceedings* were compiled by shorthand note-takers, transcribed, and produced by commercial publishers, under licence from the City of London. They were published shortly after the conclusion of each court (sessions), eight times a year until 1834, and then ten to twelve times a year thereafter. Although initially a commercial success, following the growth of newspapers and increasing publication costs the audience narrowed by the nineteenth century to a combination of lawyers and public officials, and publication was subsidized by the City of London.

Care should be taken when using the *Proceedings*, since there was no point in their long history at which they comprehensively recorded everything that was said or took place in Old Bailey trials (Emsley, Hitchcock, and Shoemaker, 2018c; Shoemaker, 2008b; Devereaux, 1996). Not every trial was reported until the mid-1680s, and editions of the *Proceedings* are missing for around a third of Old Bailey sessions between 1674 and 1714 (Emsley, Hitchcock, and Shoemaker, 2018b). From 1715 every edition of the *Proceedings* survives. In December 1729 the *Proceedings* were expanded in size and more detailed speech from prosecutors, witnesses, defendants, and judges was included. Everyday offending appears in the *Proceedings*, but more interesting and/or salacious crimes—murders, sexual offences, major robberies, and so on—were reported at greater length. Nevertheless, from the 1730s, the *Proceedings* began to be viewed as providing a legal record of the court's proceedings. In 1775, the City of London demanded that the *Proceedings* should provide a 'true, fair, and perfect narrative' of all the trials, and reports became more uniform in coverage (Devereaux 1996; Shoemaker 2008b). By the start of the nineteenth century the *Proceedings* had the status of a quasi-official publication, and legal officials relied upon it when making decisions on sentencing and pardons (Devereaux 2002; 2004, 266).

Between 2003 and 2008 the text of the *Proceedings* was digitized and made available online (https://www.oldbaileyonline.org). The *Proceedings of the Old Bailey Online* (OBO) created reliable searchable transcriptions of the full texts of the trial accounts, and added structured tagging of key information such as names of victims and defendants, their ages, gender and occupations, and offences, verdicts, and punishment sentences. This dataset is downloadable from the University of Sheffield Digital Humanities Institute Data Service (https://www.dhi.ac.uk/data/

download/oldbailey). While this structured data was the starting point for our dataset, the Old Bailey project's tagging structure was principally focused on defendants. Therefore, the Victims project enhanced the existing tagging on victims, primarily by adding missing evidence on occupations (explained below), and added additional variables, extracted from textual evidence in the *Proceedings*, providing information relating to the prosecution of these cases. Combining the existing tagging with new variables, we assembled a dataset of twenty-seven quantifiable variables, including: number, age, gender, occupation, and name of both victims and defendants; whether the victim was an individual or institution; involvement of an policing agent or prosecution agency (such as the Bank of England or NSPCC) in the trial; involvement of counsel; offence; and plea, verdict, and sentence. It should be noted that most variables do not contain relevant information for all 230,646 prosecutions, and our analysis has been attendant to the challenges of dealing with missing evidence. A data guide which lists all the variables and their characteristics is available along with the deposited data.

We would like to thank Jamie McLaughlin, Research Software Engineer at the Digital Humanities Institute, University of Sheffield, for his work in adapting the original Old Bailey Online data to meet the requirements of the Victims project.

2. *The Times* Dataset

The 1907 Criminal Appeal Act (7 Edw. VII *c.* 23) required the taking of full shorthand notes of all trials, fundamentally undermining the rationale for the *Proceedings*, leading the City of London to terminate its funding. At the conclusion of the April 1913 edition, readers found a simple statement, 'the publication of the C.C.C. Sessions Papers is now discontinued', thus bringing to an end the 239-year history of the *Proceedings* (Emsley, Hitchcock, and Shoemaker, 2018b).

In order to study cases after this date, we systematically collected data from all Old Bailey trials reported in *The Times* in two tranches (1910–25 and 1950–75). We selected *The Times* both because of its regular reporting of trials, and because it was considered by many as an authoritative source (Rowbotham, Stevenson, and Pegg, 2013, 11). Trial accounts were selected by searching the *Times Digital Archive* (https://www.gale.com/intl/c/the-times-digital-archive) for reports containing the phrases 'Central Criminal Court' or 'Old Bailey'. As explained in Chapter 1, reporting in *The Times* was selective, but we collected material on every case they reported in our chosen tranches.

We entered information from these reports into a dataset, either in the form of verbatim information (names, ages, offences) or the report was used to provide answers to binary questions (was prosecution counsel present?—yes/no/information not provided). The resulting dataset includes thirty-three quantifiable variables, most of which are the same as in the *Proceedings* dataset, but some were new, such as the presence (or not) of prosecution counsel, victim ethnicity, and one which captured the involvement (or not) of the Director of Public Prosecutions. As with the *Proceedings* dataset, a data guide was compiled listing all the variables and their characteristics; this is available with the deposited data.

Recoding schemes for the *Proceedings* and *Times* datasets

The number and complexity of the potential values for some of our variables presented significant challenges, requiring us to adopt clear and consistent recoding schemes to make it possible to carry out the quantitative analysis presented in Chapters 5 and 6.

In the case of **offences**, to enable our data to be summarized and compared internationally and historically with other studies, we chose to use the United Nations Office for Drugs and Crime 'International Classification Scheme for Statistical Purposes' (UNODC, 2015). This scheme takes about one thousand specific criminal activities and assigns them numerical codes, which are grouped into four hierarchical levels of increasing generality, culminating in the highest level, which contains eleven general categories of crime. One, 'Acts against the Natural Environment' (code 10), did not apply to any of the Old Bailey crimes analysed in this study. The others are listed in Table A.1, together with the short form labels used in the figures provided in this book.

For the *Proceedings* data, we assigned offences to the most specific relevant categories on the basis of the sixty-four specific crime categories used in the coding of trials in the OBO project. For the *Times,* offences were assigned on the basis of the language used by the newspaper in its reports. After we assigned the most specific code possible to each offence description in each dataset, they were grouped into the eleven UNODC general categories. For example, violent offences such as assault (02011), minor assault (020112), and threats (20012) were all uniquely coded and then also recorded as 'acts causing harm or intending to cause harm to the person' (02). Similarly, theft of a motor vehicle (050211), theft of livestock (05025), and theft of public property (05024) were all individually and uniquely coded, but also classified as 'acts against property only' (05) and so on.

With respect to **occupations**, we faced challenges both in identifying missing victim occupations and in classifying them into suitable categories for quantitative analysis. Victim occupations were not systematically recorded in the original trial accounts in the *Proceedings* or the reports in *The Times*, but those that were provided were identified as such in the tagging and data entry. However, the data we obtained from the OBO was limited by the fact that in the second stage of the Old Bailey project, covering the period from November 1834 to 1913, victim occupations were not comprehensively tagged. This is because for that part of the project there were fewer resources to devote to tagging, which meant that victim occupations not listed at the start of trials were not tagged. To identify these missing occupations, we used pattern matching to automatically extract from the trial accounts snippets of text following the victim's name in trial testimonies which took the form of one of forty specific expressions, including 'I am', 'I work as', 'I am employed at', 'the prisoner is my journeyman', and similar expressions. We then used a dictionary of occupations that had already been identified in the *Proceedings* (for both defendants and victims) to extract occupational labels from the identified snippets.

Table A.1: UNODC Crime Categories

UNODC Code	Category	Short Form
01	Acts leading to death, or intending to cause death	Killing
02	Acts causing harm or intending to cause harm to the person	Personal Harm
03	Injurious acts of a sexual nature	Sexual Injury
04	Acts against property involving violence or threat against a person	Property with Violence
05	Acts against property only	Property Only
06	Acts involving controlled drugs or other psychoactive substances	Drugs
07	Acts involving fraud, deception or corruption	Fraud and Deception
08	Acts against public order, authority and provisions of the state	Public Order
09	Acts against public safety and state security	Public Safety
11	Other criminal acts not elsewhere classified	Other

(Source: UNODC, 2015)

The occupational labels contained in the *Proceedings* and *The Times* were extremely varied. To classify them, we used the Historical International Classification of Occupations (HISCO), collaboratively created under the auspices of the International Institute of Social History in Amsterdam. This scheme categorizes all paid employment into twelve ranked categories, providing a classification system for 'the 1,000 most frequent male and female occupational titles in datasets from eight different countries: Belgium, Britain, Canada, France, Germany, the Netherlands, Norway and Sweden', focusing on the period from 1690 to 1970, particularly the nineteenth century (https://iisg.amsterdam/en/data/data-websites/history-of-work). The scheme is thus well suited to the occupations found in the Old Bailey data.

Each occupation in HISCO has been coded within a multilayer hierarchy, HISCLASS, similar to that created by the UNODC scheme for classifying types of crime. Our focus was on the highest level of HISCO classification, twelve groups which create a hierarchy based on whether the work is manual or non-manual, the levels of skill involved, whether the work involves the supervision of others, and whether the work involves fishing or agriculture. To these twelve groups, we added four categories for groups we felt were insufficiently distinguished in the HISCO classifications: members of the aristocracy and gentry, small manufacturers and artisans, unspecified workers, and children (when no specific occupation was provided).

As explained in Chapter 5, we then created a higher level tripartite classification (not used by HISCO) based on nineteenth-century understandings of social class. Given the underlying complexities of actual work experiences and perceptions of status, these categories are based on relatively simplistic generalizations, but they provide us with a basic overview of the socio-economic composition of victims at the Old Bailey, and allow us to assess how this changed over time. Table A.2 provides a summary of the basic HISCO categories and the social classes to which they were assigned.

The process of assigning HISCO codes to Old Bailey occupational labels was derived from the work of the Old Bailey Corpus project (see dataset 4, below), which had previously assigned HISCLASS coding to the Old Bailey data. Using the Old Bailey project trial IDs, the Victims project matched the corpus data to our Old Bailey data, and the imported HISCO codes were then spread through the entirety of the *Proceedings* dataset, assigning relevant codes to identical occupations. Remaining uncoded occupations (those not coded in the Corpus) in the *Proceedings*, and the entirety of the *Times* dataset, were coded by hand, using our amended HISCLASS classification scheme.

As discussed in Chapter 5, a significant number of victims of crimes, particularly in cases of coining, fraud, forgery, and embezzlement, were not individuals but were instead **institutions**, both state agencies and private companies. To enable these cases to be separately analysed, we introduced a separate variable, 'institution' (y/n), and coded cases accordingly. In the *Proceedings* data, we identified institutions from the list of victim names given an 'indeterminate' gender tag by the OBO project. Since, as explained above, victim names were less systematically tagged for the period from November 1834 to 1913, we added further institutions through an automated process by identifying cases in the trial accounts where the tagged victim name included one of thirty-four specific keywords or phrases, including company, society, railway, and parish. It must be noted, however, that this process failed to capture all institutions identified in the trial reports. The identification of institutional victim names in *The Times* was carried out manually.

The final recoding challenge concerns trials involving **multiple defendants, charges, verdicts, and punishment sentences.** As explained above, the basic unit of analysis in this book is the 'victim prosecution': each criminal offence linked with an identified victim. Two victims prosecuting a single offence constitute two victim prosecutions. Where the same victim charged the same defendant with more than one offence, however, this constitutes only one victim prosecution, categorized on the basis of the most serious offence charged. Multiple defendants charged by a single victim with the same offence are also deemed a single victim prosecution, but this creates difficulty when analysing differences in trial outcomes. Where two defendants of the same victim prosecution had different verdicts, these were categorized as 'mixed'. But in the case of punishment sentences, where the same victim prosecution resulted in more than one punishment (for example imprisonment plus a fine), we categorized the sentence according to the most severe punishment,

Table A.2: Class and Occupational Categories Used by the Victims Project (Numbers in brackets are not in the original HISCO scheme)

HISCLASS	Occupational Groups	Class
[0.5]	Aristocrats and gentlemen	Upper
1	Higher managers	Upper
2	Higher professionals	Upper
3	Lower managers	Middle
4	Medium skilled professionals, clerical and sales personnel	Middle
5	Lower skilled clerical and sales personnel	Middle
6	Foremen	Middle
[6.5]	Small manufacturers and artisans	Middle
7	Medium-skilled workers	Lower
8	Farmers and fishermen	Lower
9	Lower-skilled workers	Lower
10	Lower-skilled farm workers	Lower
11	Unskilled workers	Lower
12	Unskilled farm workers	Lower
[13]	Unspecified workers	Lower
[14]	Children	[N/A]

according to the following hierarchy: death, transportation, imprisonment, other (whipping, fines, community service, etc.).

We would like to thank Dr Lucy Williams, Research Associate, and Professor Barry Godfrey, both of the University of Liverpool, for assembling the data and carrying out the recoding.

3. Trial Participants dataset

To collect important information not contained within the *Proceedings* dataset, we manually compiled a sample of prosecutions containing evidence on the roles played by victims, defendants, police, and counsel in Old Bailey trials, as reported in the *Proceedings*. This dataset was confined to the nineteenth century because analysis of the *Proceedings* dataset and other evidence indicated that this was the period when crucial changes occurred in the conduct of criminal prosecutions. This dataset, derived from close reading of the trial accounts, provides more refined data on who was present and testified in trials, and whether they were the first, second, third. or fourth person to speak, thereby facilitating analysis of whose voices were most often heard, and given most prominence, in trial proceedings (discussed in Chapter 6). In addition, the dataset records when counsel were present, and whether they acted for the prosecution or defence (this information cannot be derived from the *Proceedings* dataset, which simply records the presence or absence of counsel).

Every fifth case was recorded for the January and July sessions of the *Proceedings* for every year ending in 5 or 0, starting in 1805 and ending in 1900. The resulting sample of 891 cases constitutes a sample of 0.65 percent of the 136,351 trials in the nineteenth century. For each trial sampled, we recorded the offence, victim gender, the roles of the first, second, third, and fourth speakers in the trial, and whether or not prosecution counsel, defence counsel, and the police were present (and if so, the words used to describe them). For each trial, each individual speaker was only recorded once. One hundred and ninety-two cases were labelled as 'no trial', as there was no reported speech, normally either because the defendant pleaded guilty or the trial proceedings were not reported due to the notoriety of the case (usually sexual offences); these cases were excluded from most aspects of our analysis of this dataset.

It must be acknowledged that this data is limited. Even in the nineteenth century, the *Proceedings* do not provide comprehensive transcripts of trials, so it is possible that the testimony of some trial participants was not recorded. In particular, while the presence of counsel was typically recorded, their speech in court was not. Judging by parallel accounts in other sources, however, the *Proceedings* did record the main participants in each trial, and the correct order in which they spoke, providing us with valuable evidence of how Old Bailey trials were conducted over time (Emsley, Hitchcock, and Shoemaker, 2018c).

4. The Old Bailey Corpus of Spoken Words (OBC)

The Trial Participants dataset was complemented by data on speakers in trials compiled by the Old Bailey Corpus project. Created by a team led by Magnus Huber at the University of Giessen for the purposes of linguistic analysis, the OBC contains data extracted from the original Old Bailey Online dataset and structured to document verbatim speech recorded in the *Proceedings* (https://fedora.clarin-d.uni-saarland.de/oldbailey/; Huber, Nissel, and Puga, 2016). Each speaker was tagged by their gender, occupation, role in the trial, and the order in which they appear in the trial account. The dataset is large, but not comprehensive. It includes 24.4 million spoken words recorded in trials in 637 selected sessions (meetings) of the court between 1720 and 1913, representing just over a third of all meetings of the court during that period (prior to 1720, the *Proceedings* contained relatively little verbatim speech). The number of sessions chosen per year was determined by the goal of providing a relatively similar number of spoken words in each decade.

We downloaded a copy of this dataset (available from http://fedora.clarin-d.uni-saarland.de/oldbailey/index.html) and our Research Associate, Elisa Impara (University of Essex), extracted from it the following information related to the speech of victims, judges, witnesses, and defendants: whether they were the first, second, or later person to speak in the trial, and how many words they were recorded as having spoken. For victims, we also extracted their gender, occupation, and associated HISCO coding. Unfortunately, the roles coded in the OBC do not include policing agents, and we did not use the evidence on counsel because the OBC does not differentiate between prosecution and defence counsel. Nonetheless, this data extends the chronological range of the data we compiled in the Trial Participants dataset, and, crucially, it provides information on the relative number of words spoken by victims as opposed to other trial participants. We would like to thank the Old Bailey Corpus project for making their data available, and Elisa Impara for extracting and analysing this complex dataset.

5. Parliamentary Papers Dataset

To provide the national context (England and Wales) for the evidence from the Old Bailey court, we created a sample of judicial statistics compiled by the Home Office in annual reports published in the Parliamentary Papers from 1811 to 1979. Over the course of the nineteenth century these statistics, published under a variety of titles, became more detailed, and expanded from the number of defendants committed for trial to include separate statistics for the quarter sessions and assize courts and cases heard by summary jurisdiction, as well as the number of prosecutions funded or conducted by the government. Such statistics continued to be compiled throughout the twentieth century, though the formats and types of information collected changed and in certain respects contracted, and they were substantially curtailed during both world wars. While the reliability of these statistics has been questioned, particularly those which report crimes 'known to the police', those which concern the numbers of prosecutions which took place are generally viewed as reliable (Morris, 2001).

Although they have previously been used by historians of crime, policing, and punishment (Gatrell and Hadden, 1972; Gatrell, 1980; Godfrey, 2008; Emsley, 2010), these reports have not previously been analysed by historians of victims and prosecution, a task rendered difficult owing to the fact that the number of victims per se was never reported. It was the greater understanding of the circumstances of criminals and crime, not victims, which was the impetus to collect this information (Shoemaker and Ward, 2017). Nonetheless, statistics were collected on the number of cases where the government paid the costs of prosecution, or a government agency was responsible for the prosecution, and in any case the number of defendants charged provides a rough proxy for the number of victims whose complaints led to prosecutions.

We consulted approximately every fifth annual report, from the first report, which covered 1805 to 1809, to 1979, and entered the results in this dataset. Owing to the retrospective reporting of the key statistics on commitments, this allowed us to compile the following annual series of national statistics:

- Number of criminal commitments (and individuals bailed) for trial, 1805 to 1951

- Number of individuals charged with indictable offences (including those tried both by summary jurisdiction and in the quarter sessions and assizes courts), 1857 to 1951

In addition, we collected the following statistics for approximately every fifth year:

- Numbers of cases for trial at the Central Criminal Court (Old Bailey), and at all assizes courts, 1855 to 1938
- Number of Central Criminal Court cases where the costs were paid by the government, 1856 to 1890, and the average payment per case
- Number of cases of coining prosecuted by the Mint or other government agencies, 1856 to 1979
- Number of cases prosecuted by the Director of Public Prosecutions (DPP), both on indictment and otherwise, 1886 to 1971

To understand the relationship between levels of prosecutions at the Old Bailey and these statistics, we then compared the figures in these published accounts with the annual number of defendants tried at the Old Bailey, derived from the Old Bailey Online, between 1805 and 1913. We have not been able to locate any comprehensive statistics on the number of Old Bailey cases after 1913.

Bibliography

1. Primary Source Documents

a. UK Parliamentary Papers (Accessed via Proquest UK Parliamentary Papers website) [PP]

1797–8, Twenty-Eighth Report from the Select Committee on Finance, 1798, v. 13.

1816, Select Committee on State of Police of the Metropolis; with the minutes of evidence taken before the committee; and, an appendix of sundry papers, 1816, v. 5, 510.

1818, Third Report from the Committee on State of the Police of the Metropolis; with the minutes of evidence taken before the committee; and, an appendix, 1818, v. 8, 423.

1819, Select Committee on Criminal Laws relating to Capital Punishment in Felonies. Report, Minutes of Evidence, Appendix, 1819, v. 8, 585.

1834, Report from the Select Committee on the Police of the Metropolis; with the minutes of evidence, appendix and index, 1834, v. 16, 500.

1835, Committals, England and Wales. Summary Statements of Persons Charged with Criminal Offences, Committed to the Different Gaols in England and Wales, and London and Middlesex, for Trial at the Assizes and Sessions, 1814–34, 1835, v. 45, 217.

1837–38, Select Committee on Metropolis Police Offices; with the minutes of evidence, appendix and index, 1837–8, v. 15, 578.

1852, Tables of Number of Criminal Offenders in England and Wales, 1851, v. 41, 1518.

1852–3, Second Report from the Select Committee on Police, together with the proceedings of the committee, minutes of evidence, and appendix, 1852–3, v. 36, 345.

1854, 'Public Prosecutors Bill', House of Commons (HC) Deb, 14 February, 1854, v. 130, cc. 665–72.

1854–1855, Report from the Select Committee on Public Prosecutors, together with the proceedings of the committee, minutes of evidence, appendix and index, 1854–5, v. 12, 481.

1855, 'Public Prosecutors Bill', House of Commons (HC) Deb, v. 136, 20 February, 1855, cc. 1651–59.

1856, Return of Judicial Statistics. (Part 1), England and Wales, 1857 Session 2, v. 35, 2246.

1857, Report from the Common Law (Judicial Business) Commissioners; together with the minutes of evidence and appendix, 1857 Session 2, v. 21, 2268.

1862, Report from the Select Committee on Prosecution Expenses; together with the proceedings of the committee, minutes of evidence, appendix and index, 1862, v. 11, 401.

1872, 'Public Prosecutors Bill', House of Commons (HC) Deb, 16 February 1872. v. 209, c. 593.

1874 Judicature Commission. Fifth and Final Report of the Commissioners, 1874, v. 24, C. 1090.

1882, Return of the Judicial Statistics of England and Wales, 1881, v. 75, C. 3333.

1884, Report of the Committee Appointed to Inquire into the Office of the Public Prosecutor, with minutes of evidence and appendix, 1884, v. 23, C. 4016.

1898, Judicial statistics, England and Wales, 1896. Part I.--Criminal statistics. statistics relating to criminal proceedings, police, coroners, prisons, reformatory and industrial schools, and criminal lunatics for the year 1896, 1898, v. 104, C. 8755.

1900, Judicial Statistics, England and Wales, 1898. Part I, Criminal Statistics. Statistics relating to Criminal Proceedings, Police, Coroners, Prisons, Reformatory and Industrial School and Criminal Lunatics for the year 1898, 1900, v. 103, Cd. 123.

1903a, Report of the Departmental Committee appointed to inquire into the allowances to prosecutors and witnesses in criminal prosecutions, 1903, v. 56, Cd. 1650.

1903b, Judicial statistics, England and Wales, 1901. Part I.--Criminal statistics. Statistics relating to criminal proceedings, police, coroners, prisons, reformatory and industrial schools, and criminal lunatics for the year 1901, 1903, v. 83, Cd. 1441.1588.

1977, 'Criminal Law Bill', House of Commons (HC) Deb, 3 May 1977, v. 931, c. 269.

1977, 'Confait Case', House of Commons (HC) Deb, 13 December 1977, v. 941, c. 122.

1979–80, Report of the Commissioner of Police of the Metropolis for the year 1979, 1979–80, Cmnd. 7932.

1981, 'Criminal Procedure', House of Commons (HC) Deb, 20 November, 1981, v. 13, c. 527, 554.

1990, 'Crime Victims', House of Commons (HC) Deb, 22 February 1990, v. 167, cc. 1055–7.

2021, 'Hate crime laws: Final report', Law Commission, Law Com No 402, 6 December 2021.

b. Statutes

1285 Statute of Winchester (13 Edw. I).

1554 Marian Bail Statute (1 & 2 Phil. & Mar. c. 13).

1555 Marian Committal Statute (2 & 3 Phil. & Mar. c. 10).

1692 Act for Encouraging the Apprehending of Highwaymen (4 Wm. & Mar. c. 8).

1706 Act for the Encouraging the Discovery and Apprehending of House-breakers (6 Anne c. 31).

1715 Riot Act (1 Geo. I, st. 2, c. 5).

1718 Transportation Act (4 Geo. I c. 11).

1719 Act for the Further Preventing Robbery, Burglary, and Other Felonies (6 Geo. I c. 23).
1752 An Act for the better preventing Thefts and Robberies (25 Geo. II c. 36).
1754 Offenders (Conveyance) Act 1754 (27 Geo. II c. 3).
1778 Payment of Charges of Constables Act (18 Geo. III c. 19).
1792 Middlesex Justices Act (32 Geo. III c. 53).
1803 Malicious Shooting or Stabbing Act (Lord Ellenborough's Act) (43 Geo. III c. 58).
1815 Criminal Costs (Dublin) Act (55 Geo. III c. 91).
1818 Act for Repealing Pecuniary and Other Rewards (Bennet's Act) (58 Geo. III c. 70).
1826 Criminal Law Act (7 Geo. IV c. 64).
1827 Larceny Act (7 & 8 Geo. IV c. 29).
1827 Criminal Statutes Repeal Act (7 & 8 Geo. IV c. 27).
1828 Offences Against the Person Act (Lord Lansdowne's Act) (9 Geo. IV c. 31).
1836 Prisoners' Counsel Act (6 & 7 Will. 4 c. 14).
1837 Offences Against the Person Act (1 Vict. c. 85).
1839 Metropolitan Courts Act (2 & 3 Vict. C. 71).
1841 Substitution of Punishments for Death Act (4 & 5 Vict. c. 56).
1848 Indictable Offences Act (11&12 Vict, c. 42).
1851 Prevention of Offences Act (14 & 15 Vict. c. 19).
1851 Criminal Justice Administration Act (14 & 15 Vict. c. 55).
1853 Criminal Procedure Act (16 & 17 Vict. C. 30).
1855 Criminal Justice Act (18 & 19 Vict. c. 126).
1859 Vexatious Indictments Act (22 & 23 Vict. c. 17).
1861 Larceny Act (24 & 25 Vic c. 96).
1861 Offences Against the Person Act (24 & 25 Vict. c. 100).
1866 Prosecution Expenses Act (29 & 30 Vict. C. 52).
1870 Forfeiture Act (33 & 34 Vict. c. 23).
1875 Offences Against the Person Act (38 & 39 Vict. c. 94).
1879 Prosecution of Offences Act (42 & 43 Vict. C. 22).
1879 Summary Justice Act (42 & 43 Vict. c. 49).
1882 Married Women's Property Act (45 & 46 Vict. c. 75).
1884 Prosecution of Offences Act (47 & 48 Vict. C. 58).
1885 Criminal Law Amendment Act (48 & 49 Vict. c. 69).
1889 Prevention of Cruelty to, and Protection of Children Act (52 & 53 Vict. c. 44).
1894 Prevention of Cruelty to Children Act (57 & 58 Vict. C. 41).
1904 Prevention of Cruelty to Children Act (4 Edw. VII c. 15).
1907 Criminal Appeal Act (7 Edw. VII c. 23).
1908 Children Act (8 Edw. VII c. 67).
1908 Costs in Criminal Cases Act (8 Edw. VII c. 15).
1908 Punishment of Incest Act (9 Edw. VII c. 45).
1908 Prosecution of Offenses Act (8 Edw. 7 c. 3).
1919 Sex Disqualification (Removal) Act (9 & 10 Geo. 5 c. 71).
1933 Administration of Justice (Miscellaneous Provisions) Act (23 & 24 Geo. 5 c. 36).

1948 Criminal Justice Act (11 & 12 Geo. 6 c. 58).
1956 Sexual Offences Act (4 & 5 Eliz. 2 c. 69).
1960 Indecency with Children Act (8 & 9 Eliz. II c. 33).
1967 Criminal Law Act (1967 c. 58).
1976 Domestic Violence and Matrimonial Proceedings Act (1976 c. 50).
1976 Sexual Offences (Amendment) Act (1976 c. 82).
1984 Police and Criminal Evidence Act (1984 c. 60).
1985 Prosecution of Offences Act (1985 c. 23).
1988 Criminal Justice Act (1988 c. 33).
1998 Crime and Disorder Act (1998 c. 37).
1999 Youth Justice and Criminal Evidence Act (1999 c. 23).
2003 Criminal Justice Act (2003 c. 44).
2004 Domestic Violence, Crime and Victims Act (2004 c. 28).

c. London Metropolitan Archives

LMA Solicitors Papers: COL/CCS/SO/02/01/006b.

d. Newspapers and Periodicals

Daily Telegraph
Gay International News
Gay News
Law Times
Morning Chronicle
The Standard
The Times

e. Websites

Hitchcock, T., Shoemaker, R., Emsley, C., Howard, S., McLaughlin, J. *et al.* (2018), *The Old Bailey Proceedings Online, 1674–1913* (www.oldbaileyonline.org, version 8.0).

Huber, M., Nissel, M., and Puga, K. (2016), *The Old Bailey Corpus 2.0* (http://fedora.clarin-d.uni-saarland.de/oldbailey/).

Times Digital Archive, 1785–2019 (https://www.gale.com/intl/c/the-times-digital-archive).

f. Published Primary Sources

Beveridge, W. (1942), *Social Insurance and Allied Services*. London: HMSO.

Blackstone, W. (1769), *Commentaries on the Laws of England. Book the Fourth.* Oxford.

Burn, R. (1755), *The Justice of the Peace, and Parish Officer.* London, two volumes.

Chadwick, E. (1868), 'On the Consolidation of the Police Force, and the Prevention of Crime', *Fraser's Magazine*, 77:457, p.14.

Colquhoun, P. (1796), *A Treatise on the Police of the Metropolis, Explaining the Various Crimes and Misdemeanors which at Present are felt as a Pressure upon the Community*. London.

Cottu, M. (1820), 'The administration of the criminal code in England and the spirit of the English government', *The Pamphleteer*, 16:31.

Fielding, J. (1758), *An Account of the Origins and Effects of the Police set on foot by the Duke of Newcastle in 1753. With a Plan for preserving those deserted Girls who have become prostitutes from necessity*. London.

Gisborne, T. (1794), *An Enquiry into the Duties of Men in the Higher and Middle Class of Society resulting from their respective stations, professions, and employments*. London.

Graves, C.S. (1866–7), 'Judicial Statistics', *The Law Magazine and Law Review*, 12, 104–15.

Hale, M. (1736), *Historia Placitorum Coronae: The History of Pleas of the Crown*, vols 1 and 2. London.

Joyce, H. (1893), *The History of the Post Office from Its Establishment Down to 1836*. London: R. Bentley & Son.

Maitland, F. W. (1885), *Justice and Police*. London: Macmillan.

Maule, J. B. (ed.) (1869), *The Justice of the Peace and Parish Officer [by Richard Burn]*, 13th edn, 5 vols. London: H. Sweet.

Montesquieu, C. L. de Secondat, Baron de la Brède et de Montesquieu (1949), The Spirit of the Laws. First published as *De l'Esprit des Lois* (1748).

Pizzey, E. (1974), *Scream Quietly or the Neighbours Will Hear*. London: Penguin Books.

Pizzey, E. (1975), 'Chiswick Women's Aid—a Refuge From Violence', *Royal Society of Health Journal*, 95, no. 6, 297–8.

Priestley, P. (1970), 'What About the Victim?', National Victims Association pamphlet. Cheltenham.

Savile, G. (1995), *Secret Comment: The Diaries of Gertrude Savile 1721–1757*, ed. Alan Savile, Vol. 41 (Kingsbridge: Kingsbridge History Society, Thoroton Society Record Series).

Scarman, L. G. (1982), *The Scarman Report: The Brixton Disorders 10–12 April 1981*. Harmondsworth: Penguin.

Stephen, J. F. (1863), *A General View of the Criminal Law of England*. London: Macmillan and Co.

Stephen, J. F. (1883), *A History of the Criminal Law of England*. London: Macmillan and Co.

Trusler, J. (1786), *The London Adviser and Guide: Containing Every Instruction and Information Useful and Necessary to Persons Living in London*. London.

Waddy, H. T. (1925), *The Police Court and its Work*. London: Butterworth and Co.

Wontner, T. (1833), *Old Bailey Experience: Criminal Jurisprudence and the Actual Working of our Penal Code of Laws*. London: James Fraser.

Wontner, T. (1838), *The Forensic Victimologist*. London: W. M. Clark.

2. Secondary Sources

a. Books

Auerbach, S. (2021), *Armed with Sword and Scales: Law, Culture and Local Courtrooms in London, 1860–1913*. Cambridge: Cambridge University Press.

Banks, S. (2014), *Informal Justice in England and Wales, 1760–1914*. Woodbridge: Boydell.

Barrie, D. (2008), *Police in the Age of Improvement: Police Development and the Civic Tradition in Scotland, 1775–1865*. Abingdon: Taylor & Francis.

Basannavar, N. (2021), *Sexual Violence Against Children Since 1965*. London: Palgrave Macmillan.

Beattie, J. M. (1986), *Crime and Courts in England, 1660–1800*. Princeton: Princeton University Press.

Beattie, J. M. (2001), *Policing and Punishment in London, 1660–1750*. Oxford: Oxford University Press.

Beattie, J. M. (2012), *The First English Detectives: The Bow Street Runners and the Policing of London, 1750–1840*. Oxford: Oxford University Press.

Behlmer, George K. (1982), *Child Abuse and Moral Reform, 1870–1908*. Stanford, California: Stanford University Press.

Bentley, D. (1998), *English Criminal Justice in the Nineteenth Century*. London: Hambledon.

Bland, E. (2022), *Policing Suspicion: Proactive Policing in London, 1780 to 1850*. Abingdon, Oxon: Routledge.

Bottoms, A. and Roberts, J. (eds) (2011), *Hearing the Victim: Adversarial Justice, Crime Victims and the State*. London: Routledge.

Bourke, J. (2008), *Rape: A History from 1860 to the Present Day*. London: Virago.

Box, S. (1981), *Deviance, Reality and Society*. London: Holt, Reinhardt and Winston.

Bradley, K. (2019), *Lawyers for the Poor: Legal Advice, Voluntary Action and Citizenship in England, 1890–1990*. Manchester: Manchester University Press.

Brants, C. H. and Ringnalda, A. (2011), *Issues of Convergence: Inquisitorial Prosecution in England and Wales*. Nijmegen: Wolf Legal Publishers.

Brewer, J. and Styles, J. (1980), *An Ungovernable People. The English and their Law in the Seventeenth and Eighteenth Centuries*. Tiptree, Essex: Anchor Press.

Brown, J. and Walklate, S. (eds) (2011), *Handbook on Sexual Violence*. London: Routledge.

Bunce, R. and Field, P. (2013), *Darcus Howe: A Political Biography*. London: A&C Black.

Burke, M. (1993), *Coming Out of the Blue: British Police Officers Talk about Their Lives in "The Job" as Lesbians, Gays, and Bisexuals*. London: Cassell.

Burton, M. (2008), *Legal Responses to Domestic Violence*. London: Routledge.

Cappelletti, M. and Garth, B. G. (1978), *Access to Justice. Vol.1: A World Survey*. Alphen aan den Rijn, Netherlands: Sijthoff and Noordhoff.

Chakraborti, N. and Garland, J. (eds) (2015), *Responding to Hate Crime: The Case for Connecting Policy and Research*. Bristol: Policy Press.

Chater, K. (2011), *Untold Histories: Black People in England and Wales during the Period of the British Slave Trade, c. 1660–1807*. Manchester: Manchester University Press.

Churchill, D. (2017), *Crime, Control and Everyday Life in the Victorian City*. Oxford: Oxford University Press.

Clark, A. (1987), *Women's Silence, Men's Violence: Sexual Assault in England 1770–1845*. Pandora: London.

Clark, A. (1995), *The Struggle for the Breeches: Gender and the Making of the British Working Class*. London: Rivers Oram Press.

Clark, P. (2000), *British Class and Societies, 1500–1800: The Origins of an Associational World*. Oxford: Oxford University Press.

Conley, C.A. (1991), *The Unwritten Law: Criminal Justice in Victorian Kent*. Oxford: Oxford University Press.

Cook, M., Mills, R., Trumbach, R., and Cocks, H.G. (2007), *A Gay History of Britain: Love and Sex Between Men since the Middle Ages*. Santa Barbara: Greenwood World Publishing.

Cox, P. (2002, 2013 edn), *Bad Girls in Britain: Gender, Justice and Welfare, 1900–1950*. Basingstoke: Palgrave Macmillan.

Cox, D. (2010), *A Certain Share of Low Cunning: A History of the Bow Street Runners, 1792–1839*. Milton: Willan Publishing.

Cox, P. and Walklate, S. (eds) (2022), *Victims' Access to Justice: Historical and Comparative Perspectives*. London: Routledge.

Craig, J. (1953, 2011 edn), *The Mint: A History of the London Mint from A.D. 287 to 1948*. Cambridge: Cambridge University Press.

Crew, A. (1933), *The Old Bailey: History: Constitution, Functions, Notable Trials*. London: Ivor Nicholson and Watson.

Crone, R. (2012), *Violent Victorians: Popular Entertainment in Nineteenth-Century London*. Manchester: Manchester University Press.

Daly, K. (2004), *Restorative Justice: The Real Story*. London: Ashgate.

D'Cruze, S. (1998), *Crimes of Outrage: Sex, Violence and Victorian Working Women*. London: University College London Press.

D'Cruze, S. and Jackson, L. (2009), *Women, Crime and Justice in England since 1600*. Basingstoke: Palgrave Macmillan.

Doak, J. (2008), *Victims' Rights, Human Rights and Criminal Justice: Reconceiving the Role of Third Parties*. Portland, Oregon: Hart Publishing.

Dodsworth, F. (2019), *The Security Society: History, Patriarchy, Protection*. London: Palgrave Macmillan.

Duggan, M. (ed.) (2018), *Revisiting the 'Ideal Victim': Developments in Critical Victimology*. Bristol: Policy Press.

Edwards, J. Ll. J. (1964), *The Law Officers of the Crown*. London: Sweet & Maxwell.

Elias, N. (1939, reprinted 1994), *The Civilising Process*. Oxford: Blackwell.

Emsley, C. (1991, 1996 edn), *The English Police: A Political and Social History*. Harlow: Longman.

Emsley, C. (2005), *Hard Men: The English and Violence since 1750*. London: Hambledon and London.

Emsley, C. (2010), *Crime and Society in England, 1750–1900, Fourth Edition*. Harlow: Longman.

Emsley, C. (2013a), *Crime and Society in Twentieth-Century England. Fourth Edition*. Abingdon: Routledge.

Emsley, C. (2013b), *Soldier, Sailor, Beggarman, Thief: Crime and the British Armed Services since 1914*. Oxford: Oxford University Press.

Fassin, D. and Rechtman. R (2009), *The Empire of Trauma: An Inquiry into the Condition of Victimhood*, Princeton, New Jersey: Princeton University Press.

Foster, G. C. (1941), *Misprision of Felony*. London: Herbert Jenkins.

Garland, D. (2001), *The Culture of Control: Crime and Social Order in Contemporary Society*. Oxford: Oxford University Press.

Gatrell, V. A. C. (1994), *The Hanging Tree: Execution and the English People 1770–1868*. Oxford: Oxford University Press.

Ghai, Y. and Cottrell, J. (2009), *Marginalized Communities and Access to Justice*. London: Routledge.

Gilliéron, G. (2014), *Public Prosecutors in the United States and Europe: A Comparative Analysis with Special Focus on Switzerland, France and Germany*. New York: Springer.

Gillis, J. R. (1985), *For Better, For Worse: British Marriages 1600 to the Present*. Oxford: Oxford University Press.

Godfrey, B. S., and Cox, D. J. (2013), *Policing the Factory: Theft, Private Policing and the Law in Modern England*. London: Bloomsbury.

Godfrey, B. S., Cox, D., and Farrall, S. (2007), *Criminal Lives: Family, Employment and Offending*. Oxford: Clarendon.

Godfrey, B. S., Cox, D., and Farrall, S. (2010), *Serious Offenders: A Historical Study of Habitual Criminals*. Oxford: Clarendon.

Godfrey, B. S., Cox, P., Shore, H., and Alker, Z. (2017), *Young Criminal Lives: Life Courses and Life Chances from 1850*. Oxford: Oxford University Press.

Godfrey, B. S., and Lawrence, P. (2014) *Crime and Justice since 1750*, 2nd edn. London: Routledge.

Goodey, J. (2004), *Victims and Victimology: Research, Policy and Practice*. London: Longman.

Gordon, P. (1986), *Racial Violence and Harassment*. London: Runnymede Trust.

Gordon, J. and Gordon, A. (2020), *The Role and Rights of Victims of Crime in Adversarial Criminal Justice Systems: Recommendations for Reform in England & Wales*. London: Office of the Victims Commissioner.

Gramatikov, M. (2010), *A Handbook for Measuring the Costs and Quality of Access to Justice*. Antwerp, Netherlands: Maklu.

Grant, T. (2019), *Courtroom Number One: The Old Bailey Trials that Defined Modern Britain*. London: John Murray.

Gray, D. (2009), *Crime, Prosecution and Social Relations: The Summary Courts of the City of London in the Late Eighteenth Century*. Basingstoke: Palgrave Macmillan.

Hall, M. (2017), *Victims of Crime: Construction, Governance and Policy*. Basingstoke: Palgrave Macmillan.

Harris, A. (2004), *Policing the City: Crime and Legal Authority in London, 1780–1840*. Columbus: Ohio State University Press.

Hay, D., Linebaugh, P., Rule, R., Thompson, E.P., and Winslow, C. (1975), *Albion's Fatal Tree: Crime and Society in Eighteenth-Century England*. London: Allen Lane.

Hay, D. and Snyder, F. (eds) (1989), *Policing and Prosecution in Britain 1750–1850*. Oxford: Clarendon Press.

Henderson, T. (1999), *Disorderly Women in Eighteenth-Century London*. London: Longman.

Hetherington, T (1989,) *Prosecution and the Public Interest*. London: Pergamon Press.

Hitchcock, T. and Shoemaker, R. (2015), *London Lives: Poverty, Crime, and the Making of a Modern City, 1690–1800*. Cambridge: Cambridge University Press.

Hobbs, D. (2013), *Lush Life: Constructing Organized Crime in the UK*. Oxford: Clarendon.

Houlbrook, M. (2005), *Queer London: Perils and Pleasure in the Sexual Metropolis, 1918–1957*. Chicago: University of Chicago Press.

Howson, G. (1970, 1987 edn), *Thief-taker General: The Rise and Fall of Jonathan Wild*. London: Hutchinson.

Huggins, M. (2015), *Vice and the Victorians*. London: Bloomsbury.

Ignatieff, M. (1978), *A Just Measure of Pain: The Penitentiary in the Industrial Revolution, 1750–1850*. London: Macmillan.

Innes, J. (2009), *Inferior Politics: Social Problems and Social Policies in Eighteenth-Century Britain*. Oxford: Oxford University Press.

Jacobson, J. and Cooper, P. (eds) (2020), *Participation in Courts and Tribunals: Concepts, Realities and Aspirations*. Bristol: Policy Press.

Jackson, L. (2000), *Child Sexual Abuse in Victorian England*. London: Routledge.

Jackson, R. M. (1940, 1942, 1964, and 2015 edns), *The Machinery of Justice in England*. Cambridge: Cambridge University Press.

Jarrett, S. (2020), *Those They Called Idiots: The Idea of the Disabled Mind from 1700 to the Present Day*. London: Reaktion Books.

Johnstone, G. (2002), *Restorative Justice: Ideas, Values, Debates*. Cullompton: Willan.

Jones, T., MacLean, B., and Young, J. (1986), *The Islington Crime Survey: Crime, Victimization and Policing in Inner-city London*. London: Gower.

Kilday, A. M. (2013), *A History of Infanticide in Britain, c.1600 to the Present*. Basingstoke: Palgrave Macmillan.

King, P. J. R. (2000), *Crime, Justice and Discretion in England 1740–1820*. Oxford: Oxford University Press.

King, P. J. R. (2006), *Crime and the Law in England, 1750–1840: Remaking Justice from the Margins*. Cambridge: Cambridge University Press.

Kirchengast, T. (2006), *The Victim in Criminal Law and Justice*. London: Palgrave Macmillan.

Kirchengast, T. (2010), *The Criminal Trial in Law and Discourse*. London: Palgrave Macmillan.

Kirchengast, T. (2016), *Victims and the Criminal Trial*. London: Palgrave Macmillan.

Landau, N. (1984), *The Justices of the Peace, 1670–1760*. Berkeley: University of California Press.

Langbein, J. H. (1974), *Prosecuting Crime in the Renaissance: England, Germany, France*. Cambridge, Mass: Harvard University Press.

Langbein, J. H. (2003), *The Origins of Adversary Criminal Trial*. Oxford: Oxford University Press.

Law Society (1992), *Access to Justice: The Law Society Manifesto*. London: The Law Society.

Lemmings, D. (2011), *Law and Government in England During the Long Eighteenth Century: From Consent to Command*. Basingstoke: Palgrave Macmillan.

Lewis, B. (2016), *Wolfenden's Witnesses: Homosexuality in Postwar Britain*. London: Palgrave Macmillan.

Linebaugh, P. (1991), *The London Hanged: Crime and Civil Society in the Eighteenth-Century*. Cambridge: Cambridge University Press.

Logan, A. (2008), *Feminism and Criminal Justice. A Historical Perspective*. Basingstoke: Palgrave Macmillan.

Long, L.J. (2018), *Perpetual Suspects: A Critical Race Theory of Black and Mixed-Race Experiences of Policing*. London: Palgrave Macmillan.

Lucas, I. (1998), *OutRage!: An Oral History*. London: Cassell.

Luna, E. and Wade, M. (eds) (2012), *The Prosecutor in Transnational Perspective*. Oxford: Oxford University Press.

Mawby, R. and Walklate, S. (1994), *Critical Victimology: International Perspectives*. London: Sage.

May, A. N. (2003), *The Bar and the Old Bailey, 1750–1850*. Chapel Hill: University of North Carolina.

Mayo, M., Koessl, G., and Scott, L. (2014), *Access to Justice for Disadvantaged Communities*. Bristol: Policy Press.

McConville, M., Sanders, A., and Leng, R. (1991, 2017 edn), *Case for the Prosecution: Police Suspects and the Construction of Criminality*. London: Routledge.

Miers, D. (1978), *Responses to Victimisation*. Abingdon: Professional Books.

Miers, D. (2018), *Criminal Injuries Compensation: State and Offender Compensation for Violent Crime*. Oxford University Press: Oxford.

Morgan, G. and Rushton, P. (1998), *Rogues, Thieves and the Rule of Law. The Problem of Law Enforcement in North-East England, 1718–1800*. London: University College London Press.

Myers, N. (1996), *Reconstructing the Black Past*. London: Frank Cass.

Nash, D. and Kilday, A. M. (2010), *Cultures of Shame: Exploring Crime and Morality in Britain, 1600–1900*. London, Palgrave.

Olusoga, D. (2021), *Black and British: A Forgotten History*. London: Picador.

Paley, R. (ed.) (1991), *Justice in Eighteenth-Century Hackney*. London: London Record Society, vol. 28.

Pearson, J. (2011), *Notorious: The Immortal Legend of the Kray Twins*. London. Penguin Random House.

Petrow, S. (1994), *Policing Morals: The Metropolitan Police and the Home Office, 1870–1914*. Oxford: Oxford University Press.

Philips, David (1977), *Crime and Authority in Victorian England: The Black Country, 1835–1860*. London: Croom Helm.

Radzinowicz, L. (1956), *A History of English Criminal Law and its Administration from 1750*, Vol. II. London: Stevens and Sons.

Radzinowicz, L. and Turner, J. W. C. (eds) (1950), *Symposium on the Criminal Justice Act, 1948*. London: Macmillan and Co.

Rawls, J. (1971), *A Theory of Justice*. Cambridge: Belknap Press.

Reiner, R. (1985), *The Politics of the Police*. Brighton: Wheatsheaf.

Reynolds, E. (1998), *Before the Bobbies: The Night Watch and Police Reform in Metropolitan London, 1720–1830*. Stanford, California: Stanford University Press.

Ritvo, H. (1987), *The Animal Estate: The English and Other Creatures in the Victorian Age*. Cambridge: Harvard University Press.

Robinson, L. (2007), *Gay Men and the Left in Post-War Britain: How the Personal Got Political*. Manchester: Manchester University Press.

Rock, P. (1990), *Helping Victims of Crime: The Home Office and the Rise of Victim Support in England and Wales*. Oxford: Clarendon Press.

Rock, P. (1996), *Reconstructing a Women's Prison: The Holloway Development Project, 1968–88*. Oxford: Clarendon Press.

Rock, P. (2004b), *Constructing Victims' Rights: The Home Office, New Labour, and Victims*. Oxford: Oxford University Press.

Rock, P. (2019), *The Official History of Criminal Justice in England and Wales, Volume II: Institution Building*. London: Routledge.

Roodhouse, M. (2013), *Black Market Britain, 1939–1955*. Oxford: Oxford University Press.

Rose, N. (1999), *Powers of Freedom: Reframing Political Thought*. Cambridge: Cambridge University Press.

Rowbotham, J., Stevenson, K., and Pegg, S. (2013), *Crime News in Modern Britain: Press Reportage and Responsibility, 1820–2010*. London: Palgrave Macmillan.

Rudé, G. (1985), *Criminal and Victim: Crime and Society in Early Nineteenth-Century England*. Oxford: Clarendon, Oxford University Press.

Sanders, A. (ed.) (1996), *Prosecution in Common Law Jurisdictions*. Aldershot: Dartmouth.

Seal, L. (2014), *Capital Punishment in Twentieth-Century Britain: Audience, Justice, Memory*. Abingdon: Routledge.

Shapland, J., Willmore, J. and Duff, P. (1985), *Victims in the Criminal Justice System*. London: Gower.

Shapland, J., Robinson, G., and Sorsby, A. (2011), *Restorative Justice in Practice: Evaluating What Works for Victims and Offenders*. London: Willan.

Shaw, A. G. L. (1977), *Convicts & the Colonies: A Study of Penal Transportation from Great Britain & Ireland to Australia & other parts of the British Empire*. Carlton South, Victoria: Melbourne University Press.

Shoemaker, R. B. (1991), *Prosecution and Punishment: Petty Crime and the Law in London and Rural Middlesex, c.1660–1725*. Cambridge: Cambridge University Press.

Shoemaker, R. B. (1998), *Gender in English Society, 1650–1850: The Emergence of Separate Spheres?* London: Longman.

Shoemaker, R. B. (2004), *The London Mob: Violence and Disorder in Eighteenth-Century* London: Hambledon and London.

Shore, H. (1999), *Artful Dodgers: Youth and Crime in Early Nineteenth-Century London*. Woodbridge: Boydell Press.

Shore, H. (2015), *London's Criminal Underworlds, c. 1720–1930*. Houndmills, Basingstoke: Palgrave Macmillan.

Shpayer-Makov, H. (2011), *The Ascent of the Detective in Victorian and Edwardian England*. Oxford: Oxford University Press.

Smith, G. (2020), *On the Wrong Side of The Law: Complaints Against Metropolitan Police, 1829–1964*. New York: Springer.

Sparks, R. F., Genn, H. G., and Dodd, J. D. (1977), *Surveying Victims: A Study of the Measurement of Criminal Victimization, Perceptions of Crime, and Attitudes to Criminal Justice*. Chichester: John Wiley & Sons.

Spencer, D. and Walklate, S. (eds) (2016), *Reconceptualizing Critical Victimology: Interventions and Possibilities*. New York and London: Lexington Books.

Sykes, G. M. (1958), *The Society of Captives: A Study of a Maximum Security Prison*. Princeton: Princeton University Press.

Taylor, David (1998), *Crime, Policing and Punishment, 1760–1914*. Houndmills, Basingstoke: Macmillan.

Thane, P. (2000), *Old Age in English History: Past Experiences, Present Issues*. Oxford: Oxford University Press.

Thompson, E. P. (1975), *Whigs and Hunters: The Origins of the Black Act*. London: Allen Lane.

Tobias, J. J. (1967), *Crime and Industrial Society in the 19th Century*. London: B. T. Batsford Ltd.

Toner, B. (1977), *The Facts of Rape*. London: Arrow Books.

Tonry, M (ed.) (2012), *Prosecutors and Politics: A Comparative Perspective*. Chicago, IL: University of Chicago Press.

Turner, J., Taylor, P., Morley, S., and Corteen, K. (eds) (2017), *A Companion to the History of Crime and Criminal Justice*. Bristol: Policy Press.

Wahidin, A. and Carr, N. (2013), *Understanding Criminal Justice: A Critical Introduction*. London: Routledge.

Wahrman, Dror (2004), *The Making of the Modern Self: Identity and Culture in Eighteenth-Century England*. New Haven and London: Yale.

Walklate, S. (2007), *Imagining the Victim of Crime*. Maidenhead: McGraw-Hill/Open University Press.

Walklate, S. (ed.) (2007, 2017 edn), *Handbook of Victims and Victimology*. London: Routledge.

Walklate, S. (2013), *The Victim and the Criminal Justice Process*. London: Routledge.

Walkowitiz, J. R. (1980), *Prostitution and Victorian Society*. Cambridge: Cambridge University Press.

Walkowitiz, J. R. (1992), *City of Dreadful Delight: Narratives of Sexual Danger in Late-Victorian*. London: Virago.

Ward, R. M. (2016), *Print Culture, Crime, and Justice in 18th-Century London*. London: Bloomsbury.

Watkins, E. D. (2020), *Life Courses of Young Convicts Transported to Van Diemen's Land*. London: Bloomsbury.

Watson, K. (2004), *Poisoned Lives: English Poisoners and their Victims*, London and New York: Hambledon and London.

Weeks, J. (1981), *Sex, Politics and Society: The Regulation of Sexuality Since 1800*. London: Longman.

Wiener, M. (2004), *Men of Blood: Violence, Manliness and Criminal Justice in Victorian England*, Cambridge: Cambridge University Press.

Wood, J. C. (2004), *Violence and Crime in Nineteenth-Century England: The Shadow of our Refinement*. London: Routledge.

Zehr, H. and Toews, B. (eds) (2004), *Critical Issues in Restorative Justice*. Monsey, N.J.; Cullompton: Criminal Justice Press.

b. Journal Articles and Chapters in Books

Adams, D. (1998), 'Reforming the Crown Prosecution Service', *Policy Studies*, 19:3, 223–7.

Adler, Z. (1982), 'The Intention of Parliament and the Practice of the Courts', *Modern Law Review*, 45:6, 664–75.

Allen, R. (2019), 'Class Structure and Inequality During the Industrial Revolution: Lessons from England's Social Tables, 1688–1867', *Economic History Review*, 72:1, 88–125.

Andrew, D. T. (2002), 'The Press and Public Apologies in Eighteenth-century London', in Landau, N. (ed.), *Law, Crime and English Society, 1660–1830*. Cambridge: Cambridge University Press, 208–29.

Applegate, R. (2006), 'Taking Child Witnesses Out of the Crown Court: A Live Link Initiative", *International Review of Victimology*, 13, 179–200.

Archer, J. (2008), 'Mysterious and Missing Deaths: Missing Homicides in North-West England: 1850–1900', *Crime, History & Societies*, 12:1, 45–63.

Ashworth, A. (2000), 'Developments in the Public Prosecutor's Office in England and Wales', *European Journal of Crime, Criminal Law and Criminal Justice*, 8:3, 257–82.

Baird, V. (1999), 'Changes to Section 2 of Sexual Offences Act 1976', *Medicine, Science and the Law*, 39:3, 198–208.

Baird, V. (2020), Foreword, in J. Gordon and A. Gordon, *The Role and Rights of Victims of Crime in Adversarial Criminal Justice Systems: Recommendations for Reform in England & Wales*. London: Office of the Victims Commissioner, 2–3.

Barker, V. (2007), 'The Politics of Pain: A Political Institutionalist Analysis of Crime Victims' Moral Protests', *Law and Society Review*, 41:3: 619–63.

Barrie, D. (2008), 'Patrick Colquhoun, the Scottish Enlightenment and Police Reform in Glasgow in the Late Eighteenth Century', *Crime, History & Societies*, 12:2, 55–79.

Bates, V. (2019), 'Forensic Medicine and Female Victimhood in Victorian England', *Past and Present*, 245:1, 117–51.

Beattie, J. M. (1991), 'Scales of Justice: Defense Counsel and the English Criminal Trial in the Eighteenth and Nineteenth Centuries', *Law and History Review*, 9, 221–67.

Beattie, J. M. (2007a), 'Garrow and the Detectives: Lawyers and Policemen in the Old Bailey in the Late Eighteenth Century', *Crime, History and Societies*, 11:2, 1–19. (https://journals.openedition.org/chs/212).

Beattie, J. M. (2007b), 'Sir John Fielding and Public Justice: The Bow Street Magistrates' Court, 1754–1780', *Law and History Review*, 25:1, 93–100.

Bibbings, L. (2018), 'Section 5(1) of the Criminal Law Amendment Act of 1885', in Rackley, E. and Auchmuty, R. (eds), *Women's Legal Landmarks: Celebrating the History of Women and Law in the UK and Ireland*. London: Bloomsbury, 83–9.

Bland, E. (2021), '"Flash Houses": Public Houses and Geographies of Moral Contagion in 19th-century London', *History of the Human Sciences*, 35:1, 32–55.

Bottoms, A. E. and Stevenson, S. (2016), 'What Went Wrong?': Criminal Justice Policy in England and Wales, 1945–70', in Downes, D. (ed.), *Unravelling Criminal Justice: Eleven British Studies*. Basingstoke: Macmillan, 1–45.

Bradley, K. (2009), 'Inside the Inner London Juvenile Court, c. 1909–1953', *Crimes and Misdemeanours: Deviance and the Law in Historical Perspective*, 3:2, 37–59.

Bradley, K., Logan, A., and Shaw, S. (2009), 'Youth and Crime: Centennial Reflections on the Children Act 1908', *Crimes and Misdemeanours: Deviance and the Law in Historical Perspective*, 3:2, 1–17.

Bourke, J. (2018), 'Police Surgeons and Victims of Rape: Cultures of Harm and Care', *Social History of Medicine*, 31:4, 711–31.

Bowcott, O. (2020), 'OutRage! Turns 30: LGBT Activists Seek Truth Over Police Role', *The Guardian*, 10 May.

Brown, J. (2011), 'We mind and we care but have things changed? Assessment of Progress in the Reporting, Investigating and Prosecution of Allegations of Rape', *Journal of Sexual Aggression*, 17:3, 263–72.

Cardenas, J. (1986), 'The Crime Victim in the Prosecutorial Process', *Harvard Journal of Law and Public Policy*, 9:2, 357–98.

Chadwick, R. (1991), 'Sir Augustus Stephenson and the Prosecution of Offences Act of 1884', in Gordon, W. M. and Fergus, T. D. (eds), *Legal History in the Making: Proceedings of the Ninth British Legal History Conference, Glasgow 1989*. London: Hambledon Press, 201–10.

Churchill, D. (2014), 'Rethinking the State Monopolisation Thesis: The Historiography of Policing and Criminal Justice in Nineteenth-Century England', *Crime, Histoire & Sociétés/Crime, History and Societies*, 18:1, 131–52.

Christie, N. (1977), 'Conflicts as Property', *British Journal of Criminology*, 17:1, 1–15.

Christie, N. (1986), 'The Ideal Victim', in Fattah, E. A. (ed.), *From Crime Policy to Victim Policy*. London: Macmillan, 17–30.

Clark, A. (2000), 'Domesticity and the Problem of Wifebeating in Nineteenth-century Britain: Working-class Culture, Law and Politics', in D'Cruze, S. (ed.), *Everyday Violence in Britain, 1850–1950*. Harlow: Pearson, 27–40.

Clayton, M. and Shoemaker, R. (2022), 'Blood Money and the Bloody Code: The Impact of Financial Rewards on Criminal Justice in Eighteenth-century England', *Continuity and Change*, 37, 97–125.

Conley, C. A. (1986), 'Rape and Justice in Victorian England', *Victorian Studies*, 29:4, 519–36.

Conley, C. A. (2014), 'Sexual Violence in Historical Perspective', in Gartner, R. and McCarthy, B. (eds), *The Oxford Handbook of Gender, Sex, and Crime* (online edition, 10.1093/oxfordhb/9780199838707.013.0012). Oxford: Oxford University Press, 1–20.

Cox, D. J., and Devi-Mcgleish, Y.(2020), '"Pardon Asked": Printed Apologies in British Newspapers as a Form of Public and Private Security, 1800–1900', in Churchill, D., Janiewski, D., and Leloup, P. (eds), *Private Security and the Modern State: Historical and Comparative Perspectives*. London: Routledge, 99–116.

Crewe, B. (2011), 'Depth, Weight, Tightness: Revisiting the Pains of Imprisonment', *Punishment and Society*, 13:5, 509–29.

Crymble, A. and Azid, E. (2021), 'Black Lives, British Justice: Black People in London Criminal Justice Records, 1720–1841', *Journal of Slavery and Data Preservation*, 2:2, 1–10.

D'Cruze, S. (1999), 'Sex, Violence and Local Courts: Working-class Respectability in a Mid-nineteenth-century Lancashire Town', *British Journal of Criminology*, 39:1, 39–55.

Daly, A. and Rap, S. (2019), 'Children's Participation in the Justice System', in Kilkelly, U. and Liefaard, T. (eds), *International Human Rights of Children*. Singapore: Springer, 299–319.

Daly, K. (2006), 'The Limits of Restorative Justice', in Sullivan D., and Tifft, L. (eds), *Handbook of Restorative Justice: A Global Perspective*. London: Routledge, 134–46.

Daly, K. and Bouhours, B. (2010), 'Rape and Attrition in the Legal Process: A Comparative Analysis of Five Countries', *Crime and Justice*, 39:1, 565–650.

Davis, J. (1984), 'A Poor Man's System of Justice: The London Police Courts in the Second Half of the Nineteenth Century', *The Historical Journal*, 27:2, 309–35.

Davis, J. (1989), 'Prosecutions and Their Contexts' The Use of the Criminal Law in Later Nineteenth-Century London', in Hay, D. and Snyder, F. (eds), *Policing and Prosecution in Britain 1750–1850*. Oxford: Oxford University Press, 397–426.

Davison, L. (1992), et al., 'Introduction: The Reactive State: English Governance and Society, 1689–1750' in L. Davison, et al. (eds), *Stilling the Grumbling Hive: The Response to Social and Economic Problems in England, 1689–1750*. Stroud: Alan Sutton, xi–liv.

Devereaux, S. (1996), 'The City and the Sessions Paper: "Public Justice" in London, 1770–1800', *Journal of British Studies*, 35: 466–503.

Devereaux, S. (2002), 'The Fall of the Sessions Paper: Criminal Trial and the Popular Press in Late Eighteenth-Century London', *Criminal Justice History*, 18, 57–88.

Devereaux, S. (2004), 'Peel, Pardon and Punishment: The Recorder's Report Revisited', in Devereaux, S. and Griffths, P. (eds), *Penal Practice and Culture, 1500–1900: Punishing the English*. Basingstoke: Palgrave Macmillan, 258–84.

Devereaux, S. (2013), 'England's "Bloody Code" in Crisis and Transition: Executions at the Old Bailey, 1760–1837', *Journal of the Canadian Historical Association*, 24:2, 71–113.

Devereaux, S. (2017), 'Execution and Pardon at the Old Bailey, 1730–1837', *American Journal of Legal History*, 37:4, 447–94.

Diduck, A. (2019), 'First Rape Crisis Centre, 1976', in Rackley, E. and Auchmuty, R. (eds), *Women's Legal Landmarks: Celebrating the History of Women and Law in the UK and Ireland*. London: Hart, 321.

Doak, J. (2005), 'Victims' Rights in Criminal Trials: Prospects for Participation', *Journal of Law and Society*, 32:2, 294–316.

Doak, J, Henham, R., and Mitchell, B (2009), 'Victims and the Sentencing Process: Developing Participatory Rights?' *Legal Studies*, 29:4, 651–77.

Duggan, M. (2015), 'Working with Lesbian, Gay, Bisexual and Transgender Communities to Shape Hate Crime Policy', in Chakraborti, Neil and Garland, Jon (eds), *Responding to Hate Crime: The Case for Connecting Policy and Research*. Bristol: Policy Press, 87–98.

Edwards, S. (2005), '"Kicked, Beaten, Jumped On until They are Crushed," All under Man's Wing and Protection: The Victorian Dilemma with Domestic Violence', in Rowbotham, J. and Stevenson, K. (eds), *Criminal Conversations: Victorian Crimes, Social Panic, and Moral Outrage*. Columbus: Ohio State University Press, 247–66.

Ellison, L. (2002), 'Prosecuting Domestic Violence without Victim Participation', *Modern Law Review*, 65:6, 834–58.

Emsley, C. and Storch, R. D. (1993), 'Prosecution and Police in England Since 1700', *Bulletin of the International Association for the History of Crime and Criminal Justice*, 18, 45–57.

Farrall, S. and Jennings, W. (2012), 'Policy Feedback and the Criminal Justice Agenda: An Analysis of the Economy, Crime Rates, Politics and Public Opinion in Post-War Britain', *Contemporary British History*, 26:4, 467–88.

Feeley, M. (1997), 'Legal Complexity and the Transformation of the Criminal Process: The Origins of Plea Bargaining', *Israel Law Review*, 31, 183–222.

Feeley, M. and Little, D. (1991), 'The Vanishing Female: The Decline of Women in the Criminal Process, 1687–1912', *Law & Society Review*, 25, 719–57.

Forbes, T. (1978), 'Crowner's Quest', *Transactions of the American Philosophical Society*, 68:1, 1–52.

Fry, M. (1957), 'Justice for Victims', *The Observer*, 7 July 1957, 8 [reprinted as Fry, M. (1959), 'Justice for Victims', *Journal of Public Law*, 8:1, 191–253].

Garrard, J. (1995), 'Urban Elites, 1850–1914: The Rule and Decline of a New Squirearchy?', *Albion*, 27:4, 583–621.

Gatrell, V. A. C. (1980), 'The Decline of Theft and Violence in Victorian and Edwardian England', in Gatrell, V. A. C., Lenman, B., and Parker, G. (eds), *Crime and the Law: The Social History of Crime in Early Modern Europe*, London: Europa, 238–337.

Gatrell, V. A. C. and Hadden, T. B. (1972), 'Criminal Statistics and their Interpretation', in Wrigley, E. A. (ed.), *Nineteenth-Century Society: Essays in the Use of Quantitative Methods for the Study of Social Data*. Cambridge: Cambridge University Press, 336–96.

Gay, M. J., Holtom, C. and Thomas, M. S. (1975), 'Helping the Victims', *International Journal of Offender Therapy and Comparative Criminology*, 19:3, 263–9.

Gillespie, A. A. and Ost, S. (2016), 'The "Higher" Age of Consent and the Concept of Sexual Exploitation', in Reed, A., Bohlander, M., Wake, N., and Smith, E. (eds), Consent: *Domestic and Comparative Perspectives: Substantive Issues in Criminal Law*. Routledge: London, 161–76.

Glazebrook, P. G. (1964), 'Misprision of Felony: Shadow or Phantom', *American Journal of Legal History*, 8:3, 189–208 and 8:4, 283–302.

Godfrey, B. (2008), 'Changing Prosecution Practices and their Impact on Crime Figures, 1857–1940', *British Journal of Criminology*, 48:2, 171–89.

Godfrey, B. (2011), 'Historical and Archival Research Methods', in Gadd, D. Karstedt, S., and Mesner, S. (eds), *The Handbook on Criminology Research Methods*. New York: Sage, 159–74.

Godfrey, B. (2011), 'Critical Historical Perspectives on Crime' in DeKeseredy, W. S. and Dragiewicz, M. (eds), *The Handbook of Critical Criminology*. Routledge: London, 209–23.

Godfrey, B. (2018), 'Setting the Scene: A Question of History', in Walklate, S. (ed.), *Handbook of Victims and Victimology*, 2nd edn. London: Routledge/Taylor and Francis, 13–29.

Gooderson, J. N. (1953), 'Is the Prisoner's Character Indivisible?', *Cambridge Law Journal*, 11:3, 377–94.

Gorham, D. (1978), 'The 'Maiden Tribute of Modern Babylon' Re-examined: Child Prostitution and the Idea of Childhood in Late-Victorian England', *Victorian Studies*, 21:3, 353–79.

Gray, D. (2007), 'The Regulation of Violence in the Metropolis: The Prosecution of Assault in the Summary Courts, c. 1780–1820', *London Journal*, 32, 75–87.

Green, V. (1976), 'Crisis Centre Opens', *Spare Rib*, 46, 17.

Griffiths, C. C. (2014), 'The Prisoners' Counsel Act 1836: Doctrine, Advocacy and the Criminal Trial', *Law, Crime and History*, 4:2, 28–47.

Halvorsen, V. (2014), 'Nils Christie: "Conflicts as Property"', in Dubber, M. D. (ed.), *Foundational Texts in Modern Criminal Law*, Oxford: Oxford University Press, 335–52.

Handler, P. (2007), 'The Law of Felonious Assault in England, 1803–61', *Journal of Legal History*, 28:2, 183–206.

Hanly, C. (2021a), 'Jury Selection in Victorian England', *American Journal of Legal History*, 61, 36–55.

Hanly, C. (2021b), 'Summary Jurisdiction and the Decline of Criminal Jury Trial in Victorian England', *Journal of Legal History*, 42:3, 278–303.

Harris, J. (1992), 'Political Thought and the Welfare State 1870–1940: An Intellectual Framework for British Social Policy', *Past and Present*, 135:1, 116–41.

Harwin, N. (2006), 'Putting a Stop to Domestic Violence in the United Kingdom: Challenges and Opportunities', *Violence Against Women*, 12:6, 556–67.

Harwin, N. and Barron, J. (2000), 'Domestic Violence and Social Policy: Perspectives from Women's Aid', in Hanmer, J. and Itzin, C. (eds), *Home Truths About Domestic Violence: Feminist Influences on Policy and Practice–A Reader*. London and New York: Taylor & Francis, 205–27.

Hay, D. (1975), 'Property, Authority and the Criminal Law', in Hay, D., Linebaugh, P., Rule, J., Thompson, E. P., and Winslow, C. (eds), *Albion's Fatal Tree: Crime and Society in Eighteenth-Century England*. London: Allen Lane, 17–63.

Hay, D. (1983), 'Controlling the English Prosecutor', *Osgoode Hall Law Journal*, 21, 167–80.

Hay, D. (1982), 'War, Dearth and Theft in the Eighteenth Century: The Record of the English Courts', *Past and Present*, 95, 117–60.

Hitchcock, T. and Turkel. T. (2016), 'The Old Bailey Proceedings, 1674–1913: Text Mining for Evidence of Court Behaviour', *Digital Law and History*, 34:4, 929–55.

Hodgin, R. W. (1977), 'The Criminal Injuries Compensation Board: The First Ten Years (1964–1974)', *Anglo-American Law Review*, 6:1, 34–53.

Hohl, K. and Stanko, E. A. (2015), 'Complaints of Rape and the Criminal Justice System: Fresh Evidence on the Attrition Problem in England and Wales', *European Journal of Criminology*, 12:3, 324–41.

Holdaway, S. and O'Neill, M. (2004), 'The Development of Black Police Associations: Changing Articulations of Race within the Police', *The British Journal of Criminology*, 44:6, 854–65.

Holder, R. (2018a), 'Co-producing Prosecution: Old and New Third Party Forms', in Chang, Lennon Y. C. and Brewer, R. (eds), *Criminal Justice and Regulation Revisited: Essays in Honour of Peter Grabosky*. London: Routledge, 70–84.

Holder, R. L. (2018b), 'Decoding Hegemony: Exploring the Discourse of a Prosecuting Elite', in V. Colvin and P. Stenning (eds), *The Evolving Role of the Public Prosecutor: Challenges and Innovations*. London: Routledge, 15–29.

Holder, R. L. and Kirchengast, T. (2021), 'Crime Victims' Rights Commissioners: Public Interest Entities in a Regulatory Regime', *International Journal of Comparative and Applied Criminal Justice*, 45:1, 67–87.

Hope, T. and Trickett, A. (2008), 'The Distribution of Crime Victimisation in the Population', *International Review of Victimology*, 15:1, 37–58.

Howard, P. (1930), 'Criminal Prosecutions in England', *Columbia Law Review*, 30:1, 12–59.

Hurl-Eamon, J. (2001), 'Domestic Violence Prosecuted: Women Binding over Their Husbands for Assault at Westminster Quarter Sessions, 1685–1720', *Journal of Family History*, 26, 435–54.

Iganski, P. (1999), 'Why Make 'Hate' a Crime?', *Critical Social Policy*- 19:3, 386–95.

Iganski, P. (2008), 'Criminal Law and the Routine Activity of Hate Crime', *Liverpool Law Review*, 29, 1–17.

Inwood, S. (1990), 'Policing London's Morals: The Metropolitan Police and Popular Culture, 1829–1850', *London Journal*, 15:2, 129–46.

Jackson, L. (1999), 'The Child's Word in Court: Cases of Sexual Abuse in London 1870–1914', in Arnot, M. L. and Usborne, C. (eds), *Gender and Crime in Modern Europe*. London: UCL, 222–37.

Jackson, L. (2000b), '"Singing Birds as well as Soap Suds": The Salvation Army's Work with Sexually Abused Girls in Edwardian England', *Gender and History*, 12:1, 107–27.

Joyce, P. (1993), 'The Transition from "Old" to "New: Policing in Early Nineteenth Century Manchester', *The Police Journal: Theory, Practice and Principles*, 66:2, 197–210.

Kalunta-Crumpton, A. (2005), 'How Safe is Britain's Black Community?', *Safer Communities*, 4:2, 21–8.

Kearon, T. and Godfrey, B. S. (2007), 'Setting the Scene: A Question of History', in Walklate, S. (ed.), *Handbook of Victims and Victimology*. Cullompton: Willan, 17–36.

Khan, A. N. (1986), 'Crown Prosecution Service', *The Journal of Criminal Law*, 50:3, 297–304.

King, P. (1984), 'Decision-makers and Decision-making in the English Criminal Law, 1750–1800', *The Historical Journal*, 27:1, 25–58.

King, P. J. R. (1989), 'Prosecution Associations and their Impact in Eighteenth-Century Essex', in Hay, D. and Snyder, F. (eds), *Policing and Prosecution in Britain 1750–1850*. Oxford: Clarendon Press, 171–207.

King, P. J. R. (1996), 'Punishing Assault: The Transformation of Attitudes in the English Courts', *Journal of Interdisciplinary History*, 27, 43–74.

King, P. J. R. (2002), 'War as a Judicial Resource: Press Gangs and Prosecution Rates, 1740–1830', in Landau, N. (ed.), *Law, Crime and English Society, 1660–1830*. Cambridge: Cambridge University Press, 97–116.

King, P. J. R. (2004), 'The Summary Courts and Social Relations in Eighteenth-Century England', *Past and Present*, 183, 125–72.

King, P. J. R. (2007), 'Newspaper Reporting and Attitudes to Crime and Justice in Late-Eighteenth- and Early-Nineteenth-Century London', *Continuity and Change*, 22:1, 73–112.

King, P. J. R. (2013), 'Ethnicity, Prejudice and Justice: The Treatment of the Irish at the Old Bailey, 1750–1825', *Journal of British Studies*, 52, 390–414.

King, P. J. R. and Noel, J. (1993), 'The Origins of "The Problem of Juvenile Delinquency": The Growth of Juvenile Prosecutions in London in the Late Eighteenth and Early Nineteenth Centuries', *Criminal Justice History: An International Annual*, 14, 17–41.

King, P. J. R. and Carter Wood, J. (2015), 'Black People and the Criminal Justice System: Prejudice and Practice in Later Eighteenth- and Early Nineteenth-Century London', *Historical Research*, 88: 239, 100–24.

Kurland, P. and Waters, D. W. M. (1959), 'Public Prosecutions in England, 1854–79: An Essay in English Legislative History', *Duke Law Journal*, 4, 493–562.

Lamont, R. (2022), 'The Crown against . . . : The Victim and the State in the Pursuit of Criminal Prosecution, 1840–1985', in Cox, P. and Walklate, S. (eds), *Victims' Access to Justice: Historical and Comparative Perspectives*. London: Routledge, 19–36.

Landau, N. (2002), 'The Trading Justice's Trade', in Landau, N. (ed.), *Law, Crime and English Society, 1660–1830*. Cambridge: Cambridge University Press, 46–70.

Landsman, S. (1990), 'The Rise of the Contentious Spirit: Advocacy Procedure in Eighteenth-Century England', *Cornell Law Review*, 75, 498–609.

Langbein, J. H. (1978), 'Understanding the Short History of Plea Bargaining', *Law and Society Review*, 13, 261–72.

Langbein, J. H. (1983), 'Albion's Fatal Flaws', *Past and Present*, 98:1, 96–120.

Leat, D. (1975), 'The Rise and Role of the Poor Man's Lawyer', *British Journal of Law and Society*, 2:2, 166–81.

Lewis, C. (2012), 'The Evolving Role of the English Crown Prosecution Service', in Luna, E. and Wade, M. L. (eds), *The Prosecutor in Transnational Perspective*. Oxford: Oxford University Press, 214–34.

Liddle, A. M. (1996), 'State, Masculinities and Law: Some Comments on Gender and English State Formation', *British Journal of Criminology*, 36:3, 361–80.

Loader, I. and Sparks, R. (2005), 'For an Historical Sociology of Crime Policy in England and Wales since 1968', in Matravers, M. (ed.), *Managing Modernity: Politics and the Culture of Control*. Abingdon: Routledge, 5–32.

Manikis, M. (2021), 'Conceptualising the Victim in England and Wales and the United States within a Spectrum of Public and Private Interests', *Oxford Journal of Legal Studies*, 41:1, 219–42.

Marshall, S. E. (2005), 'Victims of Crime: Their Station and Its Duties', in Matravers, M. (ed.), *Managing Modernity: Politics and the Culture of Control*. Abingdon: Routledge, 104–17.

Mason-Bish, H. (2010), 'Future Challenges for Hate Crime Policy: Lessons From the Past', in Chakraborti, N. (ed.), *Hate Crime: Concepts, Policy, Future Directions*. London: Willan, 58–77.

Mawby, R. (2022), 'The Changing Landscape of Service Delivery for Victims of Crime in England and Wales in the Last Fifty Years', in Cox, P. and Walklate, S. (eds), *Victims' Access to Justice: Historical and Comparative Perspectives*. London: Routledge, 74–98.

McCabe, S. (1977), 'Unfinished Business: A Note on the Reports of the Select Committees on Violence in Marriage and Violence in the Family', *The British Journal of Criminology*, 17:3, 280–85.

McGlynn, C. and Downes, J. (2018), 'Section 4 of the Sexual Offences (Amendment) Act 1976', in Rackley, E. and Auchmuty, R. (eds), *Women's Legal Landmarks: Celebrating the History of Women and Law in the UK and Ireland*. London: Hart, 327–32.

McGowen, R. (1983), 'The Image of Justice and Reform of the Criminal Law in Early Nineteenth-Century England', *The Buffalo Law Review*, 32:1, 89–126.

McGowen, R. (2005), 'The Bank of England and the Policing of Forgery 1797–1821', *Past and Present*, 186, 81–116.

Mellaerts, W. (2000), 'Criminal Justice in Provincial England, France and Netherlands, c. 1880–1905: Some Comparative Perspectives', *Crime, History & Societies*, 4:2, 19–52.

Mendelsohn, B. (1956), 'A New Branch of Bio-Psychological Science: La Victimology', *Revue Internationale de Criminologie et de Police Technique*, 2, 10–31.

Mendelsohn, B. (1976), 'Victimology and Contemporary Society's Trends', *Victimology: An International Journal*, 1:1, 8–28.

Miers, D. (2000), 'Taking the Law into Their Own Hands: Victims as Offenders', in Crawford, A., and Goodey, J. (eds), *Integrating a Victim Perspective within Criminal Justice*. Dartmouth: Ashgate, 77–96.

Morgan, G. and Rushton, P. (2003), 'The Magistrate, the Community and the Maintenance of an Orderly Society in Eighteenth-Century England', *Historical Research: The Bulletin of the Institute of Historical Research*, 76:191, 54–77.

Morgan, J. (1988), 'Children as Victims', in Maguire, M. and Pointing, J. (eds), *Victims of Crime: A New Deal?* Milton Keynes: Open University Press, 74–82.

Morris, R. (2001), '"Lies, Damned Lies and Criminal Statistics": Reinterpreting the Criminal Statistics in England and Wales', *Crime, History & Societies*, 5:1, 111–27.

Muir, H. (2007), 'Officers' Homophobia Hampered Murder Investigations, Says Review: Echoes of Macpherson as Met Vows to Act on Advice', *The Observer*, 15 May.

Myers, N. (1988), 'The Black Presence Through Criminal Records, 1780–1830', *Immigrants & Minorities*, 7:3, 292–307.

Newburn, T. and Stanko, E. (1994), 'When men are victims', in Newburn, T. and Stanko, E. (eds), *Just Boys Doing Business?* London, Routledge, 153–65.

O'Malley, P., Weir, L., and Shearing, C. (1997), 'Governmentality, Criticism and Politics', *Economy and Society*, 26:4, 501–17.

Paley, R. (1989), 'Thief-takers in London in the Age of the McDaniel Gang, c. 1745–1754', in Hay, D. and Snyder, F. (eds), *Policing and Prosecution in Britain 1750–1850*. Oxford: Clarendon Press, 301–41.

Pemberton, A. (2012), 'Too Readily Dismissed? A Victimological Perspective on Penal Populism', in Nelen, H. and Classen, J. C. (eds), *Beyond the Death Penalty: Reflections on Punishment*. Cambridge: Intersentia, 105–20.

Porter, A. (2019), 'Prosecuting domestic abuse in England and Wales: Crown Prosecution Service "Working Practice" and "New Public Managerialism"', *Social and Legal Studies*, 28:4, 493–516.

Philips, D. (1989), 'Good Men to Associate and Bad Men to Conspire: Associations for the Prosecution of Felons in England, 1760–1860', in Hay, D. and Snyder, F. (eds), *Policing and Prosecution in Britain 1750–1850*. Oxford: Clarendon Press, 113–70.

Reiner, R. (2001), 'The Rise of Virtual Vigilantism: Crime Reporting Since WWII', *Criminal Justice Matters*, 43, 4–5.

Reiner, R., Livingstone, L., and Allen, J. (2003), 'From Law and Order to Lynch Mobs: Crime News Since the Second World War', in Mason, P. (ed.), *Criminal Visions: Media Representations of Crime and Justice*. Cullompton: Willan, 13–32.

Rock, P. (2004a), 'Victims, Prosecutors and the State in Nineteenth-Century England and Wales', *Criminology and Criminal Justice*, 4:4, 331–54.

Rock, P. (2017), 'Theoretical Perspectives on Victimisation', in Walklate, S. (ed.), *Handbook of Victims and Victimology*, 2nd edn. London: Taylor and Francis, 37–61.

Rossner, M. (2017), 'Restorative Justice and Victims of Crime: Directions and Developments', in Walklate, S. (ed.), *Handbook of Victims and Victimology*, 2nd edn. London: Taylor and Francis, 229–46.

Rudé, G. (1956), 'The Gordon Riots: A Study of the Rioters and Their Victims', *Transactions of the Royal Historical Society*, 6, 93–114.

Sandefur, R. (2009), 'Access to Justice: Classical Approaches and New Directions', in R. Sandefur (ed.), *Access to Justice*, special edition of *Sociology of Crime, Law, and Deviance*, 12, Bingley: Emerald/JAI Press, ix–xvii.

Sarat, A and Clarke, C (2008), 'Beyond Discretion: Prosecution and the Logic of Sovereignty, and the Limits of Law', *Law and Social Inquiry*, 32:2, 387–416.

Schafer, S. (1970), 'Victim Compensation and Responsibility', *Southern California Law Review*, 43:1, 55–109.

Shapland, J., and Cohen, D. (1987), 'Facilities for Victims: The Role of the Police and the Courts', *Criminal Law Review*, January, 28–38.

Shoemaker, R. B. (2001), 'Male Honour and the Decline of Public Violence in Eighteenth-Century London', *Social History*, 26, 190–208.

Shoemaker, R. B. (2008a), 'Old Bailey', in, Cane, P. and Conaghan, J. (eds), *The New Oxford Companion to the Law*. Oxford: Oxford University Press, 848–9.

Shoemaker, R. B. (2008b), 'The Old Bailey Proceedings and the Representation of Crime and Criminal Justice in Eighteenth-Century London', *Journal of British Studies*, 47, 559–80.

Shoemaker, R. B. (2010), 'Print and the Female Voice: Representations of Women's Crime in London, 1690–1735', *Gender and History* 22:1, 75–91.

Shoemaker, R. B. (2017), 'Worrying about Crime: Experience, Moral Panics and Public Opinion in London, 1660–1800', *Past and Present*, 234, 71–100.

Shoemaker, R. B. (2022), 'Sparing the Noose: Death Sentences and the Pardoning of Old Bailey Convicts, 1763–1868', in Barclay, K. and Milka, A. (eds), *Cultural Histories of Law, Media and Emotion: Public Justice*. New York: Routledge, 237–58.

Shoemaker, R. B. and Ward, R. (2017), 'Understanding the Criminal: Record-Keeping, Statistics and the Early History of Criminology in England', *British Journal of Criminology*, 57:6, 1442–61.

Shore, H. (2002), 'Transportation, Penal Ideology and the Experience of Juvenile Offenders in the Early Nineteenth Century', *Crime, History & Societies*, 6:2, 81–102.

Shore, H. (2009), '"The Reckoning": Disorderly Women, Informing Constables, and the Westminster Justices, 1727–1733', *Social History*, 34, 409–27.

Shore, H. (2020), '"A Monstrous Innovation on the Laws": The William Sheen Case; Child Murder and Double Jeopardy at the Old Bailey', in Nash, D. and Kilday, A. M. (eds), *Fair and Unfair Trials in the British Isles, 1800–1940: Microhistories of Justice and Injustice*. London: Bloomsbury, 17–34.

Shore, H. and Williams, L. (2022), 'Divergent Victims in the Old Bailey, 1950–1979', in Cox, P. and Walklate, S. (eds), *Victims' Access to Justice: Historical and Comparative Perspectives*. London: Routledge, 37–52.

Simmonds, L. (2013), 'Lost in Transition? The Changing Face of Victim Support', *International Review of Victimology*, 19:2, 201–17.

Simpson, A. E. (1986), 'The "Blackmail Myth" and the Prosecution of Rape and its Attempt in 18th Century London: The Creation of a Legal Tradition', *Journal of Criminal Law & Criminology*, 77:1, 101–150.

Smith, B. P. (2005), 'Did the Presumption of Innocence Exist in Summary Proceedings?', *Law and History Review*, 23, 191–99.

Smith, B. P. (2006), 'The Emergence of Public Prosecution in London, 1790–1850', *Yale Journal of Law and Humanities*, 18:29, 29–62.

Smith, B. P. (2007), 'The Myth of Private Prosecution in England, 1750–1850', in Dibber, M. D., and Farmer, L. (eds), *Modern Histories of Crime and Punishment*. Stanford, California: Stanford University Press, 151–74.

Smith, G. T. (2007), 'Expanding the Compass of Domestic Violence in the Hanoverian Metropolis', *Journal of Social History*, 41:1, 31–54.

Smith, G. T. (2013), 'Introduction', in Smith, G. T. (ed.), *Summary Justice in the City: A Selection of Cases Heard at the Guildhall Justice Room, 1752–1781*. London: London Record Society, xi–xxvii.

Spencer, J. (2011), 'The Victim and the Prosecutor', in Bottoms, A. and Roberts, J. (eds), *Hearing the Victim: Adversarial Justice, Crime Victims and the State*. London: Routledge, 141–62.

Stark, F. (2013), 'The Demise of the Private Prosecution?', *The Cambridge Law Journal*, 72:1, 7–11.

Stevenson, K. (2000), 'Unequivocal Victims: The Historical Roots of the Mystification of the Female Complainant in Rape Cases', *Feminist Legal Studies*, 8, 343–66.

Stevenson, K. (2004), 'Fulfilling Their Mission: The Intervention of Voluntary Societies in Cases of Sexual Assault in the Victorian Criminal Process', *Crime History and Societies*, 8:1, 93–110.

Stevenson, K. (2005), '"Crimes of Moral Outrage": Victorian Encryptions of Sexual Violence', in Rowbotham, J. and Stevenson, K. (eds), *Criminal Conversations: Victorian Crimes, Social Panic, and Moral Outrage*. Columbus: Ohio State University Press, 232–46.

Stevenson, K. (2016), '"These Are Cases Which It Is Inadvisable to Drag into the Light of Day": Disinterring the Crime of Incest in Early Twentieth-century England', *Crime, History and Societies*, 20:2, 31–54.

Stevenson, K. (2017), '"Children of a Very Tender Age Have Vicious Propensities": Child Witness Testimonies in Cases of Sexual Abuse', *Law, Crime and History*, 7:1, 75–97.

Stone, C. and Wall, B. (2008), '"Dumb O Jemmy and Others": Deaf People, Interpreters and the London Courts in the Eighteenth and Nineteenth Centuries', *Sign Language Studies*, 8, 226–40.

Storch, R. (1976), 'The Policeman as Domestic Missionary: Urban Discipline and Popular Culture in Northern England, 1850–1880', *Journal of Social History*, 9:4, 481–502.

Tapley, J. and Davies, P. (2020), 'Victimology: A Conversion of Narratives', in Tapley, J. and Davies, P. (eds), *Victimology*. London: Palgrave Macmillan, 1–16.

Taylor, H. (1998), 'Rationing Crime: The Political Economy of Criminal Statistics Since the 1850s', *Economic History Review*, LI, 3, 569–90.

Taylor, S. (2008), 'The Crown Prosecution Service and Race Equality', in Singh Bhu, H. (ed.), *Race and Criminal Justice*. London: Sage, 66–82.

Taylor-Dunn, H. and Erol, R. (2021), 'Improving the Safety and Well-being of Domestic Abuse Survivors: The Role of a Specialist Organisation in Supporting the Work of Independent Domestic Violence Advisors', *Crime Prevention and Community Safety*, 23, 115–36.

Temkin, J. (1998), 'Medical Evidence in Rape Cases: A Continuing Problem for Criminal Justice', *Modern Law Review*, 61:6, 821–48.

Tomes, N. (1978), 'A "Torrent of Abuse": Crimes of Violence Between Working-Class Men and Women in London, 1840–1875', *Journal of Social History*, 11:3, 328–45.

Turner, D. (2012), 'Disability and Crime in Eighteenth-Century England: Physical Impairment at the Old Bailey', *Cultural and Social History*, 9:1, 47–64.

Turner, J. (2019), 'A Shocking State of Domestic Unhappiness': Male Victims of Female Violence and the Courts in Late Nineteenth Century Stafford', *Societies*, 9:2, 40.

Tyler, T. (2003), 'Procedural Justice, Legitimacy, and the Effective Rule of Law', *Crime and Justice*. 30, 283–357.

Wales, T. (2000), 'Thief-takers and Their Clients in Later Stuart London', in Griffith, P. and Jenner, M. S. R. (eds), *Londinopolis: Essays in the Cultural and Social History of Early-Modern London*. Manchester: Manchester University Press, 67–85.

Walklate, S. (2009), 'Are We All Victims Now? Crime, Justice and Suffering', *British Journal of Community Justice*, 7:2, 5–16.

Walklate, S. (2016), 'The Metamorphosis of the Victim of Crime: From Crime to Culture and the Implications for Justice', *International Journal for Crime, Justice and Social Democracy*, 5:4, 4–16.

Walkowitz, J. (1982), 'Jack the Ripper and the Myth of Male Violence', *Feminist Studies*, 8:3, 542–74.

Webster, C. (2017), 'Race, Religion, Victims and Crime', in Davies, P., Francis, P., and Greer, C. (eds), *Victims, Crime and Society: An Introduction*. London: Sage, 207–28.

Whine, M. (2011), 'The Community Security Trust: Best Practice in Combating Antisemitic Hate', *Journal of Hate Studies*, 9:1, 113–26.

Wiener, M. (1998), 'The Victorian Criminalization of Men', in Spierenburg, P. (ed.), *Men and Violence*, Columbus: Ohio State University Press, 197–231.

Williams, G. (1959), 'Comment on the Proposal. Compensation for Victims of Criminal Violence: A Round Table', *Journal of Public Law*, 8:1, 191–253.

Williams, L. and Walklate, S. (2020), 'Policy Responses to Domestic Violence, the Criminalisation Thesis and "Learning from History"', *The Howard Journal*, 59:3, 305–316.

Williamson, A. (2017), 'The Law and Politics of Marital Rape in England, 1945–1994', *Women's History Review*, 26:3, 382–413.

Zedner, L. (2002), 'Victims', in Morgan, R., Reiner, R., and Maguire, M. (eds), *The Oxford Handbook of Criminology*, 3rd edition. Oxford: Oxford University Press, 419–56.

c. Masters and Doctoral Theses

Bland, E. (2018), 'The Identification of Criminal Suspects by Policing Agents in London, 1780–1850'. PhD, University of Sheffield.

Chartrand, M. (2017), 'Gendered Justice: Women Workers, Gender, and Master and Servant Law in England, 1700–1850'. PhD, York University, Toronto.

Crymble, Adam (2015), 'Surname Analysis, Distant Reading, and Migrant Experience: The Irish in London, 1801–1820'. PhD, King's College London.

Darby, N.E.C. (2015), 'The Magistrate and the Community: Summary Proceedings in Rural England during the Long Eighteenth Century'. PhD, University of Northampton.

D'Sena, P. A. M. (1987), 'Perquisites and Pilfering in The London Docks, 1700–1795'. MPhil, Open University.

Langford, P. (1993), 'State, Law and Prosecution: The Emergence of the Modern Criminal Process, 1780–1910'. PhD, University of Warwick.

Paley, R. (1983), 'The Middlesex Justices Act of 1792: Its Origins and Effects'. PhD, University of Reading.

d. Reports

Charles, C. (2012), *Special Measures for Vulnerable and Intimidated Witnesses: Research Exploring the Decisions and Actions Taken by Prosecutors in a Sample of CPS Case Files*. London: Crown Prosecution Service.

Cox, P., Lamont, R., Sunkin, M. (2020), 'Constitutional Powers of the Victims' Commissioner for England and Wales', Report Commissioned by the Office of the Victims' Commissioner.

Fisher, Sir H. (1977), 'Report of an Inquiry by the Hon. Sir Henry Fisher into the Circumstances Leading to the Trial of Three Persons on Charges Arising out of the Death of Maxwell Confait and the Fire at 27 Doggett Road, London SE6', Report Ordered by the House of Commons. London: HMSO.

Hough, M. and Mayhew, P. (1983), *The British Crime Survey: First Report*. A Home Office Research and Planning Unit Report. London: HMSO.

Hunter, G., Jacobson, J. and Kirby, A. (2013), *Out of the Shadows: Victims' and Witnesses' Experiences of Attending the Crown Court*. Report for Institute for Criminal Policy Research, Birkbeck College, University of London.

Justice (1970), *The Prosecution Process in England and Wales: A Report*. London: Justice Educational and Research Trusts.

Macpherson, Sir W. (1999), *The Stephen Lawrence Inquiry*. Cm 4262-I. London: HMSO.

Ministry of Justice (2021), 'Delivering Justice for Victims: A Consultation on Improving Victims' Experiences of the Justice System', *CP* 574, https://assets.publishing.service.gov.uk/government/uploads/system/uploads/attachment_data/file/1039431/delivering-justice-fo-victims-consultation.pdf.

e. Online Only Sources

BBC (2021), 'Stephen Port: Met Police failings led to more deaths', 10 Dec 2021 https://www.bbc.co.uk/news/uk-england-london-59593887.

British Library Sounds (2010), Interviews with Helen Reeves, recorded 2010–11. C464/77. https://sounds.bl.uk/Oral-history/Observing-the-1980s/021M-C0464X0077XX-0005V0.

Brooke, Sir H. (2017), 'The History of Legal Aid 1945–2010'. Unpublished report, London: Fabian Society, https://fabians.org.uk/wp-content/uploads/2017/09/Bach-Commission-Appendix-6-F-1-1.pdf.

Brooks, R. and Wallis, N. (2020), 'Justice Lost in the Post', *Private Eye Online* https://www.private-eye.co.uk/special-reports/justice-lost-in-the-post.

Cox, P. (2017), 'Blamed for Being Abused: An Uncomfortable History of Child Sexual Exploitation', *The Conversation*, 18 August, 2017, https://theconversation.com/blamed-for-being-abused-an-uncomfortable-history-of-child-sexual-exploitation-82410.

Cox, P. and Lamont, R. (2020), 'Why the Courts and Police Should be Held Responsible for Failing Victims of Crime', *The Conversation*, 22 December 2020, https://theconversation.com/why-the-courts-and-police-should-be-held-responsible-for-failing-victims-of-crime-151956.

Cross, M. (2015), 'Legal Aid's Founding Text Turns 70', *Law Gazette*, 28 May 2015 https://www.lawgazette.co.uk/commentary-and-opinion/legal-aids-founding-text-turns-70/5048898.article.

Crown Prosecution Service (2019), 'Private Prosecutions' https://www.cps.gov.uk/legal-guidance/private-prosecutions (accessed 13 May 2022).

Emsley, C., Hitchcock, T., and Shoemaker, R. (2018a) 'Currency, Coinage and the Cost of Living', *Old Bailey Proceedings Online*, www.oldbaileyonline.org/static/Coinage.jsp.

Emsley, C., Hitchcock, T., and Shoemaker, R. (2018b), 'The Publishing History of the Proceedings', *Old Bailey Proceedings Online* (www.oldbaileyonline.org, version 8.0).

Emsley, C., Hitchcock, T., and Shoemaker, R. (2018c), 'The Value of the Proceedings as a Historical Source', *Old Bailey Proceedings Online* (www.oldbaileyonline.org, version 8.0).

EU Framework Directive (2001), Council of the European Union, 2001/220/JHA: Council Framework Decision of 15 March 2001 on the Standing of Victims in Criminal Proceedings. https://eur-lex.europa.eu/legal-content/EN/TXT/PDF/?uri=CELEX:32001F0220.

Fouzder, M. (2021), 'First Criminal Justice Scorecards Published', *Law Society Gazette*, 9 December 2021, https://www.lawgazette.co.uk/news/first-criminal-justice-scorecards-published/5110891.article.

Hillel, R. and Iglikowski-Broad, V. (2015), 'Rights, Resistance and Racism: The Story of the Mangrove Nine', National Archives, 21 October 2015, https://blog.nationalarchives.gov.uk/rights-resistance-racism-story-mangrove-nine/ (accessed 20 May 2022).

Jackson, L. (2015), 'Child Sexual Abuse in England and Wales: Prosecution and Prevalence 1918–1970', *History & Policy*, 18 June 2015, http://www.historyandpolicy.org/policy-papers/papers/child-sexual-abuse-in-england-and-wales-prosecution-and-prevalence-1918-197).

Jones, S. (2017), 'Private Prosecution for Causing Cyclist's Death Sees Car Driver Acquitted', *Cycling UK*, 6 April 2017, https://www.cyclinguk.org/press-release/2017-04-06/private-prosecution-causing-cyclist%E2%80%99s-death-sees-car-driver-acquitted.

Langen, N. R. (2019), 'Mangrove Nine: When Black Power Took On the British Establishment', *The Justice Gap*, 29 November 2019, https://www.thejusticegap.com/mangrove-nine-when-black-power-took-on-the-british-establishment/.

Le Marechel, C. (2014), 'Victim Support Celebrates 40 Years After its Bristol Launch in 1974', *BBC News Bristol*, 1 January 2014, https://www.bbc.co.uk/news/uk-england-bristol-25431800.

Ministry of Justice (2011), 'Increasing Community Access to Local Criminal Justice', Ministry of Justice Business Plan, https://assets.publishing.service.gov.uk/government/uploads/system/uploads/attachment_data/file/217257/increasing-access-local-criminal-justice.pdf.

Post Office (2022), 'Historical Matters FAQs' https://corporate.postoffice.co.uk/en/historical-matters/historical-matters/historical-matters-faqs.

Robins, J. (2019), 'Cases that Changed Us: Maxwell Confait', *The Justice Gap*, 21 November 2019, https://www.thejusticegap.com/cases-the-changed-us-maxwell-confait/.

Shoemaker, R. B. (2020), 'Penal Outcomes', in *The Digital Panopticon: Tracing London Convicts in Britain and Australia, 1780–1925* (www.digitalpanopticon.org/Penal_Outcomes).

UNODC (2015), 'International Classification of Crime for Statistical Purposes' https://www.unodc.org/documents/data-and-analysis/statistics/crime/ICCS/ICCS_English_2016_web.pdf.

f. Unpublished Papers

Cox, P., Impara, E., Lamont, R., and Walklate, S. (2021), 'Victims' Access to Justice: Data-mining and Victimisation Survey Data'. Unpublished paper presented to the British Society for Criminology annual conference, 7 July 2021.

Lamont, R. and Cox, P. (2021), 'Child Victims of Crime: Children's Participation in English Criminal Trials over Time', paper presented to the 'Reconceptualising Children's Rights' workshop sponsored by the *Modern Law Review*, Queen Mary, University of London, 4 Nov 2021.

Index

For the benefit of digital users, indexed terms that span two pages (e.g., 52–53) may, on occasion, appear on only one of those pages.
Tables and figures are indicated by *t* and *f* following the page number